McGraw-Hill Education

8GRE
Practice
Tests

TWENTY-THREE

McGraw-Hill Education

8GRE Practice Tests

Third Edition

Kathy A. Zahler

Christopher Thomas

New York Chicago San Francisco Athens London Madrid
Mexico City Milan New Delhi Singapore Sydney Toronto

1 2 3 4 5 6 7 8 9   LHS   23 22 21 20 19 18

ISBN   978-1-260-12247-3
MHID   1-260-12247-6

e-ISBN   978-1-260-12248-0
e-MHID   1-260-12248-4

GRE is a registered trademark of Educational Testing Service, which was not involved in the production of, and does not endorse, this product.

McGraw-Hill Education products are available at special quantity discounts for use as premiums and sales promotions, or for use in corporate training programs. To contact a representative, please visit the Contact Us pages at www.mhprofessional.com.

Contents

Getting Started

This book contains eight practice tests for the GRE General Test. They follow the test format in use for all GRE exams. Each one has been carefully crafted to match the real exam in terms of content, question types, and level of difficulty. Taking these practice tests will give you a good idea of what you'll encounter when you take the real exam. You'll learn about the test structure and content, you'll familiarize yourself with the directions for each question type, and you'll get a good idea of how well you are currently prepared for the actual GRE.

What Is the GRE General Test?

The Graduate Record Examination (GRE) General Test is required for entry by most college and university graduate programs. The General Test covers basic verbal and quantitative skills. There are also GRE tests in various specific subjects, which are required by certain graduate programs. All of these exams are created and administered by the Educational Testing Service (ETS). For complete information, including instructions for registering to take the exams, visit www.gre.org.

The following sections describe the features of the current GRE test format. More information is available at the GRE website.

Test Structure and Format

The revised GRE General Test, administered starting in August 2011, has two formats: a computer-based test and a paper-based test. The computer-based test is offered in the United States, Canada, and many other countries. The paper-based test is offered in areas of the world where computer-based testing is not available.

The revised GRE General Test has three parts:

- **Analytical Writing** (2 tasks). In this part of the test you will write two short essays in response to prompts provided. One essay will "analyze an issue" and the other will "analyze an argument." Pools of topics may be found on the GRE website. The topics on your test will be selected from these pools.

- **Verbal Reasoning** (2 sections). The questions in this part cover reading comprehension, vocabulary, and other verbal skills. Many test your ability to analyze complex concepts and ideas.
- **Quantitative Reasoning** (2 sections). The questions in this part cover a wide range of math skills. Some problems are word problems with real-life scenarios; others are straight calculations. Many test your ability to reason logically using important math concepts.

The computer-based test is partly "computer adaptive." This term means that at certain points in the test, the computer decides what questions to give you based on your performance thus far. Specifically, if you perform well on the first Verbal Reasoning section, the computer will give you a second Verbal Reasoning section that is more difficult than the one you would have gotten if you had not performed well. The same procedure is followed for the two Quantitative Reasoning sections. Within each section, however, the test is not computer adaptive; a specific set of questions is presented in a specific order. Within a section you are free to skip questions or move forwards or backwards through the question order as you wish.

On the computer-based test, you are provided with an on-screen calculator. It will help you particularly when the problems require time-consuming calculations. For many problems, however, simple reasoning will be more effective than attempting lengthy calculations, so you should use the calculator only when truly necessary. For the practice tests in this book, keep a calculator handy and use it when appropriate.

The following charts show the formats of the computer-based and paper-based revised GRE General Test.

Typical Computer-Based Revised General Test

Section	Number of Questions	Time
Analytical Writing	1 "Analyze an Issue" task and 1 "Analyze an Argument" task	30 minutes per task
Section 1: Verbal Reasoning	Approximately 20 questions	30 minutes
Section 2: Verbal Reasoning	Approximately 20 questions	30 minutes
Section 3: Quantitative Reasoning	Approximately 20 questions	35 minutes
Section 4: Quantitative Reasoning	Approximately 20 questions	35 minutes

An unidentified unscored section may be included at any point in the test. An identified unscored research section may also be included at the end of the test.

Typical Paper-Based Revised General Test

Section	Number of Questions	Time
Analytical Writing (2 sections)	1 "Analyze an Issue" task and 1 "Analyze an Argument" task	30 minutes per task
Section 3: Verbal Reasoning	Approximately 25 questions	35 minutes
Section 4: Verbal Reasoning	Approximately 25 questions	35 minutes
Section 5: Quantitative Reasoning	Approximately 25 questions	40 minutes
Section 6: Quantitative Reasoning	Approximately 25 questions	40 minutes

Verbal and Quantitative Question Types

On the revised GRE General Test, the Verbal Reasoning sections include the following question types:

- **Reading Comprehension.** These questions are based on reading passages that vary in length from one paragraph to several paragraphs. Most of the passages are fairly short. They cover topics in a wide range of subjects: the biological and physical sciences, the social sciences, literature and the arts, and the like. The number of questions per passage may vary from one to six. The questions may ask about the meaning of a word or the meaning of a sentence or a paragraph. You may be asked to draw a conclusion from the passage, to summarize the author's argument, to identify the author's viewpoint or underlying assumptions, or to identify strengths or weaknesses in the author's reasoning. Most reading-comprehension questions are standard multiple-choice questions that require you to select the single best answer. A few, however, will ask you to select more than one correct answer choice. One or two are not multiple-choice questions; instead, they will ask you to identify a sentence in the passage that matches a given description.

- **Sentence Equivalence.** Each of these questions presents a sentence containing a blank where a word is missing. Each question has six answer-choice words. You must pick two choices, each of which makes sense in the blank. The two choices must also result in sentences that have the same, or nearly the same, meaning. Both of the words that you select must be correct in order for you to receive credit for the question. There is no partial credit if you select one, but not both, correct answer choices.

- **Text Completion.** Each of these questions presents a short passage containing from one to three blanks where a word is missing. For each blank, you must select a word that makes sense in the passage in terms of its overall logic and meaning. If there is a single blank, you will be given five answer choices. If there is more than one blank, you will be given three word choices per blank. If there are two or three blanks, you must select the correct answer for all of them in order to receive credit for the question. There is no partial credit if you select one or two but not all of the words that correctly fill the blanks.

On the revised GRE General Test, the Quantitative Reasoning sections test your knowledge of mainly high-school-level arithmetic, algebra, and geometry. You may be asked questions about factoring, prime numbers, probability, coordinate geometry, systems of equations, quadratic equations, inequalities, and statistical measures such as mean, median, mode, and standard deviation. Some questions will present word problems based on everyday situations. Some will also ask you to interpret information presented in graphs, charts, or tables. The Quantitative Reasoning questions are of the following types:

- **Quantitative Comparison.** Each of these questions presents two mathematical quantities, Quantity A and Quantity B. You must decide if Quantity A is larger than Quantity B, if Quantity B is larger than Quantity A, if the two quantities are equal, or if it is impossible to determine the relationship between the two quantities. Sometimes you will be given additional mathematical information to use in your calculations.

- **Multiple Choice.** Most of these questions follow a standard format with five answer choices, of which only one is correct. A few, however, will have more than one mathematical solution, and you will be asked to select more than one correct answer from the answer choices.

- **Numeric Entry.** For these questions, you are not given a list of answer choices. Instead, you must calculate the answer and enter it in a box provided. If the answer is an integer or a decimal, you will be given a single box for your answer. If the answer is a fraction, you will be given two boxes, one for the numerator and the other for the denominator, separated by a fraction bar.

How to Use the Practice Tests

If you have enough time before you take the real GRE, you should try to work through all eight of the practice tests in this book. A good schedule is to take at least one test a week, or two if you have less time before the actual test date. The more practice you get, the better prepared you will be for the real GRE.

When you take a practice test, try to simulate actual testing conditions. Set aside at least 3½ hours to complete the entire test. Find a quiet place where you can work without being disturbed. Take one test section at a time, and if possible, follow the timing instructions exactly. Mark your answers directly on the pages of this book. (Note that when you take the real GRE, if you take the computer-based version, you will mark your answers by clicking on the computer screen.) If you finish work on a section before time is up, use the remaining minutes to go back and check your work. If you have not finished work on a section when time runs out, you may need to speed up your pacing before taking the real GRE.

Scoring the Verbal and Quantitative Test Sections

Each practice test is followed by an Answer Key and Answers and Explanations for the Verbal and Quantitative sections. Check your answers against the key, then read the explanations, paying special attention to those questions you got wrong or had to guess at. For the Quantitative questions, it pays to read all of the explanations, because there may be several ways to solve a given math problem, and the explanation may describe a solution method that was easier than the one you used.

The practice tests in this book, like all practice tests that are not the real GRE, can give you only a general idea of how well you will do on the actual exam. The percentile scores reported for the actual GRE are based on a sophisticated statistical procedure that is beyond the scope of this book. Consequently, we will not attempt to provide percentile scores for the Verbal and Quantitative sections of these practice tests. Nevertheless, by counting up the number of questions you got right and the number you got wrong, you can get a good idea of how well prepared you are for the real GRE. You can also see whether you are working too slowly and need to pick up your pacing. And finally, by studying your results to see which topics and question types gave you the most trouble and which were easiest for you, you can learn where to focus your remaining study time. Additional scaled score information is available on the GRE website.

Scoring the Analytical Writing Section

After you finish writing your essays for the Analytical Writing section of each practice test, you may want to ask a teacher, relative, or friend to score them for you, or you may score them yourself. Scoring is done by rating the essay according to a 0-to-6 scale provided by the test makers, with 6 being the highest score. Here is a simplified version of the scoring scale:

0   An essay rates a 0 if the writer does not address the assigned topic, if the essay is unintelligible, or if the writer does not submit any response.

1   An essay rates a 1 if the writing is fundamentally lacking in ideas and clarity or if most of it has nothing to do with the assigned topic. An essay at this level fails to develop any logical analysis and is filled with severe grammatical and mechanical errors that prevent understanding.

2   An essay rates a 2 if the writing has serious flaws and fails to analyze ideas or develop a logical argument. An essay at this level contains frequent grammatical and mechanical errors that impede understanding.

3   An essay rates a 3 if the writer shows some ability to develop ideas but does not analyze them clearly and displays limited organizational skills. An essay at this level contains numerous sentence-structure and usage errors.

4   An essay rates a 4 if the writer shows some competence in developing a thesis supported by relevant examples and evidence. An essay at this level displays adequate organization and good control of language, even though there may be some grammar or usage errors that impede understanding.

5   An essay rates a 5 if the writer displays the ability to analyze complex ideas soundly and thoughtfully. An essay at this level is well organized and has a well-developed main idea supported by relevant examples. The writer uses varied sentence structure and displays good control of language. Errors are minor and do not impede understanding.

6   An essay rates a 6 if the writer displays the ability to analyze complex ideas in depth, to develop a logical, tightly reasoned argument, and to support conclusions with well-chosen examples. An essay at this level is focused and well organized. The writer uses language skillfully and makes good use of vocabulary. Any grammatical or mechanical errors that may be present are minor and do not affect the meaning of the essay.

GRE Practice Test 1

SECTION 1
Analytical Writing

ANALYZE AN ISSUE

30 Minutes

You will have 30 minutes to organize your thoughts and compose a response that represents your point of view on the topic presented. Do not respond to any topic other than the one given; a response to any other topic will receive a score of 0.

You will be required to discuss your perspective on the issue, using examples and reasons drawn from your own experiences and observations.

Use scratch paper to organize your response before you begin writing. Write your response on the pages provided, or type your response using a word processor with the spell- and grammar-check functions turned off.

Issue Topic

"Art does not exist unless it is shared; it requires both artist and audience."

Discuss the extent to which you agree or disagree with the claim made above. Use relevant reasons and examples to support your point of view.

SECTION 2

Analytical Writing

ANALYZE AN ARGUMENT

30 Minutes

You will have 30 minutes to organize your thoughts and compose a response that critiques the given argument. Do not respond to any topic other than the one given; a response to any other topic will receive a score of 0.

You are not being asked to discuss your point of view on the statement. You should identify and analyze the central elements of the argument, the underlying assumptions that are being made, and any supporting information that is given. Your critique can also discuss other information that would strengthen or weaken the argument or make it more logical.

Use scratch paper to organize your response before you begin writing. Write your response on the pages provided, or type your response using a word processor with the spell- and grammar-check functions turned off.

Argument Topic

In order to vote in school elections in Lowville, you need only be a citizen, have lived in the district for 30 days, and be over the age of 18. Concerned that the turnout at recent school elections has been quite low, with only about 20 percent of eligible voters coming to the polls, school officials have discussed changing the regulations to require that voters be registered with the board of elections, as they must be for a general or municipal election. They posit that voters who are registered are already committed to the electoral process and thus are more likely to come to the polls for school elections as well.

Examine the logic of this argument by discussing what questions would need to be answered in order to decide whether the prediction and the argument on which it is based are reasonable.

_____

_____

_____

_____

_____

_____

_____

_____

_____

_____

_____

_____

_____

_____

_____

_____

_____

_____

_____

_____

_____

SECTION 3
Verbal Reasoning
Time: 35 minutes
25 questions

Questions 1 through 3 are based on this passage.

Roger Williams was a dissenter from an early age, having rebelled against his own father as a young boy to follow the path of the Puritans. He studied at Cambridge and became a cleric, but was notable even as a young chaplain for his strong belief in freedom of worship.

Line (5) After a year or two of butting his head against the strict High Church administration, Williams took his wife, Mary, and departed for Boston, arriving in 1631. Even in this new world, his radical ideas about the separation of church and state and the seizure of native land almost led to his deportation, and in 1636 he established his own colony, Providence Plantation, with a few like-minded followers.

Consider each of the choices separately and select all that apply.

1. The passage indicates that Roger Williams ran into resistance in Boston due to which of the following?

   [A] His views about the separation of church and state

   [B] His opposition to the takeover of land belonging to the tribes

   [C] His adamant and radical belief in freedom of worship

Select one answer choice.

2. Which of the following statements best summarizes the main idea of the passage?

   Ⓐ After failing as a cleric in England and then in Boston, Roger Williams left the church and struck out on his own with a small band of followers.

   Ⓑ Roger Williams left England with a small band of followers, intent on establishing his own colony and worshipping freely.

   Ⓒ Roger Williams's resistance to authority and the status quo caused him to challenge everyone from his own father to leaders in the New World.

   Ⓓ The Puritan path was no longer enough for young Roger Williams, and he set off for Boston to establish his own church there.

   Ⓔ Sensing that he was never going to succeed in the High Church, Roger Williams departed for Boston, where he seized native land to build his own colony.

3. Underline the sentence that indicates that Williams's strong beliefs caused trouble for him in England.

Question 4 is based on this passage.

Puget Sound is typically considered a bay; in fact, it is a large saltwater estuary fed by freshwater from the Cascade Range and Olympic Mountains watersheds. The sound itself was carved out by glaciers, leaving a complex series of interconnected valleys and ridges called *basins* and *sills*. The sound has an average depth of about 450 feet, but north of the city of Seattle, the basin plunges to 930 feet. Water is always circulating within the sound; at certain sills, seaward-moving surface water is sucked down to mix with incoming salt water. The result is a complicated tide pattern, made even more complex by the many islands and narrow straits that crisscross the sound. The positive result of all this churning is the deposit of fairly rich and fertile soil along the mudflats and river valleys that border the sound.

Line
(5)

(10)

Select one answer choice.

4. Which of these can be inferred about the waters of Puget Sound?

Ⓐ The sound is a constantly changing blend of salt and freshwater.

Ⓑ The sound is salt water along the surface and freshwater below.

Ⓒ The salt in the sound's water is leached away by the time it reaches shore.

Ⓓ Constant tides in Puget Sound leave salt in the basins and freshwater along the sills.

Ⓔ Seaward-moving water in the sound is saltier than incoming water.

For questions 5 through 8, complete the text by picking the best entry for each blank from the corresponding column of choices.

---

5. The 2017 Central Mexico earthquake happened to occur on the anniversary of an earthquake in 1985 that had killed thousands and had just that day been _____ with a national disaster drill.

Ⓐ	rehearsed
Ⓑ	calamitous
Ⓒ	commemorated
Ⓓ	bequeathed
Ⓔ	deracinated

6. The _____ effect of elevator music cannot be underestimated; several workers at the new office building reported being lulled into missing their floors entirely.

Ⓐ	anodyne
Ⓑ	dolorous
Ⓒ	ambient
Ⓓ	hermetic
Ⓔ	ephemeral

7. Following World War II, the Dutch manufacturer Fokker developed the _____ for a small aircraft to be used exclusively for the instruction of pilots.

Ⓐ	facsimile
Ⓑ	embodiment
Ⓒ	signifier
Ⓓ	prototype
Ⓔ	juncture

8. Raised by a father who was a noted experimental educator, the four Alcott girls received a (i) _____ education in the arts and sciences from such (ii) _____ as Ralph Waldo Emerson, Margaret Fuller, and Henry David Thoreau, all friends of the family and important thinkers (iii) _____.

Blank (i)	Blank (ii)	Blank (iii)
Ⓐ truncated	Ⓓ luminaries	Ⓖ with portfolio
Ⓑ broad	Ⓔ dilettantes	Ⓗ in their own right
Ⓒ conversant	Ⓕ novices	Ⓘ past and present

Questions 9 through 12 are based on this passage.

The fortuitous 1964 meeting of guitarist Lou Reed and keyboardist and composer John Cale would result in one of the most influential rock-and-roll collaborations of all time. The Velvet Underground (named after a book about aberrant sexual
Line practices) never succeeded by today's standards, but the recordings they made
(5) influenced everyone from Patti Smith to U2.

Cale and Reed joined with guitarist Sterling Morrison and drummer Maureen Tucker, and they played regular gigs in Greenwich Village before being spotted by artist Andy Warhol, who took them under his wing, became their manager-producer, and offered them German songstress Nico as a temporary teammate. Warhol's
(10) assistance (and stunning album-cover art) helped the Velvet Underground break out of the New York scene; they toured with Warhol's multimedia show throughout the United States and Canada in 1967.

Cale and Reed fell out over artistic differences shortly thereafter. They simply could not agree on an appropriate direction for the band. Although the Velvet
(15) Underground faded from view by the early 1970s, Lou Reed embarked on a solo career in the States, and Cale, a Welshman by birth, did the same back in the UK. They came together again briefly in 1996, when their remarkable band was inducted into the Rock and Roll Hall of Fame.

Consider each of the choices separately and select all that apply.

9. In which ways did Andy Warhol assist the Velvet Underground?

   [A] He loaned them the use of a key female singer.

   [B] He included them in films aired in his multimedia show.

   [C] He provided artwork for their early record albums.

For questions 10 through 12, select one answer choice each.

---

10. In the first sentence of the passage, what does the author mean by *fortuitous*?

    (A) Surprisingly enjoyable

    (B) Privileged to occur

    (C) Physically powerful

    (D) Unexpected but lucky

    (E) Often celebrated

11. According to the author, which is true of the Velvet Underground?

    (A)   They were pedestrian but beloved.

    (B)   They were gifted but enigmatic.

    (C)   They were avant-garde but transitory.

    (D)   They were unprofitable but influential.

    (E)   They were obscure but highly regarded.

12. Why does the author include information about the derivation of the band's name?

    (A)   To explain the evolution of their unusual sound

    (B)   To reject popular notions about the band's origin

    (C)   To hint at the band's attraction to a deviant lifestyle

    (D)   To reveal the band's appeal to all five senses

    (E)   To highlight the hippie uniform that reflected the band's style

Question 13 is based on this passage.

Jumping spiders, or salticids, are easily discerned from other types of spiders. As their name suggests, they use a different form of predation than do ordinary web-spinning spiders. Not content to sit and wait patiently for prey to cross their woven doorstep, salticids instead track their prey mercilessly and spring upon it, injecting it with venom and consuming it on the spot, or using a strand of silk to drag it back to their lair to eat. This sort of behavior requires unusually superior eyesight, and the salticids' eyes—eight of them!—are both large and complex, with long tubular eyes that provide excellent resolution combined with lateral eyes that have a broad field of vision. If you watch a salticid hunt, you will see it spot its prey with its lateral eyes and then turn to focus in with its tubular front eyes.

Line (5) ... (10) *(line markers in margin)*

13. Underline the sentence that shows step-by-step how salticids capture their prey.

For questions 14 through 17, complete the text by picking the best entry for each blank from the corresponding column of choices.

14. The Kavango people of Namibia are mainly Christian, although their religious activities often _____ elements of traditional tribal rites.

   - (A) incorporate
   - (B) replicate
   - (C) identify
   - (D) manufacture
   - (E) portend

15. If you mention seeing a bird of paradise on your journey, you must (i) _____ whether you are referring to the astonishing island bird or to the beautiful flower that is (ii) _____ to South Africa.

Blank (i)	Blank (ii)
(A) infer	(D) adaptable
(B) relinquish	(E) indigenous
(C) indicate	(F) collective

16. Due to Kandahar's (i) _____ location along the trade routes of Central and Southern Asia, it has long been the site of (ii) _____ between empires.

Blank (i)	Blank (ii)
(A) previous	(D) meeting
(B) strategic	(E) indifference
(C) unfavorable	(F) struggles

17. In addition to his more (i) _____ work as an astrophysicist, Carl Sagan helped to (ii) _____ astronomy through his writing, television series, and connection with the space program.

Blank (i)	Blank (ii)
(A) competent	(D) debate
(B) scholarly	(E) inspire
(C) acceptable	(F) popularize

Questions 18 through 20 are based on this passage.

London's Royal Opera House is frequently referred to simply as Covent Garden, but in fact, "Covent Garden" refers to the entire neighborhood in which the opera house is found, from St. Martin's Lane to Drury Lane, and encompassing St. Paul's

Line Church and the Covent Garden Market where Professor Henry Higgins and Colonel

(5) Pickering (emerging from the opera) first buy flowers from Eliza Doolittle in *My Fair Lady*. The land on which the neighborhood stands was once, in fact, a convent garden, and the fruits and vegetables raised and sold by the monks were for years a source of vitamins for Londoners. Since the 1600s, fruits and vegetables (no longer grown right there) have been sold at various sites around Covent Garden. As for

(10) the opera house, it has burned down and been rebuilt twice since George Frideric Handel presented his *Messiah* there in 1743, and it is still in continuous use.

For questions 18 through 20, select one answer choice each.

18. From what does the nickname of the opera house originally derive?

   Ⓐ The royal gardens of the queen of England

   Ⓑ A vegetable patch belonging to a religious community

   Ⓒ The flower market that was made famous in *My Fair Lady*

   Ⓓ A vegetable market that has stood nearby since the 1600s

   Ⓔ The neighborhood surrounding St. Paul's Church

19. The author apparently assumes that the reader

   Ⓐ has visited Covent Garden in the past

   Ⓑ recognizes *My Fair Lady* and the *Messiah*

   Ⓒ is familiar with many types of vegetables

   Ⓓ lives in a part of London outside Drury Lane

   Ⓔ is an aficionado of Italian and French opera

20. Which of the following best describes the function of the concluding sentence of the passage?

    (A)   It summarizes the fundamental ideas of the paragraph as a whole.

    (B)   It provides another example to support the author's premise.

    (C)   It qualifies the author's original statement concerning Covent Garden.

    (D)   It circles back to connect the opening sentence to the rest of the passage.

    (E)   It draws a conclusion about the derivation of the opera house's name.

For questions 21 through 25, select two answer choices that (1) complete the sentence in a way that makes sense and (2) produce sentences that are similar in meaning.

---

21. The earliest recorded inhabitants of the tiny island off Senegal were the Jola people, and they remain the _____ ethnic group on the island.

    [A] crowded

    [B] dominant

    [C] complex

    [D] prevailing

    [E] exceptional

    [F] established

22. In medieval England, the general population could rarely read or write, so people received news via the _____ of the town crier.

    [A] proclamations

    [B] advent

    [C] recordings

    [D] announcements

    [E] auspices

    [F] rejoinders

23. The Atlantic and Pacific Highway was an important connection between East and West coasts in the early years of automobile travel, but it was largely _____ by the development of the U.S. highway system, beginning around the mid-1920s.

    - [A] revitalized
    - [B] eradicated
    - [C] depreciated
    - [D] expanded
    - [E] eliminated
    - [F] salvaged

24. Although living benefactors may provide kidneys and bone marrow to patients who need transplants, far more organ donations _____ deceased donors than living ones.

    - [A] start out
    - [B] set off
    - [C] embark on
    - [D] derive from
    - [E] give to
    - [F] come from

25. Pioneers used clematis as a pepper substitute, and some Native Americans used small traces to cure headaches; nevertheless, the plant is _____ toxic.

    - [A] by no means
    - [B] in effect
    - [C] acutely
    - [D] essentially
    - [E] sporadically
    - [F] rarely

STOP. **This is the end of Section 3. Use any remaining time to check your work.**

SECTION 4
Verbal Reasoning
Time: 35 minutes
25 questions

For questions 1 through 4, select two answer choices that (1) complete the sentence in a way that makes sense and (2) produce sentences that are similar in meaning.

1. In 1830, Jim Bridger and his partners established a trading company that would _____ the Hudson's Bay Company and John Jacob Astor's American Fur Company for the profitable beaver-fur trade.

    [A]   adjoin

    [B]   invest in

    [C]   profit from

    [D]   compete with

    [E]   promote

    [F]   challenge

2. The ratites, a class of flightless birds, _____ both the ostrich, at more than nine feet tall, and the much smaller little spotted kiwi, at around nine inches.

    [A]   range from

    [B]   comprise

    [C]   vary with

    [D]   occupy

    [E]   characterize

    [F]   encompass

3. In the author's opinion, the reviewer's criticisms were _____, so he refused to lose sleep over the review.

   A specious

   B devastating

   C significant

   D unfounded

   E distasteful

   F comical

4. Even though she boasted a handful of advanced degrees, the professor's remarks seemed to her listeners to be somewhat _____.

   A self-centered

   B unsophisticated

   C tortuous

   D ingenuous

   E tiresome

   F abrupt

Questions 5 and 6 are based on this passage.

Although it may seem that nuclear power has declined as a means of providing electricity, the United States continues to produce the most nuclear energy of any country in the world: just under 20 percent of our electricity is produced by nuclear
Line energy. Of course, the European Union uses a much higher percent of nuclear
(5) power, at close to 30 percent, but their consumption is considerably less than that of the United States. In Europe, too, the use of nuclear power varies widely from place to place. There are no plants in Ireland, for example, but there are 16 in France. The safety of nuclear power plants continues to be a political problem for countries who wish to convert from coal or other fuels, and the question of where to put
(10) radioactive nuclear waste has still not been answered to anyone's satisfaction.

Consider each of the choices separately and select all that apply.

5. Which of these presents an accurate comparison of nuclear-energy use in the United States and the European Union?

   [A] The European Union uses more nuclear energy than the United States does.

   [B] The United States uses more nuclear energy than the European Union does.

   [C] The European Union derives more of its electricity from nuclear power than the United States does.

Select one answer choice.

6. The author's attitude toward nuclear power may best be described as

   (A) patronizing

   (B) optimistic

   (C) concerned

   (D) apathetic

   (E) animated

Question 7 is based on this passage.

The Atchison, Topeka, and Santa Fe Railway, often referred to simply as the "Santa Fe," was responsible for several cultural changes in the late nineteenth century. For example, it may be responsible for the plethora of chain restaurants we see in every U.S. city today. The Harvey House restaurants built along the path of the railroad by Fred Harvey and his company were the forerunners of the hundreds of franchise restaurants that exist along our highways today. In addition, the railroad brought tourists to a region of the Southwest they otherwise never would have seen, which in turn encouraged the spread of Hopi and Navajo artwork and products to the eastern United States.

Line
(5)

Select one answer choice.

7. Which of the following can be inferred about tourists on the Santa Fe solely on the basis of information in the passage?

   (A) They had discretionary income to spend on their journeys.

   (B) They preferred home cooking to dining on the road.

   (C) They purchased artwork as an investment strategy.

   (D) They delighted in the Western panorama, and many stayed put.

   (E) They liked to "go native" when they visited the Southwest.

Questions 8 and 9 are based on this passage.

We know him now as a fiction writer, the chronicler of California mining in the latter half of the nineteenth century; however, Bret Harte was notorious for being a muckraking journalist long before that term was coined.

Line
(5)   In 1860, a group of white miners and settlers attacked and murdered over 100 Wiyot Indian men, women, and children on an island near the settlement of Eureka, California. The Wiyots, who made their living weaving baskets and fishing, had been in the region for hundreds of years. When his editor was away, Harte wrote about the massacre in sensational language for the newspaper at which he worked. Shortly thereafter, he had to flee the region due to death threats. It appeared that everyone in
(10) the area, including his own editor, approved of the slaughter.

Consider each of the choices separately and select all that apply.

8. The passage suggests that Harte's reporting on the Wiyot massacre was

    A   daring

    B   lurid

    C   unwarranted

Select one answer choice.

9. Based on the author's word choice, a reader can infer that she finds the attack on the Wiyot Indians

    Ⓐ justified

    Ⓑ predictable

    Ⓒ repellent

    Ⓓ intriguing

    Ⓔ wearisome

> For questions 10 through 13, complete the text by picking the best entry for each blank from the corresponding column of choices.

10. The twelfth-century scientist al-Khazini, known for his work in the science of mechanics as well as his invention of several scientific instruments, lived in Merv, which was once a town in Persia but is now _____ Turkmenistan.

Ⓐ	surrounded by
Ⓑ	encompassing
Ⓒ	divided into
Ⓓ	combined with
Ⓔ	part of

11. The Florida owlet is neither a bird nor a Florida resident, although Florida _____ the southern part of its range; it is a nocturnal moth.

Ⓐ	exceeds
Ⓑ	verifies
Ⓒ	documents
Ⓓ	represents
Ⓔ	extends to

12. According to the ancient Icelandic text known as the Book of Settlement, the (i) _____ of Iceland began in the year 874, when a Norwegian chieftain sailed to the island and decided to stay (ii) _____. Over the next centuries, settlers (iii) _____ from Nordic and Celtic lands.

Blank (i)	Blank (ii)	Blank (iii)
Ⓐ pursuit	Ⓓ aboard	Ⓖ arrived
Ⓑ removal	Ⓔ permanently	Ⓗ deserted
Ⓒ colonization	Ⓕ away	Ⓘ exchanged

13. The British victory at Germantown, Pennsylvania, (i) _____ that Philadelphia, capital of the (ii) _____ United States, remained in enemy hands all winter long.

Blank (i)
(A)   ensured
(B)   concerned
(C)   verified

Blank (ii)
(D)   erstwhile
(E)   nascent
(F)   dormant

Questions 14 through 16 are based on this passage.

Every living creature produces a minor amount of electricity in its cells. Each of your brain cells fires a tiny blip of electricity, converting it from chemical energy. However, nobody makes electricity as well as one small group of marine creatures. These
Line   animals use electricity to navigate and communicate, but they also use it to sense and
(5)   stun prey. Best of all these electric predators is the electric eel, more accurately known as the electric knifefish. This large eel-like fish lives in the rivers and wetlands of South America. It eats insects, small fish, crustaceans, and even small amphibians and mammals. Its abdominal organs can produce a shock ranging up to 500 volts, as much as a high-voltage transformer—more than enough to kill you.

Consider each of the choices separately and select all that apply.

14. Based on information in the passage, which creature or creatures might an electric knifefish eat?

[A]   Angelfish

[B]   Shrew

[C]   Glass shrimp

Select one answer choice.

15. According to the passage, electric knifefish use electricity to do all of the following EXCEPT

(A)   illuminate their target

(B)   locate and discern their prey

(C)   impart information to other fish

(D)   steer a course underwater

(E)   knock out their quarry

16. Underline the sentence that discusses human energy production.

For questions 17 through 20, complete the text by picking the best entry for each blank from the corresponding column of choices.

17. Designed to _____ dehydration by replacing water and electrolytes, sports drinks have rapidly become a multimillion dollar industry.

(A)	augment
(B)	expiate
(C)	indemnify
(D)	vitalize
(E)	slake

18. Hamlet's excessively (i) _____ tone when he speaks of his late father contrasts with the forced (ii) _____ he manufactures when speaking to the uncle and mother he blames for Claudius's death.

Blank (i)		Blank (ii)	
(A)	lugubrious	(D)	affliction
(B)	trenchant	(E)	contrition
(C)	fulsome	(F)	conviviality

19. Hasidism is a (i) _____ of Orthodox Judaism that (ii) _____ its rabbis in untraditional ways as spiritual leaders and workers of miracles.

Blank (i)		Blank (ii)	
(A)	precept	(D)	exalts
(B)	branch	(E)	motivates
(C)	volume	(F)	belies

20. People who (i) _____ actor George C. Scott's portrayal of General George Patton may not (ii) _____ that the actor spent four years as a marine. While stationed in Washington, DC, he taught English and writing at the Marine Corps Institute and (iii) _____ as a guard at Arlington National Cemetery.

Blank (i)		Blank (ii)		Blank (iii)	
(A)	forget about	(D)	assume	(G)	served
(B)	look up to	(E)	recall	(H)	pursued
(C)	think highly of	(F)	realize	(I)	fought

Opera buffa was an attempt to make opera accessible to commoners. These lighter, comic operas were typically set in everyday, modern settings, rather than against classical or mythical backdrops. They might feature servants and below-stairs activities, as in commedia dell'arte, with its stock serving girls and clowns. Although the art form originated in Italy, and Donizetti's *L'elisir d'amore* remains a good example, it is Vienna's Mozart whose light comic operas endure. *Le nozze di Figaro*, *Così fan tutte*, and even *Don Giovanni* are beloved examples of the genre.

Line
(5)

Select one answer choice.

21. The author implies that opera buffa appealed to the middle class because it

  (A) emphasized the triumph of the little man

  (B) portrayed noble characters in ignoble situations

  (C) was short, amusing, and inexpensive to attend

  (D) focused on the mundane rather than the sublime

  (E) updated and modernized classical narratives

Trees that are constantly exposed to harsh, freezing winds become deformed in a manner that is so specific that it has its own name. Such trees are called *krummholz*, meaning "crooked wood." They are especially common at the tree line of subalpine or subarctic mountains. The roots and lower trunks of the trees are able to grow, but the upper trunks and branches are stunted and bent. A tree that is quite familiar in a more congenial climate—a black spruce, for example, or a balsam fir—may appear completely misshapen and shrunken in a subarctic clime. Interestingly, the recent disappearance of krummholz forests is considered a symptom of climate change.

Line
(5)

Consider each of the choices separately and select all that apply.

22. According to the passage, which fact or facts are true of krummholz trees?

  [A] They are ordinary trees that are misshapen by cold winds.

  [B] They are a subspecies found only in subalpine or subarctic zones.

  [C] Their emergence is indicative of climate change.

Questions 23 through 25 are based on this passage.

The unification of Norway took place around 880 A.D. (the exact date is unknown), when King Harald Fairhair won the Battle of Hafrsfjord. At the time, the land was divided into a series of tiny kingdoms, with the Danish king ruling some areas of eastern Norway. What we know of the era we owe to the Icelandic saga writer and historian Snorri Sturluson, whose history of the kings of Norway was completed some 300 years later. Because of the difference in dates, it is hard to accept everything Snorri wrote at face value. Nevertheless, his history remains the most valuable and detailed chronicle of these times. A more contemporaneous source of the history of the battle is Harald's court poet, Torbjørn Hornklove, who wrote a lay about the battle that is still read today.

Line (5)

(10)

Consider each of the choices separately and select all that apply.

23. The author implies which of the following about Snorri Sturluson's history of the kings of Norway?

    A   It is not necessarily reliable.

    B   It remains an indispensable artifact.

    C   It shows some Icelandic bias.

Select one answer choice.

24. In the last sentence of the passage, *contemporaneous* means

    Ⓐ modern

    Ⓑ of that era

    Ⓒ in vogue

    Ⓓ authentic

    Ⓔ permanent

25. Underline the sentence that explains why Norway required unification.

STOP. This is the end of Section 4. Use any remaining time to check your work.

SECTION 5
Quantitative Reasoning
Time: 40 minutes
25 questions

Each of Questions 1 through 9 consists of two quantities, Quantity A and Quantity B. You are to compare the two quantities. You may use additional information centered above the two quantities if additional information is given. Choose

(A) if Quantity A is greater;

(B) if Quantity B is greater;

(C) if the two quantities are equal;

(D) if the relationship cannot be determined from the information given.

Quantity A	Quantity B	
1. $\dfrac{5}{14} + \dfrac{8}{21}$	$\dfrac{26}{35} - \dfrac{3}{14}$	Ⓐ Ⓑ Ⓒ Ⓓ

n is an odd number and a multiple of 5

Quantity A	Quantity B	
2. the remainder when n is divided by 12	6	Ⓐ Ⓑ Ⓒ Ⓓ

$\lfloor x \rfloor =$ the largest integer less than or equal to x

Quantity A	Quantity B	
3. $\lfloor -1.5 \rfloor$	$-\lfloor 1.5 \rfloor$	Ⓐ Ⓑ Ⓒ Ⓓ

$$2x + y^2 > 6$$

Quantity A	Quantity B	
4. x	4	Ⓐ Ⓑ Ⓒ Ⓓ

Quantity A	Quantity B	
5. $\dfrac{2xy - x - 2x^2}{2x - 4x}$	$x - y$	Ⓐ Ⓑ Ⓒ Ⓓ

Quantity A	Quantity B	
6. the area of a square with perimeter 20	the area of a circle with radius 3	Ⓐ Ⓑ Ⓒ Ⓓ

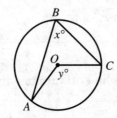

O is the center of circle ABC

Quantity A	Quantity B	
7. $2x$	y	Ⓐ Ⓑ Ⓒ Ⓓ

$$2x + 4 = 9$$

Quantity A	Quantity B	
8. $6x$	18	Ⓐ Ⓑ Ⓒ Ⓓ

	Quantity A	Quantity B	
9.	$\frac{2}{5}$ of 0.1%	0.004	Ⓐ Ⓑ Ⓒ Ⓓ

> Questions 10 through 25 have different formats. Select a single answer choice unless the directions say otherwise. For numeric-entry questions, follow these instructions:
>
> - Enter your answer in the box or boxes provided.
> - Your answer may be an integer, a decimal, a fraction, or a negative number.
> - If the answer is a fraction, you will be given two boxes: an upper one for the numerator and a lower one for the denominator.
> - Equivalent forms of the correct answer, such as 1.6 and 1.60, are all correct. You do not need to reduce fractions to lowest terms.

10. How many different diagonals can be drawn on a regular hexagon?

Ⓐ 4

Ⓑ 6

Ⓒ 8

Ⓓ 9

Ⓔ 12

For this question, write your answer in the box.

11. An agency cleans carpets at the rate of $0.05 per square foot. How much will it cost to clean a rectangular rug with a length of 25 feet and a width of 12 feet?

$ ☐

For this question, indicate all of the answer choices that apply.

12. Which of the following equations describe a line with a slope less than that of
$5y - 4x = 3$?

  [A] $4y + 5x = 3$

  [B] $4y - 2x = 3$

  [C] $y - 5x = 3$

  [D] $y + 5x = 3$

  [E] $5x - 4y = 3$

For this question, indicate all of the answer choices that apply.

13. Which of the following points are closer to $(3, 9)$ than the point $(5, 3)$ is?

  [A] $(3, 1)$

  [B] $(1, 5)$

  [C] $(-1, 8)$

  [D] $(9, 3)$

  [E] $(0, 6)$

For this question, write your answer in the boxes.

14. What fraction is equal to 0.75?

$$\frac{\boxed{}}{\boxed{}}$$

15. What is the perimeter of the below rectilinear shape?

  Ⓐ 22 feet

  Ⓑ 30 feet

  Ⓒ 32 feet

  Ⓓ 40 feet

  Ⓔ 46 feet

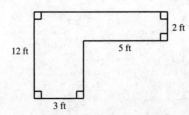

For this question, indicate all of the answer choices that apply.

16. Which of the following could be the set of lengths of a right triangle?
    - A. $\{1, \sqrt{2}\}$
    - B. $\{3, 4, 5\}$
    - C. $\{4, 5, 6\}$
    - D. $\{0.6, 0.8, 1\}$
    - E. $\{3, 4, \sqrt{7}\}$

For this question, indicate all of the answer choices that apply.

17. Let m be an odd integer and n an even integer. Which of the following must be even?
    - A. nm^2
    - B. $n + m$
    - C. $3n - 2m$
    - D. $n - m$
    - E. nm

For this question, indicate all of the answer choices that apply.

18. City A is 800 miles from City B. City B is 1,500 miles from City C. Which of the following could be the distance from City A to City C?
    - A. 600 miles
    - B. 1,000 miles
    - C. 1,200 miles
    - D. 1,500 miles
    - E. 2,000 miles
    - F. 2,500 miles

19. What is the sum of all the integers from 1 through 50 (inclusive)?

    Ⓐ 1,224

    Ⓑ 1,250

    Ⓒ 1,275

    Ⓓ 1,326

    Ⓔ 2,525

20. What is the largest prime factor of $5! \times 8!$?

    Ⓐ 5

    Ⓑ 7

    Ⓒ 13

    Ⓓ 31

    Ⓔ 37

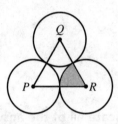

21. Equilateral triangle PQR is formed by joining the centers P, Q, and R of the three circles. Each pair of circles has exactly one point in common. If $PQ = 12$, what is the shaded area?

    Ⓐ 6π

    Ⓑ 12π

    Ⓒ 18π

    Ⓓ 24π

    Ⓔ 36π

22. $\left(\dfrac{x^7}{x^2}\right)^3 =$

    (A) x^8

    (B) x^{10}

    (C) x^{15}

    (D) x^{19}

    (E) x^{27}

Use the following figure to answer questions 23 through 25.

Household Budget

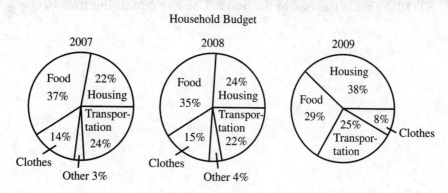

For this question, write your answer in the box.

23. What was the combined percentage of household expenses devoted to food and clothes in 2009?

24. If $4,800 was spent on clothes in 2008, how much was spent on food in 2008?

    (A) $6,480

    (B) $8,300

    (C) $9,260

    (D) $11,200

    (E) $13,800

25. Suppose the total household budget was 6% larger in 2009 than in 2007. What is the approximate percent of increase for money spent on housing from 2007 to 2009?

   (A) 16%

   (B) 21%

   (C) 73%

   (D) 83%

   (E) 170%

STOP.   This is the end of Section 5. Use any remaining time to check your work.

SECTION 6
Quantitative Reasoning
Time: 40 minutes
25 questions

Each of questions 1 through 9 consists of two quantities, Quantity A and Quantity B. You are to compare the two quantities. You may use additional information centered above the two quantities if additional information is given. Choose

(A) if Quantity A is greater;

(B) if Quantity B is greater;

(C) if the two quantities are equal;

(D) if the relationship cannot be determined from the information given.

	Quantity A	Quantity B	
1.	$0.3\overline{5}$	$0.3\overline{5}$	(A) (B) (C) (D)

	Quantity A	Quantity B	
2.	35 miles per day	7,000 feet per hour	(A) (B) (C) (D)

Suppose that, with 5% tax, Carlos's order comes to exactly $100.

	Quantity A	Quantity B	
3.	cost of Carlos's order before tax was added	$95	(A) (B) (C) (D)

The height of a triangle is 60% bigger than the height of a rectangle. The base of the triangle is 30% bigger than the base of the rectangle.

	Quantity A	Quantity B	
4.	the area of the triangle	the area of the rectangle	(A) (B) (C) (D)

	Quantity A	Quantity B	

5. $500 invested for three $575   Ⓐ Ⓑ Ⓒ Ⓓ
    years at 5% annual
    compound interest

$$5 < \sqrt{n} < 6$$

	Quantity A	Quantity B	

6. n^2 500   Ⓐ Ⓑ Ⓒ Ⓓ

$$x \clubsuit y = x^2 - y$$

	Quantity A	Quantity B	

7. $(3 \clubsuit 2) \clubsuit - 1$ 50   Ⓐ Ⓑ Ⓒ Ⓓ

$$3 : x = 7 : 10$$

	Quantity A	Quantity B	

8. x 4   Ⓐ Ⓑ Ⓒ Ⓓ

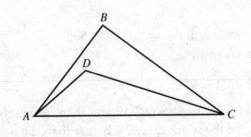

	Quantity A	Quantity B	

9. $\angle ABC$ $\angle ADC$ Ⓐ Ⓑ Ⓒ Ⓓ

Questions 10 through 25 have different formats. Select a single answer choice unless the directions say otherwise. For numeric-entry questions, follow these instructions:

- Enter your answer in the box or boxes provided.
- Your answer may be an integer, a decimal, a fraction, or a negative number.
- If the answer is a fraction, you will be given two boxes: an upper one for the numerator and a lower one for the denominator.
- Equivalent forms of the correct answer, such as 1.6 and 1.60, are all correct. You do not need to reduce fractions to lowest terms.

10. How many times 200 million is 1.2 trillion?

Ⓐ 600

Ⓑ 2,400

Ⓒ 6,000

Ⓓ 24,000

Ⓔ 60,000

For this question, write your answer in the box.

11. How many 8-inch squares will it take to tile a rectangular floor that measures 18 feet by 24 feet?

For this question, indicate all of the answer choices that apply.

12. Which of the following numbers are evenly divisible by 6?

A 35,172

B 24,834

C 28,897

D 40,356

E 49,429

13. A series of license plates will be made with two letters followed by four digits. How many different plates can be made for this series?

    (A) 26,000

    (B) 260,000

    (C) 676,000

    (D) 5,200,000

    (E) 6,760,000

14. One hundred wooden rulers have been glued together in a line to make one long stick. Each ruler is one foot long. The overlap between each adjacent pair of rulers is exactly one inch (where they were glued). What is the overall length of the long stick?

    (A) 83 feet, 6 inches

    (B) 90 feet, 8 inches

    (C) 90 feet, 9 inches

    (D) 91 feet, 9 inches

    (E) 92 feet, 6 inches

15. To use a floor cleaner, two-thirds of a cup of cleaner must be mixed with one-half gallon of water. If only one-half cup of cleaner is left, how much water should be mixed with it?

    (A) $\frac{1}{4}$ gallon

    (B) $\frac{1}{3}$ gallon

    (C) $\frac{2}{5}$ gallon

    (D) $\frac{3}{8}$ gallon

    (E) $\frac{5}{6}$ gallon

For this question, write your answer in the box.

16. What is $8^{\frac{2}{3}}$?

17. $\left(\dfrac{x^3}{y^4}\right)^{-2} \div \left(\dfrac{x^2}{y^3}\right)^{4} =$

   (A) $\dfrac{y^{20}}{x^{14}}$

   (B) $\dfrac{y^4}{x^2}$

   (C) $\dfrac{x^2}{y^4}$

   (D) $\dfrac{y^5}{x^4}$

   (E) $\dfrac{y^8}{x^5}$

18. Assuming that all pancakes are round and equally thick, how many pancakes four inches in diameter can be made with the batter of one pancake 12 inches in diameter?

   (A)   3

   (B)   4

   (C)   6

   (D)   9

   (E)   12

19. There is no solution to the system of equations $4y + 2x = 7$ and $2y = 5 + Ax$. Find A.

    (A) -2

    (B) -1

    (C) 0

    (D) 1

    (E) 2

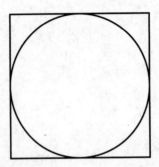

20. What is the probability that a point randomly selected in this square will be outside the circle?

    (A) $4 - \pi$

    (B) $1 - \dfrac{\pi}{4}$

    (C) $1 - \pi$

    (D) $1 - \dfrac{\pi}{8}$

    (E) $\dfrac{\pi}{4}$

For this question, write your answer in the box.

21. It takes three identical pumps working together for 8 hours to empty a 5,000-gallon tank of water. How long would it take two of these pumps to empty a 7,000-gallon tank of water at this rate?

22. An aquarium is 50 centimeters long, 30 centimeters wide, and 40 centimeters tall. How many liters of water will it take to fill to the top?

    (A) 60

    (B) 600

    (C) 6,000

    (D) 60,000

    (E) 600,000

Use the following figure to answer questions 23 through 25.

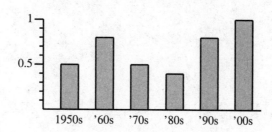

Popularity Ratings for Character X

For this question, write your answer in the box.

23. In the 1960s, how popular was character X, expressed as a percentage of X's popularity in the 2000s?

For this question, indicate all of the answer choices that apply.

24. Over which of the following time periods did character X's popularity increase?

    A   1950s to 1960s

    B   1960s to 1970s

    C   1970s to 1980s

    D   1980s to 1990s

    E   1990s to 2000s

25. How popular was character X in the 1950s, represented as a percentage of X's popularity in the 1980s?

(A) 50%

(B) 75%

(C) 120%

(D) 125%

(E) 133.$\overline{3}$%

STOP. This is the end of Section 6. Use any remaining time to check your work.

GRE Practice Test 1: Answers and Explanations

Analytical Writing: Scoring and Sample Responses

Analyze an Issue: Scoring

Score	Focus	Organization	Conventions
0	Does not address the prompt. Off topic.	Incomprehensible. May merely copy the prompt without development.	Illegible. Nonverbal. Serious errors make the paper unreadable. May be in a foreign language.
1	Mostly irrelevant to the prompt.	Little or no development of ideas. No evidence of analysis or organization.	Pervasive errors in grammar, mechanics, and spelling.
2	Unclear connection to the prompt.	Unfocused and disorganized.	Frequent errors in sentence structure, mechanics, and spelling.
3	Limited connection to the prompt.	Rough organization with weak examples or reasons.	Occasional major errors and frequent minor errors in conventions of written English.
4	Competent connection to the prompt.	Relevant examples or reasons develop a logical position.	Occasional minor errors in conventions of written English.
5	Clear, focused connection to the prompt.	Thoughtful, appropriate examples or reasons develop a consistent, coherent position. Connectors are ably used to mark transitions.	Very few errors. Sentence structure is varied and vocabulary is advanced.
6	Insightful, clever connection to the prompt.	Compelling, convincing examples or reasons develop a consistent, coherent position. The argument flows effortlessly and persuasively.	Very few errors. Sentence structure is varied and vocabulary is precise, well chosen, and effective.

Analyze an Issue:
Sample Response with a Score of 6

This essay is lucid and articulate. It addresses the prompt clearly and concisely, in this case arguing in favor of the statement and presenting and discounting a counterargument. There are no significant errors in grammar or mechanics.

If we accept the notion that art is a form of communication, which I believe to be the case, then we must admit that it needs both artist and audience to exist as art. The artist creates, but the viewer brings to the creation a wealth of background knowledge and experience that completes the artistic experience.

Even the earliest of artists—those cave dwellers who painted stories of the hunt on cavern walls—understood that they were creating something not only for themselves but for those who had not seen the hunt or witnessed the kill. They may have been more accurately described as recorders than as artists, but they were establishing a connection between creator and viewer that parallels that of any modern artist and tourist in a gallery today.

How often have we heard an artist state, "I paint for myself" or "I write for my own pleasure"? Artists may believe that they can create art in a vacuum, but writing and painting or music and dance that exist only in the shadows can never be truly whole. They can never be truly art.

The reason is simple. If no one else witnesses the performance, views the painting, or reads the poem, the artist's creation is no more than a locked diary. The artistic experience is incomplete; the artist has communicated with no one. Once the diary is unlocked, and the creation is shared, then the art comes full circle. The artist's knowledge and experience speaks to the viewer's knowledge and experience, and the connection is made. That connection, that communication between artist and audience, is what makes the creation art.

Analyze an Argument: Scoring

Score	Focus	Organization	Conventions
0	Does not address the prompt. Off topic.	Incomprehensible. May merely copy the prompt without development.	Illegible. Nonverbal. Serious errors make the paper unreadable. May be in a foreign language.
1	Little or no analysis of the argument. May indicate misunderstanding of the prompt.	Little or no development of ideas. No evidence of analysis or organization.	Pervasive errors in grammar, mechanics, and spelling.
2	Little analysis; may instead present opinions and unrelated thoughts.	Disorganized and illogical.	Frequent errors in sentence structure, mechanics, and spelling.
3	Some analysis of the prompt, but some major flaws may be omitted.	Rough organization with irrelevant support or unclear transitions.	Occasional major errors and frequent minor errors in conventions of written English.
4	Important flaws in the argument are touched upon.	Ideas are sound but may not flow logically or clearly.	Occasional minor errors in conventions of written English.
5	Perceptive analysis of the major flaws in the argument.	Logical examples and support develop a consistent, coherent critique. Connectors are ably used to mark transitions.	Very few errors. Sentence structure is varied and vocabulary is advanced.
6	Insightful, clever analysis of the argument's flaws and fallacies.	Compelling, convincing examples and support develop a consistent, coherent critique. The analysis flows effortlessly and persuasively.	Very few errors. Sentence structure is varied and vocabulary is precise, well chosen, and effective.

Analyze an Argument: Sample Response with a Score of 6

This essay is fluent and coherent. It addresses the prompt directly by dissecting the key flaws in the argument and then suggesting sensible alternatives to the proposal. There are no real errors in English usage or mechanics.

The school officials in Lowville are earnestly trying to find a way to improve their election turnout, but their proposal is flawed. By requiring voters to be registered, they presume that they will attract an electorate that is already committed to regular voting. However, they come to this conclusion based on assumptions rather than evidence.

It's logical to assume that the current electorate at Lowville school elections consists both of registered voters and of voters who merely come out for school elections rather than municipal elections, and therefore have not bothered to register with the board of elections. Let's assume for a moment that those groups are about equal in number. So 10 percent of eligible voters vote in school elections and are registered, and 10 percent of eligible voters vote in school elections and are not registered, for a total of 20 percent.

If registered voters are that much more dedicated to voting, why would they not come out to the school polls in greater numbers? Does it make sense to assume that only 10 percent of the entire electorate is registered, and that they all vote in school elections? Even if that number were closer to the total of 20 percent, it would still be extremely low. The Lowville school officials need to look closely at the turnout in municipal elections to know whether they would gain anything at all by forcing their voters to register. Do 100 percent of all registered voters typically vote in Lowville's municipal elections? It's doubtful, so the school officials' premise is flawed.

In addition, it is certainly possible that requiring registration would have a reverse effect and would in fact suppress the vote. If half of the existing vote comes from people who are not registered, or even if the percentage is less than that, it's still clear that some unregistered voters think the school election important enough to come out to vote.

There are probably good reasons to require all voters to be registered, but the assumption that registration promotes a higher turnout is unsupported by the few facts provided. Lowville school officials might look at changes in the accessibility of their polls, the date of the election, or their own promotion of the election through the media or other means as more plausible ways of increasing turnout.

GRE Practice Test 1: Answer Key

Section 3. Verbal Reasoning

1. **A, B**
2. **C**
3. After a year or two of butting his head against the strict High Church administration, Williams took his wife, Mary, and departed for Boston, arriving in 1631.
4. **A**
5. **C**
6. **A**
7. **D**
8. **B, D, H**
9. **A, C**
10. **D**
11. **D**
12. **C**
13. Not content to sit and wait patiently for prey to cross their woven doorstep, salticids instead track their prey mercilessly and spring upon it, injecting it with venom and consuming it on the spot, or using a strand of silk to drag it back to their lair to eat.
14. **A**
15. **C, E**
16. **B, F**
17. **B, F**
18. **B**
19. **B**
20. **D**
21. **B, D**
22. **A, D**
23. **B, E**
24. **D, F**
25. **B, D**

Section 4. Verbal Reasoning

1. **D, F**
2. **B, F**
3. **A, D**
4. **B, D**
5. **B, C**
6. **C**
7. **A**
8. **A, B**
9. **C**
10. **E**
11. **D**
12. **C, E, G**
13. **A, E**
14. **A, B, C**
15. **A**
16. Each of your brain cells fires a tiny blip of electricity, converting it from chemical energy.
17. **E**
18. **A, F**

19. **B, D**
20. **C, F, G**
21. **D**
22. **A**
23. **A, B**
24. **B**
25. At the time, the land was divided into a series of tiny kingdoms, with the Danish king ruling some areas of eastern Norway.

Section 5. Quantitative Reasoning

1. **A**
2. **D**
3. **B**
4. **D**
5. **A**
6. **B**
7. **C**
8. **B**
9. **B**
10. **D**
11. **$15**
12. **A, B, D**
13. **B, C, E**
14. **¾, 75/100, or any equivalent fraction**
15. **D**
16. **A, B, D, E**
17. **A, C, E**
18. **B, C, D, E**
19. **C**
20. **B**
21. **A**
22. **C**
23. **37%**
24. **D**
25. **D**

Section 6. Quantitative Reasoning

1. **B**
2. **A**
3. **A**
4. **A**
5. **A**
6. **A**
7. **C**
8. **A**
9. **B**
10. **C**
11. **972**
12. **A, B, D**
13. **E**
14. **D**
15. **D**
16. **4**
17. **A**
18. **D**
19. **B**
20. **B**
21. **16.8 hours**
22. **A**
23. **80%**
24. **A, D, E**
25. **D**

GRE Practice Test 1: Answer Explanations

Section 3. Verbal Reasoning

1. **A, B.** The answer is clarified in this phrase: "Even in this new world, his radical ideas about the separation of church and state and the seizure of native land almost led to his deportation." His belief in freedom of worship (choice C) led him to leave England, not Boston.

2. **C.** He did not leave the church (choice A), and his intention on leaving England was not to start his own colony (choice B). Choice C best summarizes all of the passage's main points.

3. **After a year or two of butting his head against the strict High Church administration, Williams took his wife, Mary, and departed for Boston, arriving in 1631.** In other words, his strong beliefs caused trouble in England, so he departed for the New World.

4. **A.** There is no support in the passage for choices B, C, or D, and choice E does not make logical sense. The entire passage suggests the mixing of salt and freshwater that is mentioned in choice A.

5. **C.** The 1985 earthquake had just been commemorated, or remembered and memorialized, with a disaster drill when the 2017 earthquake hit. None of the other choices makes sense in context.

6. **A.** An anodyne effect is a soothing effect; the lulling of the workers is caused by this soothing music. The other choices, meaning "sorrowful," "surrounding," "enclosed," and "momentary," do not fit the context.

7. **D.** Fokker did not create a duplication of something that was already there (choice A); it created a model of something brand-new, so choice D is best.

8. **B, D, H.** Use common sense to infer the correct answers. The girls' education was wide-ranging (choice B), not abridged (choice A), and their teachers were famous people (choice D), not amateurs (choices E and F). The idiom "in their own right" compares the teachers to Alcott, who was also an important thinker.

9. **A, C.** Although Warhol allowed the band to tour with him, no mention is made of using them in his films (choice B). However, he "offered them … Nico as a temporary teammate" (choice A) and created "stunning album-cover art" (choice C).

10. **D.** This is a straightforward definition of *fortuitous*, which shares a root with *fortune*.

11. **D.** Rely for your answer only on those points made by the author. The answer appears in this sentence: "The Velvet Underground … never succeeded by today's standards, but the recordings they made influenced everyone from Patti Smith to U2." In other words, they were unsuccessful financially, yet influential.

12. **C.** First, find the sentence that refers to the derivation of the band's name. That sentence states that they were "named after a book about aberrant sexual practices." That should be a good clue that the best answer is choice C; it says nothing about their sound (choice A), sensory images (choice D), or clothing (choice E).

13. **Not content to sit and wait patiently for prey to cross their woven doorstep, salticids instead track their prey mercilessly and spring upon it, injecting it with venom and consuming it on the spot, or using a strand of silk to drag it back to their lair to eat.** The sentence cited is the only one that tells step-by-step how the spiders capture their prey.

14. **A.** Religious activities of a Christian sect are more likely to include (choice A) elements of tribal rites than to duplicate them (choice B) or create them (choice D).

15. **C, E.** To paraphrase, the sentence means that people speaking of birds of paradise must tell (choice C) whether they mean birds or the flowers that are native to (choice E) South Africa.

16. **B, F.** If Kandahar's location were truly unfavorable (choice C), it would not cause trouble between empires (choice F); its location must be tactically important (choice B).

17. **B, F.** Sagan was both competent (choice A) and accepted (choice C) in both of his roles, but his astrophysics work was more scholarly (choice B). He did not so much inspire (choice E) astronomy, which already existed, as popularize it (choice F), making it accessible to the masses.

18. **B.** The answer is not stated directly but may be inferred from this phrase: "The land on which the neighborhood stands was once, in fact, a convent garden."

19. **B.** If the answer is not immediately obvious, use the process of elimination. There is no indication that the author expects the reader to know Covent Garden well (choice A) or even to live in London (choice D); if that were true, there would be no need to describe the area in detail. The author never lists types of vegetables (choice C) or mentions Italian or French operas (choice E). The passage does name *My Fair Lady* and the *Messiah* with no additional clarification, so the best answer is choice B.

20. **D.** The passage begins and ends with information about the opera house, making choice D the most logical answer.

21. **B, D.** Many of the choices might make sense in context, but only *dominant* (choice B) and *prevailing* (choice D) are synonyms.

22. **A, D.** The only pair of synonyms is *proclamations* (choice A) and *announcements* (choice D).

23. **B, E.** The sentence construction indicates that the second half of the sentence contrasts with the first. The highway was once important, but new construction largely killed it.

24. **D, F.** Here you can ignore the beginning clause if you like and just fill in the blanks based on the final clause. Choices A, B, C, and E are nonsensical; choices D and F make sense and are synonyms.

25. **B, D.** "Nevertheless" indicates a contrast; the sentence means that even though clematis is used without harm, it is actually harmful. Choices B, C, D, and E might fit, but only choices B and D are synonyms.

Section 4. Verbal Reasoning

1. **D, F.** A quick skim of the answer choices indicates that only *compete with* (choice D) and *challenge* (choice F) are synonyms.

2. **B, F.** *Range from* (A) does not work syntactically in the sentence. The only choices that fit the context and syntax and are synonyms are *comprise* (choice B) and *encompass* (choice F).

3. **A, D.** If the comments were devastating (choice B), significant (choice C), or even distasteful (choice E), the playwright might indeed lose sleep. If they were comical (choice F), he might not, but there is no synonym for *comical* among the choices. The best answer is *specious* (choice A), which means the same as *unfounded* (choice D).

4. **B, D.** The words "even though" hint at a contrast, so look for the words that contrast with the concept of advanced degrees. The best choices are *unsophisticated* (choice B) and *ingenuous* (choice D), both of which imply a level of unexpected simplicity or innocence.

5. **B, C.** The passage states clearly that the European Union uses more nuclear energy percentagewise, which nevertheless equals less consumption than that of the United States. Therefore, choices B and C are true, but choice A is not.

6. **C.** The author's concern shows in the final sentence, which discusses the problems of safety and waste.

7. **A.** To answer this question, do not roam far from the passage itself. There is no support for any of the choices but A; discretionary income would have allowed tourists to purchase food at restaurants as well as arts and crafts.

8. **A, B.** The author suggests that Harte's writing was daring (choice A) by stating that his life was in danger following publication. The phrase "sensational language" indicates that his writing was lurid (choice B). His writing may have been dangerous, but nowhere does the author suggest that it was uncalled-for or unwarranted (choice C).

9. **C.** Use the author's own language to infer her attitude. She calls the killing a "massacre" and a "slaughter," indicating strong negative feelings. *Repellent* (choice C) describes those feelings.

10. **E.** Merv was once in Persia. The assumption is that now it is in some other country. Only choice E suggests this parallel.

11. **D.** Choices A, B, C, and E sound good but make little real sense in context. Florida represents (choice D) the southern part of the moth's range.

12. **C, E, G.** Read the entire two-sentence passage before plugging in words to fit the blanks. If you do that, the logic of choices C, E, and G becomes clear.

13. **A, E.** *Ensured* (choice A) is a better, more accurate choice than *verified* (choice C). A little sense of history should tell you that the United States was, at the time of the American Revolution, a nascent (choice E), or newly born, nation.

14. **A, B, C.** The passage states: "It eats insects, small fish (choice A), crustaceans (choice C), and even small amphibians and mammals (choice B)."

15. **A.** The passage mentions all of the choices except illumination (choice A).

16. **Each of your brain cells fires a tiny blip of electricity, converting it from chemical energy.** This is the only sentence that discusses human energy production.

17. **E.** To slake thirst is to alleviate thirst. The other choices mean "add to," "atone for," "guarantee," and "energize."

18. **A, F.** Given the sentence structure, you need to find two contrasting words to finish the sentence correctly. The correct responses are *lugubrious*, meaning "mournful," and *conviviality*, meaning "warmth" or "geniality."

19. **B, D.** Hasidism is not a precept, or principle, of Judaism (choice A); it is a sect, or branch, of the religion (choice B). The sect does something that makes its rabbis appear to be workers of miracles; the only choice that suggests this is *exalts* (choice D).

20. **C, F, G.** You would look up to a person (choice B), but you might think highly of his acting (choice C). You can only recall (choice E) something you already know; the implication is that people don't realize (choice F) that George C. Scott served as a marine. Guards at the cemetery do not fight (choice I), but they do serve (choice G).

21. **D.** Do not move beyond what you are told in the passage; choices A, B, and C may be true, but there is no support for any of them. The only supported choice is D—comic operas focused on the everyday rather than the exalted themes of classical works.

22. **A.** The author states that krummholz trees may be ordinary black spruces or balsam firs, so choice B cannot be correct, and it is their disappearance, not their emergence, that indicates climate change, so choice C is wrong, too. The only correct answer is choice A.

23. **A, B.** The passage states: "Because of the difference in dates, it is hard to accept everything Snorri wrote at face value [choice A]. Nevertheless, his history remains the most valuable and detailed chronicle of these times [choice B]." There is no mention of Icelandic bias (choice C).

24. **B.** Since it was written by someone who was in the court, the lay must be of that same era (choice B).

25. **At the time, the land was divided into a series of tiny kingdoms, with the Danish king ruling some areas of eastern Norway.** The sentence indicates that Norway was not unified, suggesting that it required unification.

Section 5. Quantitative Reasoning

1. **A.** Quantity A combines to $\dfrac{31}{42}$, which is approximately 75%, while Quantity B combines to $\dfrac{37}{70}$, which is close to 50%.

2. **D.** The number n could be 15, which has a remainder of 3 when divided by 12. The number n could also be 35, which has a remainder of 11 when divided by 12.

3. **B.** The largest integer less than -1.5 is -2, the value of Quantity A. The largest integer less than 1.5 is 1, thus Quantity B is -1.

4. **D.** The inequality $2x + y^2 > 6$ can be rearranged into $x > 3 - \dfrac{y^2}{2}$. If $y = 0$, this means that $x > 3$, which means that x (Quantity A) could be 3.5 (smaller than Quantity B) or 5 (greater than Quantity B).

5. **A.** $\dfrac{2xy - x - 2x^2}{2x - 4x} = \dfrac{x(2y - 1 - 2x)}{-2x} = \dfrac{2y - 1 - 2x}{-2} = -y + \dfrac{1}{2} + x$, which is one-half more than $x - y$.

6. **B.** A square with perimeter 20 has each side of length 5, and thus an area of 25. A circle with radius 3 has area 9π, which is a little bit more than 28.

7. **C.** An angle from the center of a circle, for example $\angle AOC$, will always have double the measure of an angle from the circumference of the circle to the same endpoints, for example $\angle ABC$.

8. **B.** Solve for the equation $x = 2.5$ and plug in the value into the equation $6x = 15$. Thus 18 is greater than $6x$.

9. **B.** The fraction $\dfrac{2}{5} = 0.4$, while 0.1% $= 0.001$. When these are multiplied, the result is 0.0004, which is one-tenth of 0.004.

10. **D.** When any two of the six vertices of a hexagon are connected, the result will be one of the six edges or one of the diagonals. The number of ways of choosing 2 of 6 objects is $_6C_2 = \dfrac{6 \times 5}{2 \times 1} = 15$, thus there must be 9 diagonals. The general formula for the number of ways to choose k of n items is $_nC_k = \dfrac{n!}{(n - k)!k!}$, where $n! = n \times (n - 1) \times (n - 2) \times \cdots \times 3 \times 2 \times 1$. Another way to solve this problem would be to draw a hexagon and count all 9 diagonals.

11. **$15.** The area of the rug is $25 \times 12 = 300$ square feet. The product of 300 and 0.05 is 15.

12. **A, B, D.** The line $5y - 4x = 3$ solves to $y = \frac{4}{5}x + \frac{3}{5}$ and thus has a slope of $\frac{4}{5}$. The other lines solve to $y = -\frac{5}{4}x + \frac{3}{4}$, $y = \frac{1}{2}x + \frac{3}{4}$, $y = 5x + 3$, $y = -5x + 3$, and $y = \frac{5}{4}x - \frac{3}{4}$. These slopes are, respectively, $-\frac{5}{4}, \frac{1}{2}, 5, -5$, and $\frac{5}{4}$. All but the 5 and the $\frac{5}{4}$ are less than $\frac{4}{5}$.

13. **B, C, E.** Using the distance formula, the distance from $(3, 9)$ to $(5, 3)$ is $\sqrt{(3-5)^2 + (9-3)^2} = \sqrt{40}$. Similarly, the distance from $(3, 9)$ to $(3, 1)$ is $\sqrt{64}$, to $(1, 5)$ is $\sqrt{20}$, to $(-1, 8)$ is $\sqrt{17}$, to $(9, 3)$ is $\sqrt{72}$, and to $(0, 6)$ is $\sqrt{18}$. Thus the points $(1, 5)$, $(-1, 8)$, and $(0, 6)$ are all closer to $(3, 9)$ than $(5, 3)$ is.

14. There are many answers, including $\frac{3}{4}$ and $\frac{75}{100}$.

15. **D.** The perimeter is the sum of six sides, including the two without labels. The unlabeled horizontal side across the top measures 3 feet + 5 feet = 8 feet (the same as the two other horizontal lengths), and the unlabeled vertical edge measures 12 feet − 2 feet = 10 feet (the difference of the two other vertical lengths). Thus, going clockwise from the top left corner, the perimeter is $8 + 2 + 5 + 10 + 3 + 12 = 40$ feet.

16. **A, B, D, E.** The sets with three numbers are checked by seeing if the Pythagorean Theorem is satisfied (keeping the largest side for itself): $3^2 + 4^2 = 9 + 16 = 5^2$, $4^2 + 5^2 = 16 + 25 = 41 \neq 6^2$, $(0.6)^2 + (0.8)^2 = 0.36 + 0.64 = 1 = 1^2$, and $3^2 + \left(\sqrt{7}\right)^2 = 9 + 7 = 4^2$. In the first instance, the larger length $\sqrt{2}$ must be the hypotenuse, and $1^2 + 1^2 = \left(\sqrt{2}\right)^2$, so it also works.

17. **A, C, E.** A number is even if and only if it has a factor of 2, which includes n, nm^2, and nm. The sum of an even and odd number, for example $n + m$, will be odd. Similarly, $n - m$ is also odd. Because this question asks "which … *must* be even," you can verify these by letting m be any odd number (for example, 3) and letting n be any even number (for example, 2).

18. **B, C, D, E.** Cities A, B, and C form a triangle. Any two sides of a triangle must add up to less than the length of the third side, thus the distance from A to C must be between $1500 - 800 = 700$ and $1500 + 800 = 2300$.

19. **C.** One trick to adding $1 + 2 + 3 + \cdots + 48 + 49 + 50$ is to add $1 + 50$, $2 + 49$, $3 + 48$, and so on until $25 + 26$ in the middle. There will be a total of 25 of these pairs, each of which sums to 51, for a total of $25 \times 51 = 1275$. Another way to solve this problem would be to know this formula:
$$1 + 2 + 3 + \cdots + N = \frac{N(N+1)}{2}.$$

20. **B.** The number multiplies out to $5 \times 4 \times 3 \times 2 \times 8 \times 7 \times 6 \times 5 \times 4 \times 3 \times 2$, whose only prime factors are 2, 3, 5, and 7.

21. **A.** The angle PQR is $60°$, as one corner of an equilateral triangle. Thus the shaded area is $\dfrac{60}{360} = \dfrac{1}{6}$ of the full circle centered at R. The length $PQ = 12$ is the same as PR and QR because these are sides of an equilateral triangle. If we let p, q, and r represent the radii of circles P, Q, and R, respectively, then we see that $PQ = PR = QR$ means that $p + q = p + r = q + r$. We can therefore conclude that $p = q = r = 6$. The shaded area is thus $\dfrac{1}{6}\pi r^2 = \dfrac{1}{6}\pi 6^2 = 6\pi$.

22. **C.** The expression simplifies as: $\left(\dfrac{x^7}{x^2}\right)^3 = (x^{7-2})^3 = (x^5)^3 = x^{15}$.

23. **37%.** According to the chart, the percentage devoted to food was 29% and the percentage devoted to clothes was 8%, for a total of 37%.

24. **D.** The 2008 ratio of spending on food to spending on clothes was $\dfrac{35\%}{15\%}$, which reduces to $\dfrac{7}{3}$. Thus the amount spent on food in 2008 was $\dfrac{7}{3} \times \$4,800 = \$11,200$. Another method would be to calculate the total 2008 budget B using the equation $0.15B = 4800$, and then figure the amount spent on food as $0.35B$.

25. **D.** If the 2007 budget was B, then the amount spent on housing was $0.22B$. If the 2009 budget was 6% bigger, it was $B + 0.06B = (1.06)B$, so the amount spent on housing was $0.38(1.06)B$. The ratio between the two was thus $\dfrac{0.38(1.06)B}{0.22B} = \dfrac{0.38(1.06)}{0.22} \approx 1.83 = 183\%$. As the housing spending in 2009 was 183% of that in 2007, it increased by 83%.

Section 6. Quantitative Reasoning

1. **B.** The overline indicates that the digits repeat, thus Quantity A is $0.\overline{35} = 0.353535\ldots$ while Quantity B is $0.3\overline{5} = 0.3555\ldots$, which is almost two-thousandths larger.

2. **A.** You can convert 35 miles per day into feet per hour by multiplying by 5,280 and dividing by 24. When you multiply $\dfrac{35 \text{ miles}}{1 \text{ day}}$ by $\dfrac{5,280 \text{ feet}}{1 \text{ mile}}$ by $\dfrac{1 \text{ day}}{24 \text{ hours}}$, the miles and days cancel out, resulting in 7,700 feet per hour, which is larger than Quantity B.

3. **A.** To increase by 5% is to multiply by 1.05. Thus, to remove the 5% tax, we divide $100 \div 1.05 \approx 95.238$.

4. **A.** Increasing by 60% is the same as taking 160%, which is computed by multiplying by 1.6. Thus if the height of the rectangle is h, the height of the triangle is $1.6h$. If the base of the rectangle is b, then the base of the triangle is $1.3b$. The area of the rectangle is thus bh, while the area of the triangle is $\frac{1}{2}(1.3b)(1.6h) = \frac{2.08}{2}bh = 1.04bh$. The area of the triangle, Quantity A, is thus 4% larger than the area of the rectangle, Quantity B.

5. **A.** The easiest way to add 5% to a number is to multiply the number by 1.05. The invested $500 will receive annual interest three times, thus becoming $500(1.05)(1.05)(1.05) \approx \$578.81$. Another way is to calculate that the simple interest of 5% on $500 is $500(.05) = \$25$; so because of the compounding in the second and third years, Quantity A is automatically larger than $500 + 3 \times 25 = \$575$.

6. **A.** If you square everything in $5 < \sqrt{n} < 6$, you get $25 < n < 36$. Note: the inequalities do not change because all these numbers are positive. If you square again, you get $n^2 > 25^2 = 625$. Thus Quantity A is larger.

7. **C.** $(3 \clubsuit 2) \clubsuit -1 = (3^2 - 2) \clubsuit -1 = 7 \clubsuit -1 = 7^2 - (-1) = 50$.

8. **A.** Written as fractions, the ratio equation becomes $\frac{3}{x} = \frac{7}{10}$, which cross multiplies to $3 \times 10 = 7x$, so $x = \frac{30}{7} = 4\frac{2}{7}$. Thus Quantity A is larger.

9. **B.** $\angle ADC = 180° - \angle DAC - \angle DCA$ and $\angle ABC = 180° - \angle BAC - \angle BCA$. From the illustration, you see that $\angle DAC < \angle BAC$ and $\angle DCA < \angle BCA$. Subtracting smaller numbers produces a larger result, thus $\angle ADC = 180° - \angle DAC - \angle DCA > 180° - \angle BAC - \angle BCA = \angle ABC$. Thus $\angle ADC > \angle ABC$.

10. **C.** Divide 1.2 trillion by 200 million $= \frac{1,200,000,000,000}{200,000,000}$ and cancel out 8 zeros from the top and bottom (divide both by 10^8) to get $\frac{12,000}{2} = 6,000$.

11. **972.** First, convert the dimensions into inches; the floor measures $18 \times 12 = 216$ inches by $24 \times 12 = 288$ inches. Next, divide each dimension by 8 inches, the side of each square tile, to see that the floor measures $216 \div 8 = 27$ squares by $288 \div 8 = 36$ squares. The number of squares in a rectangle that measures 27 squares by 36 squares is $27 \times 36 = 972$.

12. **A, B, D.** A multiple of 6 must be even (this rules out 28,897 and 49,429) and divisible by 3. If the digits of a number add up to a multiple of 3, then the whole number is divisible by 3. For example, $3 + 5 + 1 + 7 + 2 = 18$, which is divisible by 3, so 35,172 is divisible by 3. Similarly $2 + 4 + 8 + 3 + 4 = 21$, so 24,834 is divisible by 3. Finally, $4 + 3 + 5 + 6 = 18$, which means that 40,356 is also divisible by 3.

13. **E.** Any of the 26 letters in the alphabet can be either the first or the second symbol, for a total of $26 \times 26 = 676$ possibilities. There are $10 \times 10 \times 10 \times 10 = 10,000$ different strings of 4 digits, so there are a total of $676 \times 10,000 = 6,760,000$ different plates.

14. **D.** When two rulers are glued together, you lose one inch for the overlap, so the total length will be 2 feet $-$ 1 inch. When three rulers are glued together, the length is 3 feet $-$ 2 inches. When all 100 are glued together, the length will be 100 feet $-$ 99 inches $= 1,200$ inches $-$ 99 inches $= 1,101$ inches $=$ 91 feet, 9 inches.

15. **D.** Viewing the problem as a ratio, you are looking for x in $\dfrac{2}{3} : \dfrac{1}{2} = \dfrac{1}{2} : x$. As fractions, this is $\dfrac{\frac{2}{3}}{\frac{1}{2}} = \dfrac{\frac{1}{2}}{x}$. If you cross multiply (multiply the means and the extremes), you get $\dfrac{2}{3}x = \dfrac{1}{2} \times \dfrac{1}{2} = \dfrac{1}{4}$. Cross multiply again and you get $8x = 3$, so you need to add $\dfrac{3}{8}$ of a gallon of water to the remaining cleaner.

16. **4.** The exponent can be viewed as $\dfrac{2}{3} = 2 \times \dfrac{1}{3}$, and thus $8^{\frac{2}{3}} = 8^{2 \times \frac{1}{3}} = \left(8^2\right)^{\frac{1}{3}} = 64^{\frac{1}{3}} = \sqrt[3]{64} = 4$.

17. **A.** $\left(\dfrac{x^3}{y^4}\right)^{-2} \div \left(\dfrac{x^2}{y^3}\right)^{4} = \dfrac{x^{3(-2)}}{y^{4(-2)}} \cdot \dfrac{y^{3 \times 4}}{x^{2 \times 4}} = \dfrac{x^{-6}y^{12}}{x^8 y^{-8}} = \dfrac{y^{12}y^8}{x^8 x^6} = \dfrac{y^{20}}{x^{14}}$.

18. **D.** The area of a circle with a 4-inch diameter is $\pi 2^2 = 4\pi$ (the radius is 2). The area of a circle with a 12-inch diameter is $\pi 6^2 = 36\pi$. Assuming that the pancakes are circles of a uniform thickness, the volume (amount of batter needed) will be relative to the area, thus the big pancake needs $\dfrac{36\pi}{4\pi} = 9$ times as much batter.

19. **B.** The solution to a system of two linear equations is given by the point on the plane where the two lines cross. There will be no solution if the two lines have the same slope and thus run forever parallel. If you solve for y, $4y + 2x = 7$ becomes $y = -\dfrac{1}{2}x + \dfrac{7}{4}$ and $2y = 5 + Ax$ becomes $y = \dfrac{A}{2}x + \dfrac{5}{2}$. The slopes will be the same when $A = -1$.

20. **B.** If the radius of the circle is r, then each side of the square will be $2r$. The area of the circle is thus πr^2 and the area of the square is $(2r)^2 = 4r^2$. The area outside the circle is thus $4r^2 - \pi r^2$, so the probability is
$$\frac{4r^2 - \pi r^2}{4r^2} = \frac{(4-\pi)}{4} \times \frac{r^2}{r^2} = \frac{4}{4} - \frac{\pi}{4} = 1 - \frac{\pi}{4}.$$

21. **16.8 hours.** Since three pumps take 8 hours to drain 5,000 gallons, then one pump would take 24 hours. Since one pump empties 5,000/24 gallons per hour, two pumps will empty 10,000/24 gallons per hour. At this rate, it will take t hours to drain the second tank, where $\dfrac{10,000}{24}t = 7,000$, thus $t = \dfrac{7,000(24)}{10,000} = $ 16.8 hours.

22. **A.** A liter is a cubic decimeter, a cube with each side 10 centimeters long, for a total of 1,000 cubic centimeters. This aquarium contains $50 \times 30 \times 40 = 60,000$ cubic centimeters, and thus 60 liters.

23. **80%.** The popularity of character X was 0.8 in the 1960s and 1 in the 2000s. As a relative percentage, this is $\dfrac{0.8}{1} = 0.8 = 80\%$.

24. **A, D, E.** These are the time intervals in which the second vertical bar is taller than the first.

25. **D.** The answer is 125%. The ratio of the popularity in the 1950s to the popularity in the 1980s is $\dfrac{0.5}{0.4} = \dfrac{5}{4} = 1.25 = 125\%$.

GRE Practice Test 2

SECTION 1
Analytical Writing

ANALYZE AN ISSUE

30 Minutes

You will have 30 minutes to organize your thoughts and compose a response that represents your point of view on the topic presented. Do not respond to any topic other than the one given; a response to any other topic will receive a score of 0.

You will be required to discuss your perspective on the issue, using examples and reasons drawn from your own experiences and observations.

Use scratch paper to organize your response before you begin writing. Write your response on the pages provided, or type your response using a word processor with the spell- and grammar-check functions turned off.

Issue Topic

"In any group effort, universal consensus is preferable to majority rule."

Discuss the extent to which you agree or disagree with the claim made above. Consider ways in which the statement might or might not hold true and explain how those affect your point of view.

SECTION 2

Analytical Writing

ANALYZE AN ARGUMENT

30 Minutes

You will have 30 minutes to organize your thoughts and compose a response that critiques the given argument. Do not respond to any topic other than the one given; a response to any other topic will receive a score of 0.

You are not being asked to discuss your point of view on the statement. You should identify and analyze the central elements of the argument, the underlying assumptions that are being made, and any supporting information that is given. Your critique can also discuss other information that would strengthen or weaken the argument or make it more logical.

Use scratch paper to organize your response before you begin writing. Write your response on the pages provided, or type your response using a word processor with the spell- and grammar-check functions turned off.

Argument Topic

To get a better sense of the recreational needs of the community, the Teeburg Town Board sent a questionnaire addressed to the "head of household" in every home in the town. The board asked a series of questions designed to zero in on residents' recreational preferences, in hopes of finding three they might fund in the upcoming year. The board was gratified to get a reasonable return rate of nearly 40 percent of all questionnaires. Based on that response, the board recommended that the following top vote getters be added to the town budget: a snowmobile trail, a skeet-shooting range, and a putting green.

Critique the reasoning used in the argument presented above by examining the stated and/or unstated assumptions of the argument and explaining the implications for the conclusion if the assumptions prove unwarranted.

SECTION 3
Verbal Reasoning
Time: 35 minutes
25 questions

For questions 1 through 4, select two answer choices that (1) complete the sentence in a way that makes sense and (2) produce sentences that are similar in meaning.

---

1. Her _____ for acting led to lessons, bit parts in independent movies, and eventually a solid career in Hollywood.

   A   aptitude

   B   weakness

   C   livelihood

   D   abhorrence

   E   talent

   F   substitute

2. The state senator's aide served as a _____ in informal meetings whenever the senator himself was unable to attend.

   A   raconteur

   B   patron

   C   courier

   D   deputy

   E   proxy

   F   surrogate

3. Refugees fleeing Myanmar appear to have been _____ targeted with antipersonnel landmines along the border with Bangladesh.

   [A] willfully

   [B] precariously

   [C] imprudently

   [D] judiciously

   [E] calculatingly

   [F] palpably

4. Rather than game rooms or free snacks, most employees at Silicon Valley's new high tech companies show a(n) _____ for professional development and flexible work schedules.

   [A] precept

   [B] dispatch

   [C] exhortation

   [D] predilection

   [E] volubility

   [F] proclivity

Questions 5 and 6 are based on this passage.

Bodiam Castle in East Sussex, England, is the quintessential child's drawing of a castle—perfectly rectangular, with crenellated towers at all four corners. Although the interior is in ruins, the exterior largely survives, having had only

Line   minimal restorations since its original construction in 1385. Built by a knight of
(5)   King Edward III, Sir Edward Dalyngrigge, it lasted through two major sieges, one during the War of the Roses and one during the English Civil War. By the eighteenth century it was overgrown and in disrepair, a favorite romantic setting for painters of the era. Not until its purchase by Lord Curzon in 1917 did the castle begin to see life again. Lord Curzon was fascinated by architectural preservation;
(10)   after restoring much of the castle's underpinnings, he willed the rebuilt structure to the National Trust. The castle, complete with museum, is now a favorite tourist destination.

Consider each of the choices separately and select all that apply.

5. The author implies which of the following about Lord Curzon?

   [A] He was a descendent of Sir Edward Dalyngrigge.

   [B] His love of architecture assisted British tourism.

   [C] He lived in Bodiam Castle from 1917 until his death.

Select one answer choice.

6. Based on the first sentence, a reader can surmise that a crenellated tower is

   (A) wooden

   (B) notched

   (C) armored

   (D) delicate

   (E) colorful

Question 7 is based on this passage.

Linguistic hypercorrection is the mistaken application of a rule to all cases, even when it is inappropriate. A common example is the mistaken assumption that the subject pronoun is more grammatically correct than the object pronoun, so that the speaker extrapolates from the correct "He and I will attend" to the incorrect "Give the lecture notes to she and I" or "Call he and I any time after three."

Line
(5)

Hyperforeignism is the mistaken application of misunderstood pronunciation rules in words that derive from foreign languages. For example, the second word in *éminence grise* should be pronounced "greez," not "gree." The composer Pierre Boulez's last name is pronounced "boo-LEZ," not "boo-LAY."

Consider each of the choices separately and select all that apply.

7. Based on the information in the passage, which of the following might be an example of hyperforeignism?

   [A] Using *whom* when *who* is the correct pronoun

   [B] Pronouncing *ballet* "bal-LAY"

   [C] Pronouncing *prix fixe* "pree fee"

Questions 8 and 9 are based on this passage.

Two of the best-known examples of neoclassical architecture are the U.S. Capitol and the White House, but other examples abound throughout the eastern United States as well as in Europe. If you classify neoclassical architecture into four main categories, the first might be the federalist style, exemplified by Charles Bulfinch's Faneuil Hall in Boston. Thomas Jefferson's Monticello is an example of the idealist style, less perfectly traditional than the federalist, but borrowing from Roman ideals of proportion and beauty. Benjamin Latrobe's Baltimore Basilica is an example of the realist style, which was more reliant on scientific principles of proportion and line than on ideals of beauty or imitations of classical works. Finally, there was the Greek Revival style. Based on Greek rather than Roman architecture and art, it was the preferred style for plantation houses, courthouses, and farmhouses from the Atlantic to the Great Lakes. Robert Mills's U.S. Treasury Building in Washington, DC, is a good example of the style.

Line (5) ... (10)

For questions 8 and 9, select one answer choice each.

---

8. The passage indicates that the U.S. Treasury Building is

   (A) based on Greek rather than on Roman design

   (B) built with scientific principles of proportion

   (C) not an example of neoclassical architecture

   (D) a good example of the idealist style

   (E) less traditional than Faneuil Hall in Boston

9. The author identifies the neoclassical subcategory for each of these buildings EXCEPT

   (A) the U.S. Treasury

   (B) the Baltimore Basilica

   (C) Monticello

   (D) Faneuil Hall

   (E) the U.S. Capitol

For questions 10 through 13, complete the text by picking the best entry for each blank from the corresponding column of choices.

---

10. The raised artificial islands known as crannogs, built in medieval times in Ireland and Scotland, _____ consist of post palisades sunk into the lake bed, all surrounding a round house set on a wooden platform.

Ⓐ	currently
Ⓑ	typically
Ⓒ	cursorily
Ⓓ	imprudently
Ⓔ	especially

11. Nahuatl was the language of the Aztecs, who _____ central Mexico during the Postclassic period.

Ⓐ	administered to
Ⓑ	dispersed among
Ⓒ	congregated at
Ⓓ	presided over
Ⓔ	reined in

12. In the case in which the Supreme Court (i) _____ the Virginia Military Institute's long-standing males-only tradition, (ii) _____ for women to enroll for the first time, Justice Thomas (iii) _____ himself, almost certainly because his son was a student there at the time the case was under consideration.

Blank (i)	Blank (ii)	Blank (iii)
Ⓐ upheld	Ⓓ bringing to mind	Ⓖ consigned
Ⓑ overturned	Ⓔ paving the way	Ⓗ involved
Ⓒ controlled	Ⓕ barring the door	Ⓘ recused

13. William Dean Howells's favorable criticism of Leo Tolstoy's work may have helped to (i) _____ the Russian writer's (ii) _____ in the United States.

Blank (i)	Blank (ii)
Ⓐ establish	Ⓓ literature
Ⓑ controvert	Ⓔ reputation
Ⓒ reward	Ⓕ acquaintance

Questions 14 through 16 are based on this passage.

The use of greenhouses dates back at least to the Middle Ages, when they were constructed to protect unusual tropical plants brought back to Europe by travelers to Africa and Asia. Italy, France, England, and Holland all developed greenhouses
Line of glass and wood or glass and iron. French orangeries were designed to protect
(5) orange trees—an enormous one was erected at the Palace of Versailles under Louis XIV—and pineries were built to protect pineapples. In Holland, gardeners grew medicinal plants under glass. As the price of glass came down, greenhouses became ever more elaborate and grand, culminating in Joseph Paxton's Crystal Palace, a 990,000-square-foot conservatory built for London's Great Exhibition of 1851.

Consider each of the choices separately and select all that apply.

14. Which of these can be inferred from the fact that the French built orangeries for certain tropical plants?

    Ⓐ Greenhouses may be used to keep plants at a moderate temperature.

    Ⓑ The climate of France is unsuited to growing tropical plants outdoors.

    Ⓒ Louis XIV was a frequent and enthusiastic traveler to Africa and Asia.

Select one answer choice.

15. It can be inferred that the author mentions pineries primarily to

    Ⓐ demonstrate how greenhouses changed over time

    Ⓑ contrast Italian and French forms of greenhouses

    Ⓒ indicate the types of fruit that Europe once imported

    Ⓓ present an example of a type of early greenhouse

    Ⓔ show that greenhouses have been around for centuries

16. Underline the sentence that suggests a practical factor in the building of larger and larger greenhouses.

For questions 17 through 20, complete the text by picking the best entry for each blank from the corresponding column of choices.

17. Photodetectors, which are also _____ light sensors, have a variety of practical uses, from pausing your garage door if you're beneath it to lighting your way along a dark driveway.

Ⓐ	considered
Ⓑ	potential
Ⓒ	former
Ⓓ	made for
Ⓔ	known as

18. Barcelona is an (i) _____ economic center, housing as it does one of Europe's most (ii) _____ Mediterranean seaports.

Blank (i)		Blank (ii)	
Ⓐ	unsuccessful	Ⓓ	active
Ⓑ	important	Ⓔ	unfinished
Ⓒ	outdated	Ⓕ	inland

19. Although they are (i) _____ U.S. citizens, residents of the U.S. Virgin Islands are (ii) _____ to vote in presidential elections.

Blank (i)		Blank (ii)	
Ⓐ	technically	Ⓓ	qualified
Ⓑ	frequently	Ⓔ	encouraged
Ⓒ	erroneously	Ⓕ	unable

20. At one million square feet in area, the Art Institute of Chicago is the second-largest art museum in the United States, (i) _____ only by the Metropolitan in New York. It (ii) _____ some of the world's most notable impressionist and postimpressionist works as well as an (iii) _____ collection of old masters that art lovers flock to see.

Blank (i)		Blank (ii)		Blank (iii)	
Ⓐ	surpassed	Ⓓ	disperses	Ⓖ	avant-garde
Ⓑ	visible	Ⓔ	houses	Ⓗ	austere
Ⓒ	familiar	Ⓕ	reserves	Ⓘ	unrivaled

Question 21 is based on this passage.

In a speech before the United Nations in 1953, President Dwight Eisenhower advocated the creation of an institution that would control and promote the peaceful use of atomic energy worldwide. The "Atoms for Peace" speech came at a difficult time. Memories of Nagasaki and Hiroshima were recent and raw, and the Cold War was very much underway. Under Truman, the U.S. military budget had increased fourfold; Eisenhower now sought to cut it back by one-third. Joseph Stalin, the feared Soviet dictator, had died earlier in the year, giving some hope that a reconciliation was possible. In his speech, Eisenhower pledged that the United States would commit itself to finding a way to "solve the fearful atomic dilemma." After several years of discussion and debate on the nonmilitary potential of nuclear energy, the UN established the International Atomic Energy Agency, which has worked ever since to inspect and set standards for nonmilitary nuclear facilities and to serve as a center for scientific inquiry into nonmilitary uses of nuclear energy.

Line (5) and *(10)* appear in left margin.

Select one answer choice.

21. Which of the following is presented as a logical reason behind the timing of President Eisenhower's "Atoms for Peace" speech?

   Ⓐ Soviets and Americans were mired in the Cold War.

   Ⓑ President Truman had expanded the military budget.

   Ⓒ The Soviet dictator Joseph Stalin had recently died.

   Ⓓ The United States had dropped bombs on Japan.

   Ⓔ The UN had established an atomic energy agency.

Question 22 is based on this passage.

Eric Rohmer became the newest of the French New Wave directors when he left his career as novelist and editor to film the first of his six "moral tales." A few earlier projects had failed to achieve the success of fellow New Wavers François Truffaut
Line and Jean-Luc Godard, but Rohmer's short film *The Bakery Girl of Monceau* was a hit.
(5) After that came *Suzanne's Career, The Collector, My Night at Maud's, Claire's Knee*, and *Chloe in the Afternoon*. All six were based on short stories or sketches Rohmer had written, and all featured his typical style and themes—long takes focused on facial features, long conversations about moral issues, temptation and its denial.
Of the six films in this series, the most popular was *My Night at Maud's*, which was
(10) a selection at Cannes and an Academy Award nominee for best foreign language film in 1969.

Consider each of the choices separately and select all that apply.

22. According to the passage, which word or words might describe Rohmer's style?

   A Dynamic

   B Dialogue-driven

   C Philosophical

Questions 23 through 25 are based on this passage.

We say that fish migrate horizontally if they migrate along rivers or across oceans. There are three main classifications of horizontally migrating fish. *Potamodromous* fish migrate only within freshwater. For example, there are over 30 species of fish
Line that migrate up and down the Mississippi River. *Oceanodromous* fish migrate only
(5) in salt water. Bluefish move from north to south; cod move from shallow to deeper water. *Diadromous* fish such as salmon and eels migrate between salt and fresh, with *anadromous* migrating from salt to fresh to breed and then back to salt to live out most of their lives, *catadromous* living mostly in fresh but breeding in salt water, and *amphidromous* moving back and forth regularly, not necessarily for breeding purposes.

Consider each of the choices separately and select all that apply.

23. Based on the information in the passage, which combination or combinations of migrations are possible in a single species?

   A Potamodromous and oceanodromous

   B Catadromous and anadromous

   C Diadromous and catadromous

Select one answer choice.

24. Which of these facts would indicate conclusively that chinook salmon are anadromous?

   Ⓐ   Chinook fry move from their freshwater breeding grounds downstream after anywhere from one to eighteen months.

   Ⓑ   Chinook salmon spend from one to eight years in the Pacific before moving back briefly to their natal streams to spawn.

   Ⓒ   Young chinook salmon feed on insects and larvae as well as on small crustaceans in their freshwater homes.

   Ⓓ   The fragile eggs of the chinook salmon require a regular flow of well-oxygenated water to survive.

   Ⓔ   Chinook salmon range as far north the arctic waters of Canada and as far south as northern California.

25. Underline the sentence that gives examples of oceanodromous fish.

STOP.   **This is the end of Section 3. Use any remaining time to check your work.**

SECTION 4
Verbal Reasoning
Time: 35 minutes
25 questions

Questions 1 through 3 are based on this passage.

Huntington's disease is by far most prevalent in people of Western European descent. Its onset typically presents as lack of coordination and a jerky gait. Often, symptoms are nonexistent until the carrier of the mutation is in his or her late 30s.

Line   After that, the patient's decline may be slow or rapid, eventually resulting in physical
(5)   and mental degeneration.

Although everyone carries the gene known as huntingtin, very few carry the mutation that results in the disease. If one parent carries the mutation, each offspring has a 50-50 chance of inheriting the mutated gene. Genetic testing and counseling are often recommended for family members of Huntington's patients. The test

(10)   uses a blood sample to isolate the huntingtin gene and count the number of CAG repetitions in that gene. Forty or more repeats usually means that the person carries the disease.

Consider each of the choices separately and select all that apply.

1. If a father of four children carries the Huntington's mutation, which of these is true?

   A Two of the four children may inherit the mutation.

   B Two of the four children may have the disease.

   C Two of the four children may end up disease free.

Select one answer choice.

2. Based on information from the passage, which of these people would be MOST likely to develop Huntington's disease?

   (A) Someone who carries the huntingtin gene

   (B) Someone whose parents come from Portugal

   (C) Someone with 25 CAG repetitions in the huntingtin gene

   (D) Someone of Romanian ancestry

   (E) Someone whose grandfather died of Huntington's disease

3. Underline the sentence that shows the unpredictability of Huntington's disease.

Question 4 is based on this passage.

The Medal of Honor, created in 1862, is the highest military decoration available in the United States. It may be bestowed on members of any of the armed forces, and it is given to those who distinguish themselves with "gallantry and intrepidity
Line   at the risk of [their lives] above and beyond the call of duty," especially when
(5)   engaged in armed conflict with an enemy of the United States. Three designs exist; one is for army members, one for navy members or marines, and one for the air force. All three involve a five-pointed star mounted on a blue ribbon. Because of its rarity and importance (there have been just over 3,400 recipients in 148 years), the Medal of Honor is always personally awarded by the president of the United States
(10)   on behalf of the Congress.

Select one answer choice.

4.   Based on the information given in the passage, which of these statements about the existing designs of the Medal of Honor is accurate?

  Ⓐ   Two of the medals feature a five-pointed star; one shows an eagle with arrows.

  Ⓑ   The naval Medal of Honor is identical to that for a member of the marine corps.

  Ⓒ   There are four designs in all, one for each division of the armed services.

  Ⓓ   At one time there was but one design, but now there are three in all.

  Ⓔ   Any design may be bestowed on any worthy member of the armed forces.

For questions 5 through 8, complete the text by picking the best entry for each blank from the corresponding column of choices.

---

5.   Born in Kent in 1866, H. G. Wells became a _____ writer in a plethora of genres, although he was best known for his futuristic works of science fiction.

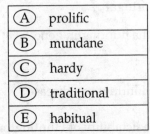

Ⓐ	prolific
Ⓑ	mundane
Ⓒ	hardy
Ⓓ	traditional
Ⓔ	habitual

6. Giovanni Arduino, sometimes called the father of Italian geology, was the first to _____ geological time, breaking the history of the earth into periods from the Primitive through the Tertiary.

Ⓐ	schedule
Ⓑ	excavate
Ⓒ	imply
Ⓓ	classify
Ⓔ	bequeath

7. In 1949, the Basketball Association of America (i) _____ with the rival National Basketball League, (ii) _____ the league that survives today, the National Basketball Association, or NBA.

Blank (i)		Blank (ii)	
Ⓐ	clashed	Ⓓ	celebrating
Ⓑ	competed	Ⓔ	concluding
Ⓒ	merged	Ⓕ	creating

8. The fact that the Republic of Malta covers only 300 square kilometers yet (i) _____ more than 410,000 citizens makes it one of the most (ii) _____ populated of European nations.

Blank (i)		Blank (ii)	
Ⓐ	exports	Ⓓ	meagerly
Ⓑ	represents	Ⓔ	densely
Ⓒ	accommodates	Ⓕ	systematically

Bull riding is called the "most dangerous eight seconds in sports"; a rider attempts to stay seated on a bucking bull for that length of time. Rules are strict: The rider must hold on with one hand and not touch the other hand to the bull for the length
Line   of the ride. The bull and rider begin the ride in a chute. In preparation for the ride,
(5)   the rider rosins one hand, wraps a braided rope around the bull's neck, and then wraps the remainder of the rope around the rosined hand. When the rider signals readiness, the chute is opened and the bull and rider fly out into the ring. The bull, selected for orneriness and speed, tries to buck the rider off before the allotted time is up. Two judges score both bull and rider on a scale of 0 to 50 points. Bulls are
(10)   scored on agility and strength, and riders earn points for control and balance. Then the scores are added together. Scores above 90 are rare; rider scores of 0 (because of a fall) are common.

Certain bulls do well enough in competition to attain a measure of fame. One example is Little Yellow Jacket, from North Dakota, who was voted best bucking
(15)   bull two years in a row. Another is the enormous bull known as Outlaw, out of Calgary. It took 58 tries by 58 different riders before one was able to hang on to him for the required eight seconds. A third bull is Red Rock, from Texas, who apparently went his entire career without a successful ride, bucking off 309 riders between 1984 and 1987.

(20)   Of course, there are dozens of famous bull riders, new ones for every generation. There are a number of rodeo circuits, and riders may work their way up to the level of the Professional Bull Riders (PBR). There they are guaranteed regular work and the possibility of many thousands of dollars in prize money. PBR bull riding is televised widely, with each event featuring the top 45 professional riders of
(25)   the year.

Consider each of the choices separately and select all that apply.

9. The passage suggests that a successful bull rider must possess which of the following qualities?

    A Extraordinary equilibrium

    B A relaxed, composed attitude

    C Skill in animal handling

For questions 10 through 12, select one answer choice each.

10. The primary purpose of the passage is to

    (A) suggest reasons why bull riding should be outlawed

    (B) compare bull riders to athletes in other endeavors

    (C) describe and explain the rules of a popular sport

    (D) list a few beloved heroes of the sport of bull riding

    (E) review and elucidate the history of bull riding

11. Based on information in the passage, what could you assume if a rider scored a 20?

    (A) He fell off the bull before eight seconds was reached.

    (B) He showed unusual agility and strength on the bull.

    (C) His agility was less than average but his balance was good.

    (D) He exhibited little control but did not fall off the bull.

    (E) His balance was not up to par but he looked strong and agile.

12. In paragraph two of the passage, the first sentence introduces the topic, and the other sentences provide

    (A) examples in support

    (B) examples in refutation

    (C) reasons for an opinion

    (D) causes and effects

    (E) comparisons and contrasts

Question 13 is based on this passage.

The Wampanoag people of southeastern Massachusetts and Rhode Island were unusual in that they were a matrilineal clan, with property passed down from mother to daughter. Although family roles were gender related, with men doing
Line the hunting and fishing and women responsible for most of the farming, women
(5) held important positions within the confederation. The sachem, or political leader, could be male or female. One of the foremost female sachems was Weetamoo, who commanded some 300 warriors during the great wars between the Wampanoag and the Puritans and Pilgrims. She joined forces with the sachem known as Philip during the time of King Philip's War, and fought valiantly for two years before
(10) drowning in the Taunton River while trying to escape English forces.

13. Underline the sentence that contrasts male and female roles in the Wampanoag clan.

For questions 14 through 17, complete the text by picking the best entry for each blank from the corresponding column of choices.

---

14. At one time, people firmly believed that the origin of contagious diseases such as the Black Death pandemic was a _____ of bad air.

Ⓐ	pathogen
Ⓑ	miasma
Ⓒ	carbuncle
Ⓓ	paroxysm
Ⓔ	catalyst

15. The (i) _____ old miser Scrooge is better known, but he is hardly the most (ii) _____ of Dickens's loathsome characters. That honor must go to Uriah Heep in *David Copperfield*, a man of such false sincerity and humility that his name elicits visions of (iii) _____ creeps.

Blank (i)	Blank (ii)	Blank (iii)
Ⓐ seditious	Ⓓ odious	Ⓖ solicitous
Ⓑ niggardly	Ⓔ sardonic	Ⓗ toadying
Ⓒ assiduous	Ⓕ indelible	Ⓘ impecunious

16. The salt we use for flavoring food or melting ice is produced in one of two ways, through the evaporation of seawater or the _____ of rock salt.

(A) production
(B) mining
(C) tasting
(D) packaging
(E) utilization

17. As leeches clamp onto a host, they rather cleverly _____ an anesthetic, which prevents the host from noticing its parasitic visitors.

(A) release
(B) collect
(C) forgo
(D) ingest
(E) allay

Questions 18 through 20 are based on this passage.

The common praying mantis is protected by a variety of self-defense mechanisms. These range from camouflage to an effective threat display. The mantis uses protective coloration to blend in with the grasses and foliage through which it moves. Some

Line mantises use mimicry to imitate the look of a leafy twig or a dead leaf. If a predator
(5) keeps coming, the mantis will exhibit several protective behaviors. It may puff itself up and spread its wings to look more threatening. It may reveal startling, colorful dots and patterns on its wings or legs. Some mantises expel air through their abdomens, making a hissing sound. If all else fails, the mantis will strike a predator with its forelegs or bite it with its strong mandibles.

For questions 18 through 20, select one answer choice each.

18. The passage focuses primarily on

(A) mimicry as an aid for the common praying mantis
(B) a range of behaviors that allow insects to survive
(C) ways in which mantises may conceal themselves
(D) protective measures used by the praying mantis
(E) defensive body structures of the praying mantis

19. Which fact about the praying mantis might be a suitable addition to the paragraph?

   (A) The praying mantis rarely flies unless it is mating season.

   (B) Standing tall and spreading its forelegs makes the mantis look menacing.

   (C) Bats, using echolocation, are a primary predator of the praying mantis.

   (D) The prey of the praying mantis ranges from beetles to small mammals.

   (E) A mantis has sharp spines on its front legs, which it uses to grip its prey.

20. Which of the following best describes the function of the first sentence of the passage?

   (A) It presents a conclusion drawn from the examples in the other sentences.

   (B) It puts forward a thesis statement that will be supported by reasons.

   (C) It offers the author's opinion about a particular behavioral characteristic.

   (D) It connects the rest of the passage to whatever has come before.

   (E) It identifies the topic that the other sentences in the passage will address.

For questions 21 through 25, select two answer choices that (1) complete the sentence in a way that makes sense and (2) produce sentences that are similar in meaning.

---

21. Because the Choctaw adopted many cultural practices of Europeans, they were _____ termed one of the "Civilized Tribes" by the very people whose descendants would later see them exiled from their homeland.

   A   callously

   B   sarcastically

   C   insensitively

   D   compassionately

   E   tolerantly

   F   reasonably

22. The school originally known as the Institute of Musical Art was moved, merged, and finally renamed after a great _____ of American music, Augustus Juilliard.

    - [A] narrator
    - [B] benefactor
    - [C] messenger
    - [D] champion
    - [E] lecturer
    - [F] architect

23. The origin of the term *Hoosier* is unknown; nevertheless, there are dozens of proposed derivations that range from logical to _____.

    - [A] lackluster
    - [B] droll
    - [C] scandalous
    - [D] convincing
    - [E] dubious
    - [F] apocryphal

24. The Japanese cartoon form known as manga covers a surprisingly _____ range of subject matter, from the typical action-adventure to the less familiar romance, horror, and business-related stories.

    - [A] restrictive
    - [B] broad
    - [C] current
    - [D] disturbing
    - [E] expansive
    - [F] inventive

25. The so-called high seas are any body of water wherein national jurisdiction no longer applies; an _____ term might be *international waters*.

    A equivalent

    B obvious

    C all-inclusive

    D analogous

    E applicable

    F appealing

STOP. This is the end of Section 4. Use any remaining time to check your work.

SECTION 5
Quantitative Reasoning
Time: 40 minutes
25 questions

Each of questions 1 through 9 consists of two quantities, Quantity A and Quantity B. You are to compare the two quantities. You may use additional information centered above the two quantities if additional information is given. Choose

Ⓐ   if Quantity A is greater;
Ⓑ   if Quantity B is greater;
Ⓒ   if the two quantities are equal;
Ⓓ   if the relationship cannot be determined from the information given.

	Quantity A	Quantity B	
1.	100,000 hours	10 years	Ⓐ Ⓑ Ⓒ Ⓓ

	Quantity A	Quantity B	
2.	the least common multiple of 6 and 10	the greatest common divisor of 80 and 140	Ⓐ Ⓑ Ⓒ Ⓓ

	Quantity A	Quantity B	
3.	the number of four-digit numbers with distinct digits	the number of three-digit numbers	Ⓐ Ⓑ Ⓒ Ⓓ

$$y = 2 - 3x$$

$$x = -2$$

	Quantity A	Quantity B	
4.	y	5	

	Quantity A	Quantity B	
5.	$(x + y)(x - y)$	$x^2 + y^2$	Ⓐ Ⓑ Ⓒ Ⓓ

x is an integer

	Quantity A	Quantity B	
6.	$\dfrac{1}{(-1)^x} - (-1)^x$	0	Ⓐ Ⓑ Ⓒ

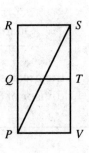

$$ST = TV$$

	Quantity A	Quantity B	
7.	the area of square PQTV	the area of triangle PSV	Ⓒ Ⓓ

A pound of walnuts costs $20.00

Quantity A	Quantity B

8. the cost of an ounce $1.25   Ⓐ Ⓑ Ⓒ Ⓓ
   of walnuts

$$|x + 2| < 5$$

Quantity A	Quantity B

9. $|x|$ 5   Ⓐ Ⓑ Ⓒ Ⓓ

Questions 10 through 25 have different formats. Select a single answer choice unless the directions say otherwise. For numeric-entry questions, follow these instructions:

- **Enter your answer in the box or boxes provided.**
- **Your answer may be an integer, a decimal, a fraction, or a negative number.**
- **If the answer is a fraction, you will be given two boxes: an upper one for the numerator and a lower one for the denominator.**
- **Equivalent forms of the correct answer, such as 1.6 and 1.60, are all correct. You do not need to reduce fractions to lowest terms.**

10. Fifty thousand grams of chemical X are equally distributed among 20 containers. How many grams of chemical X are in each container?

   Ⓐ 2.5×10^2

   Ⓑ 2.5×10^3

   Ⓒ 2.5×10^4

   Ⓓ 2.5×10^5

   Ⓔ 2.5×10^6

11. If $3A = 4B$ and $2B = 3C = 10$, then what is $\dfrac{24BC}{A}$?

(A) 15

(B) 20

(C) 30

(D) 60

(E) 100

12. The probability of event p occurring is 0.4. The probability of event q occurring is 0.25. If events p and q are independent, what is the probability that p occurs but q does not?

(A) 0.1

(B) 0.3

(C) 0.325

(D) 0.75

(E) 1.15

For this question, indicate all of the answer choices that apply.

13. For which values of n is $0.01 < \dfrac{1}{3^n} < 0.1$?

[A] 1

[B] 2

[C] 3

[D] 4

[E] 5

For this question, write your answer in the box.

14. A box has a square bottom and is twice as tall as it is wide. The volume of the box is 54. How tall is the box?

15. From 2007 to 2008, a stock increased in value by 30%. From 2008 to 2009, that stock decreased in value by 10%. What was the overall percentage change of the stock's value from 2007 to 2009?

   Ⓐ 7%

   Ⓑ 10%

   Ⓒ 17%

   Ⓓ 20%

   Ⓔ 40%

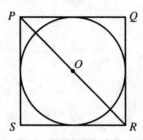

$$PR = 5$$

16. What is the area of the circle centered at O and inside of square PQRS?

   Ⓐ $\dfrac{25}{8}\pi$

   Ⓑ $\dfrac{25}{4}\pi$

   Ⓒ $\dfrac{25}{2}\pi$

   Ⓓ 25π

   Ⓔ 50π

17. In how many different ways can eight people be seated at a round table? Two ways are considered different if there are two people who are seated beside each other in one arrangement but not in the other.

   Ⓐ 630 ways

   Ⓑ 1,260 ways

   Ⓒ 2,520 ways

   Ⓓ 5,040 ways

   Ⓔ 40,320 ways

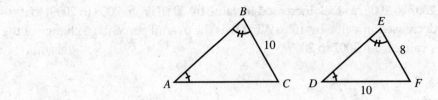

18. What is *AC*?

   Ⓐ   12

   Ⓑ   12.5

   Ⓒ   13.5

   Ⓓ   14.6

   Ⓔ   18

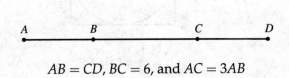

$AB = CD$, $BC = 6$, and $AC = 3AB$

19. What is *AD*?

   Ⓐ   3

   Ⓑ   6

   Ⓒ   9

   Ⓓ   12

   Ⓔ   18

For this question, indicate all of the answer choices that apply.

20. If $x = 38^n$, where n is a positive integer, which of the following digits could be the ones digit of x?

    A   0
    B   1
    C   2
    D   3
    E   4
    F   5
    G   6
    H   7
    I   8
    J   9

Use the following figure to answer questions 21 through 25.

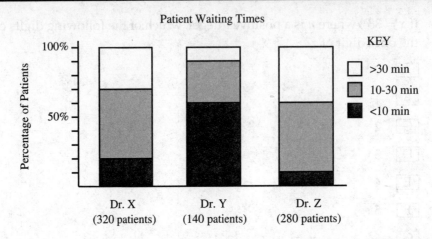

Patient Waiting Times

For this question, indicate all of the answer choices that apply.

21. Which of the following could be the median amount of time patients spent waiting for Dr. Y?

    [A] 3 minutes

    [B] 8 minutes

    [C] 10 minutes

    [D] 12 minutes

    [E] 18 minutes

For this question, write your answer in the box.

22. How many of Dr. Z's patients had to wait more than 30 minutes?

23. How many more of Dr. Y's patients were seen within 10 minutes than those of Dr. X?

    (A) 6

    (B) 20

    (C) 40

    (D) 60

    (E) 84

24. What percent of the patients of all three doctors had to wait more than 30 minutes?

    (A) 15%

    (B) 20%

    (C) 25%

    (D) 30%

    (E) 35%

25. Of the patients who waited at least 10 minutes for D. X, what percent waited over 30 minutes?

    (A) 30%

    (B) 37.5%

    (C) 40%

    (D) 42.9%

    (E) 60%

STOP.   This is the end of Section 5. Use any remaining time to check your work.

SECTION 6
Quantitative Reasoning
Time: 40 minutes
25 questions

Each of questions 1 through 9 consists of two quantities, Quantity A and Quantity B. You are to compare the two quantities. You may use additional information centered above the two quantities if additional information is given. Choose

(A) if Quantity A is greater;

(B) if Quantity B is greater;

(C) if the two quantities are equal;

(D) if the relationship cannot be determined from the information given.

Quantity A	Quantity B	
1. $\dfrac{3}{7} + \dfrac{2}{5}$	$\dfrac{3}{7} \div \dfrac{2}{5}$	Ⓐ Ⓑ Ⓒ Ⓓ

Quantity A	Quantity B	
2. $(2^3)^4$	$2^{(3^4)}$	Ⓐ Ⓑ Ⓒ Ⓓ

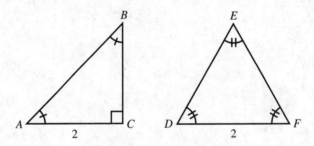

Quantity A	Quantity B	
3. the area of triangle *ABC*	the area of triangle *DEF*	Ⓐ Ⓑ Ⓒ Ⓓ

$$xy < 0$$

	Quantity A	Quantity B	
4.	$|x| + |y|$	$|x + y|$	Ⓐ Ⓑ Ⓒ Ⓓ

$$x > 4$$

	Quantity A	Quantity B	
5.	$\dfrac{x + 4}{x - 4}$	$x + 10$	Ⓐ Ⓑ Ⓒ Ⓓ

$$x^2 < x$$

	Quantity A	Quantity B	
6.	x	0	Ⓐ Ⓑ Ⓒ Ⓓ

	Quantity A	Quantity B	
7.	the distance from (2, 7) to (4, 5)	3	Ⓐ Ⓑ Ⓒ Ⓓ

	Quantity A	Quantity B	
8.	the slope of a line perpendicular to $5y - x = 2$	-5	Ⓐ Ⓑ Ⓒ Ⓓ

Quantity A	Quantity B	
9. mean of an arithmetic sequence	median of an arithmetic sequence	Ⓐ Ⓑ Ⓒ Ⓓ

Questions 10 through 25 have different formats. Select a single answer choice unless the directions say otherwise. For numeric-entry questions, follow these instructions:

- Ⓐ Enter your answer in the box or boxes provided.
- Ⓑ Your answer may be an integer, a decimal, a fraction, or a negative number.
- Ⓒ If the answer is a fraction, you will be given two boxes: an upper one for the numerator and a lower one for the denominator.
- Ⓓ Equivalent forms of the correct answer, such as 1.6 and 1.60, are all correct. You do not need to reduce fractions to lowest terms.

For this question, indicate all of the answer choices that apply.

10. Which two of the following numbers have a product that is greater than 35?

- A   −8
- B   −6
- C   4
- D   5
- E   7

For this question, indicate all of the answer choices that apply.

11. Which of the following are prime factors of 30?

    [A] 1

    [B] 2

    [C] 3

    [D] 5

    [E] 6

    [F] 7

    [G] 8

12. What is the 20th number in the sequence 3, 6, 12, 24, 48, … ?

    (A) 2×3^{20}

    (B) 3×2^{20}

    (C) 3×2^{19}

    (D) 3^{19}

    (E) 3^{20}

13. Recording studio A charges $10,000 to make the first CD and $1.50 to make each additional CD. Recording studio B charges $6,000 to make the first CD and $2 for each additional CD. How many CDs would you need to order for the bills at the two studios to be the same?

    (A) 2,001

    (B) 4,000

    (C) 4,001

    (D) 8,000

    (E) 8,001

For this question, write your answer in the box.

14. Seventy percent of the cards in a deck are green and the rest are red. Twenty percent of the green cards are rare and 50% of the red cards are rare. What percentage of all the cards are rare?

 %

For this question, indicate all of the answer choices that apply.

15. Which of the following points are on the line $3y + 2x = 5$?

   A $(0, 5)$

   B $(1, 1)$

   C $(-1, 1)$

   D $(-2, 3)$

   E $(2, 0)$

For this question, write your answer in the box.

16. How many positive integers less than 1,000 can be evenly divided by both 15 and 18?

For this question, write your answer in the box.

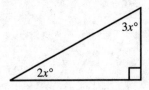

17. $x° =$

 °

For this question, write your answer in the boxes.

18. A garden center has seven female and eight male holly plants, but they aren't labeled as such. If a customer randomly purchases three plants, what is the probability of getting both male and female plants (thus holly berries, eventually)? Write your answer as a reduced fraction.

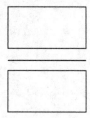

19. One inch is 2.54 centimeters. How many kilometers is one mile, rounded to the nearest thousandth?

   (A) 1.601

   (B) 1.603

   (C) 1.605

   (D) 1.607

   (E) 1.609

For this question, indicate all of the answer choices that apply.

20. $|x + 2| = |2x - 5|$

   Which of the following are possible values of x?

   A −3

   B 1

   C 2

   D 5

   E 7

21. The height of a triangle increases by 40% while the base decreases by 30%. By what percentage has the area of the triangle changed?

   (A) −10%

   (B) −2%

   (C) 0

   (D) 5%

   (E) 10%

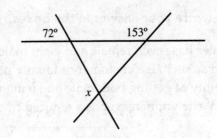

22. Find x.

   (A) 27°

   (B) 99°

   (C) 108°

   (D) 135°

   (E) 225°

For this question, indicate all of the answer choices that apply.

23. Which of the following lines are parallel to $y = 2x + 3$?

   A　$y = 3x + 2$

   B　$y - 2x = 5$

   C　$2y = 4x - 1$

   D　$y = 2x - 1$

   E　$y = 3$

Use the following figure to answer questions 24 and 25.

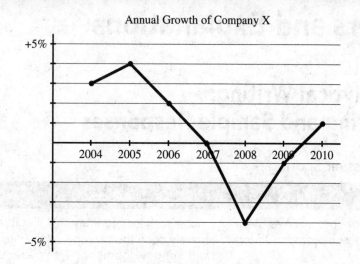

Annual Growth of Company X

24. If company X was valued at $4.6 billion at the start of 2004, what was it worth at the start of 2006, rounded to the nearest million dollars?

Ⓐ $4,876 million

Ⓑ $4,880 million

Ⓒ $4,922 million

Ⓓ $4,927 million

Ⓔ $4,928 million

25. What was the total percentage change of company X's value from the start of 2007 to the start of 2010?

Ⓐ −4.86%

Ⓑ −4.9%

Ⓒ −4.96%

Ⓓ −5%

Ⓔ −5.1%

STOP.   This is the end of Section 6. Use any remaining time to check your work.

GRE Practice Test 2: Answers and Explanations

Analytical Writing: Scoring and Sample Responses

Analyze an Issue: Scoring

Score	Focus	Organization	Conventions
0	Does not address the chosen prompt. Off topic.	Incomprehensible. May merely copy the prompt without development.	Illegible. Nonverbal. Serious errors make the paper unreadable. May be in a foreign language.
1	Mostly irrelevant to the prompt.	Little or no development of ideas. No evidence of analysis or organization.	Pervasive errors in grammar, mechanics, and spelling.
2	Unclear connection to the prompt.	Unfocused and disorganized.	Frequent errors in sentence structure, mechanics, and spelling.
3	Limited connection to the prompt.	Rough organization with weak examples or reasons.	Occasional major errors and frequent minor errors in conventions of written English.
4	Competent connection to the prompt.	Relevant examples or reasons develop a logical position.	Occasional minor errors in conventions of written English.
5	Clear, focused connection to the prompt.	Thoughtful, appropriate examples or reasons develop a consistent, coherent position. Connectors are ably used to mark transitions.	Very few errors. Sentence structure is varied and vocabulary is advanced.
6	Insightful, clever connection to the chosen prompt.	Compelling, convincing examples or reasons develop a consistent, coherent position. The argument flows effortlessly and persuasively.	Very few errors. Sentence structure is varied and vocabulary is precise, well chosen, and effective.

Analyze an Issue:
Sample Response with a Score of 6

This essay is thoughtful and rational. The writer presents an argument against consensus and offers a variety of examples. The counterargument for consensus is accepted in certain cases, but its flaws are clearly stated. There are no significant errors in grammar or mechanics.

Anyone who has ever served on a committee has felt the tension between the goal of consensus and the realities of the members' differing beliefs and attitudes. Consensus is an admirable goal, but sometimes majority rule is simply more practical.

The possibility of consensus seems likely to get smaller as the group gets bigger. Imagine if the United States Senate required universal consensus for all major decisions. You would be asking 100 people who represent vastly different constituencies to agree on a single course of action. The odds of that happening are minute.

The possibility of consensus is greatest when the group is small, is goal oriented, and represents a homogeneous population. For example, it is probably fairly easy for a club composed of 20 eighth graders to come to a consensus on the theme of a dance. The more people involved, the longer the decision will take. The less clear the goal and the more diverse the group, the less likely the group is to reach agreement in a timely manner.

Consensus may be preferable when the point of the exercise is to show the outside world a united front. For example, it is always best when parents reach consensus on the rules of a household. It is often best when a planning board reaches consensus on development goals. However, insisting on consensus may be impractical and even unwise.

When an irrational desire for consensus stalls progress toward an important goal, good leadership demands a different path. Majority rule may be the only way to break a logjam and move things forward. As much as consensus may be desirable, it is not always a reasonable goal.

Analyze an Argument: Scoring

Score	Focus	Organization	Conventions
0	Does not address the prompt. Off topic.	Incomprehensible. May merely copy the prompt without development.	Illegible. Nonverbal. Serious errors make the paper unreadable. May be in a foreign language.
1	Little or no analysis of the argument. May indicate misunderstanding of the prompt.	Little or no development of ideas. No evidence of analysis or organization.	Pervasive errors in grammar, mechanics, and spelling.
2	Little analysis; may instead present opinions and unrelated thoughts.	Disorganized and illogical.	Frequent errors in sentence structure, mechanics, and spelling.
3	Some analysis of the prompt, but some major flaws may be omitted.	Rough organization with irrelevant support or unclear transitions.	Occasional major errors and frequent minor errors in conventions of written English.
4	Important flaws in the argument are touched upon.	Ideas are sound but may not flow logically or clearly.	Occasional minor errors in conventions of written English.
5	Perceptive analysis of the major flaws in the argument.	Logical examples and support develop a consistent, coherent critique. Connectors are ably used to mark transitions.	Very few errors. Sentence structure is varied and vocabulary is advanced.
6	Insightful, clever analysis of the argument's flaws and fallacies.	Compelling, convincing examples and support develop a consistent, coherent critique. The analysis flows effortlessly and persuasively.	Very few errors. Sentence structure is varied and vocabulary is precise, well chosen, and effective.

Analyze an Argument: Sample Response with a Score of 6

This essay is short and rather light in tone, but it manages at the same time to be both comprehensive and compelling. The writer locates a possible error in data gathering that may have led to a biased conclusion and goes on to explain how that might have happened and how it might be corrected. There are no real errors in English usage or mechanics.

The oddball, rather macho trio of recreational activities that the Teeburg Town Board recommended derives from the fact that their initial sample was biased. This bias led to an unrepresentative response.

The town made the simple mistake of addressing its questionnaire to "head of household." Although households today are very likely to be "headed" by women, the response received makes it fairly clear that most people who responded to the questionnaire were the traditional "man of the house" respondents. It may be the case that the town is small and rural, or there may be some other reason that is unclear from the information given.

The questions used to derive the response are unknown, but they seem to have been personalized for the individual answering the questionnaire rather than focused on (for example) the entire family in the household. For that reason, no activities appropriate for young children are in the final three. One would hope that a town's recreation plan would be more inclusive.

If Teeburg is entirely composed of middle-aged, middle-class men, then the recommendation of the board is reasonable and proper. If, however, it is a typical small town, with women and girls, men and boys, all seeking recreational outlets, then the mailing should be redone, with questions that incorporate all family members for a truly representative response.

GRE Practice Test 2: Answer Key

Section 3. Verbal Reasoning

1. **A, E**
2. **E, F**
3. **A, E**
4. **D, E**
5. **B**
6. **B**
7. **C**
8. **A**
9. **E**
10. **B**
11. **B**
12. **B, E, I**
13. **A, E**
14. **A, B**
15. **D**
16. As the price of glass came down, greenhouses became ever more elaborate and grand, culminating in Joseph Paxton's Crystal Palace, a 990,000-square-foot conservatory built for London's Great Exhibition of 1851.

17. **E**
18. **B, D**
19. **A, F**
20. **A, E, I**
21. **C**
22. **B, C**
23. **C**
24. **B**
25. Bluefish move from north to south; cod move from shallow to deeper water.

Section 4. Verbal Reasoning

1. **A, B, C**
2. **E**
3. After that, the patient's decline may be slow or rapid, eventually resulting in physical and mental degeneration.
4. **B**
5. **A**
6. **D**
7. **C, F**
8. **C, E**
9. **A, C**
10. **C**
11. **D**
12. **A**
13. Although family roles were gender related, with men doing the hunting and fishing and women responsible for most of the farming, women held important positions within the confederation.
14. **B**
15. **B, D, H**
16. **B**
17. **A**
18. **D**
19. **B**
20. **E**
21. **A, C**
22. **B, D**
23. **E, F**
24. **B, E**
25. **A, D**

Section 5. Quantitative Reasoning

1. A
2. A
3. A
4. A
5. D
6. C
7. C
8. C
9. D
10. B
11. D
12. B
13. C, D
14. **6**
15. C
16. A
17. C
18. B
19. D
20. C, E, G, I
21. A, B
22. **112**
23. B
24. D
25. B

Section 6. Quantitative Reasoning

1. B
2. B
3. A
4. A
5. D
6. A
7. B
8. C
9. C
10. A, B
11. B, C, D
12. C
13. E
14. **29**
15. B, D
16. **11**
17. **18**
18. **4/5**
19. E
20. B, E
21. B
22. B
23. B, C, D
24. E
25. C

GRE Practice Test 2: Answer Explanations

Section 3. Verbal Reasoning

1. **A, E.** Even if some of the other choices make sense contextually, only *aptitude* (choice A) and *talent* (choice E) are synonyms.

2. **E, F.** The aide might have served as a deputy (choice D), but it's more likely that he served as a proxy (choice E) or surrogate (choice F), meaning that he represented and stood in for the senator.

3. **A, E.** The refugees have been deliberately targeted; both *willfully* (choice A) and *calculatingly* (choice E) are synonyms for *deliberately*.

4. **D, E.** The words *predilection* and *proclivity* are synonyms meaning "preference" or "liking." Of the other choices, choice A means "principle," choice B means "speed in action," choice C means "urging," and choice E means "talkativeness."

5. **B.** The author never suggests that Lord Curzon was related to the original inhabitant of the castle (choice A), nor does the passage say that Lord Curzon lived in the castle (choice C). Curzon's love of architecture led him to restore the castle and will it to the public, so the best answer is choice B.

6. **B.** To answer this, think about a child's drawing of a castle. What do the towers look like? Even if you don't know the word, you can infer that it means "notched" (choice B).

7. **C.** Choice A is hypercorrection, not hyperforeignism. Choice B might be hyperforeignism were it not absolutely correct to pronounce *ballet* without the final *t*. The only correct answer is choice C.

8. **A.** Find the mention of the U.S. Treasury Building. Then work backward to learn that it is an example of Greek Revival style, making choice A the correct answer.

9. **E.** All of the buildings except the U.S. Capitol (choice E) are presented as examples of specific substyles.

10. **B.** If they were built in medieval times, *currently* (choice A) is not a good answer. Except for *typically* (choice B), the other choices make little sense.

11. **D.** Although *administered to* (choice A) is at least possible, it is usually used to refer to a doctor's aid rather than a use of power. *Reined in* (choice E) means "held back," not "ruled." The best answer is *presided over* (choice D).

12. **B, E, I.** Read the whole passage before trying to complete it. Doing so will show that the Supreme Court must have overturned the long-standing tradition (choice B) rather than upheld it (choice A), thus paving the way (choice E) for women to enroll. Because his son attended VMI, Justice Thomas had to recuse, or disqualify, himself (choice I).

13. **A, E.** The criticism was favorable, so it helped to establish (choice A) his reputation (choice E), not controvert (choice B) it.

14. **A, B.** There is no indication that Louis XIV traveled himself to find exotic fruits (choice C). Because the French built orangeries to protect the tropical plants, both choices A and B are logical inferences.

15. **D.** Think about the author's purpose here. Although pineries were built for one particular kind of fruit, making choice C seem reasonable, the mention of them is really just another example of greenhouses, making choice D better than choice C.

16. **As the price of glass came down, greenhouses became ever more elaborate and grand, culminating in Joseph Paxton's Crystal Palace, a 990,000-square-foot conservatory built for London's Great Exhibition of 1851.** The practical factor in building bigger greenhouses is the reduced price of glass.

17. **E.** Photodetectors *are* light sensors; they are not potential (choice B) or former (choice C) or even considered (choice A) light sensors.

18. **B, D.** A seaport would not be inland (choice F). All the other choices are possible, but only choices B and D combine to make a logical sentence.

19. **A, F.** The key to this sentence is the word "although," which sets up a contrast. The residents may be technically citizens (choice A), but they are still not allowed to vote (choice F).

20. **A, E, I.** The answers here are those that are most logical and create the most sensible sentence.

21. **C.** Think about the timing of the speech and why Eisenhower made it when he did. The Cold War (choice A) did not make the timing more prudent; nor did the expansion of the military budget (choice B) or the dropping of bombs (choice D). All of these combined to make such a speech less reasonably timed, not more so. Choice E had not yet happened. Only the death of Stalin opened a door to reconciliation, making choice C the best answer.

22. **B, C.** The phrase that helps answer this question is: "All featured his typical style and themes—long takes focused on facial features, long conversations about moral issues, temptation and its denial." The style was certainly not active or dynamic (choice A); it was dialogue driven (choice B) and philosophical (choice C).

23. **C.** A single fish cannot migrate only within fresh water and only within salt water, as choice A would indicate. It cannot breed both in salt water and in fresh water, as choice B specifies. It could, however, migrate between salt and fresh while breeding in salt water, making choice C the only possible answer.

24. **B.** Anadromous fish, according to the passage, migrate from salt to fresh to breed and live out most of their lives in salt water. Only choice B indicates that this is true of the chinook salmon.

25. **Bluefish move from north to south; cod move from shallow to deeper water.** Bluefish and cod are given as examples of oceanodromous fish.

Section 4. Verbal Reasoning

1. **A, B, C.** A child of a carrier has a 50-50 chance of inheriting the mutated gene, meaning a 50-50 chance of presenting with the disease. You would expect, then, in a family of four children, that half would inherit and present (choices A, B), and half would not (choice C).

2. **E.** Everyone carries the gene (choice A). Western Europeans are more likely to inherit the mutation (choice B), but this is not the best answer of the five. The passage suggests that having more than 40 repetitions is bad, but 25 (choice C) would be normal. Eastern Europeans (choice D) are less likely that some others to inherit the mutation. However, someone whose grandfather died of the disease (choice E) is profoundly at risk.

3. **After that, the patient's decline may be slow or rapid, eventually resulting in physical and mental degeneration.** The variation in speed of the decline indicates the unpredictability of the disease.

4. **B.** All of the patterns involve a five-pointed star, making choice A incorrect. There are three designs, not four (choice C), and nothing in the passage suggests that there was once just a single design (choice D). The army gets one design, the air force a second, and the navy and marine corps share a third, making choice B correct.

5. **A.** The word "plethora" suggests abundance, so the best choice is *prolific* (choice A), meaning "very productive."

6. **D.** The second part of the sentence defines the word for you—the scientist broke the history of the Earth into segments, classifying them.

7. **C, F.** Again, you must read the whole sentence to know which choices work best. The leagues merged (choice C), creating a new league (choice F).

8. **C, E.** The little republic houses, or accommodates (choice C), many citizens, making it densely populated (choice E).

9. **A, C.** Control and balance are the skills cited by the author, making choices A and C correct. There is no mention of attitude at all (choice B).

10. **C.** Although the author names a few heroes of the sport (choice D), that is not the primary purpose of the passage, which is far more general and descriptive, without being historical (choice E).

11. **D.** A score of 0 means the rider fell off (choice A). A score of 50 indicates great balance and control. A score in between means the rider may not have had one or more of those skills but still maintained his seat on the bull.

12. **A.** The first sentence mentions certain bulls who have attained fame; the other sentences give examples of those.

13. **Although family roles were gender related, with men doing the hunting and fishing and women responsible for most of the farming, women held important positions within the confederation.** This sentence contrasts the tribal gender roles.

14. **B.** A miasma (choice B) is a mist or fog, which makes sense when applied to "bad air." The other choices would not describe bad air.

15. **B, D, H.** Read the entire two-sentence passage before plugging in words to fit the blanks. Scrooge is a miser, so he is niggardly (choice B), or stingy. Although he is bad, he is not the worst, or most odious (choice D) of loathsome characters. That honor goes to a man of false sincerity, the toadying (choice H), or fawning creep, Uriah Heep. If his sincerity were not false, he might be considered solicitous (choice G).

16. **B.** The sentence talks about production, meaning that choices C, D, and E are not correct, and choice A is redundant. The best answer is *mining* (choice B), which is one of two ways salt is produced.

17. **A.** If the leeches ingested (choice D) or collected (choice B) the anesthetic, it would affect them, not their host. They release the anesthetic (choice A), dulling the host's senses.

18. **D.** Both mimicry (choice A) and defensive body structures (choice E) may be subsumed under the more comprehensive category of protective measures, making choice D the best answer.

19. **B.** If you accept the premise that the main topic of the passage is protective measures used by the praying mantis, only choice B adds to that with a relevant detail.

20. **E.** The paragraph begins with a clear topic sentence.

21. **A, C.** When in doubt, look for the words that are synonyms. In this case, only *callously* and *insensitively* fill that bill.

22. **B, D.** It makes sense that a champion (choice D) or benefactor (choice B) of music might have a school named after him.

23. **E, F.** Think of a range from logical to something else. The words you are looking for will imply illogic, making *dubious* (choice E) and *apocryphal* (choice F) the best choices.

24. **B, E.** Think: What kind of range of subject matter goes from action-adventure to horror to business? The answer is one that is broad (choice B) or expansive (choice E).

25. **A, D.** Again, when in doubt, find the synonyms. Both *equivalent* (choice A) and *analogous* (choice D) mean "similar in meaning" here.

Section 5. Quantitative Reasoning

1. **A.** To convert from 100,000 hours into years, divide by 24 to get days, then divide by 365 to get years. With the calculator, this comes out to be about 11.4, thus 100,000 hours is more than 10 years. For a shortcut, $24 \times 365 \times 10 = 87,600$.

2. **A.** The number 6 factors into 2×3 and 10 factors into 2×5. The least common multiple of 6 and 10 is the smallest product of factors in which both of these factorizations can be found: $2 \times 3 \times 5 = 30$. The number 80 factors into $8 \times 10 = 2 \times 2 \times 2 \times 2 \times 5$, while 140 factors into $7 \times 20 = 7 \times 2 \times 2 \times 5$. The greatest common divisor of 80 and 140 is the largest product of factors which they both contain: $2 \times 2 \times 5 = 20$. The answer is A because 30 is bigger than 20.

3. **A.** To make a four-digit number with distinct digits, you have nine choices of digit for the thousands place (you cannot begin with a 0 and call it a four-digit number). Next, you can use any of the other nine digits in the hundreds place, then any of the eight remaining digits in the tens place, and any of the seven unused digits in the ones place, for a total of $9 \times 9 \times 8 \times 7 = 4,536$ possibilities. The number of three-digit numbers is $9 \times 10 \times 10 = 900$ (you can put any digit in any place except for a 0 in the hundreds place). Quantity A is bigger because $4,536 > 900$.

4. **A.** Because $x = -2$, you know that $y = 2 - 3x = 2 - 3(-2) = 2 + 6 = 8$. Thus $y = 8$ is greater than 5.

5. **D.** If you multiply out $(x + y)(x - y) = x^2 - y^2$. If $y \neq 0$, then $x^2 + y^2$ will be greater than $x^2 - y^2$. However, if $y = 0$, the two quantities will be the same. Thus you cannot determine which quantity is greater.

6. **C.** If x is an even integer, then $\dfrac{1}{(-1)^x} - (-1)^x = 1 - 1 = 0$. If x is an odd integer, then $\dfrac{1}{(-1)^x} - (-1)^x = -1 - (-1) = 0$. In either case, the two quantities are the same.

7. **C.** If the length $PV = x$, then the area of square $PQTV = x^2$. Because $ST = TV$, you know that $SV = 2x$. Thus the area of (right) triangle $PVS = \dfrac{1}{2}bh = \dfrac{1}{2}x(2x) = x^2$ as well.

8. **C.** There are 16 ounces in a pound, so an ounce of walnuts costs $\$20 \div 16 = \$1.25$.

9. **D.** We solve the inequality by $-5 < x + 2 < 5$; thus $-7 < x < 3$. This could mean that $x = -6$, so $|x| = 6$, or $x = 2$, so $|x| = 2$.

10. **B.** When 50,000 is divided by 20, the result is 2,500. This is $2.5 \times 1,000$, which is 2.5×10^3 in scientific notation.

11. **D.** If we multiply the top and bottom by 3, we can rearrange $\dfrac{3 \times 24BC}{3A} = \dfrac{3 \times (4B)2(3C)}{3A}$. We cancel out the $\dfrac{4B}{3A} = 1$ because $3A = 4B$, and we substitute $3C = 10$ to end with $3 \times 2 \times 10 = 60$.

12. **B.** If the probability of q occurring is 0.25, then the probability of q not happening is $1 - 0.25 = 0.75$. Because p and q are independent, p and not-q are also independent. Thus the probability of both p and not-q is the product of their probabilities: $0.4 \times 0.75 = 0.3$.

13. **C, D.** You are asked to find the values of n for which $\dfrac{1}{100} < \dfrac{1}{3^n} < \dfrac{1}{10}$, which is equivalent to $10 < 3^n < 100$. Your options are $n = 1, 2, 3, 4,$ and 5, which make $3^1 = 3, 3^2 = 9, 3^3 = 27, 3^4 = 81,$ and $3^5 = 243$, respectively. Of these, the values $n = 3$ and 4 make 3^n between 10 and 100.

14. **6.** If the width of the box is x, then the length is x also, because the base is a square. The height, at double the width, is then $2x$. The volume of the box is thus $x \cdot x \cdot 2x = 54$, which simplifies to $2x^3 = 54$. This is the same as $x^3 = 27$, or $x = 3$. This is the width, however, and not the height, which is $2x = 6$.

15. **C.** If you suppose that the stock started with a value of $100, an increase of 30% would bring it up to $130. Ten percent of 130 is 13, so a 10% drop in that value would take it down to $117. Thus the overall change would be an increase of 17%.

16. **A.** By symmetry, you can see that O is the center of the square. Thus, the lengths OR and OQ are both $\dfrac{5}{2}$, half of PR. The triangle QOR is thus a right triangle with two legs of length $\dfrac{5}{2}$. By the Pythagorean theorem, you calculate $\left(\dfrac{5}{2}\right)^2 + \left(\dfrac{5}{2}\right)^2 = (QR)^2$, thus $QR = \sqrt{\dfrac{50}{4}} = \dfrac{5}{\sqrt{2}}$. The diameter of the circle is the same as QR, and thus the radius is $\dfrac{5}{2\sqrt{2}}$. The area of the circle is thus $\pi \left(\dfrac{5}{2\sqrt{2}}\right)^2 = \dfrac{25}{8}\pi$.

17. **C.** There are 8! different ways that the eight seats can be filled (eight choices for the first seat, seven for the second, etc.). Each of these is essentially the same as the seven other ways obtained by rotating all guests around the table. Similarly, the mirror reflection of any arrangement will also keep everyone sitting beside the same people. Thus the number of ways is $\dfrac{8!}{8 \times 2} = \dfrac{8 \times 7 \times 6 \times 5 \times 4 \times 3 \times 2}{8 \times 2} = 7 \times 6 \times 5 \times 4 \times 3 = 2,520$.

18. **B.** The triangles have two angles in common and thus are similar. The sides opposite the corresponding angles will make the same ratio: $\frac{AC}{10} = \frac{10}{8}$. This simplifies to $AC = \frac{100}{8} = 12.5$.

19. **D.** If $x = AB$, then the equation $AC = 3AB$ can be written as $x + 6 = 3x$. This reduces to $x = 3$. The full length $AD = x + 6 + x = 12$.

20. **C, E, G, I.** The last digit of 38^1 is 8. When that number is multiplied by 38 to make 38^2, the last digit will be 4 (from $8 \times 8 = 64$). When this is multiplied by 38 to make 38^3, the last digit will be 2 (from $4 \times 8 = 32$). When this number is multiplied by 38 to make 38^4, the last digit will be 6 (from $2 \times 8 = 16$). When this number is multiplied by 38 to make 38^5, the last digit will be 8 (from $6 \times 8 = 48$). The process will then repeat, so no other last digits are possible.

21. **A, B.** Over 50% of Dr. Y's patients experienced waiting times of less than 10 minutes. Thus, the median must be in this range, which could be either 3 or 8 minutes.

22. **112 patients.** Dr. Z had 280 patients, and 40% needed to wait over 30 minutes. Thus the answer is $0.4 \times 280 = 112$.

23. **B.** Dr. Y had $0.6 \times 140 = 84$ patients who waited less than 10 minutes. Dr. X had $0.2 \times 320 = 64$. Thus, Dr. Y had $84 - 64 = 20$ more.

24. **D.** There are $320 + 140 + 280 = 740$ patients in all. Of them, $0.3 \times 320 + 0.1 \times 140 + 0.4 \times 280 = 222$ had to wait at least 30 minutes. This is thus $222/740 \approx 0.3 = 30\%$.

25. **B.** Of the patients of Dr. X, 80% waited 10 minutes or more, and 30% waited more than 30 minutes. This was $\frac{30\%}{80\%} \approx 0.375 = 37.5\%$ of them.

Section 6. Quantitative Reasoning

1. **B.** Quantity A is $\dfrac{3}{7} + \dfrac{2}{5} = \dfrac{3}{7} \times \dfrac{5}{5} + \dfrac{2}{5} \times \dfrac{7}{7} = \dfrac{15}{35} + \dfrac{14}{35} = \dfrac{29}{35}$, which is less than 1, while Quantity B is $\dfrac{3}{7} \div \dfrac{2}{5} = \dfrac{3}{7} \times \dfrac{5}{2} = \dfrac{15}{14}$, which is more than 1.

2. **B.** Quantity A is $(2^3)^4 = 2^{3 \times 4} = 2^{12}$, while Quantity B is $2^{(3^4)} = 2^{81}$. This makes Quantity B $\dfrac{2^{81}}{2^{12}} = 2^{81-12} = 2^{69}$ times as large as Quantity A.

3. **A.** Triangle ABC is an isosceles right triangle, with a base and height of 2, thus its area is $\dfrac{1}{2} \times 2 \times 2 = 2$. Triangle DEF is equilateral, so all three of its sides are 2. Because the slant height of triangle DEF is 2, its vertical height must be less than 2. Thus, the area of triangle DEF is less than that of triangle ABC.

4. **A.** If $xy < 0$, it is necessary that one of the variables, x or y, be negative while the other is positive. To add together x and y thus results in the subtraction of the smaller absolute value from the larger, with the sign of whichever has the larger absolute value. Thus Quantity B, $|x + y|$, is this subtraction made positive. Quantity A, $|x| + |y|$ is literally the sum of their absolute values. Because subtracting one positive number from another will always result in less than adding those numbers together, Quantity A will always be larger.

5. **D.** If $x = 5$, then Quantity A is 9 and Quantity B is 15, so Quantity B is larger. If $x = 4.5$, however, then Quantity A is $9.5 \div 0.5 = 19$ and Quantity B is 14.5, so Quantity A is larger. It is thus impossible to say which of the two quantities is larger.

6. **A.** The inequality $x^2 < x$ is not true if $x = 0$, so you can divide both sides by x. If $x > 0$, then the inequality will not change, resulting in $x < 1$. If $x < 0$, then the inequality will change (dividing both sides by a negative number reverses an inequality), resulting in $x > 1$—which is not possible because $x < 0$. Thus, it must be that $x > 0$ and $x < 1$. It follows that Quantity A, x, is larger than Quantity B, 0.

7. **B.** The distance from $(2, 7)$ to $(4, 5)$ is, using the distance formula, $\sqrt{(2-4)^2 + (7-5)^2} = \sqrt{4+4} = \sqrt{8}$. Because $\sqrt{8} < \sqrt{9} = 3$, Quantity B is larger than Quantity A.

8. **C.** The standard form for the equation of the line $5y - x = 2$ is $y = \dfrac{1}{5}x + \dfrac{2}{5}$, thus this line has a slope of $\dfrac{1}{5}$. The slope of a perpendicular line will be the negative reciprocal $-\dfrac{1}{\frac{1}{5}} = -5$. Thus the two quantities are equal.

9. **C.** An arithmetic sequence that begins with a, adds b each time, and has n terms is $a, a + b, a + 2b, \ldots, a + (n - 1)b$. The sum of all these terms is $na + b(1 + 2 + \ldots + n - 1) = na + b\left(\dfrac{(n-1)n}{2}\right)$; thus the mean is $\dfrac{na + \dfrac{bn(n-1)}{2}}{n} = a + \dfrac{b(n-1)}{2}$. If n is odd, then the median term is also $a + \dfrac{b(n-1)}{2}$. If n is even, then the median is the average of the two middle terms: $a + \dfrac{b(n-2)}{2}$ and $a + \dfrac{bn}{2}$. Their average is $\dfrac{a + \dfrac{b(n-2)}{2} + a + \dfrac{bn}{2}}{2} = a + \dfrac{2a + \dfrac{2bn - 2b}{2}}{2} = a + \dfrac{bn - b}{2} = a + \dfrac{b(n-1)}{2}$ once again.

10. **A, B.** If you multiply the largest two positive numbers together, you get $5 \times 7 = 35$, which is equal to, but not greater than, 35. If you multiply a positive number by a negative number, you get a negative number, all of which are less than 0 and therefore less than 35. The product of -8 and -6, however, is 48, which is greater than 35.

11. **B, C, D.** These numbers are both prime and factors of 30. The numbers 1, 6, and 8 are not prime, and the number 7 is not a factor of 30.

12. **C.** The first number in this sequence is 3 and each subsequent number is twice as large. The second number is $3 \times 2 = 6$, the third number is $3 \times 2^2 = 12$, the fourth number is $3 \times 2^3 = 24$, and the 20th number is 3×2^{19}. You multiply 3 by one power of 2 less than the place in the sequence.

13. **E.** If x is the number of CDs ordered, then studio A will charge $10{,}000 + 1.5(x - 1)$ and studio B will charge $6{,}000 + 2(x - 1)$. These bills will be the same when $10{,}000 + 1.5(x - 1) = 6{,}000 + 2(x - 1)$, thus $4{,}000 = 0.5(x - 1)$ and $x - 1 = 8{,}000$, so $x = 8{,}001$.

14. **29.** The percentage which are rare green cards is $70\% \times 20\% = 0.7 \times 0.2 = 0.14 = 14\%$. The percentage which are rare red cards is $30\% \times 50\% = 0.3 \times 0.5 = 0.15 = 15\%$. Thus the total percentage which are rare is $14\% + 15\% = 29\%$.

15. **B, D.** The easiest way to check would be to plug in the x and y values and see if the equation is true. If $x = 0$ and $y = 5$, then $3y + 2x = 15$, not 5. If $x = 1$ and $y = 1$, then $3y + 2x = 5$ is satisfied. If $x = -1$ and $y = 1$, then $3y + 2x = 1$, not 5. If $x = -2$ and $y = 3$, then $3y + 2x = 5$. If $x = 2$ and $y = 0$, then $3y + 2x = 4$, not 5.

16. **11.** Any number that is a multiple of $15 = 3 \times 5$ and $18 = 3 \times 3 \times 2$ must be a multiple of $3 \times 3 \times 5 \times 2 = 90$. Because $1{,}000/90 \approx 11.11$, there are 11 positive numbers less than 1,000 that can be divided by both 15 and 18.

17. **18°.** The angles of a triangle sum to 180°, so $2x° + 3x° + 90° = 180°$. This simplifies to $5x = 90°$, thus $x = 18°$.

18. $\frac{4}{5}$. The probability that all the plants will be female is $\frac{7}{15} \times \frac{6}{14} \times \frac{5}{13} = \frac{1}{13}$ because the customer must pick one of the seven (out of 15) female plants first, then one of the six (out of 14) remaining female plants second, etc. The probability that all the plants will be male is $\frac{8}{15} \times \frac{7}{14} \times \frac{6}{13} = \frac{8}{5 \times 13}$. Together, the probability that the plants will be either all male or all female is thus $\frac{1}{13} + \frac{8}{5 \times 13} = \frac{13}{5 \times 13} = \frac{1}{5}$. Thus the probability that this does *not* happen (that there will be a mix of both male and female plants) will be $\frac{4}{5}$.

19. **E.** One mile $= 5,280$ feet $= 5,280$ feet $\times \dfrac{12\ \text{in}}{1\ \text{ft}} = 63,360$ inches $= 63,360$ inches $\times \dfrac{2.54\ \text{cm}}{1\ \text{in}} = 160,934.4$ centimeters $= 1,609.344$ meters $= 1.609344$ kilometers.

20. **B, E.** Absolute values leave positive numbers alone and reverse negative numbers by multiplying by -1. Thus $|x+2| = |2x-5|$ represents $x+2 = 2x-5$ and $x+2 = -(2x-5)$. The first simplifies to $x = 7$, the second to $x+2 = -2x+5$ and thus $x = 1$.

21. **B.** The height changes from h to $1.4h$ while the base changes from b to $0.7b$. The area thus changes from $\frac{1}{2}bh$ to $\frac{1}{2}(1.4h)(0.7b) = (1.4 \times 0.7)\frac{1}{2}bh = 0.98 \times \frac{1}{2}bh$. This is a decrease of 2%.

22. **B.** The upper left corner of the triangle in the figure measures $72°$, because vertical angles have the same measure. The upper right corner of the triangle is supplementary to one measuring $153°$, thus measures $180° - 153° = 27°$. The bottom angle of the triangle thus measures $180° - 72° - 27° = 81°$. As the angle marked x is supplementary to this, it measures $x = 180° - 81° = 99°$.

23. **B, C, D.** The line $y = 2x + 3$ has a slope of 2. Every other line with a slope of 2 will be parallel. The line $y = 3x + 2$ has a slope of 3. The line $y - 2x = 5$ is the same as $y = 2x + 5$, which has a slope of 2. The line $2y = 4x - 1$ is the same as $y = 2x - \frac{1}{2}$, which has a slope of 2. The line $y = 2x - 1$ has a slope of 2. The line $y = 3$ has a slope of 0. Thus, the parallel lines are $y - 2x = 5$, $2y = 4x - 1$, and $y = 2x - 1$.

24. **E.** The company grew 3% in 2004 and 4% in 2005. If it began 2004 valued at \$4.6 billion, then at the end of 2005 it was worth \$4.6 billion $\times (1.03) \times (1.04) = $ \$4.92752 billion $=$ \$4,927.52 million, which rounds to \$4,928 million.

25. **C.** The value did not change in 2007, lost 4% in 2008, and lost 1% in 2009. Thus, the ending value was $0.96 \times 0.99 = 0.9504 = 95.04\%$, a loss of $100\% - 95.04\% = 4.96\%$.

GRE Practice Test 3

SECTION 1
Analytical Writing

ANALYZE AN ISSUE

30 Minutes

You will have 30 minutes to organize your thoughts and compose a response that represents your point of view on the topic presented. Do not respond to any topic other than the one given; a response to any other topic will receive a score of 0.

You will be required to discuss your perspective on the issue, using examples and reasons drawn from your own experiences and observations.

Use scratch paper to organize your response before you begin writing. Write your response on the pages provided, or type your response using a word processor with the spell- and grammar-check functions turned off.

Issue Topic

"Allowing our children to spend hours a day IM'ing and employing social media is bound to impede their social skills as they enter adulthood and the workforce."

Discuss the extent to which you agree or disagree with the claim made above. In developing your position, address any counterarguments that might be used to challenge your point of view.

SECTION 2

Analytical Writing

ANALYZE AN ARGUMENT

30 Minutes

You will have 30 minutes to organize your thoughts and compose a response that critiques the given argument. Do not respond to any topic other than the one given; a response to any other topic will receive a score of 0.

You are not being asked to discuss your point of view on the statement. You should identify and analyze the central elements of the argument, the underlying assumptions that are being made, and any supporting information that is given. Your critique can also discuss other information that would strengthen or weaken the argument or make it more logical.

Use scratch paper to organize your response before you begin writing. Write your response on the pages provided, or type your response using a word processor with the spell- and grammar-check functions turned off.

Argument Topic

A resident of Coburn sent the following letter to the editor:

"I strongly object to the proposed placement of walking trails in Coburn. Although the trails will use land that belongs to the railroads, it is land that adjoining neighbors are accustomed to using for their own purposes. In addition, it is clear that people bent on nefarious purposes such as robbery will be able to use the trails to access the houses that back onto that land. Walking trails that steal land and protect criminals have no place in Coburn."

Critique the reasoning used in the argument presented above by examining the underlying assumptions of the argument. Explain how the argument depends on those assumptions and describe the implications for the argument should the assumptions prove unwarranted.

SECTION 3
Verbal Reasoning
Time: 35 minutes
25 questions

Questions 1 through 3 are based on this passage.

Uriah Phillips Levy fought anti-Semitism to rise through the ranks and become a commodore of the U.S. Navy. He first went to sea at age 10, returning only for his bar mitzvah three years later before taking off again. He was 20 years old by the
Line   time the War of 1812 began, and he served as sailing master aboard the USS *Argus*,
(5)   was captured with his crew, and spent 16 months in a British prison. His naval career was never smooth sailing; he was court-martialed and dismissed for refusing to use corporal punishment. Only the intervention of President Tyler enabled his reinstatement. As commodore, Levy commanded the Mediterranean fleet and abolished flogging as a form of naval discipline. Today, Levy is better known as the
(10)   person who purchased Monticello from Thomas Jefferson's daughter—and whose heirs turned the property over to the people as a museum and memorial—than as a naval hero.

Consider each of the choices separately and select all that apply.

1. The assertion made in the first sentence of the passage could best be supported by the inclusion of which of the following?

    [A] Examples of anti-Semitism in the navy

    [B] A synopsis of Levy's career as commodore

    [C] A complete chart of naval ranks

Select one answer choice.

2. Assuming that the final sentence of the passage is true, which of these suppositions might explain it?

   (A) Thomas Jefferson's daughter is well known as a contributor to American arts and letters.

   (B) Commodore Levy renamed Monticello after himself following his purchase of the estate from the Jefferson heirs.

   (C) There are many naval heroes in American history, and it is difficult to keep them all straight.

   (D) In general, Americans study Jefferson and his home far more commonly than they study naval history.

   (E) People tend to remember one's latest or last achievement, to the detriment of all that have gone before.

3. Underline the sentence that suggests that Levy's career relied in some degree on patronage.

Question 4 is based on this passage.

Klezmer, a name that means "song instrument," is a musical tradition that developed in southeastern Europe more than 600 years ago. Itinerant musicians known as klezmorim would perform at celebrations. Instruments for more modern
Line klezmer typically include violins, flutes, piccolos, accordions, hammered dulcimers,
(5) clarinets, cellos or double basses, and occasionally small drums. The object of klezmer is to make music that imitates the human voice, whether wailing or laughing. Over the years, a variety of cultural influences have shaped klezmer, from Yiddish songs to Russian folk music and from early jazz to Gypsy dances. Most klezmer music is meant for dancing, but there are several improvisational forms
(10) of klezmer that are meant to serve as a backdrop for a wedding banquet or other solemn occasion.

Select one answer choice.

4. The primary purpose of the passage is to

   (A) compare and contrast klezmer with other musical formats

   (B) define and illustrate a particular genre of eastern European music

   (C) show the influences that led to the klezmer we know today

   (D) explain how klezmer music adapted and changed over time

   (E) persuade the reader to listen to and enjoy a new form of music

> For questions 5 through 8, complete the text by picking the best entry for each blank from the corresponding column of choices.

5. After World War I, League of Nations mandates divided Cameroon, _____ a German colony, between France and England.

Ⓐ	ruled
Ⓑ	covertly
Ⓒ	becoming
Ⓓ	perhaps
Ⓔ	previously

6. Dengue fever, unlike many other tropical diseases, is equally _____ in cities and in rural areas.

Ⓐ	welcomed
Ⓑ	distinguished
Ⓒ	worse
Ⓓ	prevalent
Ⓔ	iniquitous

7. Wallaroos are (i) _____ in size between kangaroos and wallabies, and their name is (ii) _____ a blend of those two animal names.

Blank (i)		Blank (ii)	
Ⓐ	correlated	Ⓓ	in fact
Ⓑ	superior	Ⓔ	by means of
Ⓒ	intermediate	Ⓕ	other than

8. The term *quattrocento*, referring to the 1400s, is used to (i) _____ art of the late Middle Ages and early Renaissance, (ii) _____ art that rejected Gothic and Byzantine forms and instead (iii) _____ the classical patterns of the ancient Greeks and Romans.

Blank (i)		Blank (ii)		Blank (iii)	
Ⓐ	label	Ⓓ	by no means	Ⓖ	initiated
Ⓑ	rank	Ⓔ	particularly	Ⓗ	spurned
Ⓒ	package	Ⓕ	necessarily	Ⓘ	revived

Questions 9 through 12 are based on this passage.

From the early 1700s through the 1800s, having one's paintings shown at the annual Salon de Paris was de rigueur for any serious artist. From 1748, a panel of judges awarded prizes to the artworks they considered best. The public was welcome to visit, and art critics sprang up, writing essays for the Paris newspapers about their favorite and least favorite artists of the day.

The conservative nature of the juried exhibitions proved harmful at first to the impressionists, whose work did not meet with the panels' favor. For several years, important new artists saw their works rejected. In 1863, Napoléon III ordered the opening of the Salon des Refusés, which hung paintings that had been turned down by the official Salon. Perhaps the most famous painting hung in the Salon des Refusés in that first year was Manet's *Le déjeuner sur l'herbe*, which titillated and scandalized viewers with its focus on a nude woman lunching in a park with fully dressed male companions. Painters such as Whistler, Cézanne, Manet, and Cassatt would continue to exhibit in their own salons in the years to come, and eventually the government of France stopped sanctioning the official Salon de Paris.

Consider each of the choices separately and select all that apply.

9. Which of the following statements about the Salon de Paris is supported by the passage?

    [A] For a while, the Salon was an extremely important venue for painters in France.

    [B] Salon judges appreciated art that was forward thinking and nonconformist.

    [C] Among other firsts, the Salon helped to establish a culture of art criticism.

For questions 10 through 12, select one answer choice each.

---

10. In the first sentence of the passage, what does the author mean by "de rigueur"?

    (A) Required by convention

    (B) A demanding test

    (C) Nothing at all

    (D) Always a pleasure

    (E) Enforced by law

11. The author implies that the original Salon de Paris eventually lost favor with the government because

   (A) it became enmeshed in scandal

   (B) it prized artists who were not French

   (C) it stopped featuring current artists

   (D) it was controversial and political

   (E) it failed to be inclusive and relevant

12. In the first sentence of paragraph two, the author implies that

   (A) the impressionists had trouble succeeding without the Salon's support

   (B) juried exhibitions are a poor way to advance the production of art

   (C) although the people liked impressionist art, the judges did not

   (D) over and over, the impressionists failed to follow the judges' rules

   (E) despite their conservative bent, the impressionists were not well received

Question 13 is based on this passage.

Neoteny refers to the retention of certain juvenile characteristics in adulthood. An example is the axolotl, a salamander that remains aquatic as it matures. Most salamanders move from an aquatic juvenile stage to a land-based adult phase, but the axolotl retains its gills and stays in the water. In birds, ostriches and emus are considered to be neotenous descendants of flying birds. Baby birds do not fly; nor do ratites. In mammals, neoteny is all those babylike qualities that lead to the "oh how cute" response. We breed for neotenous qualities in dogs, for example—big, round eyes and floppy ears rather than the more wolf like traits of feral dogs.

Line (5)

Consider each of the choices separately and select all that apply.

13. Based on information from the passage, which of the following might be considered a neotenous feature?

   [A] minimal body hair on humans

   [B] rear-facing toes on sparrows

   [C] whiskers on rabbits

For questions 14 through 17, complete the text by picking the best entry for each blank from the corresponding column of choices.

---

14. Aspirin's ability to _____ the production of thromboxane, a clotting factor, makes it useful in the prevention of stroke and heart attack in people prone to blood clots.

Ⓐ	prolong
Ⓑ	create
Ⓒ	solidify
Ⓓ	pilfer
Ⓔ	inhibit

15. The Wildlife Conservation Society originated in 1895 as the New York Zoological Society, _____ to teach zoology, conserve wildlife, and establish a top-notch zoo.

Ⓐ	consented
Ⓑ	authorized
Ⓒ	endeavored
Ⓓ	materialized
Ⓔ	appraised

16. Under the so-called literary inquisition in imperial China, intellectuals could be (i) _____ for their writings if even one word in a volume was (ii) _____ offensive.

Blank (i)		Blank (ii)	
Ⓐ	persecuted	Ⓓ	proved
Ⓑ	corrected	Ⓔ	deemed
Ⓒ	extolled	Ⓕ	discounted

17. Because they are so (i) _____ to changes in temperature, coral reefs are among the world's most (ii) _____ ecosystems.

Blank (i)		Blank (ii)	
Ⓐ	accustomed	Ⓓ	popular
Ⓑ	sensitive	Ⓔ	fragile
Ⓒ	impervious	Ⓕ	diverse

Questions 18 through 20 are based on this passage.

If you are visiting the Netherlands in springtime, take an extra day to visit Keukenhof garden outside Lisse. Billed as the largest garden in the world, it features over 7 million bulb plants, often, it seems, all flowering at once. The park itself is a beautiful site, with sculptures, fountains, and ponds abounding. Visitors may bring a picnic lunch or enjoy one of the several cafés. Although the gardens spread over 70 acres, the walking is easy. Of course, tulips are the most prominent flower on display, but you will also see daffodils, hyacinths, a greenhouse full of orchids, and a variety of flowering trees. Each weekend offers a special theme, from a flower parade to a national costume display. If you love color and sheer abundance, there is no better place to be in late April or early May.

Line
(5)

(10)

For questions 18 through 20, select one answer choice each.

18. In addition to bulb plants, Keukenhof also apparently displays

   Ⓐ daffodils and hyacinths

   Ⓑ orchids and flowering trees

   Ⓒ tulips and daffodils

   Ⓓ flowering trees and roses

   Ⓔ African violets and orchids

19. The author of the passage probably mentions the cafés in order to

   Ⓐ suggest that a visit to the gardens is an all-day affair

   Ⓑ explain that the gardens are not just for professional florists

   Ⓒ show how the gardens are used to complement other structures

   Ⓓ provide a further reason for the reader to visit the gardens

   Ⓔ offer an alternative for readers who prefer not to view flowers

20. Which of the following best describes the function of the concluding sentence of the passage?

   Ⓐ It provides a final example to support the author's premise.

   Ⓑ It softens the author's opening statement about Keukenhof.

   Ⓒ It repeats and summarizes some of the author's key points.

   Ⓓ It draws a conclusion about the joys of springtime gardening.

   Ⓔ It sums up the author's persuasive argument for the reader.

> For questions 21 through 25, select two answer choices that (1) complete the sentence in a way that makes sense and (2) produce sentences that are similar in meaning.

21. *Plenipotentiary* is one of those _____ titles given to government officials whose job one does not quite understand.

    - A irrational
    - B arcane
    - C affable
    - D esoteric
    - E imperious
    - F paltry

22. Her work was always _____, with every *i* dotted and every *t* crossed.

    - A cogent
    - B incongruous
    - C tenacious
    - D meticulous
    - E opportune
    - F punctilious

23. In order that we better taste all of the flavors in the wine, the instructor recommended _____ each sample with a small crust of bread.

    - A dunking
    - B removing
    - C following
    - D chasing
    - E balancing
    - F sprinkling

24. Of the various cue sports, pool is probably the best known in America, whereas snooker is the _____.

   [A]   most popular

   [B]   least competitive

   [C]   most amusing

   [D]   least demanding

   [E]   most exotic

   [F]   least familiar

25. The plants known as cycads are often _____ palms, but in fact they are only distantly related.

   [A]   recognized as

   [B]   adjacent to

   [C]   confused with

   [D]   on a par with

   [E]   akin to

   [F]   taken for

STOP.   **This is the end of Section 3. Use any remaining time to check your work.**

SECTION 4
Verbal Reasoning
Time: 35 minutes
25 questions

> For questions 1 through 4, select two answer choices that (1) complete the sentence in a way that makes sense and (2) produce sentences that are similar in meaning.

1. The nocturnal birds we know as nightjars are sometimes called goatsuckers due to the erroneous but _____ belief that they milk goats in the night.

    A mistaken

    B irrational

    C widespread

    D popular

    E accurate

    F entertaining

2. Referenda, by which the general population may approve or _____ a proposed law, have been allowed in California since 1849.

    A reject

    B amend

    C turn down

    D facilitate

    E compose

    F nominate

3. The long-running comic strip *Blondie* gave rise to a series of feature films,
   _____ a radio show and a television sitcom.

   A suggested by

   B on top of

   C featuring

   D following

   E in lieu of

   F as well as

4. Their speed was notable, but because clipper ships were narrow and could hold
   only a limited amount of freight, they were used mainly for goods that were
   small and had to be moved _____.

   A with care

   B economically

   C rapidly

   D deliberately

   E repeatedly

   F expeditiously

Questions 5 and 6 are based on this passage.

On a recent list of the ten most corrupt world leaders, defined as those who have
embezzled the most from their own countries, the Philippines is the only country
that has the dubious honor of being named twice. Ferdinand Marcos, president
from 1965 to 1986, was estimated to have stolen anywhere between 5 and 10 billion
in U.S. dollars from his native land before being overthrown in the People Power
Revolution. Marcos's wife, the devious Imelda, symbolizes corruption in the minds
of many who survived that era. In 2001, President Joseph Estrada—a former movie
star—was removed from office after serving only two and a half years and stealing
perhaps $80 million. He was convicted of "plunder" but granted executive clemency
by President Gloria Macapagal-Arroyo. He continues to strive for a political role in
that hapless, looted nation.

Line
(5)

(10)

5. Underline the sentence that indicates the author's opinion about a person rather
   than a place.

Select one answer choice.

6. The author's attitude toward the nation of the Philippines might be described as

Ⓐ enraged

Ⓑ sanguine

Ⓒ casual

Ⓓ sympathetic

Ⓔ enthusiastic

Question 7 is based on this passage.

Band Aid was the 1984 brainchild of Irish singer-songwriter Bob Geldof and his friend Jim "Midge" Ure. Its original purpose was to raise money for famine relief in Ethiopia. Geldof called on a variety of British and Irish singers (with a couple of Americans mixed in) to record a single for free. The song, "Do They Know It's Christmas?," was released on November 29 and went on to sell a million copies in its first week. It would remain the best-selling single in UK history for another 13 years. Sales of the record raised nearly $144 million for the Ethiopian cause. Geldof and Ure ran into trouble with the British government, however, which refused to waive taxes on the record until public sentiment forced its hand.

Line (5)

Select one answer choice.

7. Which of the following can be inferred about Band Aid solely on the basis of information in the passage?

Ⓐ After 13 years, it succeeded in ending famine in Ethiopia.

Ⓑ No sales of "Do They Know It's Christmas?" occurred in 1998.

Ⓒ The musicians on the record worked for minimum wage.

Ⓓ The single easily reached number one on the U.S. pop charts.

Ⓔ Geldof and Ure timed the song's release for the holiday season.

Questions 8 and 9 are based on this passage.

It appears on most lists of hard-to-spell words, but the beautiful flowering plant known as the fuchsia is actually named for Leonhart Fuchs, chair of medicine at the University of Tübingen in Germany from 1535 until 1566. He did not name
Line   the plant; an admirer of his work with medicinal plants did so in 1703. French
(5)   botanist Charles Plumier had taken a long trip through the Americas and was in the process of producing a significant volume of new plant species. He brought back fuchsia seeds from Hispaniola, and the plant quickly became popular in France and England. Today, about 100 species of fuchsia have been identified. Once you know the origin of the plant's name, of course, it should be simple to
(10)   spell that name correctly.

Consider each of the choices separately and select all that apply.

8. Which of the following inferences can be made from the information given in the passage?

   A   Leonhart Fuchs probably never actually saw a fuchsia plant.

   B   Charles Plumier was a student of Fuchs's at Tübingen.

   C   Plumier's book of plants included species from the Caribbean.

Select one answer choice.

9. The author uses the word "significant" to mean

   Ⓐ hasty

   Ⓑ noteworthy

   Ⓒ scientific

   Ⓓ illustrated

   Ⓔ ponderous

For questions 10 through 13, complete the text by picking the best entry for each blank from the corresponding column of choices.

10. Famous authors who used pen names to disguise their true identities include Samuel Clemens, who wrote as Mark Twain, and Mary Ann Evans, who wrote _____ George Eliot.

Ⓐ	for the author
Ⓑ	under the name
Ⓒ	as well as
Ⓓ	instead of
Ⓔ	about the character

11. _____ the Dutch East India Company, Henry Hudson explored the region around what is now New York City, searching for a western route to Asia.

Ⓐ	Without further ado from
Ⓑ	In the offing with
Ⓒ	On the shoulders of
Ⓓ	Under the auspices of
Ⓔ	Giving a wide berth to

12. The traditional, casual peacoat is military by birth; it was (i) _____ worn by European sailors. Its name apparently (ii) _____ from the Dutch word for the kind of cloth used to (iii) _____ the coat—*pij* cloth.

Blank (i)	Blank (ii)	Blank (iii)
Ⓐ presently	Ⓓ derives	Ⓖ envisage
Ⓑ formally	Ⓔ denotes	Ⓗ wear
Ⓒ initially	Ⓕ departs	Ⓘ construct

13. As its name suggests, a box canyon is a small (i) _____ with steep walls on three sides, allowing entry or (ii) _____ from only one direction. Long ago, buffalo hunters might drive a herd into a box canyon, (iii) _____ trapping them and making them easy to butcher.

Blank (i)	Blank (ii)	Blank (iii)
Ⓐ knoll	Ⓓ egress	Ⓖ however
Ⓑ gullet	Ⓔ opening	Ⓗ thereby
Ⓒ ravine	Ⓕ connection	Ⓘ meanwhile

Questions 14 through 16 are based on this passage.

Does your state have a secretary of state? Most states do. If you live in Massachusetts, Virginia, or Pennsylvania, the official in that position is called secretary of the commonwealth. If you live in Alaska, Hawaii, or Utah, there is no such position; the
Line duties of that office are given to the lieutenant governor. The duties vary widely from
(5) state to state. In most states, the secretary of state has a responsibility to ensure fair and free elections. Typically, too, the office of the secretary of state houses all official state documents, from executive orders to statutes and regulations. Some states make the office a licensing bureau, giving it the power to issue anything from marriage licenses to licenses for general contractors, and three states even issue
(10) driver's licenses through the office of the secretary of state.

Consider each of the choices separately and select all that apply.

14. Which of these inferences about the office of secretary of state can be made from the information given in the passage?

   A   In most cases, the office includes duties involving foreign affairs.

   B   The office is equivalent in status and duties to that of lieutenant governor.

   C   The secretary of state frequently functions as the state's record keeper.

Select one answer choice.

15. According to the passage, it can be inferred that a department of state headed by a secretary of state exists in all of these capital cities EXCEPT

Ⓐ Albany

Ⓑ Santa Fe

Ⓒ Salt Lake City

Ⓓ Bismarck

Ⓔ Austin

16. Underline the sentence that provides an exception to the assertion presented in sentence two.

> **For questions 17 through 20, complete the text by picking the best entry for each blank from the corresponding column of choices.**

17. According to legend, Damocles enjoyed switching places with King Dionysius II and acting in his _____, until he glanced upward and noticed the sword dangling over his head.

Ⓐ	kitchen
Ⓑ	throne
Ⓒ	stead
Ⓓ	drama
Ⓔ	camp

18. The French Quarter in New Orleans is (i) _____ with old, historic architecture, which is why the entire neighborhood was long ago (ii) _____ historic landmark status.

Blank (i)		Blank (ii)	
Ⓐ	acquainted	Ⓓ	relegated
Ⓑ	magnified	Ⓔ	shown
Ⓒ	replete	Ⓕ	assigned

19. Punishing drug possession with (i) _____ sentences is beginning to be viewed as a (ii) _____ use of resources that is often discriminatory.

Blank (i)		Blank (ii)	
A	draconian	D	judicious
B	curtailed	E	felonious
C	tribunal	F	profligate

20. In an effort to remove (i) _____ from the streets of Delhi prior to the Commonwealth Games, the government vowed to catalog all (ii) _____ adults and children it found bothering tourists and then to retrain and rehabilitate them.

Blank (i)		Blank (ii)	
A	offal	D	tenacious
B	opprobrium	E	impecunious
C	mendicants	F	venal

Question 21 is based on this passage.

Regulation of food and drugs has often—perhaps always—derived from an accidental adulteration of said food and drugs that resulted in consumer deaths. A classic example is the Bradford sweets poisoning of 1858. In this case, a confectionary
Line   salesman known as "Humbug Billy" purchased the sweets sold at his stand from
(5)   a wholesaler, Joseph Neal. To hold down costs, Neal cut the expensive sugar in his candy with daft, which may have been a less-than-nutritious combination of crushed limestone and plaster of paris. On the occasion in question, a series of circumstances led Neal's daft supplier to substitute 12 pounds of the wrong powder. The candy was mixed with arsenic trioxide rather than daft, and 20 people died after consuming the
(10)   sweets. It took another 10 years, but the Pharmacy Act in 1868 restricted the sale and availability of poisons.

Select one answer choice.

21. The author of the passage cites the Bradford sweets case primarily in order to

  Ⓐ illustrate what can happen when food sellers are motivated by profit

  Ⓑ offer an example of an adulteration of foods that led to a new law

  Ⓒ narrate a sensational, long-ago story of greed and corruption

  Ⓓ reveal the effects of arsenic trioxide on an unsuspecting public

  Ⓔ clarify why it is inadvisable to store foodstuffs near poisons

Question 22 is based on this passage.

Tourists from America are often surprised to learn that a kipper is not a particular
kind of fish but rather a fish prepared a certain way. Kippers are herring that have
been split down the spine, salted or pickled, and then smoked. Kippering, then, is
Line   the process of salting prior to smoking. You can kipper things other than fish; for
(5)   example, kippered beef is much like beef jerky. In British cuisine, kippers are often
served with scrambled eggs and toast for breakfast or with potatoes and buttered
bread for lunch. Many kipper aficionados believe that the best kippers in the world
come from the Isle of Man. Many kippers are available online and in gourmet shops
throughout the world.

Consider each of the choices separately and select all that apply.

22.   Based on the information in the passage, it can be inferred that a dictionary
definition of *kipper* might include which of the following?

 A   A treat involving fish with eggs and toast

 B   Herring that has been salted and smoked

 C   The act of curing by salting and smoking

Questions 23 through 25 are based on this passage.

Dorence Atwater went to war as a Union soldier when he was only 16. He served as
a scout but was taken prisoner by a pair of Confederate soldiers in disguise. Thrown
into the Confederates' most notorious prison at Andersonville, he was chosen for his
Line   admirable penmanship to be the keeper of the "death list," a list of prisoners who
(5)   died. Fearing that the official list would never be shared with the Union, Atwater
kept a duplicate list. Following his release from Andersonville, he smuggled the list
north, eventually sharing it with Clara Barton, who wished to mark the graves of the
Union dead—some 13,000 names from Andersonville alone. Atwater's refusal to turn
the list over to the War Department led to his arrest, but Barton intervened on his
(10)   behalf, and editor Horace Greeley finally published the entire list of names. President
Johnson rewarded Atwater for his patriotism by sending him as consul to the
Seychelles at the age of only 23. Later he was reassigned as consul to Tahiti, where he
would live for some 40 years.

Consider each of the choices separately and select all that apply.

23.   The author implies which of the following about the Andersonville prison?

 A   It was well known as a terrible place.

 B   It housed Union prisoners of war.

 C   More than half of its prisoners died.

Select one answer choice.

24. In the passage, the author is primarily concerned with

    Ⓐ demonstrating the ways in which good deeds may often be rewarded

    Ⓑ documenting the life and adventures of a little-known American hero

    Ⓒ adding to the reader's understanding of the remarkable nurse Clara Barton

    Ⓓ comparing and contrasting the treatment of prisoners during wartime

    Ⓔ clarifying the importance of retaining accurate lists of casualties of war

25. Underline the sentence that provides the motivation behind Atwater's copying of the "death list."

STOP. This is the end of Section 4. Use any remaining time to check your work.

SECTION 5
Quantitative Reasoning
Time: 40 minutes
25 questions

Each of questions 1 through 9 consists of two quantities, Quantity A and Quantity B. You are to compare the two quantities. You may use additional information centered above the two quantities if additional information is given. Choose

Ⓐ if Quantity A is greater;

Ⓑ if Quantity B is greater;

Ⓒ if the two quantities are equal;

Ⓓ if the relationship cannot be determined from the information given.

	Quantity A	Quantity B	
1.	15% of 50	20% of 40	Ⓐ Ⓑ Ⓒ Ⓓ

$d = 3.17486$ and $\boxed{d}$ is the decimal expression for d rounded to the nearest thousandth

	Quantity A	Quantity B	
2.	$\boxed{d} - d$	0.001	Ⓐ Ⓑ Ⓒ Ⓓ

$\lfloor x \rfloor$ = the largest integer less than or equal to x

	Quantity A	Quantity B	
3.	$\frac{1}{2}\lfloor x \rfloor$	$\lfloor \frac{1}{2}x \rfloor$	Ⓐ Ⓑ Ⓒ Ⓓ

$$x = \frac{x+1}{x}$$

Quantity A	Quantity B	
4. $\dfrac{1}{x}$	$x - 1$	Ⓐ Ⓑ Ⓒ Ⓓ

$$x > 1$$

Quantity A	Quantity B	
5. $\dfrac{2x+10}{7}$	$x + 1$	Ⓐ Ⓑ Ⓒ Ⓓ

$$\Delta a = 2 - a^2$$

Quantity A	Quantity B	
6. $\Delta(\Delta 2)$	0	Ⓐ Ⓑ Ⓒ Ⓓ

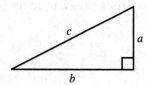

Quantity A	Quantity B	
7. $(a + b)^2$	c^2	Ⓐ Ⓑ Ⓒ Ⓓ

X is a collection of positive integers

Quantity A	Quantity B	
8. median of X	twice the mean of X	Ⓐ Ⓑ Ⓒ Ⓓ

A shirt that normally costs $20 is on sale for $14

	Quantity A	Quantity B	
9.	The discount on the shirt, expressed as a percentage of the original price	30%	(A) (B) (C) (D)

Questions 10 through 25 have different formats. Select a single answer choice unless the directions say otherwise. For numeric-entry questions, follow these instructions:

- Enter your answer in the box or boxes provided.
- Your answer may be an integer, a decimal, a fraction, or a negative number.
- If the answer is a fraction, you will be given two boxes: an upper one for the numerator and a lower one for the denominator.
- Equivalent forms of the correct answer, such as 1.6 and 1.60, are all correct. You do not need to reduce fractions to lowest terms.

10. If a car gets 26 miles per gallon and gasoline costs $2.79 per gallon, then approximately how far can the car go on $40 of gasoline?

(A) 200 miles

(B) 300 miles

(C) 400 miles

(D) 500 miles

(E) 600 miles

11. In how many ways can 4 of 10 colors be selected where the order in which they are chosen is unimportant?

(A) 40

(B) 180

(C) 210

(D) 360

(E) 5,040

12. Two hundred milliliters of pure water is added to 300 milliliters of a solution which is 12% salt. What is the percentage of salt in the resulting solution?

 (A) 6.0%

 (B) 6.5%

 (C) 6.9%

 (D) 7.2%

 (E) 7.5%

13. Tim went through 25 diapers per week for his first year and 10 diapers per week for his second and third years. How many diapers did he use in his first three years?

 (A) 1,040

 (B) 1,300

 (C) 1,820

 (D) 2,340

 (E) 3,640

For this question, write your answer in the box.

14. What is the total surface area of a box with length 5, width 4, and height 6?

For this question, indicate all of the answer choices that apply.

15. The operation $\otimes$ is defined for all integers x and y as $x \otimes y = y - x^2 + 1$. Which of the following *must* be zero?

 A $1 \otimes 0$

 B $0 \otimes 1$

 C $x \otimes x^2$

 D $(x - 1) \otimes x (x - 2)$

 E $x \otimes (x^2 - 1)$

16. If $-1 < mn < 0$, then which of the following can be true?

   (A) $m < 0$ and $n < 0$

   (B) $m < 1$ and $n < 1$

   (C) $m > 1$ and $n < -1$

   (D) $m > 1$ and $n > 1$

   (E) $-1 < m < 0$ and $n < 0$

17. If $2y - x = 1$ and $y - x = 2$, then which of the following is true?

   (A) $x = -3$ and $y = 2$

   (B) $x = 1$ and $y = 1$

   (C) $x = 1$ and $y = 3$

   (D) $x = -3$ and $y = -1$

   (E) $x = -1$ and $y = -2$

For this question, indicate all of the answer choices that apply.

18. Which of the following numbers are multiples of both 4 and 6?

   [A] 1

   [B] 2

   [C] 3

   [D] 12

   [E] 18

   [F] 36

19. What is the tenth term of this geometric sequence?

$$abr, ab^2 r^3, \ldots$$

   (A) $ab^9 r^{19}$

   (B) $ab^{10} r^{13}$

   (C) $ab^{10} r^{20}$

   (D) $a^{10} b^{10} r^{30}$

   (E) $ab^{10} r^{19}$

20. The radius of circle *A* is one more than the radius of circle *B*. What is the difference between the circumferences of circle *A* and circle *B*?

   (A) 1

   (B) 2

   (C) π

   (D) 2π

   (E) 4π

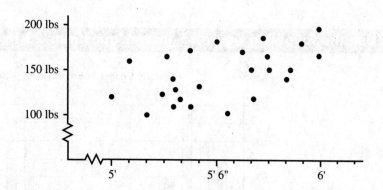

21. The dots on the graph indicate the heights and weights for a sample of 25 people. What percentage of these people are no more than 5'4" and under 150 pounds?

   (A) 7%

   (B) 14%

   (C) 25%

   (D) 28%

   (E) 36%

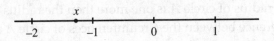

22. Which of the following would be the best estimate for the value of x?

Ⓐ −2.7

Ⓑ −2.3

Ⓒ −1.7

Ⓓ −1.3

Ⓔ −0.7

Use the following figure to answer questions 23 through 25.

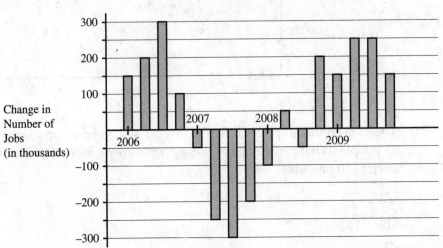

For this question, write your answer in the box.

23. How many jobs did state X gain in the first quarter of 2009?

24. How many jobs did state X gain in the four quarters of 2006?

    Ⓐ   150,000

    Ⓑ   300,000

    Ⓒ   600,000

    Ⓓ   650,000

    Ⓔ   750,000

25. Suppose state X had 2.5 million jobs at the beginning of 2008. How many jobs did the state have at the beginning of 2007?

    Ⓐ   1.6 million

    Ⓑ   2.0 million

    Ⓒ   2.8 million

    Ⓓ   3.3 million

    Ⓔ   3.4 million

STOP.   **This is the end of Section 5. Use any remaining time to check your work.**

SECTION 6
Quantitative Reasoning
Time: 40 minutes
25 questions

Each of questions 1 through 9 consists of two quantities, Quantity A and Quantity B. You are to compare the two quantities. You may use additional information centered above the two quantities if additional information is given. Choose

(A) if Quantity A is greater;

(B) if Quantity B is greater;

(C) if the two quantities are equal;

(D) if the relationship cannot be determined from the information given.

	Quantity A	Quantity B	
1.	0.25%	$\dfrac{1}{4}$	Ⓐ Ⓑ Ⓒ Ⓓ

	Quantity A	Quantity B	
2.	π	3.14	Ⓐ Ⓑ Ⓒ Ⓓ

	Quantity A	Quantity B	
3.	$8^{\frac{2}{3}}$	$\left(\dfrac{1}{2}\right)^{-2}$	Ⓐ Ⓑ Ⓒ Ⓓ

N is divisible by both 12 and 15.

	Quantity A	Quantity B	
4.	The last digit of *N*	5	Ⓐ Ⓑ Ⓒ Ⓓ

$$f(x) = \frac{5x^2 - 9.2x^4}{25.7 + x^6}$$

Quantity A	Quantity B	
5. $f(2.38)$	$f(-2.38)$	Ⓐ Ⓑ Ⓒ Ⓓ

$$xy < 0$$

Quantity A	Quantity B	
6. $(x + y)^2$	$(x - y)^2$	Ⓐ Ⓑ Ⓒ Ⓓ

Quantity A	Quantity B	
7. $\sqrt{x + 5}$	$\sqrt{x} + 2$	Ⓐ Ⓑ Ⓒ Ⓓ

Quantity A	Quantity B	
8. the surface area of a cylindrical can with height 2 and radius 1	4π	Ⓐ Ⓑ Ⓒ Ⓓ

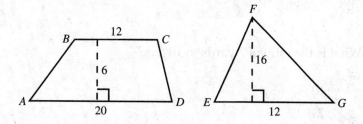

Quantity A	Quantity B	
9. the area of trapezoid ABCD	the area of triangle EFG	Ⓐ Ⓑ Ⓒ Ⓓ

Questions 10 through 25 have different formats. Select a single answer choice unless the directions say otherwise. For numeric-entry questions, follow these instructions:

- Enter your answer in the box or boxes provided.
- Your answer may be an integer, a decimal, a fraction, or a negative number.
- If the answer is a fraction, you will be given two boxes: an upper one for the numerator and a lower one for the denominator.
- Equivalent forms of the correct answer, such as 1.6 and 1.60, are all correct. You do not need to reduce fractions to lowest terms.

10. How many digits are in $2^8 \times 5^{10}$, when written out completely?

   (A) 8

   (B) 10

   (C) 13

   (D) 18

   (E) 80

11. $5\% \times 5\% =$

   (A) 25%

   (B) 2.5%

   (C) 0.25%

   (D) 250%

   (E) 0.025%

12. What is the ratio of 7 yards to 10 feet?

   (A) $\dfrac{7}{10}$

   (B) $\dfrac{21}{10}$

   (C) 1

   (D) $\dfrac{11}{10}$

   (E) $\dfrac{42}{5}$

13. What is the fiftieth digit after the decimal point when $\frac{1}{7}$ is written out as a decimal?

   (A) 1

   (B) 2

   (C) 4

   (D) 5

   (E) 7

14. $\dfrac{x+2}{x-1} + \dfrac{x-2}{x+1} =$

   (A) 1

   (B) $\dfrac{2x}{x^2-1}$

   (C) $\dfrac{2(x^2+3x+2)}{x^2-1}$

   (D) $\dfrac{6x}{x^2-1}$

   (E) $2\left(\dfrac{x^2+2}{x^2-1}\right)$

15. There are 12 people in a wedding party. How many different ways can five of them be arranged from left to right for a photograph?

   (A) 60

   (B) 120

   (C) 792

   (D) 95,040

   (E) 47,901,600

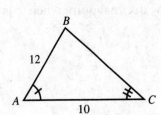 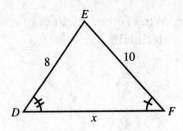

16. Find x.

Ⓐ 6

Ⓑ $6\frac{2}{3}$

Ⓒ $8\frac{1}{3}$

Ⓓ 12

Ⓔ 15

17. Suppose that set S consists of all points in the plane whose coordinates (x, y) have both x and y in the set $\{0, 1, 2\}$. If three points are randomly selected from set S, what is the probability that they are collinear?

Ⓐ $\dfrac{3}{41}$

Ⓑ $\dfrac{2}{21}$

Ⓒ $\dfrac{1}{63}$

Ⓓ $\dfrac{2}{63}$

Ⓔ $\dfrac{1}{84}$

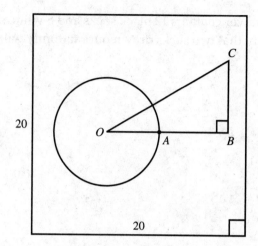

18. *O* is the center of the circle. *A* is the midpoint of $\overline{OB}$. $OB = BC = 8$. If a point is randomly chosen from the square, what is the probability it will be in both the circle and the triangle?

    Ⓐ $\dfrac{1}{25}$

    Ⓑ $\dfrac{\pi}{25}$

    Ⓒ $\dfrac{4}{25}$

    Ⓓ $\dfrac{\pi}{100}$

    Ⓔ $\dfrac{\pi}{200}$

19. Which of the following points is closest to $(9, -4)$?

    Ⓐ $(8, 5)$

    Ⓑ $(10, 2)$

    Ⓒ $(5, 5)$

    Ⓓ $(2, -2)$

    Ⓔ $(4, 6)$

20. A sock drawer contains 12 black socks and 8 white socks. What is the probability that two socks drawn out randomly will be the same color?

   Ⓐ $\dfrac{1}{6}$

   Ⓑ $\dfrac{13}{25}$

   Ⓒ $\dfrac{47}{95}$

   Ⓓ $\dfrac{49}{96}$

   Ⓔ $\dfrac{2}{3}$

For this question, write your answer in the box.

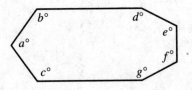

21. $a° + b° + c° + d° + e° + f° + g° =$

For this question, write your answer in the box.

22. If $\dfrac{28^5}{2^x}$ is an integer, what is the greatest possible value of x?

Use the following figure to answer questions 23 through 25.

Budget Changes 2000–2005

	Education	Transportation	Health	Police	Other
State A	+3%	+1%	−4%	+1%	−2%
State B	+4%	+10%	−5%	+1%	−10%
State C	+1%	−3%	+1%	−1%	−5%
State D	−1%	−2%	−2%	0%	−1%

23. If state B spent $380 million on education in 2005, how much did that state spend in 2000 (rounded to the nearest tenth of a million)?

    (A) $364.8 million

    (B) $365.4 million

    (C) $368.9 million

    (D) $391.4 million

    (E) $395.2 million

For this question, indicate all of the answer choices that apply.

24. Which of the following must be true?

    [A] The total budget of state B was the same in 2000 and 2005.

    [B] The total budget of state D was lower in 2005 than it was in 2000.

    [C] If state A spent as much in 2000 on health and education combined as on the police, then the total spent on those three areas in 2005 was the same as in 2000.

25. Suppose that from 2005 to 2010, state C increases spending in all areas by 3%. How much will state C spend in 2010 on transportation, as a percentage of its spending in 2000 (rounded to the nearest tenth of a percent)?

    (A) 99.9%

    (B) 100%

    (C) 100.1%

    (D) 103%

    (E) 106%

STOP. This is the end of Section 6. Use any remaining time to check your work.

GRE Practice Test 3: Answers and Explanations

Analytical Writing: Scoring and Sample Responses

Analyze an Issue: Scoring

Score	Focus	Organization	Conventions
0	Does not address the prompt. Off topic.	Incomprehensible. May merely copy the prompt without development.	Illegible. Nonverbal. Serious errors make the paper unreadable. May be in a foreign language.
1	Mostly irrelevant to the prompt.	Little or no development of ideas. No evidence of analysis or organization.	Pervasive errors in grammar, mechanics, and spelling.
2	Unclear connection to the prompt.	Unfocused and disorganized.	Frequent errors in sentence structure, mechanics, and spelling.
3	Limited connection to the prompt.	Rough organization with weak examples or reasons.	Occasional major errors and frequent minor errors in conventions of written English.
4	Competent connection to the prompt.	Relevant examples or reasons develop a logical position.	Occasional minor errors in conventions of written English.
5	Clear, focused connection to the prompt.	Thoughtful, appropriate examples or reasons develop a consistent, coherent position. Connectors are ably used to mark transitions.	Very few errors. Sentence structure is varied and vocabulary is advanced.
6	Insightful, clever connection to the prompt.	Compelling, convincing examples or reasons develop a consistent, coherent position. The argument flows effortlessly and persuasively.	Very few errors. Sentence structure is varied and vocabulary is precise, well chosen, and effective.

Analyze an Issue:
Sample Response with a Score of 6

This essay, which counters the premise given in the prompt, is sensible and well argued. The writer uses personal examples to present a strong case, while acknowledging and responding to other opinions. There are no significant errors in grammar or mechanics.

Whether the constant use of instant messaging and social media by young people is a plus or a minus is a topic of great debate in our country. In my opinion, the new technology is less an impediment to socialization than it is an extension of possibilities for socialization.

My contemporaries and I are glued to our phones and PDAs in a way that our parents find hard to fathom. We may contact one another several times a day to check in, ask advice, share opinions, and so on. We may log into our Facebook or other social-media accounts to learn about the escapades of friends, to post photographs or links to articles that interest us, or just to connect to people far away. In a single day, in a matter of minutes, I can ask my boss about my hours for tonight's shift, share a picture of myself and my friends with my grandmother in Buenos Aires, and read and critique the opening paragraph of my sister's senior thesis. This is not a lessening of social contact; it is an expansion of it.

Critics of this kind of instant electronic contact tend to believe that it is both impersonal and careless. Granted, it takes less time to blast out an instant message than to write a formal letter. It is possible to respond so instantly that the response seems unthinking and perfunctory. We have all learned that it is wise to slow down and reread before hitting the Send button.

I think that people who suggest that our ability to use English properly is waning due to the use of social media are misguided. I do not know anyone who confuses the abbreviated language of IM with the formal language of business. I do not know anyone whose ability to use thumbs on a keypad makes them unable to carry on a conversation face-to-face. These criticisms, it seems to me, are exaggerated.

Indeed, I think the case might be made that social media and instant messaging represent the current and future means of communicating, whether in college or in the workplace. Those people who are able to communicate and socialize in multiple modes are those most likely to succeed in the twenty-first century.

Analyze an Argument: Scoring

Score	Focus	Organization	Conventions
0	Does not address the prompt. Off topic.	Incomprehensible. May merely copy the prompt without development.	Illegible. Nonverbal. Serious errors make the paper unreadable. May be in a foreign language.
1	Little or no analysis of the argument. May indicate misunderstanding of the prompt.	Little or no development of ideas. No evidence of analysis or organization.	Pervasive errors in grammar, mechanics, and spelling.
2	Little analysis; may instead present opinions and unrelated thoughts.	Disorganized and illogical.	Frequent errors in sentence structure, mechanics, and spelling.
3	Some analysis of the prompt, but some major flaws may be omitted.	Rough organization with irrelevant support or unclear transitions.	Occasional major errors and frequent minor errors in conventions of written English.
4	Important flaws in the argument are touched upon.	Ideas are sound but may not flow logically or clearly.	Occasional minor errors in conventions of written English.
5	Perceptive analysis of the major flaws in the argument.	Logical examples and support develop a consistent, coherent critique. Connectors are ably used to mark transitions.	Very few errors. Sentence structure is varied and vocabulary is advanced.
6	Insightful, clever analysis of the argument's flaws and fallacies.	Compelling, convincing examples and support develop a consistent, coherent critique. The analysis flows effortlessly and persuasively.	Very few errors. Sentence structure is varied and vocabulary is precise, well chosen, and effective.

Analyze an Argument: Sample Response with a Score of 6

This essay is well organized and cogent. The writer notes distortions and assumptions that detract from the letter's persuasive argument. There are no real errors in English usage or mechanics.

The Coburn resident is obviously extremely concerned about the proposed placement of walking trails. However, he or she shows the dangers of making unfounded assumptions, and the conclusion, which describes the development of trails as a process that "steals land and protects criminals," is a distortion of the situation.

First, the trails will use land that belongs to the railroads. This being true, only the railroads can determine that land use. Just because the neighbors are accustomed to using that land "for their own purposes" does not make it their land, no matter how long that state of affairs has existed.

Second, people bent on robbery or other "nefarious" deeds are presumably already able to access the houses from the rear—or from the front, for that matter. The railroad beds already supply a means of access, as do the roads that run in front of the houses. Suggesting that robbery is a natural by-product of trail building is illogical. If the writer had proof that criminal activity was common in other places where trails had been established, this argument might be more believable. As it is, the robbery issue seems more like a red herring designed to spread fear and distract readers from the real issue.

The final sentence is a gross exaggeration. The trails do not "steal land"; the land does not belong to the neighbors. There is no evidence given that supports the idea that the trails "protect criminals." This writer would do better to think of a few realistic reasons for his or her position—perhaps the noise factor of having a walking trail, or concerns that the neighbors might have to provide upkeep—and write a letter that expresses genuine concerns rather than overstated fears.

GRE Practice Test 3: Answer Key

Section 3. Verbal Reasoning

1. **A**
2. **D**
3. Only the intervention of President Tyler enabled his reinstatement.
4. **B**
5. **E**
6. **D**
7. **C, D**
8. **A, E, I**
9. **A, C**
10. **A**
11. **E**
12. **A**
13. **A**
14. **E**
15. **B**
16. **A, E**
17. **B, E**
18. **B**
19. **D**
20. **E**
21. **B, D**
22. **D, F**
23. **C, D**
24. **E, F**
25. **C, F**

Section 4. Verbal Reasoning

1. **C, D**
2. **A, C**
3. **B, F**
4. **C, F**
5. Marcos's wife, the devious Imelda, symbolizes corruption in the minds of many who survived that era.
6. **D**
7. **E**
8. **A, C**
9. **B**
10. **B**
11. **D**
12. **C, D, I**
13. **C, D, H**
14. **C**
15. **C**
16. If you live in Alaska, Hawaii, or Utah, there is no such position; the duties of that office are given to the lieutenant governor.
17. **C**
18. **C, F**
19. **A, F**
20. **C, E**
21. **B**
22. **B, C**
23. **A, B**
24. **B**
25. Fearing that the official list would never be shared with the Union, Atwater kept a duplicate list.

Section 5. Quantitative Reasoning

1.	B	14.	148
2.	B	15.	A, D, E
3.	D	16.	B
4.	C	17.	D
5.	B	18.	D, F
6.	B	19.	E
7.	A	20.	D
8.	B	21.	D
9.	C	22.	D
10.	C	23.	150,000
11.	C	24.	E
12.	D	25.	D
13.	D		

Section 6. Quantitative Reasoning

1.	B	14.	E
2.	A	15.	D
3.	C	16.	C
4.	B	17.	B
5.	C	18.	E
6.	B	19.	B
7.	D	20.	C
8.	A	21.	900
9.	C	22.	10
10.	B	23.	B
11.	C	24.	B
12.	B	25.	A
13.	C		

GRE Practice Test 3: Answer Explanations

Section 3. Verbal Reasoning

1. **A.** Because sentence one covers the time prior to Levy's becoming commodore, choice B is not accurate, and choice C would not support the assertion, although it might add interesting information. The best answer is choice A.

2. **D.** The last sentence says that Levy is better known for taking over Monticello than for being a naval hero. If that is assumed to be true, the only sentence that really explains it is choice D.

3. **Only the intervention of President Tyler enabled his reinstatement.** The implication is that Levy relied on Tyler's patronage to resume his career.

4. **B.** No comparisons are made (choice A), and influences and adaptations (choices C and D) are only a small part of the passage. The passage is not particularly persuasive (choice E), so the best all-encompassing answer is choice B.

5. **E.** Cameroon was a German colony until it was divided, so *previously* (choice E) makes the most sense.

6. **D.** A disease would be neither welcomed (choice A) nor distinguished (choice B); nor would it be called sinful, or iniquitous (choice E). *Worse* does not fit the context. The disease is common, or prevalent, in both city and countryside, so choice D is correct.

7. **C, D.** The key word here is "between," which indicates that the wallaroo is intermediate in size (choice C). Only choice D makes sense in the second blank.

8. **A, E, I.** A term is usually used to label (choice A) rather than to rank (choice C). If in doubt about the other choices, read the sentence aloud, incorporating each choice in turn.

9. **A, C.** The Salon was clearly important for artists (choice A), and the last sentence in paragraph one details the creation of a critical following (choice C). However, it seems that the juries did not admire avant-garde art, meaning that choice B is not correct.

10. **A.** Whether or not you recognize the term, applying the five choices in context should clarify its meaning.

11. **E.** Napoléon III opened a new salon to hang the paintings of those artists rejected by the original salon. The implication is that he found the original salon narrow-minded and no longer important.

12. **A.** Read the sentence in question and compare it to the answer choices. The Salon's conservative nature "harmed" the Impressionists, which is approximately what choice A suggests.

13. **A.** Neoteny is defined as the retention of immature characteristics in mature animals. Neither rear-facing toes (choice B) nor whiskers (choice C) could be considered immature, but hairlessness (choice A) could be.

14. **E.** Work backward. If aspirin prevents stroke in people prone to blood clotting, it must do that in a way that keeps blood from clotting—that inhibits clotting (choice E).

15. **B.** Pay attention to the way in which the sentence is constructed; its syntax immediately eliminates choices A, C, and D. Choice B makes the most sense.

16. **A, E.** Look at the sentence as a whole to determine the answers that work together. Writers could be persecuted (choice A) if their work was deemed (choice E) offensive.

17. **B, E.** Again, looking at the sentence as a whole will guide you to the best answer. Because they are sensitive (choice B), coral reefs are fragile (choice E).

18. **B.** To answer correctly, it helps to know or guess that daffodils, tulips, and hyacinths are bulb plants. Even if you had no idea that this was so, you could eliminate roses and violets (choices D and E), which are never mentioned, and infer from what remains that choice B is correct.

19. **D.** The passage as a whole is persuasive, and the author mentions the cafés as a nice place to lunch if visitors don't bring their own food. This is not meant to take visitors away from the flowers (choice E) or to suggest that the visit is a long ordeal (choice A); it's simply another reason to visit, making choice D the best answer.

20. **E.** Read the last sentence. It does not support a premise (choice A) or draw a conclusion (choice D); it essentially sums up the writer's belief that visitors should see the gardens (choice E).

21. **B, D.** Many of the choices might make sense in context, but only *arcane* (B) and *esoteric* (D) are synonyms, both meaning "mysterious" or "obscure."

22. **D, F.** The only pair of synonyms is *meticulous* (D) and *punctilious* (F), both meaning "thorough" and "painstaking."

23. **C, D.** You can dunk in but not dunk with (choice A). Although some of the other words might fit the context, only *following* (choice C) and *chasing* (D) mean the same thing.

24. **E, F.** The word "whereas" suggests a contrast, so you should look for something that contrasts with "best known." Both choices E and F denote unfamiliarity.

25. **C, F.** Any of the choices might work in context, but keeping the meaning of the whole sentence in mind will lead you to choose synonyms *confused with* (choice C) and *taken for* (choice F).

Section 4. Verbal Reasoning

1. **C, D.** The belief may be erroneous, but it is also something else. *Mistaken* (choice A) means the same thing as *erroneous*, so that cannot be the answer, and no belief can be both erroneous and accurate (choice E). The best choice is *widespread* (choice C) and its synonym *popular* (choice D).

2. **A, C.** When in doubt, look for the synonyms. Here, a few choices are possible, but only *reject* (choice A) and *turn down* (choice C) are synonymous.

3. **B, F.** *On top of* (choice B) is an idiomatic phrase that means "in addition to" or "as well as" (choice F). There are no other synonyms in this list of answer choices.

4. **C, F.** Again, there are several possible choices, but only two synonyms—*rapidly* (choice C) and *expeditiously* (choice F).

5. **Marcos's wife, the devious Imelda, symbolizes corruption in the minds of many who survived that era.** There are sentences in the passage that give an opinion about the Philippines, but only this one opines about a person.

6. **D.** The author refers to the Philippines as "hapless" and "looted," suggesting some sympathy (choice D). To be sanguine (choice B) is to be hopeful, and there is no such sense here.

7. **E.** There is no support for choices A, B, or D in the passage, and choice C is belied by the fact that the singers worked "for free." You can infer that the November release of a single about Christmas was due to the chance for holiday sales, making choice E correct.

8. **A, C.** It is highly unlikely that Fuchs would have traveled to the newly settled Caribbean in his lifetime, and he lived over a century before fuchsia plants arrived on the Continent (choice A). Because he lived so much earlier than Plumier, he could not have taught him, making choice B incorrect. Since Hispaniola is part of the Caribbean, choice C makes sense.

9. **B.** Locate the use of the word in the passage and compare it to the choices, some of which would work in a slightly different context. The best answer is that Plumier's catalog of plants was noteworthy (choice B).

10. **B.** Assume that the sentence contains parallel construction, which means that Clemens wrote as Mark Twain and Mary Ann Evans wrote as George Eliot. The only choice that fulfills this meaning is choice B.

11. **D.** In this example, you must simply find the answer that makes the most sense. Hudson sailed under the auspices (with the support) of the Dutch East India Company, so choice D is correct.

12. **C, D, I.** If the coat is casual, it cannot be formally worn (choice B). The cloth is used to make the coat (choice I), not to imagine (choice G) or dress in (choice H) it.

13. **C, D, H.** A gullet (choice B) is a body part, not a geographical feature. The other answers should be clear if you read the sentence aloud and substitute each one in order.

14. **C.** There is no mention of foreign affairs (choice A), which is a duty of the United States Secretary of State, not of any individual state's. Although certain states assign duties of the secretary of state to their lieutenant governor, that does not mean that those jobs are always equivalent (choice B). The only correct response is choice C.

15. **C.** If you don't know your capital cities, use the process of elimination. Albany is the capital of New York, Santa Fe is the capital of New Mexico, Bismarck is the capital of North Dakota, and Austin is the capital of Texas. All of these states have secretaries of state. Salt Lake City (choice C) is the capital of Utah, which has no such position.

16. **If you live in Alaska, Hawaii, or Utah, there is no such position; the duties of that office are given to the lieutenant governor.** The assertion in question is that most states have secretaries of state. The exception appears in the sentence quoted here.

17. **C.** The clue is "switching places"; Damocles acted in the king's place, or stead (choice C).

18. **C, F.** Basic vocabulary skills come into play here. *Replete* (choice C) means "full." *Relegated* (choice D) means "demoted," so *assigned* (choice F) works better here.

19. **A, F.** The sentences are draconian (choice A), or excessively harsh, and the use of resources is profligate (choice F), or wasteful.

20. **C, E.** Reading the whole sentence will help you here. The government wanted all mendicants (choice C), or beggars, removed. So they vowed to catalog all impecunious (choice E), or poor, adults and children.

21. **B.** Keep the first sentence of the passage in mind as you answer; it contains the author's purpose and main focus. That helps you understand that the case is mentioned as an example of food adulteration that led to a change in the law (choice B).

22. **B, C.** The author defines *kipper* in the passage both as herring that is treated (choice B) and the process of so treating it (choice C). The treat that contains kippers (choice A) is not called a kipper, at least not here.

23. **A, B.** Andersonville was the site of the South's "most notorious prison," meaning that it was known to be terrible (choice A). Since Atwater was housed there as a Union soldier, you can infer that choice B is correct. Although the number 13,000 is mentioned, there is no way of knowing what percentage of the prisoners this represents, so choice C cannot be accepted as true.

24. **B.** Each answer represents a small part of the passage, but only choice B reflects the passage as a whole.

25. **Fearing that the official list would never be shared with the Union, Atwater kept a duplicate list.** This sentence tells why Atwater copied the list—his motivation was fear that the original would never be shared with the Union.

Section 5. Quantitative Reasoning

1. **B.** Quantity A is $0.15 \times 50 = 7.5$, while Quantity B is $0.2 \times 40 = 8$.

2. **B.** When 3.17486 is rounded to the nearest thousandth, the result is 3.175. Quantity A is thus $3.175 - 3.17486 = 0.00014$, which is less than 0.001.

3. **D.** If $x = 0$, then both quantities will be 0. If $x = 5$, however, then $\frac{1}{2}\lfloor 5 \rfloor = \frac{1}{2} \times 5 = 2.5$ while $\lfloor \frac{1}{2} \times 5 \rfloor = \lfloor 2.5 \rfloor = 2$. There is thus no way to tell whether the two quantities are equal or not.

4. **C.** If $x = \dfrac{x+1}{x}$, then $x - 1 = \dfrac{(x+1)}{x} - \dfrac{x}{x} = \dfrac{1}{x}$.

5. **B.** If you multiply both quantities by 7, then Quantity A is $2x + 10$ and Quantity B is $7x + 7$. If you subtract $2x$ from both quantities, then Quantity A is 10 and Quantity B is $5x + 7$. Because $x > 1$, it follows that $5x + 7 > 10$, so Quantity B is larger than Quantity A.

6. **B.** To evaluate $\Delta(\Delta 2)$, you first evaluate $\Delta 2 = 2 - 2^2 = -2$. It follows that $\Delta(\Delta 2) = \Delta(-2) = 2 - (-2)^2 = -2$. Thus 0, Quantity B is greater than -2, Quantity A.

7. **A.** Quantity A is $(a + b)^2 = a^2 + 2ab + b^2$. Quantity B is c^2 which equals $a^2 + b^2$ by the Pythagorean theorem. Because a and b are positive lengths, it follows that Quantity A is $2ab$ greater than Quantity B.

8. **B.** Suppose that the median of X is M. This means that half of X consists of numbers $\leq M$ and the other half of numbers $\geq M$. The smallest mean for such a collection will occur when all of these numbers are as small as possible (the ones smaller all 1s and the bigger ones all M's): $X = \{1, 1, \ldots, 1, M, M, \ldots, M\}$. For the median to be M, over half of these numbers must be M (including either the one or two in the middle); thus the mean is larger than $\dfrac{M+1}{2}$. Double this is $M + 1$, which is always larger than the mean M.

9. **C.** The shirt was discounted $6 which, relative to the original price, is $\dfrac{6}{20} = \dfrac{30}{100} = 30\%$.

10. **C.** If the three numbers are written out with units, they are $\dfrac{26 \text{ mi}}{\text{gal}}$, $\dfrac{\$2.79}{\text{gal}}$, and $\$40$. Because the units are all different, these numbers cannot be added or subtracted.

    If you flip the 2.79 to its reciprocal and multiply the three numbers, the result is $\dfrac{26 \text{ mi}}{\text{gal}} \times \dfrac{\text{gal}}{\$2.79} \times \dfrac{\$40}{1} = \dfrac{26 \times 40}{2.79}$ miles (the other units all cancel out). Because $\dfrac{26}{2.79}$ is a little less than 10, the result is a little less than 400 miles.

11. **C.** The formula for the number of ways to choose k of n items, where the order in which they are chosen is unimportant, is $\dfrac{n!}{(n-k)!k!}$, where $n!$ is the factorial, representing $n \times (n-1) \times (n-2) \times \cdots \times 3 \times 2 \times 1$. In this case, the number of ways to choose 4 of 10 colors is $\dfrac{10!}{(10-4)!4!} = \dfrac{10 \times 9 \times 8 \times 7 \times 6 \times 5 \times 4 \times 3 \times 2 \times 1}{6 \times 5 \times 4 \times 3 \times 2 \times 1 \times 4 \times 3 \times 2 \times 1} = \dfrac{10 \times 9 \times 8 \times 7}{4 \times 3 \times 2 \times 1} = 10 \times 3 \times 7 = 210$.

12. **D.** A 300 mL solution which is 12% salt contains $0.12 \times 300 = 36$ mL of salt. When 200 mL of pure water is added, the result will be 500 mL of liquid, of which 36 mL is salt. This means that the percentage of salt is $\dfrac{36}{500} = \dfrac{72}{1000} = 0.072 = 7.2\%$.

13. **D.** Tim used $25 \times 52 = 1{,}300$ diapers in the 52 weeks of his first year and $10 \times 52 = 520$ diapers in each of his next two years, for a total of $1300 + 520 + 520 = 2{,}340$.

14. **148.** The top and bottom of the box each have area $5 \times 4 = 20$. The front and back of the box each have area $4 \times 6 = 24$. The remaining two sides each have area $5 \times 6 = 30$. The total surface area is thus $2 \times 20 + 2 \times 24 + 2 \times 30 = 148$. It is also possible to use the formula $2lw + 2hw + 2lh$ for the surface area of a box with length l, width w, and height h.

15. **A, D, E.** If we work out each possibility in order, we get $1 \otimes 0 = 0 - 1^2 + 1 = 0$, $0 \otimes 1 = 1 - 0^2 + 1 = 2$, $x \otimes x^2 = x^2 - x^2 + 1 = 1$, $(x-1) \otimes x(x-2) = x(x-2) - (x-1)^2 + 1 = x^2 - 2x - x^2 + 2x - 1 + 1 = 0$, and $x \otimes (x^2 - 1) = x^2 - 1 - x^2 + 1 = 0$.

16. **B.** It is not possible for m and n to be both negative or both positive, because this would make $mn > 0$, which is not the case. This rules out $m < 0$ and $n < 0$, $m > 1$ and $n > 1$, and $-1 < m < 0$ and $n < 0$. Furthermore, $m > 1$ and $n < -1$ is not possible because then the product mn would be less than -1, which is also not the case. Thus $m < 1$ and $n < 1$ is the only possibility which could be true.

17. **D.** Because $y - x = 2$, you know that $y = 2 + x$. You can substitute this into $2y - x = 1$ to make it $2(2 + x) - x = 1$, which simplifies to $4 + x = 1$ or $x = -3$. You then substitute $y = 2 + x = 2 + (-3) = -1$ and conclude that $x = -3$ and $y = -1$.

18. **D, F.** The number 12 is either 4×3 or 6×2, and the number 36 is either 4×9 or 6×6. None of the other options are multiples of both 4 and 6.

19. **E.** A geometric sequence multiplies a constant k each time, so $(abr)k = ab^2r^3$. Divide both sides by abr, and we see $k = br^2$. To obtain the tenth term, we multiply abr by k nine times to get $(abr)(br^2)^9 = abrb^9r^{18} = ab^{10}r^{19}$.

20. **D.** If the radius of circle B is r, then the radius of circle A is $r + 1$. The circumference of circle B is $2\pi r$ and the circumference of circle A is $2\pi(r + 1) = 2\pi r + 2\pi$. Thus, the circumference of circle A is 2π more than the circumference of circle B.

21. **D.** There are 7 dots on the graph which are below the 150-pound mark and directly above or to the left of the 5'4" mark. The percentage of 7 out of 25 is $\frac{7}{25} = \frac{28}{100} = 0.28 = 28\%$.

22. **D.** The point marked x is between -2 and -1, which rules out -2.7 and -2.3 (less than -2) and also -0.7 (greater than -1). Furthermore, x appears closer to -1 than to -2, which makes -1.3 a better estimate than -1.7.

23. **150,000.** The first bar at 2009 rises up to the point marked 150. Because this scale is measured in thousands, the answer is 150,000.

24. **E.** The four bars of employment growth in 2006 reach 150, 200, 300, and 100, for a total of 750,000.

25. **D.** From 2007 to 2008, state X lost 50,000, 250,000, 300,000, and 200,000 jobs in the four quarters. These sum up to a total job loss of 800,000. If there were 2.5 million jobs at the beginning of 2008, then there must have been 800,000 more at the beginning of 2007, for a total of 3.3 million.

Section 6. Quantitative Reasoning

1. **B.** The fraction $\frac{1}{4} = 0.25$, while $0.25\% = 0.0025$.

2. **A.** The ratio of a circle's circumference to its diameter, written π, is $\pi = 3.1415926\ldots$ and goes on forever without ever repeating. While 3.14 is a handy approximation, it is a bit less than the actual number.

3. **C.** Quantity A is $8^{\frac{2}{3}} = \left(8^{\frac{1}{3}}\right)^2 = \left(\sqrt[3]{8}\right)^2 = 2^2 = 4$. Quantity B is $\left(\frac{1}{2}\right)^{-2} = \dfrac{1}{\left(\frac{1}{2}\right)^2} = \dfrac{1}{\left(\frac{1}{4}\right)} = 4$.

4. **B.** Because N is a multiple of 12, N is even. Because N is a multiple of 15, it is a multiple of 5. Together N must be a multiple of 10; thus its last digit is 0.

5. **C.** It is not necessary to make any computation. In the function's equation, all of the powers of x are even (2, 4, and 6), so plugging in $x = 2.38$ and its negative, $x = -2.38$, will give the same result.

6. **B.** Quantity A is $(x + y)^2 = x^2 + 2xy + y^2$ and Quantity B is $(x - y)^2 = x^2 - 2xy + y^2$. Because $xy < 0$, you know $2xy < 0$ and $-2xy > 0$, thus Quantity B is larger.

7. **D.** If $x = 0$, then Quantity A is $\sqrt{5}$, which is greater than Quantity B, which is 2. If $x = 1$, then Quantity A is $\sqrt{6}$, which is less than Quantity B, which is $\sqrt{1} + 2 = 3.$

8. **A.** The top and bottom of the can are circles with radius 1, for a combined area of $2 \times \pi 1^2 = 2\pi$. If the side of the can is cut vertically, the result unrolls into a rectangle with the same height as the can, 2, and the same width as the circumference of the circles, 2π, for an area of $2 \times 2\pi = 4\pi$. Quantity A is thus $2\pi + 4\pi = 6\pi$, larger than Quantity B.

9. **C.** The area of trapezoid $ABCD$ is $\frac{1}{2} \times (12 + 20) \times 6 = 96$. The area of triangle EFG is $\frac{1}{2}(12)(16) = 96$.

10. **B.** The trick is to pair up as many 2s and 5s as possible, in order to make 10s, thus $2^8 \times 5^{10} = 2^8 \times 5^8 \times 5^2 = (2 \times 5)^8 \times 25 = 10^8 \times 25 = 2{,}500{,}000{,}000$. This number has 10 digits.

11. **C.** The product is $5\% \times 5\% = 0.05 \times 0.05 = 0.0025 = 0.25\%$.

12. **B.** In order to compute the ratio, you must first convert everything to the same units. Because one yard is three feet, 7 yards is 21 feet, and thus the ratio is $\dfrac{21}{10}$.

13. **C.** If you divide 1 by 7 with a calculator, the result is $0.142857143\ldots$, although that last 3 is the result of rounding up a 2. The real result is $\frac{1}{7} = 0.\overline{142857}$, a decimal that repeats every 6 digits. Because $50 \div 6 = 8$ with a remainder of 2, the fiftieth digit of $\frac{1}{7}$ will be the second of this six-digit repeating sequence, a 4.

14. **E.** By finding a common denominator, you can calculate $\dfrac{x+2}{x-1}+\dfrac{x-2}{x+1}=$

$\dfrac{x+2}{x-1}\times\left(\dfrac{x+1}{x+1}\right)+\dfrac{x-2}{x+1}\times\left(\dfrac{x-1}{x-1}\right)=\dfrac{x^2+3x+2}{x^2-1}+\dfrac{x^2-3x+2}{x^2-1}=\dfrac{2x^2+4}{x^2-1}=$

$2\left(\dfrac{x^2+2}{x^2-1}\right)$.

15. **D.** There are 12 people who can be chosen to stand in the first place. After this person is chosen, there are 11 choices as to who stands in the second spot. Next, there are 10, 9, and then 8 ways to fill each of the remaining three spots. The total number of ways is $12\times11\times10\times9\times8=95{,}040$.

16. **C.** The two triangles are similar because they have a pair of angles in common, thus all angles in common. The side $AC=10$ corresponds with the side $DF=x$. The side $AB=12$ corresponds with $EF=10$ (not DE, because angle A is the same as angle F, not angle D). This means that $\dfrac{10}{x}=\dfrac{12}{10}$. Cross multiplication results in $12x=100$, so $x=\dfrac{100}{12}=\dfrac{25}{3}=8\dfrac{1}{3}$.

17. **B.** There are nine points in S: (0, 0), (0, 1), (0, 2), (1, 0), (1, 1), (1, 2), (2, 0), (2, 1), and (2, 2). These make a 3×3 array of points much like the available spaces in the game Tic-Tac-Toe. Similarly, the collinear arrangements are the ways to win: three horizontal, three vertical, and two diagonal. These eight "successes" are out of as many possibilities as choosing three of nine items: $\dbinom{9}{3}=\dfrac{9!}{3!(9-3)!}=\dfrac{9\cdot8\cdot7}{3\cdot2}=84$. Thus the probability that three random points are collinear is $\dfrac{8}{84}=\dfrac{2}{21}$.

18. **E.** Because $OB=BC$, the triangle is isosceles, thus $\angle COB=45°$. The radius of the circle is $OA=\dfrac{1}{2}OB=4$. Thus the area contained in both the circle and the triangle is $\dfrac{45}{360}=\dfrac{1}{8}$ of the whole circle's area of $\pi4^2=16\pi$, thus 2π. The whole area of the square is 400. The probability that a point chosen from the square will be inside both the circle and the triangle is $\dfrac{2\pi}{400}=\dfrac{\pi}{200}$.

19. **B.** The distance from (9, −4) to (8, 5) is $\sqrt{(9-8)^2+(-4-5)^2}=\sqrt{82}$, to (10, 2) is $\sqrt{(9-10)^2+(-4-2)^2}=\sqrt{37}$, to (5, 5) is $\sqrt{(9-5)^2+(-4-5)^2}=\sqrt{97}$, to (2, −2) is $\sqrt{(9-2)^2+(-4-(-2))^2}=\sqrt{53}$, and to (4, 6) is $\sqrt{(9-4)^2+(-4-6)^2}=\sqrt{125}$. Thus the nearest of these points to (9, −4) is (10, 2).

20. **C.** There are a total of 20 socks and 12 of them are black, so the probability of pulling out a black sock is $\frac{12}{20} = \frac{3}{5}$. If this happens, there will be 19 socks left, 11 of which are black, so the probability of pulling out a second black sock will be $\frac{11}{19}$. The probability that both of these happen (two black socks are pulled) will be $\frac{3}{5} \times \frac{11}{19} = \frac{33}{95}$. Similarly, the probability of pulling out a white sock first is $\frac{8}{20} = \frac{2}{5}$ and the probability of pulling out a second white sock is $\frac{7}{19}$, so the probability of pulling out two white socks is $\frac{2}{5} \times \frac{7}{19} = \frac{14}{95}$. The probability of pulling out two socks of the same color is the sum of the probabilities of getting either two black or two white socks: $\frac{33}{95} + \frac{14}{95} = \frac{47}{95}$.

21. **900°.** It is possible to draw 4 diagonals from the vertex marked $a°$ to the vertices marked $d°, e°, f°$, and $g°$. This slices the heptagon into 5 triangles. The angle sum of these 5 triangles is $5 \times 180° = 900°$, which is also the angle sum of the heptagon: $a° + b° + c° + d° + e° + f° + g°$. It is also possible to use the formula $(n - 2) \times 180°$ for the total angle sum of a figure with n sides.

22. **10.** When 28^5 is factored into primes, the result is $(2 \times 2 \times 7)^5 = (2^2 \times 7)^5 = 2^{10} \times 7^5$. The largest power of 2 by which this number can be divided and still remain an integer is thus 2^{10}.

23. **B.** According to the chart, education spending in state B went up by 4% from 2000 to 2005. Thus if the amount spent in 2000 was x, then the amount spent in 2005 was $x + 0.04x = 1.04x = 380$ million. The answer (in millions) is thus $380 \div 1.04$, approximately 365.4.

24. **B.** Even though all the percentages listed for state B add up to 0, there is no way of knowing whether they really balance each other out. If the transportation budget was much larger than the "other" category, for example, then the 10% increase in transportation could not be offset by the 10% decrease in other. Thus, choice A is not necessarily true. Similarly, if much more was spent on education than on health in state A, then the overall change need not be −1%, enough to balance out the increase in police spending. However, all of the areas in state D's budget decreased or stayed the same from 2000 to 2005, and thus it is certain that the total budget was lower in 2005 than in 2000. Note: if all of state D's spending was on the police, then the budget would have stayed level; however, in this event the spending on the other departments would not have been listed as reduced.

25. **A.** If state C spent $100 million on transportation in 2000, then it spent 3% less, for a total of $97 million in 2005. After a 3% increase between 2005 and 2010, the budget will end up at $97 \times 1.03 = 99.91$ million dollars. Rounded to the nearest tenth of a percent, this is 99.9% of the 2000 budget for transportation.

GRE Practice Test 4

SECTION 1
Analytical Writing

ANALYZE AN ISSUE

30 Minutes

You will have 30 minutes to organize your thoughts, and compose a response that represents your point of view on the topic presented. Do not respond to any topic other than the one given; a response to any other topic will receive a score of 0.

You will be required to discuss your perspective on the issue, using examples and reasons drawn from your own experiences and observations.

Use scratch paper to organize your response before you begin writing. Write your response on the pages provided, or type your response using a word processor with the spell- and grammar-check functions turned off.

Issue Topic

"It is not possible for one person to succeed without another, somewhere, failing."

Discuss the extent to which you agree or disagree with the claim made above. In your response, use specific examples and explain how those examples shape your position.

SECTION 2
Analytical Writing

ANALYZE AN ARGUMENT

30 Minutes

You will have 30 minutes to organize your thoughts and compose a response that critiques the given argument. Do not respond to any topic other than the one given; a response to any other topic will receive a score of 0.

You are not being asked to discuss your point of view on the statement. You should identify and analyze the central elements of the argument, the underlying assumptions that are being made, and any supporting information that is given. Your critique can also discuss other information that would strengthen or weaken the argument or make it more logical.

Use scratch paper to organize your response before you begin writing. Write your response on the pages provided, or type your response using a word processor with the spell- and grammar-check functions turned off.

Argument Topic

The state school-board association sent this note to its constituent school-board members.

"It is clear that the proposed 10 percent cuts to state aid affect poor districts more than wealthy districts. If the statewide average cut per student is $500, wealthy districts' cuts are far below that average, whereas the poorest upstate districts will receive cuts that are nearly twice that average. Since state aid is distributed now in a way that gives more to the poor districts than to the wealthy districts, shouldn't cuts in state aid be similarly equitable?"

Examine the logic of this argument by discussing what questions would need to be answered in order to decide whether the recommendation and the argument on which it is based are reasonable.

SECTION 3
Verbal Reasoning
Time: 35 minutes
25 questions

For questions 1 through 4, select two answer choices that (1) complete the sentence in a way that makes sense and (2) produce sentences that are similar in meaning.

---

1. The bank clerk moved in a _____ manner meant to disguise the movement of cash from one drawer to the other.

    A   clandestine

    B   importunate

    C   sycophantic

    D   preternatural

    E   desultory

    F   surreptitious

2. Dressing with understatement rather than _____ is desirable in a first-year attorney at most of our downtown firms.

    A   fastidiousness

    B   panache

    C   élan

    D   deviation

    E   severity

    F   homogeneity

3. Of the eight Ivy League universities, Cornell is the youngest; the others were _____ when the British still ruled the 13 colonies.

   [A] endorsed

   [B] inhabited

   [C] founded

   [D] established

   [E] discharged

   [F] secured

4. In the upper Midwest, especially in Wisconsin, Minnesota, and North Dakota, a surprising percentage of the population claims to be of Norwegian _____.

   [A] descent

   [B] patronage

   [C] extraction

   [D] idiom

   [E] society

   [F] pursuit

Questions 5 and 6 are based on this passage.

Boston's major airport was once simply named Boston Airport. In 1944 it became Commonwealth Airport, and in 1956 it was renamed Logan Airport, after a famous local general who became a judge and legislator. Now some Massachusetts

Line

(5) residents want to rename it once more, this time in honor of the late Ted Kennedy, Massachusetts's longtime senator. The controversy surrounding the name change may remind some of that surrounding the 1998 change from Washington National Airport to Ronald Reagan Washington National Airport. Some said that renaming an airport after one president (Reagan) when it was already named for another (Washington) was inappropriate. If Logan does undergo a name change, it will

(10) probably merge the old and new and reemerge as Logan-Kennedy or Kennedy-Logan Airport.

Consider each of the choices separately and select all that apply.

5. Why does the author compare Logan Airport to Ronald Reagan Airport?

    A   To indicate what may happen when a local airport goes national

    B   To demonstrate how changing familiar names may be contentious

    C   To present an applicable and parallel example as a cautionary tale

Select one answer choice.

6. In the final sentence, the author suggests that

    (A) it is never good politics to remove an old name and substitute a new one

    (B) at this point, it seems unlikely that Logan Airport will receive a new name

    (C) Bostonians are equally divided on the two possible names for their airport

    (D) the renaming of Boston's airport will likely require a compromise solution

    (E) as U.S. airports age, more of them will adopt hyphenated monikers

Question 7 is based on this passage.

The Professional Children's School was founded in 1914 by reformers who hoped to give a decent education to those children who worked on the Broadway stage. Today its students include professional musicians; stage, television, and film
Line   actors; and dancers. Unlike the School of Performing Arts, which trains pupils for
(5)   performance, the Professional Children's School is a typical college prep school. Probably the main difference between it and other prep schools is the fact that children are expected to be absent for professional reasons, sometimes for extended periods of time. Famous alumni of the school include actors Sarah Jessica Parker and Christopher Walken, dancers Suzanne Farrell and Darci Kistler, and musicians
(10)   Yo-Yo Ma and Beverly Sills.

Consider each of the choices separately and select all that apply.

7. Based on the information in the passage, which of these can be inferred about the Professional Children's School?

    [A] Its community of learners has broadened from that of the school's inception.

    [B] It features a flexible schedule that enables actors to make films or appear in plays.

    [C] Its sliding fee scale is largely based on whether its students are currently employed.

Questions 8 and 9 are based on this passage.

In the old days, twine held the reed in place in a single-reed instrument. This twine was called a ligature, as in the thread used to tie up an artery in surgery. Mouthpieces were designed with grooves in place to hold the twine. Instrument maker Iwan Müller invented a metal ligature for clarinets in the early 1800s, and this is the sort of ligature that is widely used today. Metal ligatures held on with screws, similar to those that Müller designed, are used on saxophones as well. Despite the ease of use that a metal ligature provides, some clarinet purists prefer to use twine because the resulting resonance of the reed is not quite so metallic in tone.

Line
(5)

For questions 8 and 9, select one answer choice each.

8. A comprehensive summary of the passage could most easily omit

    (A) the allusion to the ligatures used in surgery

    (B) the discussion of Iwan Müller's invention

    (C) the reference to the use of ligatures in saxophones

    (D) the description of early reed-instrument mouthpieces

    (E) the fact that some clarinet players still use twine

9. According to the author, certain clarinet players prefer twine to metal ligatures due to the difference in

(A) user-friendliness

(B) convenience

(C) sound quality

(D) expenditure

(E) reiteration

For questions 10 through 13, complete the text by picking the best entry for each blank from the corresponding column of choices.

---

10. Mercury is a (i) _____ of many scientific instruments, but in recent times, concerns about its (ii) _____ have led to its replacement by equally accurate digital or alcohol-based substitutes.

Blank (i)	Blank (ii)
(A) rival	(D) precision
(B) function	(E) toxicity
(C) component	(F) empiricism

11. *Hanja* is the Korean name for Chinese characters that have been (i) _____ from Chinese, given Korean pronunciation, and then (ii) _____ into the Korean language.

Blank (i)	Blank (ii)
(A) rescued	(D) incorporated
(B) lifted	(E) condensed
(C) deciphered	(F) submerged

12. Richard II ascended to the throne at the age of 10, ruled 22 years, and was _____ in 1399 by Henry Bolingbroke, whom he had earlier exiled.

Ⓐ	crowned
Ⓑ	invaded
Ⓒ	exceeded
Ⓓ	vindicated
Ⓔ	deposed

13. Of the five uniformed armed forces of the United States, only four are within the Department of Defense; the coast guard now resides within the Department of Homeland Security, but it may _____ to naval control if the Congress declares war.

Ⓐ	revert
Ⓑ	accede
Ⓒ	descend
Ⓓ	reply
Ⓔ	correspond

Questions 14 through 16 are based on this passage.

Members of elite families in ancient Rome might be tapped to become *flamines maiores*, the trio of high priests who served the major deities. The Flamen Dialis oversaw the cult of Jupiter, king of the gods. The Flamen Martialis oversaw the cult of Mars, god of war and agriculture. The Flamen Quirinalis oversaw the cult of
Line
(5) Quirinus, a major god of early Rome who was later deemed to be the reincarnation of Romulus, Rome's founder. The altar to peace known as the Ara Pacis, built in 13 BC to honor Augustus, features friezes that illustrate the *flamines* of the time as well as a variety of secular characters, from senators and magistrates, to children of the ruling class.

Consider each of the choices separately and select all that apply.

14. Which of these facts could most logically be added somewhere within the passage?

   A   Each member of the triad was chosen, not elected, by the pontifical college.

   B   Romulus and his twin, Remus, were deemed to be the sons of Mars.

   C   In Augustan Rome, the god Janus was given the epithet Quirinus.

Select one answer choice.

15. The author introduces the Ara Pacis in the last sentence primarily to

   (A) suggest that flamines were kept apart from the rest of Roman society

   (B) contrast the religious and secular personages of ancient Rome

   (C) discuss the classes of Romans who lived in the time of Augustus

   (D) illustrate one extant resource for learning more about flamines

   (E) show that by the era of Augustus's reign, flamines were in decline

16. Underline the sentence that mentions a change in the public's perception of a particular deity.

For questions 17 through 20, complete the text by picking the best entry for each blank from the corresponding column of choices.

---

17. John Wesley led his young Methodist movement to take a leadership role in many of the political issues of the day, including prison reform and abolitionism; in this way, he _____ many political preachers of the twentieth century.

(A)	mimicked
(B)	countered
(C)	involved
(D)	denoted
(E)	presaged

18. A fjord is an inlet formed when glaciers cut valleys into the bedrock (i) _____ the ocean; many were (ii) _____ during the last ice age.

Blank (i)		Blank (ii)	
(A)	overhanging	(D)	removed
(B)	beneath	(E)	saturated
(C)	adjoining	(F)	formed

19. Scottish Gaelic was once the (i) _____ language of the Outer Hebrides, but it has been (ii) _____ by English in most areas. Today, many places on the islands have (iii) _____ signage in Gaelic and English.

Blank (i)	Blank (ii)	Blank (iii)
(A) verbalized	(D) omitted	(G) recurring
(B) sponsored	(E) supplanted	(H) new
(C) predominant	(F) reclaimed	(I) dual

20. Strangely enough, there are no albino horses, (i) _____ there are occasionally horses that are white with pink skin. It appears that the gene that (ii) _____ albinism is (iii) _____ to horses, and affected embryos spontaneously abort.

Blank (i)	Blank (ii)	Blank (iii)
(A) considering	(D) causes	(G) common
(B) meaning	(E) exposes	(H) lethal
(C) although	(F) guards	(I) extended

Question 21 is based on this passage.

Few screenwriter–directors are as closely allied with a city as Barry Levinson is with his hometown of Baltimore. Although they were not his best-attended films, the Baltimore trilogy of *Diner* (1982), *Tin Men* (1987), and *Avalon* (1990) forms a
Line
(5)
deeply personal panorama with a sharply focused sense of place. With *Liberty Heights* (1999), a coming-of-age story set in the 1950s, Levinson returned to the Baltimore of his youth. Throughout the 1990s, he helped produce the TV series *Homicide: Life on the Street*, a police procedural set in Baltimore. Unlike most series, *Homicide* was filmed almost entirely on site in Baltimore, making the city itself a prominent focus of the drama.

Select one answer choice.

21. The primary purpose of the passage is to

    (A) list award-winning films and television shows set in Baltimore

    (B) contrast Levinson's early films with his later television writing

    (C) reveal how one director's work is informed by a sense of place

    (D) express a critical opinion about the films of Barry Levinson

    (E) develop a film theory connecting setting to plot and characterization

Question 22 is based on this passage.

Everyone has heard of the Texas Rangers, but Arizona had its own rangers, too. At the turn of the twentieth century, Arizona was a fairly lawless place. This was a political liability, as the territory wished to apply for statehood. Governor Murphy
Line suggested to the legislature that they organize a posse of rangers to clean things up.
(5) The Arizona Rangers, some of them veterans of the Spanish-American War, rode through the territory from 1901 until 1909. They consisted of the best marksmen and horsemen money could buy, and they had relative autonomy to do what they had to do. The Arizona Rangers rounded up cattle rustlers, put down rioters in labor disputes, and made some 4,000 arrests before they were disbanded. The territory
(10) became the forty-eighth state three years later.

Consider each of the choices separately and select all that apply.

22. It can be inferred from the passage that the main reasons behind the formation of the Arizona Rangers included which of the following?

   ☐A☐ Issues involving immigration and the misuse of itinerant labor

   ☐B☐ A desire to make the Arizona Territory more acceptable for statehood

   ☐C☐ The need to address illegalities in a vast, unsupervised region

Questions 23 through 25 are based on this passage.

When Aristotle wrote, "The whole is more than the sum of its parts," he laid the foundation for today's systems biology. Systems biologists study the integrated and interactive web of structures and systems that make up a living organism.
Line To do that, they must fuse disciplines to create a "big picture" outlook. For
(5) example, Harvard's new Department of Systems Biology welcomes students in applied mathematics and engineering as well as the usual biology or chemistry. Rather than looking at how individual components of an organism function, systems biologists view the interactions of components. Rather than explaining or predicting the action of a system based on an understanding of its parts,
(10) systems biologists explain the function of the parts based on the behavior of the system. Identifying and modeling the effects of a new drug on genes, proteins, cell structure, and so on is one way to use systems biology in the marketplace.

Consider each of the choices separately and select all that apply.

23.   The author mentions applied mathematics and engineering in order to

   ☐A   indicate the need for an interdisciplinary approach when considering problems of systems biology

   ☐B   make the point that systems biologists are not necessarily biologists at all

   ☐C   suggest that the expected paths of study are not always required of students applying to the Harvard program

Select one answer choice.

24.   Based on the information in the article, it can be inferred that the principles of systems biology are based on

   Ⓐ   reductionism, an approach to understanding the nature of complex things by reducing them to the interactions of their parts

   Ⓑ   structuralism, the process of determining and analyzing the basic, stable structural elements of a system

   Ⓒ   empiricism, the pursuit of knowledge through observation, experimentation, and sensory experience

   Ⓓ   realism, the doctrine that suggests that physical objects exist even if they cannot be readily perceived

   Ⓔ   holism, the theory that the parts of any whole cannot be understood except in their relation to the whole

25.   Underline the sentence that presents an example of systems biology in practice.

STOP.   This is the end of Section 3. Use any remaining time to check your work.

SECTION 4
Verbal Reasoning
Time: 35 minutes
25 questions

Questions 1 through 3 are based on this passage.

More than half of all birds fall into the category of perching birds, or passerines. Most, but not all, passerines are also categorized as songbirds. This includes seedeaters, insectivores, and birds that sip nectar. As you can tell, the order is remarkably diverse, ranging from ravens to wrens, from wagtails to warblers. They have some physical characteristics in common: all have three toes that point forward and one that points backward (enabling perching), and all have 12 tail feathers. Passerine eggs are often pastel in color, as opposed to the white eggs of most other birds. Passerines are described as *altricial*, which means that they produce young that remain in a helpless or immature condition for some time, requiring much parental care.

Line
(5)

Consider each of the choices separately and select all that apply.

1. Based on the definition given in the passage, which of these might be considered altricial species?

   [A] Dogs

   [B] Humans

   [C] Horses

Select one answer choice.

2. If an unfamiliar bird laid a blue egg, which other trait or attribute would best indicate that it was almost certainly a passerine?

   (A) Insects and arthropods as a major part of the diet

   (B) One backward-facing and three forward-facing toes

   (C) Overdeveloped vocal organs adapted to singing

   (D) Elaborate tail wagging during the mating season

   (E) A beak adapted for the easy opening of seeds

3. Underline the sentence that directly contrasts an attribute of passerines with that of other birds.

Question 4 is based on this passage.

Enzo Ferrari was a car racer for Alfa Romeo, eventually running his own team of drivers. Before the war, he left Alfa Romeo to set up an auto parts company and build race cars. In 1947 he reconfigured the company and gave it his name. By the early 1950s, his Ferrari race cars were taking titles in Grand Prix and Le Mans races. His love for race cars endured all his life, but to make a decent profit, Ferrari had to diversify into street cars as well. Today, a new Ferrari often retails for between $200,000 and $300,000, putting them well out of the reach of most consumers.

Line (5)

Select one answer choice.

4. Which of these statements about Ferraris is NOT supported by information in the passage?

(A) The cars are named for the man who owned the company that built them.

(B) The cars have frequently won races both at Le Mans and the Grand Prix.

(C) The cars are too high-priced for ordinary buyers in Europe or elsewhere.

(D) The cars that sell for everyday use contain the same engines as the race cars.

(E) Ferrari race cars managed to outpace Alfa Romeo race cars in the 1950s.

For questions 5 through 8, complete the text by picking the best entry for each blank from the corresponding column of choices.

---

5. Although rococo style (i) _____ in the decorative arts and interior design, it (ii) _____ painting and music of the time as well.

Blank (i)	Blank (ii)
(A) changed	(D) implicated
(B) paled	(E) influenced
(C) originated	(F) goaded

6. The Little House series of books by Laura Ingalls Wilder are usually
   (i) _____ as historical novels, although the later books are nearly
   entirely (ii) _____.

Blank (i)		Blank (ii)	
(A)	overlooked	(D)	autobiographical
(B)	classified	(E)	fictional
(C)	rendered	(F)	chronological

7. The Cuban conga drum has staves like a barrel, suggesting that congas were
   once perhaps made from _____ barrels.

(A)	similar
(B)	salvaged
(C)	musical
(D)	tinted
(E)	prehistoric

8. The three-day bombing of Dresden in 1945 remains _____, both for its
   disproportionate use of heavy ordnance and for its apparent targeting of
   civilians.

(A)	inconclusive
(B)	celebrated
(C)	controversial
(D)	clandestine
(E)	eminent

Questions 9 through 12 are based on this passage.

Although Norway is today a Lutheran nation and thus not much associated with saints and miracles, the legend of Sunniva survives there as a testament to earlier values. On the island of Selja, there remain ruins of a great Christian center. Churches dating back
Line to the 900s and a large monastery from somewhat later are part of the Selja ruins. On the
(5) island, too, is a large cave, where the legend is mostly set.

Sunniva was the Christian daughter of the Irish king Otto. She was pursued by a heathen Viking, who wanted her hand in marriage. Seeking asylum, she set off in three ships with her followers, but her ships foundered without sails or oars, and she was castaway on the island of Selja. There she lived with her followers, pious
(10) men and women known as the *seljumun*, or "holy ones." The islanders suspected the strangers of eating their grazing animals, and they called on Earl Håkon to attack them and remove them from the island. Sunniva and her followers hid in a cave, but as their pursuers came near, the cave collapsed.

After that came a series of miracles. People reported seeing rays of light and
(15) smelling sweet odors emanating from the cave. The new Christian king Olaf had the cave opened and found Sunniva's intact body, which he placed in a crypt inside a church he built for her. The island became a site for pilgrimages and a major focus of Olaf's Christianization of Norway. Sunniva is now the patron saint of Western Norway and particularly of Bergen.

Consider each of the choices separately and select all that apply.

9. Paragraph two of the passage suggests that Sunniva and her followers might have survived and thrived were it not for

  A   mysticism

  B   intolerance

  C   royal decree

For questions 10 through 12, select one answer choice each.

---

10. It can be inferred that Sunniva rejected her Viking would-be lover because of her

  (A) faith

  (B) purity

  (C) royal blood

  (D) love for another

  (E) Irish heritage

11. Ancient Norwegians considered the fact that Sunniva's body was intact to be a miracle, but another logical explanation might be that

(A) the rays of light came from flaming volcanic lava

(B) King Olaf kept her body interred in a crypt

(C) the cave offered natural properties of preservation

(D) Earl Håkon never managed to find Sunniva

(E) Sunniva did not perish when the cave-in occurred

12. How might the organization of the passage be described?

(A) Paragraph one introduces the topic; paragraph two tells the story; paragraph three presents the moral.

(B) Paragraph one introduces the topic; paragraphs two and three narrate the legend.

(C) Paragraphs one and two narrate the legend; paragraph three summarizes the story.

(D) Paragraphs one and two introduce the topic; paragraph three extends the topic to the present day.

(E) Paragraph one defines the terms; paragraph two tells the story; paragraph three offers an alternative.

Question 13 is based on this passage.

Bushwhackers versus Jayhawkers may sound like an invitation to a basketball game, but it was a serious matter in the Midwest during the Civil War. The Bushwhackers were Confederate guerrillas, and the Jayhawkers were militant abolitionists. When
Line those two teams clashed, innocent civilians often died. Jayhawkers from Kansas
(5) raided into Missouri, murdering slave owners and stealing horses and provisions. Bushwhackers from Missouri pillaged Lawrence, Kansas, killing nearly all the male population. In retaliation, the Union Army emptied four Missouri counties that bordered Kansas, ordering everyone to vacate the area no matter where their sympathies lay. Homes were burned to the ground, and entire flourishing
(10) communities became ghost towns overnight.

13. Underline the sentence that describes atrocities committed by Confederate guerrillas.

For questions 14 through 17, complete the text by picking the best entry for each blank from the corresponding column of choices.

14. In heraldry, the dexter side of the shield is considered the _____ side, as in the case of the Great Seal of the United States, in which the eagle clutches an olive branch in its dexter talon and arrows in its sinister talon.

Ⓐ	honorable
Ⓑ	negative
Ⓒ	analogous
Ⓓ	martial
Ⓔ	dominant

15. Caught up in the ongoing Russian _____, certain associates close to the administration seemed eager to turn state's evidence.

Ⓐ	paradigm
Ⓑ	polemic
Ⓒ	imbroglio
Ⓓ	rostrum
Ⓔ	persiflage

16. Although the Microscopic Septet officially (i) _____ in 1992, they (ii) _____ 14 years later, getting together for several performances, and have played together in New York (iii) _____ ever since, despite the fact that their founder now lives in Australia.

Blank (i)	Blank (ii)	Blank (iii)
Ⓐ devolved	Ⓓ acceded	Ⓖ sporadically
Ⓑ coalesced	Ⓔ reconciled	Ⓗ imperceptibly
Ⓒ sundered	Ⓕ palliated	Ⓘ abstemiously

17. The term *in medias res* is a Latin (i) _____ referring to the narrative technique in which a story is told not from the beginning, (ii) _____ from a point in the middle of the action. The technique is especially common in epic poetry, two well-known (iii) _____ being the *Iliad* and *Paradise Lost*.

Blank (i)	Blank (ii)	Blank (iii)
(A) adage	(D) but rather	(G) canons
(B) theme	(E) instead of	(H) conventions
(C) phrase	(F) rather than	(I) exemplars

Questions 18 through 20 are based on this passage.

Line
(5)

(10)

The Leonese language, like many endangered languages, has a handful of proponents who are desperately trying to keep it alive. In the case of Leonese, these speakers and history lovers have banded together to create an online encyclopedia in the Leonese language. Titled *Llionpedia*, the encyclopedia is a wiki, allowing collaborative writing and editing. Leonese is derived directly from Latin and is spoken in a handful of Spanish provinces and Portuguese villages—the area that in the Middle Ages made up the Kingdom of León. Much of the monastic history of the kingdom remains in texts written in Leonese. Although the language is in some ways very similar to Spanish, in other ways it is closer to the original Latin. An example is the verb *to make*, which in Latin and Leonese is *facere*, but in Castilian Spanish is *hacer*.

> For questions 18 through 20, select one answer choice each.

18. In the first sentence of the passage, what does the word *proponents* most precisely mean?

   (A) Advocates

   (B) Underwriters

   (C) Benefactors

   (D) Collaborators

   (E) Orators

19. Which of the following can be inferred from the passage about the text known as *Llionpedia*?

 Ⓐ *Llionpedia* is a narrative history of a region of Spain and Portugal.

 Ⓑ The encyclopedia will be available in print and digital formats.

 Ⓒ Special software will be required to read the online encyclopedia.

 Ⓓ The text is being written in Spanish and translated lovingly to Leonese.

 Ⓔ Anyone who speaks or writes Leonese may participate in the project.

20. Which of the following best describes the function of the last sentence of the passage?

 Ⓐ It presents a conclusion drawn from prior examples.

 Ⓑ It offers supporting evidence for the author's earlier judgment.

 Ⓒ It puts forward a thesis statement that will be supported by reasons.

 Ⓓ It provides a case in point confirming the preceding supposition.

 Ⓔ It summarizes a hypothesis by reiterating the passage's premise.

For questions 21 through 25, select two answer choices that (1) complete the sentence in a way that makes sense and (2) produce sentences that are similar in meaning.

---

21. The _____ Rubik's Cube measures about 2¼ inches on each side, with 26 smaller, pivoting cubes making up the puzzle; however, there are many accepted variations.

 Ⓐ multihued

 Ⓑ amazing

 Ⓒ classic

 Ⓓ perplexing

 Ⓔ instructive

 Ⓕ standard

22. Because one-fifth of its landmass lies below sea level, the process of land reclamation is _____ to the existence of the Netherlands.

    [A] imperative

    [B] endemic

    [C] essential

    [D] secondary

    [E] immaterial

    [F] lethal

23. Della Reese began her career as a singer of gospel and jazz, but she _____ hosted a talk show and acted in a television drama.

    [A] previously

    [B] predictably

    [C] later

    [D] subsequently

    [E] moreover

    [F] in point of fact

24. While thousands of Americans keep tropical birds as pets, the birds' natural need for warmth makes them _____ to chills caused by drafts and power outages.

    [A] susceptible

    [B] contributory

    [C] impervious

    [D] causative

    [E] detrimental

    [F] vulnerable

25. The timber rattlesnake has the _____ Latin name *Crotalus horridus*, which vividly captures human revulsion to this most dangerous of snakes.

   [A] official

   [B] fitting

   [C] familiar

   [D] distinctive

   [E] apt

   [F] droll

STOP.   This is the end of Section 4. Use any remaining time to check your work.

SECTION 5
Quantitative Reasoning
Time: 40 minutes
25 questions

Each of questions 1 through 9 consists of two quantities, Quantity A and Quantity B. You are to compare the two quantities. You may use additional information centered above the two quantities if additional information is given. Choose

Ⓐ if Quantity A is greater;

Ⓑ if Quantity B is greater;

Ⓒ if the two quantities are equal;

Ⓓ if the relationship cannot be determined from the information given.

	Quantity A	Quantity B	
1.	$\dfrac{21}{29}$	$\dfrac{5}{7}$	Ⓐ Ⓑ Ⓒ Ⓓ

	Quantity A	Quantity B	
2.	2^5	5^2	Ⓐ Ⓑ Ⓒ Ⓓ

$$1 - 3x > 7$$

	Quantity A	Quantity B	
3.	x^2	$10x$	Ⓐ Ⓑ Ⓒ Ⓓ

$x, x^2,$ and $\sqrt{x}$ are distinct odd integers less than 100

Quantity A	Quantity B	
4. $x + 5$	$2x$	Ⓐ Ⓑ Ⓒ Ⓓ

Quantity A	Quantity B	
5. $\sqrt{x^2 + 2x + 1}$	$|x + 1|$	Ⓐ Ⓑ Ⓒ Ⓓ

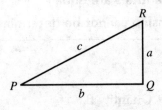

$\angle PQR$ is obtuse

Quantity A	Quantity B	
6. $a^2 + b^2$	c^2	Ⓐ Ⓑ Ⓒ Ⓓ

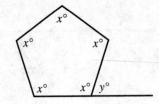

Quantity A	Quantity B	
7. $3y$	$2x$	Ⓐ Ⓑ Ⓒ Ⓓ

12 oranges cost \$3.30

Quantity A	Quantity B	
8. The price of 8 oranges	\$2.50	Ⓐ Ⓑ Ⓒ Ⓓ

p and q are distinct prime numbers

Quantity A	Quantity B	
9. The number of divisors of p^3q	The number of divisors of p^2q^2	Ⓐ Ⓑ Ⓒ Ⓓ

Questions 10 through 25 have different formats. Select a single answer choice unless the directions say otherwise. For numeric-entry questions, follow these instructions:

- **Enter your answer in the box or boxes provided.**
- **Your answer may be an integer, a decimal, a fraction, or a negative number.**
- **If the answer is a fraction, you will be given two boxes: an upper one for the numerator and a lower one for the denominator.**
- **Equivalent forms of the correct answer, such as 1.6 and 1.60, are all correct. You do not need to reduce fractions to lowest terms.**

---

10. $(10 - 9 + 8 - 7) - (6 - 7 + 8 - 9) =$

    Ⓐ −2

    Ⓑ −1

    Ⓒ 0

    Ⓓ 2

    Ⓔ 4

For this question, indicate all of the answer choices that apply.

11. Which of the following equations are for lines which are perpendicular to the line $y = 2x + 4$?

A $2y + x = 5$

B $2y - x = 3$

C $x + 2y = 7$

D $x - 2y = 4$

E $4y + 2x = 0$

12. A circle has an area of A. A second circle has a diameter four times that of the first circle. What is the area of the second circle?

(A) $2A$

(B) $4A$

(C) $8A$

(D) $16A$

(E) $32A$

For this question, write your answer in the box.

13. A high school has 36 students on the debate team, 45 students on the football team, and 8 students on both. If there are 490 students in the whole school, how many are on neither the football team nor the debate team?

14. A moment is randomly selected in the week. What is the probability that this moment will occur during normal business hours (Monday through Friday between 8 a.m. and 5 p.m.)?

    (A) $\dfrac{1}{3}$

    (B) $\dfrac{3}{8}$

    (C) $\dfrac{5}{7}$

    (D) $\dfrac{5}{21}$

    (E) $\dfrac{15}{56}$

15. In a certain collection, there are 74 coins, each with 0.3 ounces of pure gold. If gold costs $800 per ounce, what is the value of the coins?

    (A) $13,760

    (B) $14,760

    (C) $15,760

    (D) $16,760

    (E) $17,760

For this question, write your answer in the box.

16. The cost of a car repair is $220 for parts and $180 for labor. What percentage of the total repair bill is the labor?

    Give your answer rounded to the nearest whole percent.

     %

For this question, indicate all of the answer choices that apply.

17. If $0 < x < 1$, which of the following must be true?

    A $\quad x < \dfrac{1}{x}$

    B $\quad -x < x$

    C $\quad x^2 < x^3$

    D $\quad x^2 < x$

    E $\quad x < x + 2$

18. Approximately how many feet per minute is 30 miles per hour?

    Ⓐ 2,000 feet per minute

    Ⓑ 2,500 feet per minute

    Ⓒ 3,000 feet per minute

    Ⓓ 3,500 feet per minute

    Ⓔ 4,000 feet per minute

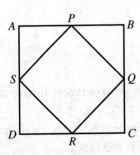

19. Square $ABCD$ has area 50. The points P, Q, R, and S are the midpoints of $\overline{AB}$, $\overline{BC}$, $\overline{DC}$, and $\overline{AD}$ respectively. What is the area of square $PQRS$?

    Ⓐ 12.5

    Ⓑ 25

    Ⓒ $20\sqrt{2}$

    Ⓓ $25\sqrt{2}$

    Ⓔ 37.5

20. For which of the following values of x does $\dfrac{5}{3-x}$ have the least value?

    (A) 2

    (B) 2.5

    (C) 3.5

    (D) 4

    (E) 5

21. If $x^4 = 19$, what is the arithmetic mean of 1, x^2, $x^3(x-1)$, $x(x+1)(x-1)$, and $x(1-x)$?

    (A) 4

    (B) $4x$

    (C) $\dfrac{x+1}{5}$

    (D) 5

    (E) $\dfrac{x-1}{5}$

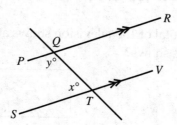

22. If $\overline{PR} \parallel \overline{SV}$ and $y = 3x$, what is x?

    (A) 30

    (B) 45

    (C) 60

    (D) 90

    (E) 180

Use the following figure to answer questions 23 through 25.

Television Programming at Station X, by Genre

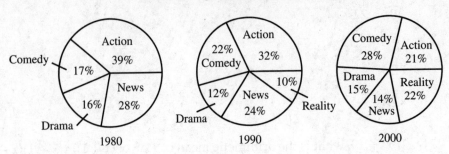

23. What was the leading genre of television at station X in 2000?

    Ⓐ Action

    Ⓑ Comedy

    Ⓒ Drama

    Ⓓ News

    Ⓔ Reality

For this question, write your answer in the box.

24. If there were a total of 150 television shows at station X in 1990, how many of them were news shows?

25. How much of station X's programming in 2000 was devoted to reality programs, represented as a percentage of X's reality programming in 1990?

    Ⓐ 12%

    Ⓑ 22%

    Ⓒ 120%

    Ⓓ 122%

    Ⓔ 220%

STOP. This is the end of Section 5. Use any remaining time to check your work.

SECTION 6
Quantitative Reasoning
Time: 40 minutes
25 questions

> Each of questions 1 through 9 consists of two quantities, Quantity A and Quantity B. You are to compare the two quantities. You may use additional information centered above the two quantities if additional information is given. Choose
>
> (A) if Quantity A is greater;
> (B) if Quantity B is greater;
> (C) if the two quantities are equal;
> (D) if the relationship cannot be determined from the information given.

	Quantity A	Quantity B	
1.	four-fifths of two-thirds	two-thirds of four-fifths	(A) (B) (C) (D)

	Quantity A	Quantity B	
2.	-3^2	$(-3)^2$	(A) (B) (C) (D)

	Quantity A	Quantity B	
3.	the largest prime factor of 351	the greatest common factor of 42 and 140	(A) (B) (C) (D)

In a school of 350 students, there are 90 basketball players and
65 members of the math club.

Quantity A	Quantity B	
4. The number of people on the basketball team and math club combined	100	Ⓐ Ⓑ Ⓒ Ⓓ

Quantity A	Quantity B	
5. $(x-1)(x+1)$	$(x+3)(x-3)$	Ⓐ Ⓑ Ⓒ Ⓓ

$$|x| < 1$$

Quantity A	Quantity B	
6. x^2	x^3	Ⓐ Ⓑ Ⓒ Ⓓ

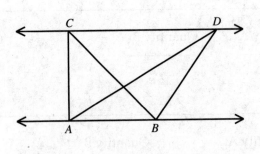

$$\overrightarrow{AB} \parallel \overrightarrow{CD}$$

Quantity A	Quantity B	
7. the area of triangle ABC	the area of triangle ABD	Ⓐ Ⓑ Ⓒ Ⓓ

$$4x - y = 7 \text{ and } 2x + 2y = 4$$

Quantity A	Quantity B	
8. x	2	Ⓐ Ⓑ Ⓒ Ⓓ

M and N are real numbers.

Quantity A	Quantity B	
9. $|M - N|$	$M + N$	Ⓐ Ⓑ Ⓒ Ⓓ

Questions 10 through 25 have different formats. Select a single answer choice unless the directions say otherwise. For numeric-entry questions, follow these instructions:

- Enter your answer in the box or boxes provided.
- Your answer may be an integer, a decimal, a fraction, or a negative number.
- If the answer is a fraction, you will be given two boxes: an upper one for the numerator and a lower one for the denominator.
- Equivalent forms of the correct answer, such as 1.6 and 1.60, are all correct. You do not need to reduce fractions to lowest terms.

---

10. What is the smallest natural number which is a multiple of all the numbers from 1 through 10 (inclusive)?

Ⓐ 55

Ⓑ 2,520

Ⓒ 5,040

Ⓓ 12,600

Ⓔ 3,628,800

For this question, indicate all of the answer choices that apply.

11. Which are between $0.\overline{41}$ and $0.5\overline{2}$?

    A 0.525

    B 0.411

    C 0.424

    D 0.409

    E 0.519

12. A regular polygon will be drawn with a number of sides randomly chosen from the whole numbers 3 through 10. What is the probability that the internal angles will be greater than 110°?

    (A) $\dfrac{1}{8}$

    (B) $\dfrac{1}{4}$

    (C) $\dfrac{3}{8}$

    (D) $\dfrac{1}{2}$

    (E) $\dfrac{5}{8}$

13. The information on a cereal box states that 28 grams of cereal contains 45% of the daily recommended amount of iron. How much of this cereal must be eaten in order to obtain 100% of the daily recommended amount of iron? Round your answer to the nearest gram.

    (A) 62 g

    (B) 63 g

    (C) 64 g

    (D) 65 g

    (E) 66 g

14. Uranium is present in seawater at a concentration of 3 parts per billion. If a process is available to extract this uranium, how many kilograms of seawater would need to be processed in order to obtain 50 kilograms of uranium? Round your answer to two significant digits.

   Ⓐ 17 million kilograms

   Ⓑ 150 million kilograms

   Ⓒ 17 billion kilograms

   Ⓓ 150 billion kilograms

   Ⓔ 17 trillion kilograms

15. A play has two roles for men and four roles for women. If five men and 12 women try out for these parts, in how many different ways can the director choose people for the roles?

   Ⓐ 60

   Ⓑ 480

   Ⓒ 4,950

   Ⓓ 59,400

   Ⓔ 237,600

16. Which of the following data sets has the largest standard deviation?

   Ⓐ 7, 6, 8, 4, 5

   Ⓑ 7, 9, 6, 9, 8

   Ⓒ 12, 13, 17, 14, 13

   Ⓓ 1, 2, 9, 8, 9

   Ⓔ 3, 3, 3, 4, 3

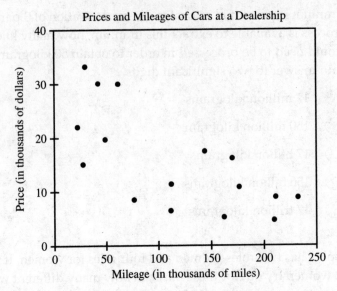

17. If a car at the dealership has less than 100,000 miles on it, what is the probability that it costs less than $25,000? Round your answer to the nearest percent.

    (A) 50%

    (B) 57%

    (C) 63%

    (D) 67%

    (E) 71%

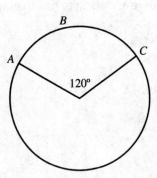

18. If arc *ABC* measures 8π, what is the area of the circle?

    (A) 12π

    (B) 16π

    (C) 24π

    (D) 144π

    (E) 256π

$\overline{AB} \parallel \overline{CD}$, $AB = 5$, $AE = 7$, and $ED = 10$

19. What is CD?

    (A) $3\frac{1}{2}$

    (B) $7\frac{1}{7}$

    (C) $8\frac{1}{3}$

    (D) $10\frac{5}{7}$

    (E) 14

20. What is the area of an equilateral triangle with a side of length 2?

    (A) $\sqrt{3}$

    (B) 2

    (C) $2\sqrt{3}$

    (D) 3

    (E) $3\sqrt{3}$

For this question, indicate all of the answer choices that apply.

21. Which of the following equations have graphs that are parallel to $2y - 6x = 7$.

    [A] $x = \dfrac{5 + y}{3}$

    [B] $2x = 6y + 1$

    [C] $\dfrac{3}{y} = \dfrac{1}{x + 1}$

    [D] $\dfrac{1}{3}y - 2x = 5$

    [E] $(x - 6)(y - 2) = 1$

For this question, indicate all of the answer choices that apply.

22. If $3x^2 + 3 = 2x^2 - x + 15$, which of the following are possible values of x?

    [A] -4

    [B] -2

    [C] 2

    [D] 3

    [E] 4

For this question, indicate all of the answer choices that apply.

23. Which of the following are factors of 240?

    [A] 6

    [B] 9

    [C] 12

    [D] 20

    [E] 36

    [F] 45

Use the following figure to answer questions 24 and 25.

Monthly Production (in thousands)

Product

		A	B	C	D	E
Factory	W	15	12	17	9	14
	X	8	9	6	7	5
	Y	0	5	31	0	0
	Z	6	4	5	9	1

For this question, write your answer in the box.

24. How much of product C is made in factory Z each year?

For this question, write your answer in the box.

25. What percentage of the monthly production of product D is made in factory X?

┌─────────────┐
│   │ %
└─────────────┘

STOP.   This is the end of Section 6. Use any remaining time to check your work.

GRE Practice Test 4: Answers and Explanations

Analytical Writing: Scoring and Sample Responses

Analyze an Issue: Scoring

Score	Focus	Organization	Conventions
0	Does not address the prompt. Off topic.	Incomprehensible. May merely copy the prompt without development.	Illegible. Nonverbal. Serious errors make the paper unreadable. May be in a foreign language.
1	Mostly irrelevant to the prompt.	Little or no development of ideas. No evidence of analysis or organization.	Pervasive errors in grammar, mechanics, and spelling.
2	Unclear connection to the prompt.	Unfocused and disorganized.	Frequent errors in sentence structure, mechanics, and spelling.
3	Limited connection to the prompt.	Rough organization with weak examples or reasons.	Occasional major errors and frequent minor errors in conventions of written English.
4	Competent connection to the prompt.	Relevant examples or reasons develop a logical position.	Occasional minor errors in conventions of written English.
5	Clear, focused connection to the prompt.	Thoughtful, appropriate examples or reasons develop a consistent, coherent position. Connectors are ably used to mark transitions.	Very few errors. Sentence structure is varied and vocabulary is advanced.
6	Insightful, clever connection to the prompt.	Compelling, convincing examples or reasons develop a consistent, coherent position. The argument flows effortlessly and persuasively.	Very few errors. Sentence structure is varied and vocabulary is precise, well chosen, and effective.

Analyze an Issue:
Sample Response with a Score of 6

In this essay, the writer counters the premise given in the prompt, using examples both from history and from the writer's own experience. While acknowledging the original argument, the writer provides strong opposing cases in point. There are no significant errors in grammar or mechanics.

The notion that one person cannot succeed without someone else failing is passionately held by those who decry big-box development and Wall Street greed. However, if we look back at our history, there are many examples that belie this simplistic premise.

Look, for example, at immigration in the United States in the nineteenth and twentieth centuries. One success bred another as formerly impoverished immigrants reached back to pull up their siblings and other relatives, and the result was wide-ranging success and the rise of the middle class.

The civil-rights movements of the twentieth century provide another example of success breeding success. As more women rose in the workforce, they reached down to pull up their sisters. As Jim Crow was struck down, African Americans began to take their rightful places in businesses, legislatures, and universities, and America as a whole benefited.

Those who believe that the success of one means the failure of another might point to affirmative action as an example— if an African American with a B average takes the place of a white American with an A average, that African American depends on the failure of the white American. There is no question that examples like this one exist. Small businesses are often driven out by large ones. The rich do get richer, while their workers must survive on 2 percent raises—or none at all.

There is inequity and unfairness in our system. Despite that, there are many, many cases that prove that one person's success can snowball, allowing others to stand upon his shoulders. My personal example is my grandfather, who arrived here from Haiti in the 1960s. He found a job as a restaurant worker and rose from busboy to waiter to manager. In time, he saved enough to purchase part of a franchise, the profits from which enabled him to send his son and daughter to college. The son joined the business and soon brought over his cousins from Haiti to join as well. The daughter, my mother, became an immigration lawyer. Her success has led to the achievements of hundreds of immigrants she has helped through the system. The culmination of all these successes could be seen in 2010, when three generations of my family traveled back to Haiti to provide assistance after the earthquake there. We are one family, but our success has enabled others to succeed and thrive as well.

Analyze an Argument: Scoring

Score	Focus	Organization	Conventions
0	Does not address the prompt. Off topic.	Incomprehensible. May merely copy the prompt without development.	Illegible. Nonverbal. Serious errors make the paper unreadable. May be in a foreign language.
1	Little or no analysis of the argument. May indicate misunderstanding of the prompt.	Little or no development of ideas. No evidence of analysis or organization.	Pervasive errors in grammar, mechanics, and spelling.
2	Little analysis; may instead present opinions and unrelated thoughts.	Disorganized and illogical.	Frequent errors in sentence structure, mechanics, and spelling.
3	Some analysis of the prompt, but some major flaws may be omitted.	Rough organization with irrelevant support or unclear transitions.	Occasional major errors and frequent minor errors in conventions of written English.
4	Important flaws in the argument are touched upon.	Ideas are sound but may not flow logically or clearly.	Occasional minor errors in conventions of written English.
5	Perceptive analysis of the major flaws in the argument.	Logical examples and support develop a consistent, coherent critique. Connectors are ably used to mark transitions.	Very few errors. Sentence structure is varied and vocabulary is advanced.
6	Insightful, clever analysis of the argument's flaws and fallacies.	Compelling, convincing examples and support develop a consistent, coherent critique. The analysis flows effortlessly and persuasively.	Very few errors. Sentence structure is varied and vocabulary is precise, well chosen, and effective.

Analyze an Argument:
Sample Response with a Score of 6

This essay is short but complete. The writer uses a comprehensible mathematical example to point out a possible flaw in the original reasoning and follows up with a suggestion about future study. No errors in English usage or mechanics detract from the argument.

The state school-board association presents an impassioned argument in favor of modifying state cuts to schools to make them more equitable. Since the cut per student is less at rich schools than at poor schools, they argue, the cuts are harmful to poor schools. To determine whether the association is correct, these questions must be asked: Are the cuts what is harmful? Is there a break-even point between the cuts and state aid? Is something else standing in the way of equity?

The problem is that as things stand, the state already gives less per student to wealthy districts, who presumably then make up that difference using their own existing wealth. So a rich district might receive $2000 per student from the state, while an average district gets, say, $5000 per student. A cut of 10 percent to that rich district's aid then limits their payment to $1800 per student, while the average district still gets $4500. Yes, the cut to the rich district is only $200 per student, while the cut to the average district is $500. However, the result is still a 2:5 ratio of aid—exactly the same ratio as before the cut was made.

Despite this, the school board is not entirely wrong in its supposition that poor schools will be harmed. They will be harmed not because of an inequitable aid cut but because they do not have the money to supplement state aid. The state school-board association would be better off addressing that fundamental inequity. If school districts have to make up the difference through property taxes, or if they are simply unable to make up the difference at all and therefore have less to offer their students than wealthy districts do, that's a real problem that warrants everyone's immediate attention.

GRE Practice Test 4: Answer Key

Section 3. Verbal Reasoning

1. **A, F**
2. **B, C**
3. **C, D**
4. **A, C**
5. **B, C**
6. **D**
7. **A, B**
8. **A**
9. **C**
10. **C, E**
11. **B, D**
12. **E**
13. **A**
14. **A**
15. **D**
16. The Flamen Quirinalis oversaw the cult of Quirinus, a major god of early Rome who was later deemed to be the reincarnation of Romulus, Rome's founder.

17. **E**
18. **C, F**
19. **C, E, I**
20. **C, D, H**
21. **C**
22. **B, C**
23. **A, B, C**
24. **E**
25. Identifying and modeling the effects of a new drug on genes, proteins, cell structure, and so on is one way to use systems biology in the marketplace.

Section 4. Verbal Reasoning

1. A, B
2. B
3. Passerine eggs are often pastel in color, as opposed to the white eggs of most other birds.
4. D
5. C, E
6. B, D
7. B
8. C
9. B
10. A
11. C
12. B
13. Bushwhackers from Missouri pillaged Lawrence, Kansas, killing nearly all the male population.

14. A
15. C
16. C, E, G
17. C, D, I
18. A
19. E
20. D
21. C, F
22. A, C
23. C, D
24. A, F
25. B, E

Section 5. Quantitative Reasoning

1. A
2. A
3. A
4. B
5. C
6. B
7. C
8. B
9. B
10. E
11. A, C, E
12. D
13. 417

14. E
15. E
16. 45%
17. A, B, D, E
18. B
19. B
20. C
21. A
22. B
23. B
24. 36
25. E

Section 6. Quantitative Reasoning

1.	C	14.	C
2.	B	15.	E
3.	B	16.	D
4.	D	17.	B
5.	A	18.	D
6.	D	19.	B
7.	C	20.	A
8.	B	21.	A, C
9.	D	22.	A, D
10.	B	23.	A, C, D
11.	C, E	24.	60,000
12.	E	25.	28%
13.	A		

GRE Practice Test 4: Answer Explanations

Section 3. Verbal Reasoning

1. **A, F.** Even if some of the other choices make sense contextually, only *clandestine* (choice A) and *surreptitious* (choice E) are synonyms, with both meaning "secret."

2. **B, C.** The contrast is between understatement and style. *Panache* (choice B) and *élan* (choice C) are both synonyms for a spirited sort of style or flair.

3. **C, D.** The other seven universities were set up before the country was a nation; the best choices are C and D.

4. **A, C.** Choice A should be an easy one; *extraction* (choice C) is a synonym in this context.

5. **B, C.** Choice A does not apply to the passage. The comparison shows that changing names can cause trouble (choice B); it is a parallel situation raised to make that point (choice C).

6. **D.** A quick rereading of the final sentence should be enough to indicate that the author suggests a compromise merger of two names for the airport.

7. **A, B.** Choice A refers to the first two sentences; the school started by educating Broadway children but now educates dancers, musicians, and stars of television and film. Choice B refers to this line: "Probably the main difference between it and other prep schools is the fact that children are expected to be absent for professional reasons, sometimes for extended periods of time." There is no mention of a sliding fee scale, so choice C cannot be correct.

8. **A.** To determine which detail could be omitted, look for the one that does not support the main idea. Choice A is an interesting detail, but it is not necessary.

9. **C.** According to the passage, "the resulting resonance of the reed is not quite so metallic in tone." In other words, the sound quality is preferable.

10. **C, E.** If there were concerns about mercury's precision (choice D), the author would not call the other elements "equally accurate." The choices here are straightforward.

11. **B, D.** Read the whole sentence before making your choices. The characters have been borrowed, or lifted (choice B), from Chinese and then integrated, or incorporated (choice D), into Korean.

12. **E.** Richard was already on the throne, so he would not have been crowned (choice A). A person cannot be invaded (choice B), and the proper word would be *succeeded*, not *exceeded* (choice C). The best choice is *deposed* (choice E), meaning "removed from office."

13. **A.** Understanding the entire meaning of the sentence will help you choose correctly. The coast guard "now" resides in a different department; presumably it was once with the other armed forces. It may go back, or revert (choice A), to naval control in times of war.

14. **A.** To decide which details to add, think about the main idea of the passage. The passage is mostly about the triad of *flamines maiores*. Choice A tells more about them; the other choices are extraneous to the passage as a whole.

15. **D.** Again, think about the main idea of the passage, which is a discussion of the *flamines maiores*. Although the author names some other classes of Romans, as choices A, B, and C discuss, the main reason for bringing up the altar is because it shows pictures of the flamines.

16. **The Flamen Quirinalis oversaw the cult of Quirinus, a major god of early Rome who was later deemed to be the reincarnation of Romulus, Rome's founder.** Quirinus apparently went through some kind of reassessment between the time of early Rome and "later."

17. **E.** He could not mimic (choice A) a group that came after him. Instead, he foreshadowed, or presaged (choice E), later preachers.

18. **C, F.** If the bedrock were beneath the ocean (choice B), the fjords would not form inlets. The most logical choices are C and F.

19. **C, E, I.** Reading the whole passage should make the meaning clear: Gaelic was once the major language (choice C), but it was replaced by English (choice E). However, there remain signs in both languages (choice I).

20. **C, D, H.** If you have trouble, work backward. The fact that embryos spontaneously abort indicates that the gene is lethal (choice H). The other choices should become clear from that point.

21. **C.** The primary purpose of the paragraph is indicated fairly clearly in the first sentence.

22. **B, C.** The clues are in this portion of the passage: "Arizona was a fairly lawless place. This was a political liability, as the territory wished to apply for statehood." There is no support for choice A.

23. **A, B, C.** The author gives those disciplines as examples of the fusing of disciplines that makes up systems biology (choice A), but the phrase "as well as the usual biology and chemistry" implies that systems biologists need not be biologists (choice B) and that the path to systems biology is not always the expected one (choice C).

24. **E.** Holism is exactly the concept behind systems biology, which studies the whole by looking at the interaction of components.

25. **Identifying and modeling the effects of a new drug on genes, proteins, cell structure, and so on is one way to use systems biology in the marketplace.** This is the only sentence in the passage that indicates a practical use for the discipline.

Section 4. Verbal Reasoning

1. **A, B.** Dogs and humans give birth to helpless creatures that require adult help for some time. Baby horses are born with eyes open, fully formed, and ready to stand; they cannot be considered altricial.

2. **B.** Based on information from the passage, only choice B indicates that the bird is certainly passerine.

3. **Passerine eggs are often pastel in color, as opposed to the white eggs of most other birds.** This is the only sentence that directly compares passerines to other birds.

4. **D.** Choices A, B, C, and E are supported by details from the passage, but no mention is made of the engines in the street cars versus those in the race cars.

5. **C, E.** Try saying the sentence aloud with the choices in place; that will make clear that only choices C and E make sense.

6. **B, D.** Remember that *although* sets up a contrast. Even though the later books are true, or autobiographical (choice D), the series is usually classified (choice B) as historical fiction.

7. **B.** Here the best choice is the one that is most logical. Congas may have been made from recycled, or salvaged (choice B), barrels.

8. **C.** The second half of the sentence makes your choice clear. Targeting civilians and overusing ordnance would make the bombing controversial (choice C), not celebrated (choice A), and certainly not secret, or clandestine (choice D).

9. **B.** Sunniva and her followers seem to have been targeted because they were strangers, making choice B the best selection.

10. **A.** The Viking was a "heathen," making him inappropriate as a husband for a good Christian woman.

11. **C.** You are asked to find another reason why Sunniva's body might have been intact when it was discovered by King Olaf. Therefore, choice B cannot be correct. Choices A and D are irrelevant to the condition of her body, and choice E does not make sense. Only choice C provides a logical explanation.

12. **B.** The first paragraph introduces Sunniva and ends by announcing the legend. The following paragraphs detail that legend.

13. **Bushwhackers from Missouri pillaged Lawrence, Kansas, killing nearly all the male population.** The "Confederate guerrillas" were the Bushwhackers. This is the only sentence that describes their violent acts.

14. **A.** The second half of the sentence helps you choose correctly. The dexter talon clutches a symbol of peace; the sinister talon clutches a symbol of war. Therefore, the dexter talon must have a positive meaning, making choice A the likely possibility.

15. **C.** An imbroglio is a scandal. Choice C is the only choice that fits the context.

16. **C, E, G.** The band broke apart (choice C) but then got back together (choice E) and have played together occasionally (choice G) ever since.

17. **C, D, I.** *In media res* is not an adage, or proverb (choice A); nor is it a theme, or premise (choice B). It is simply a phrase that refers to a particular narrative technique. The other choices should be easy to determine if you read the passage aloud.

18. **A.** The people trying to keep Leonese alive are its advocates.

19. **E.** The clue is here: "Titled *Llionpedia*, the encyclopedia is a wiki, allowing collaborative writing and editing." In other words, anyone who speaks the language may help out. There is no support for any of the other choices.

20. **D.** The last sentence gives an example of how Leonese is closer in some ways to Latin than to Spanish, which was the author's preceding premise.

21. **C, F.** Look for the synonyms. The author is referring to the typical, or classic (choice C), cube, which might also be called the standard (choice F) cube.

22. **A, C.** Land reclamation is vital to the survival of the nation—it is imperative (choice A), or essential (choice C).

23. **C, D.** Although several choices fit the context, only two of the choices are synonyms.

24. **A, F.** The birds are at risk of, or susceptible (choice A) to, chills; they are vulnerable (choice F) to them.

25. **B, E.** The rattlesnake's name is fitting (choice B) or apt (choice E) because it captures human revulsion to the animal.

Section 5. Quantitative Reasoning

1. **A.** When the fractions are converted to have common denominators, they become $\dfrac{21}{29} = \dfrac{21 \times 7}{29 \times 7} = \dfrac{147}{203}$ and $\dfrac{5}{7} = \dfrac{5 \times 29}{7 \times 29} = \dfrac{145}{203}$. Alternatively, you could divide the numerators by the denominators and compare the resulting decimals. Quantity A is thus larger.

2. **A.** Quantity A is $2^5 = 2 \times 2 \times 2 \times 2 \times 2 = 32$, which is larger than Quantity B: $5^2 = 5 \times 5 = 25$.

3. **A.** The inequality $1 - 3x > 7$ simplifies to $1 - 7 > 3x$, which is $-6 > 3x$, and thus $x < -2$. Because x is a negative number, Quantity A, x^2, will always be positive, while Quantity B, $10x$, will always be negative. Thus A is greater than B.

4. **B.** For x^2 to be less than 100, x must be less than 10. For $\sqrt{x}$ to be an odd integer, x must further be either 1 or 9. If $x = 1$, then x, x^2, and $\sqrt{x}$ will all be the same, and thus not distinct. Thus x must be 9, which makes Quantity B 18 and Quantity A 14.

5. **C.** Quantity A can be simplified: $\sqrt{x^2 + 2x + 1} = \sqrt{(x+1)^2} = |x+1|$. Thus the two quantities are equal.

6. **B.** If $\angle PQR$ were right, then the Pythagorean theorem would state that $a^2 + b^2 = c^2$. However, because $\angle PQR$ is obtuse, the side c is too long for this equality to be true. Thus Quantity B, c^2, is larger than Quantity A, $a^2 + b^2$.

7. **C.** The total angle measure of a five-sided pentagon is $(5 - 2) \times 180° = 540°$, thus $x = 540 \div 5 = 108$. The angles x and y add up to a straight $180°$, thus $y = 180 - 108 = 72$. Quantity A is thus $3y = 216$ and Quantity B is $2x = 216$.

8. **B.** The price of 8 oranges is $\frac{8}{12} = \frac{2}{3}$ the price of 12 oranges. Thus 8 oranges cost $\frac{2}{3} \times \$3.30 = 2 \times \$1.10 = \$2.20$.

9. **B.** The number $p^3 q$ has eight different factors: $1, p, p^2, p^3, q, qp, qp^2$, and qp^3. The number $p^2 q^2$ has nine factors $1, p, q, p^2, q^2, pq, p^2 q, pq^2$, and $p^2 q^2$.

10. **E.** The easiest method is to see that both sets of parentheses contain a -9, a $+8$, and a -7. Because the second set is being subtracted from the first, these will all cancel out, leaving: $(10 - 9 + 8 - 7) - (6 - 7 + 8 - 9) = 10 - 6 = 4$. This could also be calculated directly.

11. **A, C, E.** The slope of the line $y = 2x + 4$ is $m = 2$. The slope of a perpendicular line will be the negative reciprocal, $m = -\frac{1}{2}$. When the five candidate equations are solved for y, they become $y = -\frac{1}{2}x + \frac{5}{2}$, $y = \frac{1}{2}x + \frac{3}{2}$, $y = -\frac{1}{2}x + \frac{7}{2}$, $y = \frac{1}{2}x - 2$, and $y = -\frac{1}{2}x$. The first, third, and fifth of these all have slope $m = -\frac{1}{2}$.

12. **D.** If the first circle has a radius of r, then the area is $A = \pi r^2$. The diameter of that circle will be $2r$. The diameter of the second circle is $8r$, so its radius is $4r$ and its area is $\pi(4r)^2 = 16\pi r^2 = 16A$.

13. **417.** If we add the sizes of the two teams, $36 + 45 = 81$, we double-count the eight students on both. Thus there are $81 - 8 = 73$ students on the two teams together. This means that $490 - 73 = 417$ students are on neither team.

14. **E.** There are 9 hours between 8 a.m. and 5 p.m., thus a total of 45 such hours from Monday to Friday. In a week, there are a total of $24 \times 7 = 168$ hours. Thus the probability that a moment in a week falls during these business hours is $\frac{45}{168} = \frac{15}{56}$.

15. **E.** Each coin is worth $0.3 \times \$800 = \$240$. The value of all 74 coins is thus $74 \times \$240 = \$17,760$.

16. **45%.** The total repair bill is $\$220 + \$180 = \$400$. The percent due to labor is $\dfrac{180}{400} = \dfrac{18}{40} = \dfrac{9}{20} = \dfrac{45}{100} = 45\%$.

17. **A, B, D, E.** The statement $x < x + 2$ is true for every real number, so it is true here. The statement $-x < x$ is true for all positive numbers. Because $0 < x < 1$, you know that $\dfrac{1}{x}$ is a positive number which is greater than one, and thus $x < \dfrac{1}{x}$. Finally, multiplying by a number between 0 and 1 always yields a smaller number, thus $x \cdot x < x$, so $x^2 < x$. By the same token, $x^3 < x^2$, so $x^2 < x^3$ is false.

18. **B.** To convert $\dfrac{30\,\text{mi}}{1\,\text{h}}$ into feet per minute, you need to multiply by 5,280 to convert miles into feet and divide by 60 to convert hours into minutes: $\dfrac{30\,\text{mi}}{1\,\text{h}} \times \dfrac{5,280\,\text{ft}}{1\,\text{mi}} \times \dfrac{1\,\text{h}}{60\,\text{min}}$. Because $\dfrac{30}{60} = \dfrac{1}{2}$, the answer will be half of 5,280, which is closer to 2,500 than to 3,000.

19. **B.** The easiest solution is to draw the line segments $\overline{PR}$ and $\overline{SQ}$, dividing the square $ABCD$ into eight congruent triangles. The square $PQRS$ consists of 4 of these triangles, and thus has half the area of square $ABCD$. A more complicated solution would be to calculate that $AB = \sqrt{50}$ and $AP = \dfrac{\sqrt{50}}{2}$, then use the Pythagorean theorem on triangle APS to find that $PS = \sqrt{25}$. To find the area of square $PQRS$, we square PS to get 25.

20. **C.** The numbers $x = 3.5$, $x = 4$, and $x = 5$ will make $\dfrac{5}{3 - x}$ have a negative value, all of which will be smaller than the positive numbers obtained by $x = 2$ and $x = 2.5$. You can calculate $\dfrac{5}{3 - 3.5} = -10$, $\dfrac{5}{3 - 4} = -5$, and $\dfrac{5}{3 - 5} = -2.5$. Thus $x = 3.5$ makes $\dfrac{5}{3 - x}$ have the least value.

21. **A.** To get the mean, we add all the terms and then divide by 5. When multiplied out, the sum is $1 + x^2 + x^4 - x^3 + x^3 - x + x - x^2$, which reduces to $1 + x^4$. Because $x^4 = 19$, the mean is $20/5 = 4$.

22. **B.** The transversal $\overline{QT}$ crosses the parallel lines $\overline{PR}$ and $\overline{SV}$, making the angles marked with $x°$ and $y°$ supplementary (they sum to $180°$). Thus $x + y = x + 3x = 180$, so $4x = 180$ and $x = 45$.

23. **B.** On the pie chart representing 2000, the largest sector is devoted to Comedy.

24. **36.** In 1990, 24% of the programming was news shows. If there were 150 shows, then $150 \times 0.24 = 36$ of them would be news.

25. **E.** Reality shows made up 22% of the programming in 2000 and 10% in 1990. Thus the amount in 2000, relative to that in 1990, was $\dfrac{22}{10} = \dfrac{220}{100} = 220\%$.

Section 6. Quantitative Reasoning

1. **C.** Quantity A is $\dfrac{4}{5} \times \dfrac{2}{3} = \dfrac{8}{15}$ and Quantity B is $\dfrac{2}{3} \times \dfrac{4}{5} = \dfrac{8}{15}$.

2. **B.** Quantity A is -9 and Quantity B is $(-3)(-3) = 9$.

3. **B.** The number 351 can be divided by 9 because its digits sum to $3 + 5 + 1 = 9$. When divided, $351 \div 9 = 39$. This makes it easy to see that the prime factorization of 351 is $3 \times 3 \times 3 \times 13$, so Quantity A is 13. Similarly, 42 factors into $2 \times 3 \times 7$ and 140 factors into $2 \times 2 \times 5 \times 7$, so their greatest common factor is $2 \times 7 = 14$. Thus Quantity B is 14, larger than 13, Quantity A.

4. **D.** It cannot be ruled out that all members of the math club play basketball, in which case the two together would total 90. It would also be possible for the two teams to be disjoint, in which case their total would be $90 + 65 = 155$.

5. **A.** Quantity A is $(x - 1)(x + 1) = x^2 - 1$ and Quantity B is $(x + 3)(x - 3) = x^2 - 9$, so Quantity B will always be 8 units less than Quantity A.

6. **D.** It is possible for $x = 0$, because $|0| < 1$, in which case quantities A and B will both equal 0. However, if $x = \dfrac{1}{2}$, which also satisfies $\left|\dfrac{1}{2}\right| < 1$, then Quantity A is $\left(\dfrac{1}{2}\right)^2 = \dfrac{1}{4}$, while Quantity B is $\left(\dfrac{1}{2}\right)^3 = \dfrac{1}{8}$. Thus it is impossible to say which quantity is larger.

7. **C.** Because $\overrightarrow{AB} \parallel \overrightarrow{CD}$, the vertical distance between these two lines is always the same, and thus the heights of the two triangles are equal. Both triangles have the same base $\overline{AB}$. With the same heights and bases, the triangle areas are equal.

8. **B.** If you solve $4x - y = 7$ for y, you obtain $y = 4x - 7$. When you substitute this in for y in $2x + 2y = 4$, you obtain $2x + 2(4x - 7) = 4$, which simplifies to $10x = 18$, so $x = \dfrac{18}{10} = \dfrac{9}{5}$. Thus Quantity B is $\dfrac{1}{5} = 0.2$ bigger than Quantity A.

9. **D.** In a case like $M = N = 0$, the quantities are equal. In a case like $M = N = 1$, we have $|M - N| = 0$ and $M + N = 2$. Thus the relationship cannot be determined.

10. **B.** The trick is to factor all the numbers into primes: 2, 3, 2 × 2, 5, 2 × 3, 7, 2 × 2 × 2, 3 × 3, 2 × 5. The smallest multiple will need to have enough copies of each prime to cover all of these: 2 × 2 × 2 × 3 × 3 × 5 × 7 = 2,520.

11. **C, E.** The numbers between $0.\overline{41} = 0.41414...$ and $0.5\overline{2} = 0.5222...$ include 0.424 and 0.519, but 0.525 is too big and both 0.411 and 0.409 are too small.

12. **E.** The internal angle of a regular polygon with n sides is $\dfrac{(n-2)180}{n}$, so when $n = 3$ the angles are 60°, when $n = 4$ the angles are 90°, when $n = 5$ the angles are 108°, and when $n = 6$ the angles are 120°. As n increases, so will these angles, thus the polygons with six, seven, eight, nine, and 10 sides will all have angles greater than 110°. Thus the probability is $\dfrac{5}{8}$.

13. **A.** If x is the amount of cereal needed to get 100% of the recommended amount of iron, you can find x by solving $\dfrac{28}{45} = \dfrac{x}{100}$. Thus $x = \dfrac{2800}{45} = 62.\overline{2}$, which is 62 grams when rounded to the nearest gram.

14. **C.** If x is the number of kilograms of water processed, then $\dfrac{3}{1,000,000,000} x = 50$, so $x = \dfrac{50,000,000,000}{3} = 16,666,666,666.\overline{6}$ kilograms. This rounds to 17 billion kilograms.

15. **E.** The first male role can be filled by any of the five men, and the second by any of the remaining 4, for a total of 5 × 4 = 20 choices. Similarly, there are 12 options for the first female role, 11 for the next, 10 for the third, and 9 for the last. The total number of possibilities is thus 5 × 4 × 12 × 11 × 10 × 9 = 237,600.

16. **D.** Rather than compute the standard deviation of each data set, it is enough to look at their ranges. Data set A ranges from 4 to 8, thus its data cannot deviate more than 2 (half of the difference) up and down from its mean. Data set B ranges from 6 to 9, C from 12 to 17, D from 1 to 9, and E from 3 to 4. Data set D varies by 8, far more than all the others. Furthermore, all of the data is at the extremes, either 1, 2, 8, or 9. This means that the standard deviation of data set D is close to 4, more than would be possible with any of the other data sets.

17. **B.** There are 7 cars with less than 100,000 miles on them, and 4 of them cost less than \$25,000. Thus, the probability is $\frac{4}{7} \approx 57\%$.

18. **D.** An arc that measures 120° is $\frac{120}{360} = \frac{1}{3}$ of the circle's circumference. Because arc ABC measures 8π, the whole circumference of the circle is $3 \times 8\pi = 24\pi$. You can find the radius r of the circle by solving $2\pi r = 24\pi$, which gives $r = 12$. The area of the circle is thus $\pi 12^2 = 144\pi$.

19. **B.** Because $\overline{AB} \parallel \overline{CD}$, you know that $\angle A \cong \angle D$ and $\angle B \cong \angle C$, thus triangle ABE is similar to triangle DCE. The side $AB = 5$ corresponds to $CD = x$, and the side $AE = 7$ corresponds to $ED = 10$. Thus, you only have to solve $\frac{5}{x} = \frac{7}{10}$ to find that $x = \frac{50}{7} = 7\frac{1}{7}$.

20. **A.** If the height h of the triangle is drawn, it will form a right triangle with base 1 and hypotenuse 2. By the Pythagorean theorem, $1^2 + h^2 = 2^2$, so $h^2 = 3$ and $h = \sqrt{3}$. Because the full base of the triangle is 2, the area is $\frac{1}{2}(2)\sqrt{3} = \sqrt{3}$.

21. **A, C.** We solve $2y - 6x = 7$ as $y = 3x + \frac{7}{2}$ to see that this is a straight line with slope 3. Any line parallel will also have a slope of 3. Equation A rearranges to $y = 3x - 5$. Equation B is $y = \frac{1}{3}x - \frac{1}{6}$. Equation C cross-multiplies to $3x + 3 = y$. Equation D is equivalent to $y = 6x + 15$. Equation E multiplies out to $xy - 2x - 6y + 12 = 1$, which is not even a straight line. Thus only equations A and C have slope 3.

22. **A, D.** When everything is brought to one side of the equation and simplified, the result is $x^2 + x - 12 = 0$. This factors into $(x + 4)(x - 3) = 0$, which has two solutions: $x = -4$ and $x = 3$.

23. **A, C, D.** The number 240 factors into $240 = 24 \times 10 = 6 \times 4 \times 10$, for a prime factorization of $2 \times 3 \times 2 \times 2 \times 5 \times 2$. You can find the factors of $6 = 2 \times 3$ in this, as well as both $12 = 2 \times 2 \times 3$ and $20 = 2 \times 2 \times 5$. However, there is only one 3, and thus you cannot make $9 = 3 \times 3$, $36 = 3 \times 3 \times 2 \times 2$, or $45 = 3 \times 3 \times 5$. Thus 240 can be evenly divided by 6, 12, and 20, but not by 9, 36, or 45.

24. **60,000.** The number 5 in the column marked C and the row marked Z represents 5,000, as the title of the table indicates.

25. **28%.** The total monthly production of product D is $9,000 + 7,000 + 9,000 = 25,000$. The percentage made in factory X is thus $\frac{7}{25} = \frac{28}{100} = 28\%$.

GRE Practice Test 5

SECTION 1
Analytical Writing

ANALYZE AN ISSUE

30 Minutes

You will have 30 minutes to organize your thoughts and compose a response that represents your point of view on the topic presented. Do not respond to any topic other than the one given; a response to any other topic will receive a score of 0.

You will be required to discuss your perspective on the issue, using examples and reasons drawn from your own experiences and observations.

Use scratch paper to organize your response before you begin writing. Write your response on the pages provided, or type your response using a word processor with the spell- and grammar-check functions turned off.

Issue Topic

"Television is entirely democratic in that its content is controlled by what the people want."

Discuss the extent to which you agree or disagree with the claim made above. In developing your position, address both the pro and the con viewpoints and explain the reasons for your choice.

SECTION 2

Analytical Writing

ANALYZE AN ARGUMENT

30 Minutes

You will have 30 minutes to organize your thoughts and compose a response that critiques the given argument. Do not respond to any topic other than the one given; a response to any other topic will receive a score of 0.

You are not being asked to discuss your point of view on the statement. You should identify and analyze the central elements of the argument, the underlying assumptions that are being made, and any supporting information that is given. Your critique can also discuss other information that would strengthen or weaken the argument or make it more logical.

Use scratch paper to organize your response before you begin writing. Write your response on the pages provided, or type your response using a word processor with the spell- and grammar-check functions turned off.

Argument Topic

Senator Winston Diehard recently delivered a speech at West Point, from which this is excerpted:

"I could not disagree more with Senators Weeks and Bland, who are lobbying Congress day and night to dismantle the Triton Missile Program. Yes, at $10 billion spent so far in research and development, Triton is expensive, but what price freedom? Would your tax dollars really be better spent propping up a variety of social programs than in defending our nation from the enemy abroad? Furthermore, why would you simply throw that $10 billion down the drain?"

Critique the strength and logic of the argument presented above. Discuss some questions that should be posed and answered in order to evaluate the recommendation.

SECTION 3
Verbal Reasoning
Time: 35 minutes
25 questions

Questions 1 through 3 are based on this passage.

The College of Arms is an official regulatory commission established in 1484 by King Richard III. Its purpose is to design and register new coats of arms and to establish and confirm pedigrees, particularly for families of English and Welsh descent. It does
Line not receive funds from the government; it is kept in business via the fees it charges,
(5) and the heralds who perform the services are paid small salaries by the queen.

It may seem an anachronistic service in the twenty-first century, but in 2005, Camilla, the Duchess of Cornwall, requested and received a new coat of arms to denote her role as wife of the heir to the throne. The arms consist of an amalgam of her father's existing arms; the arms of her husband, the Prince of Wales; and a crown
(10) with a single arch, signifying since 1661 a noblewoman's position as the consort of the heir apparent.

Consider each of the choices separately and select all that apply.

1. Based on the information given in the passage, which potential customers would be most likely to need the services of the College of Arms?

    A   A distant cousin of a minor duke who wishes to use the family coat of arms

    B   Heirs of an ancient Scottish clan wishing to know the pattern of the family tartan

    C   A woman descended from foreign nobility marrying into British nobility

Select one answer choice.

2. In the final sentence of the passage, the author is primarily concerned with

    (A) suggesting that coats of arms are indeed an archaic fashion

    (B) providing a description of a modern woman's coat of arms

    (C) showing how coats of arms have changed over the centuries

    (D) comparing the duchess's coat of arms to that of her father

    (E) explaining why a woman's coat of arms is different from a man's

3. Underline the sentence that expresses and then contradicts a particular point of view.

Question 4 is based on this passage.

The term *grand slam*, originally used in golf, has been part of the tennis world since the late 1930s. It refers to the accomplishment of a single player (or doubles team) who wins the top four tennis contests in a single year. Those contests are the Australian Open in January, the French Open in May and June, Wimbledon in June and July, and the U.S. Open in August and September. Rod Laver performed this remarkable feat in 1962 and again in 1969. Steffi Graf did it in 1988 and won the Olympic gold medal as well, giving her a so-called golden grand slam. Doubles team Martina Navratilova and Pam Shriver did it in 1984. Today the grand slam may refer to any four consecutive wins in the four major tournaments, not necessarily within a single year. It's still remarkable, but does it have the same cachet?

Line

(5)

(10)

Select one answer choice.

4. Based on the direction of the rest of the passage, the word *cachet* in the final sentence is apparently used to mean

Ⓐ snob appeal

Ⓑ class

Ⓒ effect

Ⓓ prestige

Ⓔ seal of approval

For questions 5 through 8, complete the text by picking the best entry for each blank from the corresponding column of choices.

---

5. Rio de Janeiro is not only the second-largest city in Brazil; it is the third-largest _____ area in all of South America.

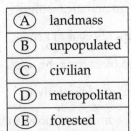

Ⓐ	landmass
Ⓑ	unpopulated
Ⓒ	civilian
Ⓓ	metropolitan
Ⓔ	forested

6. In hang gliding, the pilot _____ control over the vehicle by shifting his or her body weight in opposition to a control frame.

Ⓐ	relinquishes
Ⓑ	anticipates
Ⓒ	varies
Ⓓ	decreases
Ⓔ	maintains

7. The Civil War saw a number of important (i) _____ in naval warfare, including the (ii) _____ of torpedo boats.

Blank (i)		Blank (ii)	
Ⓐ	mishaps	Ⓓ	production
Ⓑ	setbacks	Ⓔ	discovery
Ⓒ	innovations	Ⓕ	replication

8. By far the largest of the penguins, the emperor penguin is (i) _____ to Antarctica, where it (ii) _____ over many miles of ice to its breeding ground, and later (iii) _____ for food hundreds of miles away to bring back to its single chick.

Blank (i)		Blank (ii)		Blank (iii)	
Ⓐ	pervasive	Ⓓ	submerges	Ⓖ	forages
Ⓑ	endemic	Ⓔ	treks	Ⓗ	arranges
Ⓒ	devoted	Ⓕ	strays	Ⓘ	pursues

Questions 9 through 12 are based on this passage.

At over 195,000 square miles, Canada's Baffin Island is the fifth-largest island in the world—more than twice the size of Great Britain. As large as it is, Baffin Island is home to only about 11,000 people, primarily due to its harsh climate. It is surrounded
Line   by sea ice and the Arctic Ocean, and the temperature rarely gets above 50 degrees
(5)   Fahrenheit, even in July. In the center of the island, summer temperatures hover below 10 degrees Fahrenheit. In winter, temperatures throughout the island average well below zero.

Geologically speaking, Baffin Island represents a continuation of the Canadian Shield, an expanse of land scoured by glaciers that extends from the Arctic
(10)   Archipelago south into the north-central United States, and from the Northwest Territories all the way east to Labrador. The geography of the island features rocky bluffs, a coastal strip of marshland, and a wide plains region that turns into a large plateau at the northern end of the island. Despite its inclement weather, it is a breeding ground for a remarkable variety of seabirds and a wintering place for
(15)   narwhals, belugas, and walruses.

Things are changing on Baffin Island. Hunters are beginning to see melting of the sea ice. Trekkers are finding glaciers turned to slush in some places. Rock surfaces that have never seen the light of day are starting to emerge from the ice-covered tundra. The last decade has not warmed Baffin Island to the point where it is
(20)   habitable for any but the hardiest souls—but it has definitely warmed it.

Consider each of the choices separately and select all that apply.

9. Which of the following statements about the climate on Baffin Island is supported by the passage?

    A The climate is intolerable for all but the toughest of animals and humans.

    B Recent changes in the climate have led to changes in local topography.

    C It is rare for temperatures at the island's center to climb above freezing.

For questions 10 through 12, select one answer choice each.

---

10. In the first sentence of paragraph two ("Geologically speaking … Labrador"), the author implies that

    (A) Baffin Island is huge, but it is dwarfed by its surroundings

    (B) at one time, Baffin Island was joined to the Canadian mainland

    (C) glaciers separate Baffin Island from the mainland of Canada

    (D) a single glacier helped to carve out Baffin Island and Labrador

    (E) Baffin Island is physically similar to some parts of northern Michigan

11. From the passage, it can be inferred that descriptions of changes on Baffin Island are mostly the product of

(A) scientific study

(B) satellite surveillance

(C) journalists' reports

(D) anecdotal observation

(E) pioneer narratives

12. Which of the following evidence would most strengthen the author's argument that things are changing on Baffin Island?

(A) Archaeological proof that the Vikings visited natives on Baffin Island

(B) Increased immigration from the provinces to Baffin's major city, Iqaluit

(C) Growth of warm-water lake algae in formerly frozen Baffin lakes

(D) Pods of belugas feeding off the coast of Baffin Island

(E) Continuous sunlight from May to July in the northeast part of the island

Question 13 is based on this passage.

Gettysburg saw the highest number of casualties of any battle in the Civil War, but the lesser-known Battle of Chickamauga followed close behind. The Army of the Cumberland met the Confederate Army of Tennessee at West Chickamauga Creek
Line in Georgia. The Union goal had been to capture Chattanooga, Tennessee, which it
(5) had essentially done by the time of the battle. The Confederate goal was to protect the city and prevent the Union army from proceeding further south. In three days of sustained fighting, the Union Army lost 16,000 troops and the Confederate Army lost 18,000. The Confederates claimed a win, as they forced the Union troops back northward, but since the Union Army retained its positions in Tennessee,
(10) Chickamauga was essentially a draw.

Consider each of the choices separately and select all that apply.

13. Which of these facts about Chickamauga best support the author's suggestion that the battle was not a Confederate victory?

[A] The battle resulted in more Confederate casualties than Union casualties.

[B] The Confederate Army did not allow Union soldiers to cross further into Georgia.

[C] The Union Army was able to hold on to land it had seized north of Chickamauga.

For questions 14 through 17, complete the text by picking the best entry for each blank from the corresponding column of choices.

14. The Midway Plaisance is a long strip of parkland along the southern boundary of the University of Chicago, _____ Washington Park on the west to Jackson Park on the east.

Ⓐ	linking
Ⓑ	separating
Ⓒ	integrating
Ⓓ	moving
Ⓔ	forming

15. One modern _____ of the Book of Job took place as scholars, inspired by the suffering of refugees around the world, argued that Job's submission is really an excuse for authoritarianism.

Ⓐ	polemic
Ⓑ	unorthodoxy
Ⓒ	altercation
Ⓓ	exegesis
Ⓔ	abatement

16. *Time* magazine once called dictator Idi Amin "a strutting (i) _____," which makes him seem more a figure of fun than the dangerous leader who annihilated his enemies and (ii) _____ the Ugandan economy.

Blank (i)		Blank (ii)	
Ⓐ	martinet	Ⓓ	decimated
Ⓑ	pariah	Ⓔ	machinated
Ⓒ	slaughterer	Ⓕ	impugned

17. You can easily tell a damselfly from a dragonfly (i) _____; the former has similar-sized upper and lower wings that fold easily together when at rest, (ii) _____ the latter has larger lower wings and holds its wings outstretched.

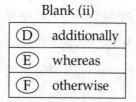

Blank (i)	Blank (ii)
(A) single-handedly	(D) additionally
(B) at a distance	(E) whereas
(C) by a long shot	(F) otherwise

Questions 18 through 20 are based on this passage.

Is there intelligent life elsewhere in the Milky Way? The odds seem to favor a positive response, but scientists like numbers and proofs. For that reason, radio astronomer Frank Drake created a formula that has become fundamental for many in the field of
Line SETI—the search for extraterrestrial intelligence.
(5)   The 1961 Drake equation begins with N = the number of intelligent civilizations, defined as those with whom we might communicate. It finds N by multiplying the rate of star formation in our galaxy, which Drake calculated as 10 per year, by the fraction of stars with planets, about one-half. That in turn is multiplied by the number of planets per star that might be capable of sustaining life, which
(10) Drake figured as two, and by the fraction of those planets that will develop life, which he considered to be 100%. Finally, that is multiplied by the percentage of those life-bearing planets that might develop intelligent life, the percentage of that life that might be able to communicate, and the length of time during which such life might send communications into space. Drake's figures, being 50 years old, have since been
(15) superseded by more accurate predictions.

> **For questions 18 through 20, select one answer choice each.**

18. Which of these premises did Drake NOT include in his calculations?

    (A) Not every life-form can communicate.

    (B) The time during which communication might occur is finite.

    (C) Not every planet is capable of sustaining life.

    (D) Not every planet is orbited by satellites.

    (E) Not every star is orbited by planets.

19. In the last sentence of the passage, the author probably mentions the age of Drake's equation to

    (A) show how long a single hypothesis may prove valid and useful

    (B) indicate that some variables within the hypothesis have changed

    (C) suggest that intelligent life should have been found by now

    (D) provide a timeline to use when calculating the odds of intelligent life

    (E) surprise the reader with the unexpected age of a forward-looking model

20. NASA now calculates that the rate of star formation in our galaxy is closer to seven per year than to Drake's original calculation. If that were the only change, how would it affect Drake's equation?

    (A) The fraction of stars with planets would decline about 30 percent.

    (B) The number of planets per star capable of housing life would decline.

    (C) The number of intelligent civilizations would decline by 30 percent.

    (D) The number of planets per star capable of housing life would increase.

    (E) The number of intelligent civilizations would increase by 70 percent.

For questions 21 through 25, select two answer choices that (1) complete the sentence in a way that makes sense and (2) produce sentences that are similar in meaning.

---

21. Luging, a sport in which you lie faceup and feetfirst on a tiny sled, is _____ dangerous; a Georgian athlete died in 2008 while preparing for Olympic competition.

    [A] extremely

    [B] plainly

    [C] tragically

    [D] frequently

    [E] obviously

    [F] surprisingly

22. Whether newspapers survive as a medium is largely _____ on how well they adapt to the age of social media and instant news.

  [A] fixed

  [B] contingent

  [C] dependent

  [D] amassed

  [E] colluded

  [F] intent

23. Like many artists who _____ Islam in midlife, the jazz drummer and bandleader Art Blakey took an Arabic name, in his case Abdullah Ibn Buhaina.

  [A] espoused

  [B] converted

  [C] resumed

  [D] initiated

  [E] embraced

  [F] renounced

24. Marsupials, from the kangaroo to the opossum, are characterized by the pouch in which the mother _____ her young throughout their infancy.

  [A] clasps

  [B] nourishes

  [C] transports

  [D] suspends

  [E] surrounds

  [F] conveys

25. Brazil produces one-third of the world's sugarcane, a perennial grass with thick, _____ stalks that contain raw sugar crystals.

   A   rigid

   B   stringy

   C   jointed

   D   hardy

   E   succulent

   F   fibrous

STOP.   **This is the end of Section 3. Use any remaining time to check your work.**

SECTION 4
Verbal Reasoning
Time: 35 minutes
25 questions

For questions 1 through 4, select two answer choices that (1) complete the sentence in a way that makes sense and (2) produce sentences that are similar in meaning.

---

1. Umbriel and Ariel are two moons of Uranus, first _____ on the same day, October 24, 1851, by the renowned British astronomer William Lassell.

    A   upheld

    B   classified

    C   christened

    D   espied

    E   observed

    F   asserted

2. Before running for president on the Democratic ticket, Woodrow Wilson had been governor of New Jersey as well as a leading _____ and university president.

    A   academic

    B   cleric

    C   supervisor

    D   disciplinarian

    E   entrepreneur

    F   scholar

3. When a sentence is deferred and probation is not violated, a judge may decide to throw out the original guilty plea and sentence, thus _____ the crime from the defendant's record.

   [A] detaching

   [B] absolving

   [C] removing

   [D] censuring

   [E] expunging

   [F] atoning

4. The earliest known pharmacological compilation was the *Sushruta Samhita*, which listed a variety of medicinal plants and minerals along with their _____ properties.

   [A] therapeutic

   [B] detrimental

   [C] curative

   [D] noteworthy

   [E] ministerial

   [F] communal

Questions 5 and 6 are based on this passage.

A cable ferry, sometimes called a floating bridge, is a simple means of crossing a fast-flowing or shallow river. As the name suggests, the transport itself is propelled using cables that are secured at either side of the river. The simplest type is hand operated—a crank system or pulley guides the craft across. Some cable ferries are motorized, but others simply use the power of the current to propel the craft. The ferries may carry up to half a dozen cars, or they may be for foot traffic only, depending on their size. In most cases, the cables are visible, but some ferries have underwater cables.

Line
(5)

5. Underline the sentence that suggests another designation for the form of transportation discussed in the passage.

Select one answer choice.

6. From the information give, it can be concluded that cable ferries are

   (A) tethered to shore

   (B) enclosed

   (C) inefficient

   (D) preprogrammed

   (E) safe

Question 7 is based on this passage.

Line
(5)

The Washington Bullets changed their admittedly insensitive name to the Wizards. The Marquette University Warriors are now the Golden Eagles. Yet some teams retain their names and mascots despite criticism. The worst offenders are those involving Native American symbols. The Cleveland Indians are still the Indians, the Washington Redskins have kept their disrespectful name, and fans of the Atlanta Braves still do the offensive "tomahawk chop" to spur their team to victory. It appears that tradition trumps consideration when it comes to our nation's sports.

Select one answer choice.

7. The author's choice of words indicates a belief that the teams mentioned in the second-to-last sentence are

   (A) innocent

   (B) incompatible

   (C) inconsistent

   (D) powerful

   (E) inconsiderate

> **Questions 8 and 9 are based on this passage.**

It's hard to imagine who first looked at a pineapple and decided it looked edible. The fruit is hidden inside a tough, waxy rind and protected by sharp, needle-tipped leaves. When unripe, the fruit is quite toxic, and even when ripe, the cores can cause

Line   damage to the digestive tract. Pineapple juice is acidic enough to be used in cleaning
(5)   metal, and it contains enough anticoagulants that hemophiliacs should avoid consuming it. Despite all this, the pineapple trade is enormous, with major fruit-producing areas including Hawaii, Brazil, Malaysia, Taiwan, Mexico, the Philippines, Thailand, Costa Rica, South Africa, and Puerto Rico; and pineapples are considered a delicacy in many places. There are dozens of varieties, some better for canning and
(10)   others sold fresh or as juice, either processed or fresh-squeezed.

Consider each of the choices separately and select all that apply.

8. Which of the following inferences can be made from the information given in the passage?

   [A] The best pineapple-growing regions are in the tropical or subtropical zones.

   [B] Because of its acidity, pineapple juice must be processed before drinking.

   [C] People with certain blood disorders might do well to avoid pineapples.

Select one answer choice.

9. In the passage, the author is primarily concerned with

   (A) contrasting one fruit's unpleasant qualities with its popular status

   (B) explaining why a certain popular fruit should be eaten with care

   (C) making a point about toxic foods and their attractiveness to humans

   (D) comparing tropical fruits in terms of sales and cultivation sites

   (E) expressing an opinion about the paradoxical reputation of one tropical fruit

For questions 10 through 13, complete the text by picking the best entry for each blank from the corresponding column of choices.

10. Mammals diversified and rose to prominence only after the land-dwelling dinosaurs _____, opening up a variety of niches for other species.

Ⓐ	took over
Ⓑ	thrived
Ⓒ	arrived
Ⓓ	died out
Ⓔ	disembarked

11. The large number of inscribed, commemorative markers, or *stelae*, surviving from ancient Egypt and Mesoamerica provide some of the most _____ information available on those civilizations.

Ⓐ	stockpiled
Ⓑ	comprehensive
Ⓒ	intuitive
Ⓓ	deliberate
Ⓔ	indeterminate

12. His 1946 book *Baby and Child Care* remains one of the biggest best sellers (i) _____, but Dr. Benjamin Spock was more than a pediatrician and author. He was a (ii) _____ antiwar crusader, an outspoken (iii) _____ of nuclear proliferation, and an activist in the Committee for a Sane Nuclear Policy.

Blank (i)		Blank (ii)		Blank (iii)	
Ⓐ	in his day	Ⓓ	potential	Ⓖ	student
Ⓑ	of all time	Ⓔ	chronic	Ⓗ	critic
Ⓒ	forevermore	Ⓕ	dedicated	Ⓘ	member

13. It was theater manager Richard D'Oyly Carte who first (i) _____ a short comic opera from W. S. Gilbert and Arthur Sullivan, and when a later collaboration (ii) _____ beyond his wildest dreams, D'Oyly Carte initiated a (iii) _____ with the talented duo that brought fame and fortune to them all.

Blank (i)	Blank (ii)	Blank (iii)
(A) composed	(D) resounded	(G) composition
(B) attended	(E) succeeded	(H) songbook
(C) commissioned	(F) embellished	(I) partnership

Questions 14 through 16 are based on this passage.

As parks close due to budget constraints, many hearken back to the glory days of the Civilian Conservation Corps (CCC), a New Deal agency born of the Great Depression. This work corps for the unemployed quickly moved able-bodied
Line enrollees from induction sites to work camps all over the country. Federal agencies
(5) worked in tandem, with the Labor Department handling applications and the Departments of Agriculture and the Interior developing the work plans. By 1935, there were half a million men (and a few women, briefly) at work in 2,600 camps. They reforested land, extended roads, erected fire towers, built campgrounds, worked on soil-erosion and flood-control programs, and improved parklands all over
(10) the United States. Until the advent of war, when its funding was diverted to defense, this peacetime army was one of the most successful of all government programs.

Consider each of the choices separately and select all that apply.

14. Which of the following statements about the CCC is supported by the passage?

[A] The Civilian Conservation Corps's success relied on interagency cooperation.

[B] Among their many successes, CCC members served as smoke jumpers.

[C] World War II would see the dissolution of the Civilian Conservation Corps.

Select one answer choice.

15. The passage suggests that diversion of funding at the beginning of the war led to the end of the CCC, but another likely reason may have been

    Ⓐ   the conversion of state and national parks to staging grounds for war

    Ⓑ   Roosevelt's untimely death and the loss of critical support

    Ⓒ   scandals leading to indictments in the Department of the Interior

    Ⓓ   a steady reduction in the need for new infrastructure

    Ⓔ   increased employment opportunities for able-bodied young men

16. Underline the sentence that connects the topic of the passage to present-day events.

For questions 17 through 20, complete the text by picking the best entry for each blank from the corresponding column of choices.

---

17. The river Thames flows through London, of course, but it also _____ other important towns, including Oxford and Windsor.

Ⓐ	bypasses
Ⓑ	circumvents
Ⓒ	corrals
Ⓓ	barricades
Ⓔ	traverses

18. Daniel Webster twice firmly (i) _____ the vice presidential side of the Whig Party ticket; in both cases, he may have regretted his (ii) _____, for both presidents died in office.

Blank (i)		Blank (ii)	
Ⓐ	offered	Ⓓ	office
Ⓑ	received	Ⓔ	decision
Ⓒ	declined	Ⓕ	hesitation

19. The (i) _____ culture of a four-year college may seem (ii) _____ to young, rural students whose towns often house fewer people than a single campus lecture hall does and whose world view may be limited by geography.

Blank (i)	Blank (ii)
(A) intrinsic	(D) daunting
(B) rarefied	(E) multifarious
(C) amicable	(F) torpid

20. If there is any effect of Hurricane Maria that may be considered (i) _____, it is the fact that Puerto Rico's power grid must now be entirely (ii) _____ rather than simply patched.

Blank (i)	Blank (ii)
(A) salutary	(D) assuaged
(B) cataclysmic	(E) bifurcated
(C) anomalous	(F) reconstituted

Question 21 is based on this passage.

There aren't many professional coopers left; it's practically an extinct profession. There was a time when every town and village had a cooper. He used wood and metal to bang out containers. A dry cooper would make barrels to hold dry goods such as tobacco or cereal. A drytight cooper made watertight casks that might hold flour or gunpowder. A wet cooper made containers that could withstand pressure and hold liquids like vinegar or beer. A white cooper concentrated on washtubs, butter churns, and buckets of all sizes. These days, coopers exist primarily to accommodate the wine industry; certain fine wines and cognacs are still aged in oak barrels, most made by machine, not by hand.

Line (5)

Select one answer choice.

21. Based on the information in the passage, it can be inferred that in modern times, the most common cooper is

(A) a dry cooper

(B) a drytight cooper

(C) a wet cooper

(D) either a dry or a drytight cooper

(E) either a wet or a white cooper

Question 22 is based on this passage.

The small herbivorous mammal known as the hyrax is something of a mystery, for it mixes complexity with extremely primitive characteristics. For example, although it is warm-blooded, it has very poor temperature regulation. For warmth, hyraxes often bask in the sun or huddle in groups. The male hyrax's testes do not descend, and the foot of the hyrax resembles that of an elephant rather than another small mammal's. The hyrax looks at first glance like a guinea pig, but its complex stomach is more like that of a camel or a deer. In summary, the hyrax is unlike any animal on earth; it is unique enough to have its own taxonomic order.

Line
(5)

Consider each of the choices separately and select all that apply.

22. Which of the following characteristics are used to support the author's contention that the hyrax is in some ways quite primitive?

   [A] Its temperature regulation

   [B] Its testes

   [C] Its stomach

Questions 23 through 25 are based on this passage.

Josiah Bushnell Grinnell, the founder of Grinnell College, was a Republican member of Congress from Iowa in 1866 when he was assaulted in the House by a fellow congressman, Unconditional Unionist Lovell Harrison Rousseau of Kentucky. Grinnell had committed the unpardonable sin of challenging Rousseau's Civil War record, accusing him of "blowing his own horn." Speaker of the House Schuyler Colfax had chastised Grinnell at the time, but that was not enough for Rousseau. With armed supporters beside him, Rousseau beat Grinnell with an iron-tipped cane, bruising and battering him. A special committee called for both men to be reprimanded, but in the end, charges against Grinnell were dropped. Rousseau resigned after his reprimand, but—remarkable even by House standards—he was then reappointed to fill the seat he had left. By March of 1867, both men had retired from the House to pursue other interests. Grinnell went off to run the Rock Island Railroad, and Rousseau served in Alaska as a brigadier general.

Line
(5)

(10)

Consider each of the choices separately and select all that apply.

23. On which of the following facts does the author express a sardonic opinion or viewpoint?

    [A] Grinnell challenged Rousseau's war record.

    [B] Rousseau beat Grinnell with his iron-tipped cane.

    [C] Rousseau was reappointed after he resigned.

Select one answer choice.

24. The author probably includes details about Grinnell College and the Rock Island Railroad to

    (A) give the reader a better sense of the time and place in which the incident occurred

    (B) suggest that Grinnell should not be remembered merely for this one incident

    (C) compare and contrast the postcongressional lives of Grinnell and Rousseau

    (D) help the reader better understand the motivation behind Grinnell's actions

    (E) demonstrate the wide-ranging interests of elected officials in Congress in the 1860s

25. Underline the sentence that alludes to the original incentive for the attack in the House chambers.

STOP.   This is the end of Section 4. Use any remaining time to check your work.

SECTION 5
Quantitative Reasoning
Time: 40 minutes
25 questions

Each of questions 1 through 9 consists of two quantities, Quantity A and Quantity B. You are to compare the two quantities. You may use additional information centered above the two quantities if additional information is given. Choose

Ⓐ if Quantity A is greater;

Ⓑ if Quantity B is greater;

Ⓒ if the two quantities are equal;

Ⓓ if the relationship cannot be determined from the information given.

	Quantity A	Quantity B	
1.	$\dfrac{\left(\frac{3}{5}\right)\left(\frac{3}{4}\right)}{\left(\frac{2}{5}\right)\left(\frac{1}{4}\right)}$	$\dfrac{\left(\frac{1}{3}\right)\left(\frac{5}{6}\right)}{\left(\frac{2}{3}\right)\left(\frac{1}{6}\right)}$	Ⓐ Ⓑ Ⓒ Ⓓ

$$2x - y = 5$$
$$4x = 10 + 2y$$

	Quantity A	Quantity B	
2.	x	5	Ⓐ Ⓑ Ⓒ Ⓓ

A group of 20 students has average age 18. A disjoint group of 16 students has average age 20.

	Quantity A	Quantity B	
3.	The average age of the 36 students in the two groups combined	19	Ⓐ Ⓑ Ⓒ Ⓓ

The greatest common divisor of N and 500 is 20.

Quantity A	Quantity B	
4. The greatest common divisor of N and 100	The greatest common divisor of N and 2,500	Ⓐ Ⓑ Ⓒ Ⓓ

Line L has equation $3x + 2y = 7$; line M has equation $y - 5x - 4 = 0$

Quantity A	Quantity B	
5. the y-intercept of line L	the y-intercept of line M	Ⓐ Ⓑ Ⓒ Ⓓ

Quantity A	Quantity B	
6. the volume of a box with length 14, width 8, and height 5	the volume of a box with length 7, width 8, and height 10.	Ⓐ Ⓑ Ⓒ Ⓓ

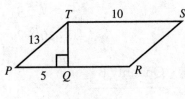

$PQ = 5$

Quantity A	Quantity B	
7. the area of parallelogram PRST	120	Ⓐ Ⓑ Ⓒ Ⓓ

$$10 - 3x = -2x - 5$$

	Quantity A	Quantity B	
8.	x	3	Ⓐ Ⓑ Ⓒ Ⓓ

	Quantity A	Quantity B	
9.	$\left(\dfrac{x^2}{x^5}\right)^4$	x^{12}	Ⓐ Ⓑ Ⓒ Ⓓ

Questions 10 through 25 have different formats. Select a single answer choice unless the directions say otherwise. For numeric-entry questions, follow these instructions:

- Enter your answer in the box or boxes provided.
- Your answer may be an integer, a decimal, a fraction, or a negative number.
- If the answer is a fraction, you will be given two boxes: an upper one for the numerator and a lower one for the denominator.
- Equivalent forms of the correct answer, such as 1.6 and 1.60, are all correct. You do not need to reduce fractions to lowest terms.

---

10. Formula X is 500,000 times as concentrated as formula Y. Formula Y is 80,000 times as concentrated as formula Z. How many times as concentrated as formula Z is formula X?

    Ⓐ 4×10^6

    Ⓑ 4×10^7

    Ⓒ 4×10^8

    Ⓓ 4×10^9

    Ⓔ 4×10^{10}

11. If $4:5 = 6:x$, what is x?

(A) 7

(B) 7.5

(C) 8

(D) 8.5

(E) 10

12. At the start of an insect study, 40% of the flies have red eyes, and the rest have white eyes. By the end of the study, the number of flies with red eyes has tripled, and the number of white-eyed flies has increased by 220%. If there are 2,184 flies at the end of the study, how many have red eyes?

(A) 840

(B) 1,040

(C) 1,144

(D) 1,310

(E) 1,365

13. From 8 a.m. to 5 p.m., Lee makes $15 per hour. From 7 p.m. to 10 p.m., Lee makes $25 per hour. How much does Lee make in 5 days?

(A) $1,050

(B) $1,125

(C) $1,200

(D) $1,250

(E) $1,375

For this question, write your answer in the box.

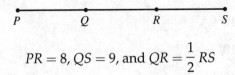

$$PR = 8, QS = 9, \text{ and } QR = \frac{1}{2}RS$$

14. $PS =$

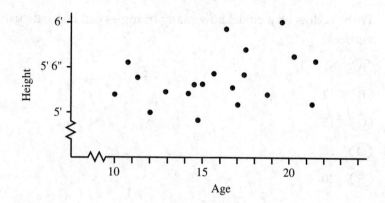

15. This scatter plot compares the ages and heights of 20 randomly selected people. What percentage of these people are under 5 feet 6 inches tall and between 14 and 20 years old?

   (A)   10%

   (B)   25%

   (C)   30%

   (D)   45%

   (E)   50%

For this question, indicate all of the answer choices that apply.

16. If $x \neq 0$, which of the following must be true?

   A $\dfrac{1}{x} < x$

   B $-x < x$

   C $x^3 < x^5$

   D $x < x^2 + 2$

   E $-|x| < |x|$

For this question, indicate all of the answer choices that apply.

17. Which <u>two</u> of the following numbers have a quotient that is greater than 3?

   A   −8

   B   −4

   C   −2

   D   4

   E   8

18. With six dots on a circle, how many triangles can be made using these points as vertices?

(A) 6

(B) 12

(C) 15

(D) 18

(E) 20

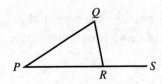

$$PQ = QR = PR$$

19. What is the measure of $\angle QRS$?

(A) 45°

(B) 60°

(C) 90°

(D) 110°

(E) 120°

20. If $n = pr^2$, and p and r are distinct prime numbers, how many factors does n have?

(A) 2

(B) 3

(C) 4

(D) 5

(E) 6

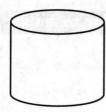

21. This cylinder has a volume of V. What is the volume of a cylinder that is twice as wide and three times as tall?

    Ⓐ 5V

    Ⓑ 6V

    Ⓒ 8V

    Ⓓ 12V

    Ⓔ 18V

22. What is the distance from the point (3, 1) to the point (6, 5)?

    Ⓐ 3

    Ⓑ 4

    Ⓒ 5

    Ⓓ 6

    Ⓔ 7

Use the following figure to answer questions 23 through 25.

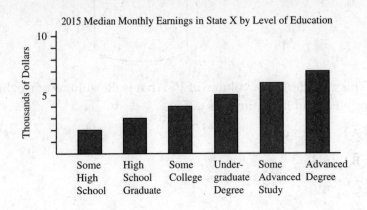

2015 Median Monthly Earnings in State X by Level of Education

For this question, write your answer in the box.

23. What was the median annual income in state X in 2015 for people with an advanced degree?

$ [   ]

24. Suppose that, in state X, a high school graduate earning the median income rate in 2015 spends $120,000 in earning a college degree and then gets a new job at the median rate for college graduates. How many years will it take for the difference in these two salaries to cover the college expenses? Please ignore interest and taxes, and assume that income levels remain fixed at 2015 levels.

    Ⓐ 5 years

    Ⓑ 8 years

    Ⓒ 10 years

    Ⓓ 20 years

    Ⓔ 60 years

25. How much more, as a percent, is the median income of a person with an advance degree compared to a person with an undergraduate degree (but no advanced study) in state X in 2015? Round your answer to the nearest multiple of 10 percent.

    (A) 10%

    (B) 20%

    (C) 30%

    (D) 40%

    (E) 50%

STOP. This is the end of Section 5. Use any remaining time to check your work.

SECTION 6
Quantitative Reasoning
Time: 40 minutes
25 questions

Each of questions 1 through 9 consists of two quantities, Quantity A and Quantity B. You are to compare the two quantities. You may use additional information centered above the two quantities if additional information is given. Choose

(A) if Quantity A is greater;
(B) if Quantity B is greater;
(C) if the two quantities are equal;
(D) if the relationship cannot be determined from the information given.

Quantity A	Quantity B	

1. $\dfrac{1}{1+\dfrac{1}{1+\dfrac{1}{3}}}$ $\qquad$ $\dfrac{1}{1+\dfrac{1}{1+\dfrac{1}{2}}}$ $\qquad$ (A) (B) (C) (D)

Quantity A	Quantity B	

2. 5^{-2} $\qquad$ 10^{-1} $\qquad$ (A) (B) (C) (D)

$$2x + y = 30$$

Quantity A	Quantity B	

3. $x + y$ $\qquad$ $x - y$ $\qquad$ (A) (B) (C) (D)

$$3 < x < 6$$

Quantity A	Quantity B		

4. $\dfrac{x+5}{x-2}$ $\dfrac{x+9}{x-1}$ Ⓐ   Ⓑ   Ⓒ   Ⓓ

Quantity A	Quantity B		

5. x^2 2^x Ⓐ   Ⓑ   Ⓒ   Ⓓ

$$xy < 0$$

Quantity A	Quantity B		

6. $x^2 + y^2$ $(x+y)^2$ Ⓐ   Ⓑ   Ⓒ   Ⓓ

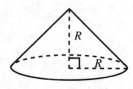 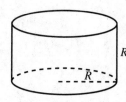 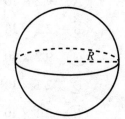

Quantity A	Quantity B		

7. the combined volumes of a cone and a cylinder, each with base radius R and height R the volume of a sphere with radius R Ⓐ   Ⓑ   Ⓒ   Ⓓ

Quantity A	Quantity B		

8. the circumference of a circle with diameter D the perimeter of an equilateral triangle with side D Ⓐ   Ⓑ   Ⓒ   Ⓓ

Quantity A	Quantity B

9. x^2 $\sqrt{x}$ Ⓐ Ⓑ Ⓒ Ⓓ

Questions 10 through 25 have different formats. Select a single answer choice unless the directions say otherwise. For numeric-entry questions, follow these instructions:

- Enter your answer in the box or boxes provided.
- Your answer may be an integer, a decimal, a fraction, or a negative number.
- If the answer is a fraction, you will be given two boxes: an upper one for the numerator and a lower one for the denominator.
- Equivalent forms of the correct answer, such as 1.6 and 1.60, are all correct. You do not need to reduce fractions to lowest terms.

10.   What is the product of 4.2×10^7 and 5×10^8, written in scientific notation?

Ⓐ 9.2×10^7

Ⓑ 2.1×10^8

Ⓒ 9.2×10^8

Ⓓ 2.1×10^{15}

Ⓔ 2.1×10^{16}

For this question, indicate all of the answer choices that apply.

11.   Suppose you have two coupons for a certain store. One gives you 20% off any purchase; the other gives you $20 off any purchase of $60 or more. For which of the following purchase amounts (at that store) would you save more money with the 20% off coupon than with the $20 off coupon?

    Ⓐ $50

    Ⓑ $60

    Ⓒ $80

    Ⓓ $100

    Ⓔ $120

For this question, write your answer in the box.

12. Of the $3.2 billion earned by company X last year, $720 million came from division D. A pie chart is made to represent the breakdown of the earnings at company X by division. How many degrees is the sector of the pie chart representing division D?

13. How many numbers between 1 and 1,000 are either a multiple of 28 or a multiple of 32 (or both)?

   (A) 60

   (B) 62

   (C) 64

   (D) 66

   (E) 68

For this question, write your answer in the box.

14. $x^2 - 3x - 10 = 0$ and $4x + 3 > 15$. Find x.

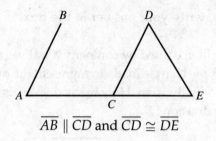

$\overline{AB} \parallel \overline{CD}$ and $\overline{CD} \cong \overline{DE}$

15. If $\angle BAC = 48°$, what is the measure of $\angle CDE$?

   (A) 36°

   (B) 42°

   (C) 48°

   (D) 84°

   (E) 132°

16. A bag of grass seed covers 10,000 square feet of lawn. How many bags will be needed to cover a rectangular field that measures 250 feet by 150 feet?

   (A) 2

   (B) 3

   (C) 4

   (D) 5

   (E) 6

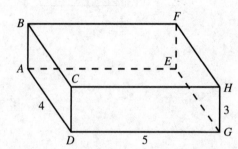

17. What is the distance from point A to point H through the interior of this box?

   (A) $5\sqrt{2}$

   (B) $\sqrt{41}$

   (C) $4 + \sqrt{34}$

   (D) 10

   (E) 12

For this question, indicate all of the answer choices that apply.

18. Which of the following would take less than three hours?

    A driving 200 miles at 65 mph

    B driving 140 miles at 45 mph

    C driving 250 miles at 85 mph

    D driving 100 miles at 35 mph

    E driving 400 miles at 75 mph

Use the following figure to answer questions 19 and 20.

Changes in Spending in State X, by Category

	1990–1995	1995–2000	2000–2005	2005–2010
Education	+8%	+9%	+1%	–3%
Transportation	+2%	+5%	–3%	–5%
Police	+3%	+4%	+0%	–2%
Health	+5%	+8%	+7%	+9%
Other	+2%	+7%	–10%	–8%

19. If $870 million was spent on transportation in 1995, how much was spent on transportation in 2005 (rounded to the nearest million)?

    (A) $853 million

    (B) $886 million

    (C) $887 million

    (D) $889 million

    (E) $913 million

20. What was the total change in health spending from 1990 to 2010, as a percentage (rounded to the nearest tenth)?

    (A) 29.0%

    (B) 29.2%

    (C) 30.7%

    (D) 31.5%

    (E) 32.3%

21. What is the probability that a whole number chosen randomly from the numbers 1 through 20 (inclusive) will be prime?

    (A) 40%

    (B) 45%

    (C) 50%

    (D) 55%

    (E) 60%

For this question, write your answer in the box.

22. The numbers 4, x, 5, 4, x, 9, 7, and 5 have a mean of 6. Find x.

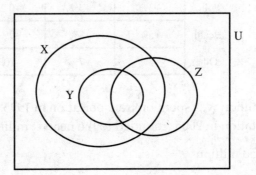

23. Which of the following is not true for the above Euler diagram?

    (A) Some Z are X.

    (B) All Y are X.

    (C) Some X are Z.

    (D) All Z are Y.

    (E) Some Y are Z.

For this question, indicate all of the answer choices that apply.

24. Which of the following equations are equivalent to $x^2 + 1 = 2x$?

    $\boxed{A}$ $x^2 + 2x + 1 = 0$

    $\boxed{B}$ $(x - 1)^3 = 0$

    $\boxed{C}$ $x + 1 = 2$

    $\boxed{D}$ $0 = 0$

    $\boxed{E}$ $x^2 = 1$

25. When company X ships a dozen eggs, there is a 3% chance that exactly one egg will be broken, a 0.5% chance that the whole dozen will be broken, but no chance that any other number of eggs will be broken. If 1,000 dozen eggs are ordered from company X, how many broken eggs should be expected?

    Ⓐ 8

    Ⓑ 35

    Ⓒ 80

    Ⓓ 90

    Ⓔ 630

STOP.   This is the end of Section 6. Use any remaining time to check your work.

GRE Practice Test 5:
Answers and Explanations

Analytical Writing: Scoring and Sample Responses

Analyze an Issue: Scoring

Score	Focus	Organization	Conventions
0	Does not address the prompt. Off topic.	Incomprehensible. May merely copy the prompt without development.	Illegible. Nonverbal. Serious errors make the paper unreadable. May be in a foreign language.
1	Mostly irrelevant to the prompt.	Little or no development of ideas. No evidence of analysis or organization.	Pervasive errors in grammar, mechanics, and spelling.
2	Unclear connection to the prompt.	Unfocused and disorganized.	Frequent errors in sentence structure, mechanics, and spelling.
3	Limited connection to the prompt.	Rough organization with weak examples or reasons.	Occasional major errors and frequent minor errors in conventions of written English.
4	Competent connection to the prompt.	Relevant examples or reasons develop a logical position.	Occasional minor errors in conventions of written English.
5	Clear, focused connection to the prompt.	Thoughtful, appropriate examples or reasons develop a consistent, coherent position. Connectors are ably used to mark transitions.	Very few errors. Sentence structure is varied and vocabulary is advanced.
6	Insightful, clever connection to the prompt.	Compelling, convincing examples or reasons develop a consistent, coherent position. The argument flows effortlessly and persuasively.	Very few errors. Sentence structure is varied and vocabulary is precise, well chosen, and effective.

Analyze an Issue:
Sample Response with a Score of 6

In this essay, the writer recognizes the reason for the claim given in the prompt but refutes it with specific examples, even coming up with a perhaps more appropriate analogy. The essay contains no significant errors in grammar or mechanics.

The suggestion has been made that television is a democratic medium because its content is controlled by the will of the people. Although this is a supposition that probably makes television executives sleep well at night, it is flawed. I believe television is less a democracy than it is a federal republic.

Power in the world of television is centralized, with subdivisions of that power granted to franchises, or affiliates. The central powers that be dictate the programming to the affiliates, and only recently have certain affiliates gained the power to fight back or to insert their own programming when they disagree with the networks' plan.

The notion that television is democratic is based on the fact that programming is determined by Nielsen ratings, in which people are polled on their likes and dislikes. However, since Nielsen ratings do not entail the vote of every single household, or even every single household with a television, how are they democratic? We do not vote for someone to represent our tastes in a Nielsen rating. The raters are themselves chosen, perhaps at random but perhaps not, by the company doing the polling. It is also obvious to anyone that certain elements of the television-watching population have a greater pull than others. Since television depends on advertising sales, people who consume certain products have more of a vote in programming than people who do not.

So the centralized powers in the television world use a biased rating system to determine programming for the affiliates, who then pass this on to the masses. An affiliate gets a certain amount of airtime in which to place local advertising that presumably appeals more directly to its viewers, but most of the advertising is national, supporting my contention that television is a federal republic. As citizens, our only real power is the power to turn the TV off.

Analyze an Argument: Scoring

Score	Focus	Organization	Conventions
0	Does not address the prompt. Off topic.	Incomprehensible. May merely copy the prompt without development.	Illegible. Nonverbal. Serious errors make the paper unreadable. May be in a foreign language.
1	Little or no analysis of the argument. May indicate misunderstanding of the prompt.	Little or no development of ideas. No evidence of analysis or organization.	Pervasive errors in grammar, mechanics, and spelling.
2	Little analysis; may instead present opinions and unrelated thoughts.	Disorganized and illogical.	Frequent errors in sentence structure, mechanics, and spelling.
3	Some analysis of the prompt, but some major flaws may be omitted.	Rough organization with irrelevant support or unclear transitions.	Occasional major errors and frequent minor errors in conventions of written English.
4	Important flaws in the argument are touched upon.	Ideas are sound but may not flow logically or clearly.	Occasional minor errors in conventions of written English.
5	Perceptive analysis of the major flaws in the argument.	Logical examples and support develop a consistent, coherent critique. Connectors are ably used to mark transitions.	Very few errors. Sentence structure is varied and vocabulary is advanced.
6	Insightful, clever analysis of the argument's flaws and fallacies.	Compelling, convincing examples and support develop a consistent, coherent critique. The analysis flows effortlessly and persuasively.	Very few errors. Sentence structure is varied and vocabulary is precise, well chosen, and effective.

Analyze an Argument:
Sample Response with a Score of 6

This essay is solid and well organized. The writer dissects the speaker's claims one by one and then suggests ways of making his argument stronger. There are practically no errors in English usage or mechanics.

Senator Diehard toes the party line in standing up for an expensive missile program, but as he does so, he manufactures a flood of fallacies with which to bamboozle his listeners.

"What price freedom?" cries the senator. Well, most of us would nod and agree that freedom is, in fact, priceless. However, that begs the question of whether the $10 billion spent so far on Triton is a reasonable price for freedom—or, more important, whether Triton represents freedom at all. The senator's emotional appeal is a red herring, pulling his listeners' attention away from the facts at hand.

The senator goes on to ask, "Would your tax dollars really be better spent propping up a variety of social programs than in defending our nation from the enemy abroad?" Here the senator presents his listeners with a false dilemma—you may have either social programs or defense but not both. There is absolutely nothing to indicate that if the Triton program were canceled today, its funding would switch over to support Medicare or housing in the inner cities. The only reason to present such a dichotomy is to sow confusion and fear.

The senator concludes with the suggestion that to stop the program now would be to throw $10 billion "down the drain." This is a very common argument from Washington and our state capital. However, just as two wrongs don't make a right, so throwing good money after bad doesn't correct a situation that is possibly wrongheaded to begin with.

Instead of appealing to fear and ridicule, the senator would do better to present what he sees as the positive values of the Triton Missile Program. What advances has the funding provided? What is the role of the program in our overall defense? Can costs be controlled and deadlines met? Standing up for his beloved program with facts and figures might prove more successful than covering up the program's faults with swaggering, fallacious obfuscation.

GRE Practice Test 5: Answer Key

Section 3. Verbal Reasoning

1. **A, C**
2. **B**
3. It may seem an anachronistic service in the twenty-first century, but in 2005, Camilla, the Duchess of Cornwall, requested and received a new coat of arms to denote her role as wife of the heir to the throne.
4. **D**
5. **D**
6. **E**
7. **C, D**
8. **B, E, G**
9. **A, B, C**
10. **E**
11. **D**
12. **C**
13. **A, C**
14. **A**
15. **D**
16. **A, D**
17. **B, E**
18. **D**
19. **B**
20. **C**
21. **B, E**
22. **B, C**
23. **A, E**
24. **C, F**
25. **B, F**

Section 4. Verbal Reasoning

1. **D, E**
2. **A, F**
3. **C, E**
4. **A, C**
5. A cable ferry, sometimes called a floating bridge, is a simple means of crossing a fast-flowing or shallow river.
6. **A**
7. **E**
8. **A, C**
9. **A**
10. **D**
11. **B**
12. **B, F, H**
13. **C, E, I**
14. **A, C**
15. **E**
16. As parks close due to budget constraints, many hearken back to the glory days of the Civilian Conservation Corps (CCC), a New Deal agency born of the Great Depression.
17. **E**
18. **C, E**
19. **B, D**
20. **A, F**
21. **C**
22. **A, B**
23. **A, C**
24. **B**
25. Grinnell had committed the unpardonable sin of challenging Rousseau's Civil War record, accusing him of "blowing his own horn."

Section 5. Quantitative Reasoning

1. **A**
2. **D**
3. **B**
4. **C**
5. **B**
6. **C**
7. **C**
8. **A**
9. **D**
10. **E**
11. **B**
12. **A**
13. **A**
14. **14**
15. **D**
16. **D, E**
17. **A, C**
18. **E**
19. **E**
20. **E**
21. **D**
22. **C**
23. **84,000**
24. **A**
25. **D**

Section 6. Quantitative Reasoning

1. **B**
2. **B**
3. **D**
4. **D**
5. **D**
6. **A**
7. **C**
8. **A**
9. **D**
10. **E**
11. **A, E**
12. **81**
13. **B**
14. **5**
15. **D**
16. **C**
17. **A**
18. **C, D**
19. **B**
20. **E**
21. **A**
22. **7**
23. **D**
24. **B, C**
25. **D**

GRE Practice Test 5: Answer Explanations

Section 3. Verbal Reasoning

1. **A, C.** The organization has to do with English and Welsh nobility, so either choice A or choice C might benefit from its services, but choice B would not.

2. **B.** The sentence describes the coat of arms belonging to the Duchess of Cornwall.

3. **It may seem an anachronistic service in the twenty-first century, but in 2005, Camilla, the Duchess of Cornwall, requested and received a new coat of arms to denote her role as wife of the heir to the throne.** The word "but" denotes contrast; the author is saying that although the service seems outdated, it clearly still is useful.

4. **D.** *Cachet* means "status" or "reputation"; the author is using it to suggest that the new, more easily obtained grand slam may not have the same prestige that the old one had.

5. **D.** The correct choice will make the two parts of the sentence parallel—Rio is not only the second-largest city in Brazil, it is the third-largest city in all of South America.

6. **E.** A pilot would not wish to relinquish (choice A), vary (choice C), or decrease (choice D) control of the vehicle; he or she would wish to maintain (choice E) control.

7. **C, D.** Torpedo boats were not discovered (choice E), but they were produced (choice D), marking a useful innovation (choice C).

8. **B, E, G.** Choosing correctly here may involve recognizing the correct use of prepositions in idiomatic phrases. A species may be "endemic to" an area (choice B), but we don't say it is "pervasive to" the area (choice A). Similarly, animals may "forage for" food (choice G), but they don't "pursue for" food (choice I).

9. **A, B, C.** Choice A is found at the end of paragraph three. Choice B appears at the beginning of paragraph three. Choice C appears toward the end of paragraph one.

10. **E.** Reread the entire sentence and compare it to the answer choices. The only choice that is supported by the sentence is choice E—Baffin Island is part of a geological shield that extends down into the northern United States, meaning that it shares physical traits with those northern states.

11. **D.** The information cited comes from hunters and trekkers, making it anecdotal rather than scientific.

12. **C.** The author mentions changes that indicate a warming trend, so your choice should support that supposition. Choices C and E are possibilities, but the continuous sunlight is typical of the Arctic and would not represent a change.

13. **A, C.** Choice B is the reason the Confederates *did* see this as a victory. The other two facts support the author's contention that it was not.

14. **A.** The preposition "to" helps you identify the correct choice as A rather than choice B (which would take the word *from*) or choice C (which would take the word *with*).

15. **D.** An exegesis (choice D) is a critical interpretation. The other words mean "argument" (choice A), "deviation" (choice B), "fight" (choice C), and "reduction" (choice E).

16. **A, D.** Amin was a strutting despot who destroyed the economy.

17. **B, E.** This is one of those fill-in-the-blank questions that will become clear as it is read aloud.

18. **D.** Drake incorporated "the percentage of that life that might be able to communicate" (choice A), "the length of time during which such life might send communications into space" (choice B), "the number of planets per star that might be capable of sustaining life" (choice C), and "the fraction of stars with planets" (choice E). He did not include the satellites surrounding planets (choice D), as that would presumably have no effect on intelligent life on planets.

19. **B.** The last sentence states: "Drake's figures, being 50 years old, have since been superseded by more accurate predictions." The author means that since the figures are old, some parts of them have been recalculated.

20. **C.** Drake suggested that 10 stars were formed each year; the real number is 30 percent fewer. Since Drake used that 10 as a factor in his formula, reducing it to 7 would reduce the final figure, number of intelligent civilizations, by 30 percent.

21. **B, E.** Since several of the choices make sense, look for the synonyms. Only choices B and E lead to sentences that share the same meaning.

22. **B, C.** Whether newspapers survive depends on how well they adapt; choices B and C supply that meaning.

23. **A, E.** Blakey took an Arabic name, suggesting that he took up Islam rather than renouncing it (choice F). The words that share that meaning are *espoused* (choice A) and *embraced* (choice E). You can convert to Islam, but you cannot convert Islam (choice B).

24. **C, F.** The mother carries her young in the pouch; she transports (choice C) or conveys (choice F) them.

25. **B, F.** Any of the choices might fit, but only *stringy* (choice B) and *fibrous* (choice F) are synonyms.

Section 4. Verbal Reasoning

1. **D, E.** *Classified* (choice B) and *christened* (choice C) do not mean the same thing, but *espied* (choice D) and *observed* (choice E) do.

2. **A, F.** Find the synonyms. Only choices A and F produce sentences that mean the same thing.

3. **C, E.** The crime is taken off the record; it is removed (choice C) or expunged (choice E).

4. **A, C.** The compendium told about the medicinal properties of plants and minerals; it makes sense that it should list their therapeutic (choice A) or curative (choice C) properties. *Ministerial* (choice E) does not mean "administered by a doctor"; it means "serving as a minister" or "characteristic of government."

5. **A cable ferry, sometimes called a floating bridge, is a simple means of crossing a fast-flowing or shallow river.** The "other designation" is "floating bridge."

6. **A.** Choice A is the only answer supported by information in the passage.

7. **E.** The author uses the words "disrespectful" and "offensive" to indicate that the teams are insulting or inconsiderate (choice E).

8. **A, C.** The countries listed in the passage are in the tropical or subtropical regions of the world, making choice A correct. The final sentence suggests that juice may be fresh-squeezed, making choice B untrue. The author writes that "hemophiliacs should avoid consuming it," meaning that choice C is correct.

9. **A.** The passage begins with a description of the pineapple's unpleasant characteristics but switches midstream to say that "despite all this," the pineapple is quite popular. Choice A is closest to the form and function of the passage as presented.

10. **D.** What did the dinosaurs do that opened a variety of niches for other species? They died out (choice D).

11. **B.** There are many stelae and therefore lots of information, so the best answer is choice B.

12. **B, F, H.** The book "remains" a best seller, so it is not limited to "his day" (choice A), but *forevermore* is excessive (choice C). The other choices should be clear if you read the sentences aloud.

13. **C, E, I.** D'Oyly Carte might have composed an opera for Gilbert and Sullivan or attended an opera by Gilbert and Sullivan, but the preposition "from" indicates that he commissioned the opera (choice C). The other choices should be clear from a close reading of the passage as a whole.

14. **A, C.** Choice A is supported by this sentence: "Federal agencies worked in tandem, with the Labor Department handling applications and the Departments of Agriculture and the Interior developing the work plans." Choice C is supported by this sentence: "Until the advent of war, when its funding was diverted to defense, this peacetime army was one of the most successful of all government programs." Choice B has no support in the passage.

15. **E.** Your job is to find the reason that is most likely, given what you know about history and what you learned from the passage. The CCC was a "work corps for the unemployed," so as jobs opened up in wartime, there was a place for those unemployed outside the CCC. This is a far more likely choice than any of the others.

16. **As parks close due to budget constraints, many hearken back to the glory days of the Civilian Conservation Corps (CCC), a New Deal agency born of the Great Depression.** The passage opens with a connection of present-day woes to those surrounding the creation of the CCC.

17. **E.** The word "also" implies a parallel, so look for a word that means "flows through."

18. **C, E.** Read the whole sentence before making a choice. If Webster "firmly declined" the position, he did not regret his hesitation (choice F)—he did not hesitate. He may have regretted his decision (choice E).

19. **B, D.** In other words, the highbrow, refined culture of college may seem intimidating to rural students.

20. **A, F.** Read the whole sentence first to interpret its meaning. The author is saying that instead of being simply patched, the power grid must be completely redone (choice F), which is a beneficial effect (choice A).

21. **C.** Today, according to the passage, "coopers exist primarily to accommodate the wine industry," meaning that they are wet coopers.

22. **A, B.** Some of the qualities mentioned support the notion that the hyrax is primitive, whereas others support the notion that it is complex. Its poor temperature regulation (choice A) and undescended testes (choice B) are two of the former; its complex stomach (choice C) is among the latter.

23. **A, C.** The author sardonically calls Grinnell's challenge of Rousseau's war record an "unpardonable sin" (choice A) and remarks that Rousseau's reappointment was "remarkable even by House standards." No such snarky remark is made about the fight itself (choice B).

24. **B.** Grinnell founded a college before going to the House and ran a railroad afterward. This suggests that he had other memorable events in his life besides the one fight in Congress.

25. **Grinnell had committed the unpardonable sin of challenging Rousseau's Civil War record, accusing him of "blowing his own horn."** This was Rousseau's motive for attacking Grinnell.

Section 5. Quantitative Reasoning

1. **A.** If you multiply the top and bottom of Quantity A by $5 \times 4 = 20$, it reduces to $\frac{9}{2}$. Similarly, if you multiply the top and bottom of Quantity B by $3 \times 6 = 18$, it reduces to $\frac{5}{2}$.

2. **D.** Both equations, when solved for y, are $y = 2x - 5$. It follows that x can have any value, thus there is no way to tell if it is more or less than 5.

3.   **B.** The total age sum of the 20 students is $20 \times 18 = 360$, and the total age sum of the 16 students is $16 \times 20 = 320$. Thus the total age sum of the 36 students must be $360 + 320 = 680$, for an average of $680 \div 36 \approx 18.888\dots.$

4.   **C.** Because $20 = 2^2 \times 5$ and $500 = 2^2 \times 5^3$, we know that N has at least two 2s but only one 5 (and possibly prime factors other than 2 and 5). Because $100 = 2^2 \times 5^2$ and $2{,}500 = 2^2 \times 5^4$, we can see that the greatest common divisor of these numbers with N will also be $2^2 \times 5 = 20$.

5.   **B.** If you solve each equation for y, you get $y = -\dfrac{3}{2}x + \dfrac{7}{2}$ for line L and $y = 5x + 4$ for line M. The y-intercept of line L is thus $\dfrac{7}{2}$ and the y-intercept of line M is 4.

6.   **C.** One way to see this would be to multiply out the two volumes: $14 \times 8 \times 5 = 560$ and $7 \times 8 \times 10 = 560$. A faster way would be to recognize that the two boxes have the same width, but that one has twice the height and the other has twice the length. The volumes will thus come out to be equal.

7.   **C.** You can calculate the height TQ of the parallelogram with the Pythagorean theorem: $5^2 + (TQ)^2 = 13^2$. The answer is $TQ = \sqrt{169 - 25} = \sqrt{144} = 12$. The area of a parallelogram is base $\times$ height, and thus the area of $PRST$ is $10 \times 12 = 120$.

8.   **A.** If you add $3x$ and 5 to both sides of the equation, you obtain $15 = x$.

9.   **D.** Quantity A simplifies: $\left(\dfrac{x^2}{x^5}\right)^4 = (x^{2-5})^4 = (x^{-3})^4 = x^{-12}$. There is no way to tell whether this is greater than, less than, or equal to x^{12} without knowing the value of x. If $x = 1$, the two quantities are equal. If $x = 2$, then Quantity B is far larger than Quantity A.

10.   **E.** Formula X is $500{,}000 \times 80{,}000$ times as concentrated as formula Z. This is $500{,}000 \times 80{,}000 = 40{,}000{,}000{,}000 = 4 \times 10^{10}$.

11.   **B.** Written as a fraction, the ratio is $\dfrac{4}{5} = \dfrac{6}{x}$, which cross multiplies to $4x = 30$. This simplifies to $x = 7.5$.

12.   **A.** The flies at the start of the study have a ratio of red eyes to white eyes of 40:60. At the end, the ratio of red:white is equivalent to $40(3):[60 + 2.2(60)]$, which simplifies to 120:192. The number R with red eyes can be solved via the proportion $\dfrac{120}{120 + 192} = \dfrac{R}{2{,}184}$. Thus $R = \dfrac{120(2{,}184)}{120 + 192} = 840$.

13. **A.** In the nine hours from 8 a.m. to 5 p.m., Lee makes $9 \times \$15 = \$135$. In the three hours from 7 p.m. to 10 p.m., Lee makes $3 \times \$25 = \$75$ more, for a total of $\$210$ each day. In five such days, Lee will make $5 \times \$210 = \$1,050$.

14. **14.** If $QR = x$, then $RS = 2x$, so $QS = 3x = 9$, thus $x = 3$. Thus $QR = 3$ and $RS = 6$. The whole length is $PS = PR + RS = 8 + 6 = 14$.

15. **D.** There are nine points on the scatter plot which are below the 5'6" level and between the lines for 14 and 20 years old. Of all 20 points, these represent $\frac{9}{20} = \frac{45}{100} = 45\%$.

16. **D, E.** The inequality $\frac{1}{x} < x$ is not true if x is a positive number less than 1, for example $x = \frac{1}{2}$. The inequality $-x < x$ is not true if x is negative. The inequality $x^3 < x^5$ is not true if x is between 0 and 1 or less than -1. The equation $x < x^2 + 2$ is true when x is negative (because $x^2 + 2$ is always positive) and when $x \le 2$. When $x > 2$, you can divide both sides of $x < x^2 + 2$ by x to get $1 < x + \frac{2}{x}$, which is true (because $x > 2$). Thus $x < x^2 + 2$ is always true. Finally, $-|x| < |x|$ is always true except when $x = 0$, but this case has been specifically excluded.

17. **A, C.** The quotient of a negative and a positive number will be negative, thus not more than 3. The quotient of the only two positive numbers is either $8 \div 4 = 2$ or else $4 \div 8 = \frac{1}{2}$, neither of which is more than 3. If you take -8 and -2, however, you can form the quotient $-8 \div -2 = 4$, which is more than 3.

18. **E.** Any three points on the circle can be connected to form a triangle. The number of ways this can be done is the number of ways 3 of 6 things can be chosen: $\frac{6!}{(6-3)!3!} = \frac{6 \times 5 \times 4 \times 3 \times 2 \times 1}{3 \times 2 \times 1 \times 3 \times 2 \times 1} = 5 \times 4 = 20$.

19. **E.** Not drawn to scale, the triangle PQR is equilateral because all three of its sides have the same length. Thus $\angle QRP = 60°$, and so the measure of $\angle QRS$ is $180° - 60° = 120°$.

20. **E.** The prime factorization of n is $p \times r \times r$. The factors of n are thus $1, p, r, r^2$, pr, and pr^2. Another way to solve this problem would be to choose values for p and r. With $p = 3$ and $r = 2$, the questions asks how many factors $3 \times 2^2 = 12$ has. There are six factors: 1, 2, 3, 4, 6, and 12.

21. **D.** If this cylinder has a radius of r and a height of h, its volume is $V = \pi r^2 h$. A cylinder that is twice as wide and three times as tall will have a radius of $2r$, a height of $3h$, and a volume of $\pi(2r)^2(3h) = 12\pi r^2 h = 12V$.

22. **C.** Using the distance formula, the distance from $(3, 1)$ to $(6, 5)$ is
$$\sqrt{(6-3)^2 + (5-1)^2} = \sqrt{9+16} = 5.$$

23. **84,000.** The information is in the height of the fourth bar from the left: $7,000 per month. To convert to an annual rate, we multiply $12 \times 7,000 = 84,000$.

24. **A.** The difference between making $3,000 and $5,000 per month is $2,000 per month or $24,000 per year. Thus in $\dfrac{120,000}{24,000} = 5$ years, this difference will cover the $120,000 in college expenses.

25. **D.** From 5,000 per month to 7,000 is an increase of $\dfrac{2,000}{5,000} = 40\%$.

Section 6. Quantitative Reasoning

1. **B.** Quantity A simplifies: $\dfrac{1}{1+\frac{1}{1+\frac{1}{3}}} = \dfrac{1}{1+\frac{1}{\frac{4}{3}}} = \dfrac{1}{1+\frac{3}{4}} = \dfrac{1}{\frac{7}{4}} = \dfrac{4}{7}$. Quantity B simplifies

   to $\dfrac{1}{1+\frac{1}{1+\frac{1}{2}}} = \dfrac{1}{1+\frac{1}{\frac{3}{2}}} = \dfrac{1}{1+\frac{2}{3}} = \dfrac{1}{\frac{5}{3}} = \dfrac{3}{5}$. Because $\dfrac{4}{7} = \dfrac{4}{7} \times \dfrac{5}{5} = \dfrac{20}{35}$ and

   $\dfrac{3}{5} = \dfrac{3}{5} \times \dfrac{7}{7} = \dfrac{21}{35}$, Quantity B is larger.

2. **B.** Quantity A is $5^{-2} = \dfrac{1}{5^2} = \dfrac{1}{25}$, which is smaller than Quantity B: $10^{-1} = \dfrac{1}{10}$.

3. **D.** If x and y are both positive, as with $x = y = 10$, then $x + y$ is clearly bigger than $x - y$. However, as soon as y is negative, as when $x = 20$ and $y = -10$, then $x - y$ becomes larger.

4. **D.** As x varies from 3 to 6, Quantity A will vary from $\dfrac{3+5}{3-2} = 8$ to $\dfrac{6+5}{6-2} = \dfrac{11}{4}$.

   At the same time, Quantity B will vary from $\dfrac{3+9}{3-1} = 6$ to $\dfrac{6+9}{6-1} = 3$. Because these ranges overlap, there is no way to tell which quantity is greater. For

   example, when $x = 4$, Quantity A is $\dfrac{9}{2}$ which is larger than Quantity B, $\dfrac{13}{3}$.

   However, when $x = 5$, Quantity A is $\dfrac{10}{3}$, which is less than Quantity B, $\dfrac{7}{2}$.

5. **D.** If $x = 0$, then Quantity A is $0^2 = 0$, which is less than Quantity B, $2^0 = 1$.

   However, if $x = -1$, then Quantity A is $(-1)^2 = 1$, which is larger than Quantity

   B, $2^{-1} = \dfrac{1}{2}$.

6. **A.** If you multiply out Quantity B, you get $(x + y)^2 = x^2 + 2xy + y^2$. Because $xy < 0$, you know that $2xy$ is negative, thus this is less than Quantity A, $x^2 + y^2$.

7. **C.** The volume of the cone is $\frac{1}{3}\pi R^2 R = \frac{1}{3}\pi R^3$, the volume of the cylinder is $\pi R^2 R = \pi R^3$, and the volume of the sphere is $\frac{4}{3}\pi R^3$. Because $\frac{1}{3}\pi R^3 + \pi R^3 = \frac{4}{3}\pi R^3$, Quantities A and B are equal.

8. **A.** Quantity A is πD and Quantity B is $3D$. Because $\pi \approx 3.14$, Quantity A is larger.

9. **D.** If $x = 0$ then the two quantities will be the same. If $x = 4$ then Quantity A is 16 and Quantity B is 2. Thus there is no way to tell which quantity is larger.

10. **E.** To calculate $4.2 \times 10^7 \times 5 \times 10^8$, you multiply the powers of ten separately, obtaining $4.2 \times 5 \times 10^7 \times 10^8 = 21 \times 10^{15}$. In scientific notation, this is 2.1×10^{16}.

11. **A, E.** The $20 off coupon cannot be used on a $50 purchase, so for that one the 20% off coupon is best. The coupons will be of equal value on a purchase of value x where $0.2x = 20$, so $x = 100$. For the larger amount of $120, the 20% coupon will save more money.

12. **81.** We take the fraction of earnings from division D and multiply by 360 degrees to get $\left(\dfrac{720,000,000}{3,200,000,000}\right)360 = \left(\dfrac{720}{3,200}\right)360 = 81$.

13. **B.** The number 28 factors into $2 \times 2 \times 7$ and 32 factors into $2 \times 2 \times 2 \times 2 \times 2$, so their least common multiple is $2 \times 2 \times 2 \times 2 \times 2 \times 7 = 224$. Because $1,000 \div 28 \approx 35.7$, there are 35 multiples of 28 from 1 to 1,000. Because $1,000 \div 32 = 31.25$, there are 31 multiples of 32 from 1 to 1,000. Because $1,000 \div 224 \approx 4.5$, there are four numbers between 1 and 1,000 that are multiples of both 28 and 32. This means that if you count all the multiples of 28 and all the multiples of 32, you will double-count four of them. Thus there are $35 + 31 - 4 = 62$ numbers between 1 and 1,000 that are either a multiple of 28 or a multiple of 32.

14. **5.** The equation $x^2 - 3x - 10 = 0$ factors into $(x - 5)(x + 2) = 0$, so $x = 5$ or $x = -2$. The inequality $4x + 3 > 15$ simplifies to $x > 3$, which eliminates the possibility that $x = -2$. Thus, the only possible answer is $x = 5$.

15. **D.** Because $\overline{AB} \parallel \overline{CD}$, you know $\angle DCE$ measures 48°. Because $\overline{CD} \cong \overline{DE}$, the triangle CDE is isosceles, thus $\angle DEC$ also measures 48°. Because the angles of a triangle must sum to 180°, this means that $\angle CDE$ measures $180° - 48° - 48° = 84°$.

16. **C.** The area of the lawn is $250 \times 150 = 37,500$ square feet, and so it will take 4 bags of grass seed to cover it (there will be some left over).

17. **A.** The distance from A to G can be found by applying the Pythagorean theorem to the right triangle ADG: $4^2 + 5^2 = (AG)^2$, so $AG = \sqrt{41}$. The distance from A to H can then be calculated by applying the Pythagorean theorem to the right triangle AGH, $(AG)^2 + (GH)^2 = (AH)^2$. Thus $(\sqrt{41})^2 + 3^2 = (AH)^2$, so $AH = \sqrt{50} = 5\sqrt{2}$.

18. **C, D.** In both cases, the number of miles to drive is less than three times the speed (which would be 255 miles and 105 miles, respectively). The other options all have distances greater than what can be traveled in three hours at the given rate.

19. **B.** From 1995 to 2000, spending increased by 5%, from $870 million to $1.05 \times \$870 = \$913.5$ million. From 2000 to 2005, spending decreased by 3%, from $913.5 million to $0.97 \times \$913.5 = \$886.095$ million.

20. **E.** To increase by 5% is the same as to multiply by 1.05. Increasing by 5%, then 8%, then 7%, and then 9% is the same as multiplying by $(1.05) \times (1.08) \times (1.07) \times (1.09) \approx 1.32258$. This is the same as increasing by 32.258%, which is 32.3% when rounded to the nearest tenth of a percent.

21. **A.** The eight prime numbers from 1 through 20 are 2, 3, 5, 7, 11, 13, 17, and 19. Thus the probability that a whole number chosen randomly from 1 through 20 will be prime is $\dfrac{8}{20} = \dfrac{4}{10} = 40\%$.

22. **7.** In order to have a mean of 6, it must be that $\dfrac{4 + x + 5 + 4 + x + 9 + 7 + 5}{8} = 6$. This is equivalent to $2x + 34 = 48$, thus $x = 7$.

23. **D.** Of the answer choices, choice A is true because Z overlaps X, choice B is true because Y is entirely inside X, choice C is true because X overlaps Z, and choice E is true because Y overlaps Z. Choice D is not true because there are parts of region Z that are outside of Y.

24. **B, C.** The equation $x^2 + 1 = 2x$ can be rewritten as $x^2 - 2x + 1 = 0$, factored into $(x - 1)^2 = 0$, and simplified into $x - 1 = 0$ by taking the square root of both sides. Thus any equation whose only solution is $x = 1$ will be equivalent to this one. This is the case for $(x - 1)^3 = 0$ and $x + 1 = 2$. Choice E also has $x = -1$ as a solution. Choice D is true no matter what x may be, not just $x = 1$.

25. **D.** You would expect $0.03 \times 1000 = 30$ cartons to contain a single broken egg and $0.005 \times 1000 = 5$ cartons to be entirely smashed. This is a total of $30 + 5 \times 12 = 90$ broken eggs.

GRE Practice Test 6

SECTION 1
Analytical Writing

ANALYZE AN ISSUE

30 Minutes

You will have 30 minutes to organize your thoughts and compose a response that represents your point of view on the topic presented. Do not respond to any topic other than the one given; a response to any other topic will receive a score of 0.

You will be required to discuss your perspective on the issue, using examples and reasons drawn from your own experiences and observations.

Use scratch paper to organize your response before you begin writing. Write your response on the pages provided, or type your response using a word processor with the spell- and grammar-check functions turned off.

Issue Topic

"A formal education is nothing more than the relentless revelation of one's own ignorance."

Discuss the extent to which you agree or disagree with the claim made above. In developing your position, address some reasons or examples that might be used to challenge your point of view.

SECTION 2

Analytical Writing

ANALYZE AN ARGUMENT

30 Minutes

You will have 30 minutes to organize your thoughts and compose a response that critiques the given argument. Do not respond to any topic other than the one given; a response to any other topic will receive a score of 0.

You are not being asked to discuss your point of view on the statement. You should identify and analyze the central elements of the argument, the underlying assumptions that are being made, and any supporting information that is given. Your critique can also discuss other information that would strengthen or weaken the argument or make it more logical.

Use scratch paper to organize your response before you begin writing. Write your response on the pages provided, or type your response using a word processor with the spell- and grammar-check functions turned off.

Argument Topic

Presented with a serious deficit, the county administrator in Kindle County suggested reducing sanitation workers' pay by 1 percent to avoid layoffs. The union balked and called for a raise, as in previous years, of 4 percent. The county board decided it would be only fair to split the difference, and agreed to a 2.5 percent increase in wages along with a slight increase in the county's share of health benefits.

Evaluate the reasoning used in the argument presented above by suggesting some questions that would need to be answered to determine whether the solution and the argument on which it was based are reasonable.

_____

_____

_____

_____

_____

_____

_____

_____

_____

_____

_____

_____

_____

_____

_____

_____

_____

_____

_____

_____

SECTION 3
Verbal Reasoning
Time: 35 minutes
25 questions

For questions 1 through 4, select two answer choices that (1) complete the sentence in a way that makes sense and (2) produce sentences that are similar in meaning.

1. When they purchased the hilltop property, they were blissfully _____ of the fact that it stood directly in the flight path of the local airport.

   - [A] ignorant
   - [B] apprised
   - [C] chary
   - [D] unconscious
   - [E] staggered
   - [F] extolled

2. Morels are related to cup fungi, but they are both more anatomically complex and more widely _____ for their flavor.

   - [A] sought
   - [B] valued
   - [C] promoted
   - [D] confiscated
   - [E] idyllic
   - [F] prized

3. Over the course of just a few years, the Works Progress Administration (WPA) constructed parks, bridges, and _____ buildings in neighborhoods all over America.

   - [A] school
   - [B] innovative
   - [C] refurbished
   - [D] municipal
   - [E] prominent
   - [F] public

4. Emily Post, who died fifty years ago, was probably the best-known _____ on American manners and etiquette; her books are still in use today.

   - [A] writer
   - [B] authority
   - [C] expert
   - [D] spokesperson
   - [E] mentor
   - [F] strategist

Questions 5 and 6 are based on this passage.

In 2007, *Mother Jones* published an article on "the ethanol effect," showing the negative ramifications of switching from foreign oil to corn-based ethanol. It pointed out that over just five years, the amount of corn used for ethanol had risen from 7 percent to 20 percent. That led to a rise in the price of corn, which in turn led to a rise in food prices. Since so much corn was used to manufacture ethanol, less was exported. This meant less corn on the global market and the potential of an increase in global hunger. Ironically, the production of corn requires a great deal of gasoline for tractors and harvesters, reducing the energy savings to below that of gasoline.

Consider each of the choices separately and select all that apply.

5. According to the passage, what are some negatives involved in switching from foreign oil to ethanol?

   A The amount of corn needed means less corn available as food.

   B It takes more and more corn to manufacture a single gallon of ethanol.

   C Production of corn in general is surprisingly energy inefficient.

Select one answer choice.

6. In the final sentence, the author suggests that

   Ⓐ using ethanol in place of gasoline does not ultimately save energy

   Ⓑ producing corn for ethanol rather than for food uses more energy

   Ⓒ retrofitting cars and tractors to run on ethanol is surprisingly costly

   Ⓓ farm equipment cannot be retrofitted to run on corn-based fuel

   Ⓔ gasoline is far more energy efficient than most people believe

Question 7 is based on this passage.

You're more likely to see a tavern or restaurant named the Whistle Post than to notice the little signs along the tracks marked with a *W* or an *X*. The whistle-post signs tell train engineers where to begin blowing a warning prior to crossing an intersection.

Line They are especially useful where the railroad crossing has no automatic barrier—on
(5) rarely traveled crossings or when approaching rail yards, for example. Train whistles have largely been replaced by air horns, but the rules of rail travel still call for two short, one long, and one short blast of the horn to be repeated until the train reaches the crossing. The noise may be a nuisance, but studies have shown that accidents double when the horn is not used.

Consider each of the choices separately and select all that apply.

7. Based on the information in the passage, which of these can be inferred about whistle posts?

   A They have been largely replaced in modern times by air horns.

   B They alert an engineer to begin a series of two short, one long, and one short blast of the horn.

   C Their occasional removal or ban has led to observable increases in train-automobile collisions.

Questions 8 and 9 are based on this passage.

Line
(5)

(10)

Water beetles have a number of adaptations that make them able to live in water rather than on land as their countless beetle cousins do. Their spiracles open and close to take in air when they are on the surface and keep water out when they are underwater. Whirligig beetles have a clever division in their eyes that allows them to see above and below the surface at the same time. A number of water beetles, especially those that dive to find prey, trap and carry air bubbles with them on their abdomens, much as scuba divers carry air in their oxygen tanks. The legs of water beetles differ from those of their landlubber cousins. Often they are covered with fringelike hairs that help them speed across the water's surface. Like all beetles, water beetles are capable of flight, but they usually use this skill only to escape predators or to move from puddle to pond.

For questions 8 and 9, select one answer choice each.

---

8. The sentence in the passage that connects LEAST to the main idea is probably

   (A) the sentence about spiracles that open and close

   (B) the sentence about seeing above and below the surface

   (C) the sentence about trapping and carrying air bubbles

   (D) the sentence about fringelike hairs

   (E) the sentence about water-beetle flight

9. It can be inferred that the author mentions scuba divers primarily to

   (A) argue that members of the animal world have a good deal in common

   (B) give the reader a clear visual reference that will help clarify a point

   (C) contrast a natural means of diving with an artificial mode of diving

   (D) explain how scientists have analyzed the water beetle's motility

   (E) provide a humorous aside in an otherwise serious study

> For questions 10 through 13, complete the text by picking the best entry for each blank from the corresponding column of choices.

10. Neurogenesis, the (i) _____ by which the brain generates neurons, is most (ii) _____ during prenatal development.

Blank (i)	Blank (ii)
Ⓐ situation	Ⓓ insensible
Ⓑ process	Ⓔ active
Ⓒ experience	Ⓕ noteworthy

11. The downward trend of voter turnout indicates that the citizenry has a (i) _____ reaction to the vagaries of politics. Of course, the smaller the voting population, the greater the (ii) _____ of each vote.

Blank (i)	Blank (ii)
Ⓐ cursory	Ⓓ incertitude
Ⓑ trenchant	Ⓔ ramifications
Ⓒ phlegmatic	Ⓕ vacillations

12. Throughout Washington, DC, it is common to see young interns serving as _____, serving coffee, fetching dry cleaning, taking notes at meetings, or performing whatever chores their bosses might impose.

Ⓐ mercenaries
Ⓑ factotums
Ⓒ compeers
Ⓓ bureaucrats
Ⓔ urbanites

13. Maui is the second largest of the Hawaiian islands, _____ only the Big Island (Hawaii) in size.

Ⓐ exceeding
Ⓑ surpassing
Ⓒ trailing
Ⓓ engaging
Ⓔ reducing

Questions 14 through 16 are based on this passage.

His name has become synonymous with seduction, but many people fail to realize that Casanova was not a fictional character but rather a real, fascinating person. The book about his escapades is a memoir, not a novel. He was the son of an actress and her paramour, born in Venice in 1725. His patrons sent him to the University of Padua when he was only 12 years old, and he graduated with a degree in law, although he was far more interested in medicine. He became a professional gambler (not a good one), and he lived off the kindness of patrons, moving from city to city across Europe, often one step ahead of the law or his own debts. It was in his later years that he began writing the enormous and unfinished memoir that would be his legacy. His chronicling of the famous people he met along his way makes his memoir a valuable document of an era.

Line (5)

(10)

Consider each of the choices separately and select all that apply.

14. The author of the passage would most likely agree with which of the following statements?

   A. Casanova's low birth predestined that every step upward would be a struggle.

   B. Casanova's reputation as a roué is only a small element of his vibrant personality.

   C. Casanova's memoir provides an intriguing portrait of eighteenth-century life and manners.

Select one answer choice.

15. The author uses a parenthetical element primarily to

   (A) point out that Casanova's talents were not in the area of self-finance

   (B) contrast amateur gambling with Casanova's more professional gaming

   (C) support the notion that Casanova was not cut out for an ordinary life

   (D) suggest that Casanova would have been a better doctor than a gambler

   (E) engage the reader in an ongoing analysis of Casanova's descent

16. Underline the sentence that suggests that Casanova was unusually precocious.

For questions 17 through 20, complete the text by picking the best entry for each blank from the corresponding column of choices.

17. In 1881's *Egbert v. Lippmann*, the Supreme Court determined that public use of an invention (in this _____, corset steels) meant that one could be barred from patenting the invention.

Ⓐ	position
Ⓑ	instance
Ⓒ	setting
Ⓓ	prospect
Ⓔ	viewpoint

18. The Adirondack range in upstate New York is frequently (i) _____ part of the Appalachians by geographers, but geologists point to its close geological (ii) _____ to Canada's Laurentian Mountains.

Blank (i)		Blank (ii)	
Ⓐ	taken into	Ⓓ	familiarity
Ⓑ	regarded as	Ⓔ	immediacy
Ⓒ	kept in mind	Ⓕ	resemblance

19. The Eighty Years' War, sometimes (i) _____ the Dutch War of Independence, started as a (ii) _____ against Philip II of Spain. Led by William of Orange, residents of the Low Countries (iii) _____ Spanish taxes and the presence of Spanish troops.

Blank (i)		Blank (ii)		Blank (iii)	
Ⓐ	alluded to	Ⓓ	revolt	Ⓖ	forfeited
Ⓑ	talked about	Ⓔ	fiat	Ⓗ	rejected
Ⓒ	known as	Ⓕ	tribunal	Ⓘ	hindered

20. The horizontal lines of the (i) _____ of architecture called the Prairie School are supposed to (ii) _____ the horizon of the flat prairie grassland. The (iii) _____ of this style was that architecture should rise naturally out of its site.

Blank (i)	Blank (ii)	Blank (iii)
(A) focus	(D) equate	(G) premise
(B) brand	(E) reveal	(H) tenor
(C) style	(F) evoke	(I) belief

Question 21 is based on this passage.

A novel sequence is a form prominent in the nineteenth century, in which a series of novels by an author share themes or settings or even a main character. However, the novels are not necessarily organized chronologically, nor must they be read
Line in a certain order. Some works by James Fenimore Cooper fall into this category.
(5) His Leatherstocking Tales feature a single protagonist, Natty Bumppo, but their publication dates have nothing to do with the order of events in Natty Bumppo's life. Honoré de Balzac's many novels and stories in La Comédie Humaine contain recurring characters, but Balzac's intent was to look at a broad swath of humanity. Although he had a plan and outlined how he thought the works might fit together,
(10) the reader can plunge into the novels at any point.

Select one answer choice.

21. The primary purpose of the passage is to

(A) distinguish between serial novels and novel sequences

(B) contrast American novel sequences with that of French writers

(C) express a critical opinion about the works of Cooper and Balzac

(D) provide an outline for the reading of Cooper's and Balzac's novels

(E) define and provide examples of a particular literary form

Question 22 is based on this passage.

The pluses of polycarbonate plastics are easy to see. A child's cup now bounces
rather than shatters when it's tossed out of the high chair. People with terrible
eyesight can wear featherweight glasses rather than massive, heavy glass lenses.
People like polycarbonates for their lightweight clarity and their toughness under
fire. Nevertheless, polycarbonates appear to have some minuses, too. Until recently,
when a few manufacturers changed their processing, all polycarbonates were found
to leach a chemical called bisphenol A (BPA). This chemical, once studied as a
potential estrogen replacement, is believed to inhibit the endocrine system and to be
especially harmful to young children. It is possible now to buy BPA-free products,
but the consumer should assume that BPA is in a polycarbonate product unless it is
labeled otherwise.

Consider each of the choices separately and select all that apply.

22. Which of the following generalizations is supported by the passage?

   A   All polycarbonates are durable and light.

   B   All polycarbonates leach bisphenol A.

   C   All children should avoid bisphenol A.

Questions 23 through 25 are based on this passage.

Geographic labels for lunar features often suggest, wrongly, that the moon is covered
with bodies of water. Blame early astronomers, who were unable to distinguish lava
flows from seas or oceans. Primarily to blame is probably Giovanni Riccioli, a priest
and astronomer whose nomenclature for Francesco Grimaldi's lunar map is still
used today. The *Mare Tranquillitatis*, or Sea of Tranquility, is really a volcanic basalt
basin surrounded by high walls. The *Oceanus Procellarum*, the Ocean of Storms, is a
vast, flat lowland that some call the Great Plains of the moon. The *Lacus Felicitatis*,
the Lake of Happiness, is another low-lying patch of lava, and the *Palus Putredinis*, or
Marsh of Decay, is a lava flow with a crater on one end and a mountain on the other.
The dampness implied by the names is simply an illusion; basalt reflects less light
than the surrounding rock, making these regions appear dark and deep.

Consider each of the choices separately and select all that apply.

23. According to the author, what did Giovanni Riccioli do wrong?

    A Named moon structures for bodies of water

    B Mistook lava flows for marine features

    C Renamed objects on Grimaldi's lunar map

Select one answer choice.

24. Based on the passage as a whole, the author most likely feels that the mistakes made by the early astronomers were

    Ⓐ problematic

    Ⓑ inconsequential

    Ⓒ deliberate

    Ⓓ preventable

    Ⓔ understandable

25. Underline the sentence that provides a logical explanation for the early astronomers' errors.

STOP. This is the end of Section 3. Use any remaining time to check your work.

SECTION 4
Verbal Reasoning
Time: 35 minutes
25 questions

Questions 1 through 3 are based on this passage.

Paris in the Twentieth Century is the title of Jules Verne's "lost novel." His second work of fiction after *Five Weeks in a Balloon*, the manuscript was deemed too pessimistic and dark by his editor, and Verne never revised it, forging ahead instead with such blockbusters as *A Journey to the Center of the Earth* and *Twenty Thousand Leagues Under the Sea.* The lost novel, first penned in 1863, was rediscovered and published in 1994. Like most of Verne's science fiction, it accurately predicts certain technological advances, among them modern subways, air conditioning, fax machines, and television. Unlike many of Verne's more mature works, it lacks strong characterization and plot development. The hero of the book is a kind of Luddite, a humanities scholar who fails to connect to the Soviet-style technoworld that is Verne's imagined 1960s Paris.

Line
(5)

(10)

Consider each of the choices separately and select all that apply.

1. According to the passage, how does *Paris in the Twentieth Century* differ from Verne's later works?

   A   It contains eerily precise predictions about technological advances.

   B   The action in the book is not particularly well developed.

   C   It was not a runaway success while the author was alive.

Select one answer choice.

2. When the author refers to the protagonist of *Paris in the Twentieth Century* as a Luddite, she primarily means that he

   (A) fails to separate the political from the personal

   (B) cannot perform the simplest of mechanical tasks

   (C) prefers arts and literature to science and mathematics

   (D) hides behind a romantic vision of man's possibilities

   (E) opposes technological development in principle

3. Underline the sentence that explains why the novel was "lost."

Question 4 is based on this passage.

George Westinghouse and Nikola Tesla believed in alternating current (AC). Thomas Edison was a proponent of direct current (DC). The resulting rivalry became known as the War of the Currents. Although it was clear that AC offered advantages in transmitting electricity over long distances, Edison's DC was the U.S. standard at the time, and the loss of patents he faced if conversion took place would mean a devastating financial blow. He mounted a fierce media campaign against AC, using faked data to indicate its dangers. He hired a man, Harold Brown, to travel around electrocuting animals on stage to prove that AC current was uncontrollable and hazardous. Brown even succeeded in convincing Auburn State Prison to use a Westinghouse generator to electrocute an ax-murderer in the first electric-chair execution.

Line (5)

(10)

Select one answer choice.

4. It can be inferred that which of these was the motivation behind Edison's fakery?

   Ⓐ   Absolute belief in the dangers of alternating current

   Ⓑ   Concern that widespread use of alternating current would eat into profits

   Ⓒ   Strong dislike for the methods of Tesla and Westinghouse

   Ⓓ   Conviction that direct current was an improvement over alternating current

   Ⓔ   Distress over the fact that Westinghouse and Tesla faked data

---

For questions 5 through 8, complete the text by picking the best entry for each blank from the corresponding column of choices.

---

5. Undersea life decreases with _____ depth; in very deep waters, light levels, salinity, and amount of oxygen tend to limit the number of species available.

Ⓐ	impending
Ⓑ	diminishing
Ⓒ	subterranean
Ⓓ	minimal
Ⓔ	increasing

6. Atlantic puffins are _____; each pair of parents stays together for years and shares duties involving the incubation of eggs and the feeding of chicks.

(A)	monogamous
(B)	gregarious
(C)	aggressive
(D)	heterogeneous
(E)	indistinguishable

7. The Lebanese Civil War lasted 15 years and (i) _____ in a quarter of a million civilian casualties, nearly 1 million wounded citizens, and the total (ii) _____ of the capital city, Beirut.

Blank (i)		Blank (ii)	
(A)	terminated	(D)	deprivation
(B)	colluded	(E)	destruction
(C)	resulted	(F)	defamation

8. Nearly 90 percent of the earth's crust is (i) _____ of silicate minerals, which vary enormously yet all (ii) _____ silicon and oxygen.

Blank (i)		Blank (ii)	
(A)	abundance	(D)	inhibit
(B)	deficient	(E)	contain
(C)	composed	(F)	exchange

Questions 9 through 12 are based on this passage.

The first Philippine Revolution occurred at the end of the 1800s, but it was fueled in part by a movement that had grown up earlier. Filipinos who had emigrated to Europe, either in exile or to study, began to come together to strive for equal rights for Filipino and Spanish citizens in the Philippines. They asked for representation in the Spanish parliament, freedoms of speech and assembly, and equal opportunities for Filipinos when it came to getting jobs in government.

Line
(5)

La Solidaridad, a newspaper published in Spain by exiled Filipinos, was the main organ of this Propaganda Movement. La Solidaridad was the name of an organization as well as a newspaper, but it was the paper that mattered more. Between the years 1889 and 1895, the little paper, whose ambitions were modest and whose readership was small, lit a fire of nationalist pride under those few individuals who would go on to lead the Filipino people in their fight against Spanish exploitation.

(10)

Perhaps the most prominent member of the Propaganda Movement was José Rizal. A scientist by trade, he strove scientifically to refute Europeans' notions of Filipinos as an inferior people. His papers and orations were important, but his two novels, *Noli Me Tangere* (1886) and *El Filibusterismo* (1891), were even more influential. Their heavy-handed symbolism portrayed corruption and abuse in the Spanish-led government and clergy of the Philippines. Although Rizal mainly wanted equality and representation, his books led to a sense of Filipino self-respect that stimulated true revolution.

(15)

(20)

Consider each of the choices separately and select all that apply.

9. Paragraph two of the passage suggests that *La Solidaridad* was a success because it

    [A] had modest goals that it stuck to year after year

    [B] reached thousands of people who longed for leadership

    [C] touched a handful of leaders who took up its cause

For questions 10 through 12, select one answer choice each.

10. It can be inferred from the passage that in the Philippines around the year 1890,

    Ⓐ *La Solidaridad* became the most important local newspaper

    Ⓑ Filipino exiles returned to their impoverished nation

    Ⓒ José Rizal produced experiments showing Filipino superiority

    Ⓓ Spanish-born residents had more rights than the natives had

    Ⓔ a revolution broke out with the goal of separation from Spain

11. The author suggests that the sense of cultural pride engendered by Rizal's books helped to goad Filipinos into revolution, but another possibility might be that

   Ⓐ Rizal's scientific refutation of European biases angered the Spanish

   Ⓑ Rizal's call for equality and representation was scorned by Filipinos

   Ⓒ Rizal's descriptions of Spanish abuses aroused anger and bitterness

   Ⓓ Rizal's books did more to convince Spaniards than to reassure Filipinos

   Ⓔ Rizal's novels were thinly concealed biographies of real Filipinos

12. How might the organization of the passage be described?

   Ⓐ Paragraph one introduces the topic; paragraphs two and three present examples in support.

   Ⓑ Paragraph one introduces the topic; paragraphs two and three present reasons in support.

   Ⓒ Paragraphs one and two present an argument; paragraph three summarizes the argument.

   Ⓓ Paragraphs one and two introduce the topic; paragraph three offers alternatives.

   Ⓔ Paragraph one introduces a cause; paragraphs two and three provide effects in order.

Question 13 is based on this passage.

It ended with a whimper rather than a bang, plagued by debt, allegations of abuse, and the death of its founder. Yet in its day, the Boys Choir of Harlem was a marvel of precision and vocal superiority, and its boys traveled the world.

Line
(5)

Dr. Walter Turnbull organized the choir at his church in Harlem in 1968. Within a few years, the choir had its own school, where hundreds of children received training in academics and music. The choir performed at the White House and sang for the pope. It recorded music for award-winning films. Its demise troubles its alumni and former board members, but no one seems able to resurrect the lifeless organization.

13. Underline the sentence that presents the author's perspective on the original Boys Choir.

> For questions 14 through 17, complete the text by picking the best entry for each blank from the corresponding column of choices.

14. Epiphytes, or air plants, may develop roots for attachment to host plants or objects (i) _____ for the movement of nutrients. Instead of using roots, they (ii) _____ their nutrition from the air or from rain, often collecting moisture in (iii) _____ structures.

Blank (i)	Blank (ii)	Blank (iii)
(A) on behalf of	(D) eliminate	(G) formalized
(B) as well as	(E) obtain	(H) authorized
(C) rather than	(F) restore	(I) specialized

15. Far more (i) _____ than the counterfeiting of money or bonds is the counterfeiting of consumer goods, especially those that are popular and costly but easy to (ii) _____ cheaply; this is a worldwide and fairly open phenomenon.

Blank (i)	Blank (ii)
(A) clandestine	(D) reproduce
(B) intricate	(E) advertise
(C) prevalent	(F) sanction

16. The Blacksmith Institute issues annual reports on the world's worst-polluted places, _____ of life-threatening hot spots all over the globe.

(A)	combinations
(B)	inventories
(C)	fundamentals
(D)	abridgments
(E)	allegories

17. It's such a _____ concept that it seems to have been around for all time, but packaged sliced bread has only been available since the late 1920s.

(A) radical
(B) fresh
(C) primitive
(D) hollow
(E) meaningless

Questions 18 through 20 are based on this passage.

There were four Hiram Binghams, each more exceptional than the last. The first two were among the earliest Hawaiian missionaries. Hiram Bingham II had a son, Hiram III, who went to the mainland for his education. He was teaching
Line   South American history at Yale when he traveled to Peru and, with the help of
(5)   locals, rediscovered the lost city of Machu Picchu. He later became governor of Connecticut for a single day, for he was also elected senator to fill a vacancy just a month after the November election. He married a Tiffany heiress, and they had seven sons. The first son, Hiram IV, would be a hero of World War II, secretly helping Jewish refugees to escape from Nazi-occupied France in his position as vice-consul in
(10)   Marseille.

> For questions 18 through 20, select one answer choice each.

18. In the first sentence of the passage, what does the word *exceptional* most precisely mean?

    (A) Abnormal

    (B) Superior

    (C) Rare

    (D) Objectionable

    (E) Extraordinary

19. Which of the following can be inferred from the passage about Hiram Bingham I?

  Ⓐ His son and grandson were educated in the United States.

  Ⓑ He traveled widely in South America in the late 1800s.

  Ⓒ He helped introduce Christianity to the Hawaiian Islands.

  Ⓓ His son served as a junior senator from Connecticut.

  Ⓔ He was born around the time of the Civil War.

20. Which of these sentences could most appropriately conclude the paragraph?

  Ⓐ Hiram's brother Jonathan served in Congress for nearly twenty years.

  Ⓑ Hiram and his wife, Rose—a drama teacher—had eleven children.

  Ⓒ Hiram Bingham III is buried at Arlington National Cemetery.

  Ⓓ The four Hirams spanned and influenced critical eras in American history.

  Ⓔ A World War II ship was christened the SS *Hiram Bingham*.

For questions 21 through 25, select two answer choices that (1) complete the sentence in a way that makes sense and (2) produce sentences that are similar in meaning.

---

21. A variety of children's dictionaries are available for school or home use, ranging from the simplest of picture dictionaries for the very young prereader to quite _____ versions for middle schoolers that include the latest in slang and technical vocabulary.

  Ⓐ verbose

  Ⓑ cumbersome

  Ⓒ satisfactory

  Ⓓ educational

  Ⓔ minimal

  Ⓕ acceptable

22. Hieroglyphics had three main functions in ancient Egypt—they might _____ an idea, a phonogram, or a semantic category.

    [A] represent

    [B] construct

    [C] prefigure

    [D] address

    [E] denote

    [F] catalog

23. For centuries, the first gospel was _____ to St. Matthew, probably incorrectly; most scholars today believe it was written by an anonymous author at the end of the first century.

    [A] endorsed

    [B] dedicated

    [C] forged

    [D] attributed

    [E] petitioned

    [F] credited

24. As retail centers fail and expire across America, online e-tailers continue to _____, offering ease and discounted goods rarely available in the malls of yesterday.

    [A] fester

    [B] burgeon

    [C] reciprocate

    [D] transmogrify

    [E] rejuvenate

    [F] proliferate

25. In early modern Europe, the slightest _____ might lead men to seek satisfaction through the barbaric formality known as the duel.

    A   dereliction

    B   complicity

    C   aversion

    D   aspersion

    E   defamation

    F   aberration

STOP.   This is the end of Section 4. Use any remaining time to check your work.

SECTION 5
Quantitative Reasoning
Time: 40 minutes
25 questions

Each of questions 1 through 9 consists of two quantities, Quantity A and Quantity B. You are to compare the two quantities. You may use additional information centered above the two quantities if additional information is given. Choose

(A) if Quantity A is greater;

(B) if Quantity B is greater;

(C) if the two quantities are equal;

(D) if the relationship cannot be determined from the information given.

A job involves working 40 hours per week, 50 weeks per year

	Quantity A	Quantity B	
1.	$20 per hour	$40,000 per year	Ⓐ Ⓑ Ⓒ Ⓓ

	Quantity A	Quantity B	
2.	$\dfrac{\frac{2}{3}+5}{1-\frac{1}{6}}$	$\dfrac{8+\frac{1}{4}}{\frac{3}{4}+1}$	Ⓐ Ⓑ Ⓒ Ⓓ

$$4x < 3 - 2y$$

	Quantity A	Quantity B	
3.	$2x + y$	2	Ⓐ Ⓑ Ⓒ Ⓓ

	Quantity A	Quantity B	
4.	$(2x + 1)(2x - 1) - (x^2 + 1)$	$3x^2$	Ⓐ Ⓑ Ⓒ Ⓓ

x, $2y$, and $2z - 1$ are consecutive integers

	Quantity A	Quantity B	
5.	y	z	Ⓐ Ⓑ Ⓒ Ⓓ

There are 14 girls and eight boys in a classroom

	Quantity A	Quantity B	
6.	the number of ways to choose two of the girls	the number of ways to choose three of the boys	Ⓐ Ⓑ Ⓒ Ⓓ

	Quantity A	Quantity B	
7.	the sum of the areas of two circles 10 inches in diameter	the area of a circle 16 inches in diameter	Ⓐ Ⓑ Ⓒ Ⓓ

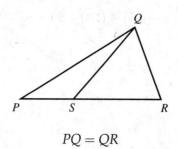

$$PQ = QR$$

Quantity A	Quantity B

8. the measure of ∠QRS   the measure of ∠QSR   Ⓐ   Ⓑ   Ⓒ   Ⓓ

Quantity A   Quantity B

9. $\dfrac{3}{10} + \dfrac{7}{12}$ $\dfrac{11}{6} - \dfrac{4}{5}$ Ⓐ   Ⓑ   Ⓒ   Ⓓ

> **Questions 10 through 25 have different formats. Select a single answer choice unless the directions say otherwise. For numeric-entry questions, follow these instructions:**
>
> - **Enter your answer in the box or boxes provided.**
> - **Your answer may be an integer, a decimal, a fraction, or a negative number.**
> - **If the answer is a fraction, you will be given two boxes: an upper one for the numerator and a lower one for the denominator.**
> - **Equivalent forms of the correct answer, such as 1.6 and 1.60, are all correct. You do not need to reduce fractions to lowest terms.**

For this question, indicate all of the answer choices that apply.

10. Which of the following are less than 99?

    Ⓐ   30% of 200

    Ⓑ   20% less than 150

    Ⓒ   20% more than 80

    Ⓓ   60% of 150

    Ⓔ   320% of 40

11. $(99 - 98 - 97 - 96 - 95) - (100 - 99 - 98 - 97 - 96) =$

　　Ⓐ −2

　　Ⓑ 1

　　Ⓒ 2

　　Ⓓ 3

　　Ⓔ 4

12. Among 23,280 discarded lottery tickets, about 1.8% are found to be worth $1, about 0.02% are found to be worth $2, and all the rest are worthless. Approximately how much are all the lottery tickets worth?

　　Ⓐ $400

　　Ⓑ $425

　　Ⓒ $450

　　Ⓓ $500

　　Ⓔ $525

13. A teacher has two classes. In the first class, there are 14 students. In the second class, there are 22 students. The mean age of the first class is 25. The mean age of the second class is 19. What is the mean age of the two classes put together (rounded to the nearest tenth)?

　　Ⓐ 20.9

　　Ⓑ 21.3

　　Ⓒ 21.7

　　Ⓓ 22.0

　　Ⓔ 22.6

For this question, write your answer in the box.

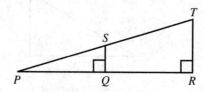

$PQ = 6, QR = 9,$ and $QS = 5$

14. $RT =$

For this question, indicate all of the answer choices that apply.

15. If $n = 6 \times 15$, which of the following are prime factors of n?

    A   2

    B   3

    C   7

    D   9

    E   15

16. A book has undergone two printings. The second was for three times as many books as the first. The cost of printing, per book, was 20% cheaper during the second printing. If the total cost of the two printings was $12,240, what was the cost of the second printing?

$

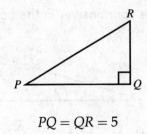

$$PQ = QR = 5$$

17. What is the perimeter of triangle PQR?

   (A) $5\sqrt{2}$

   (B) $10 + 5\sqrt{2}$

   (C)   15

   (D)   25

   (E) $10 + \sqrt{2}$

18. If $\dfrac{36^x}{3^{11}}$ is an integer, what is the smallest possible integer value of x?

   (A)   1

   (B)   4

   (C)   6

   (D)   11

   (E)   12

19. Let $x \lozenge y = y^2 - 2x$. What is the value of $5 \lozenge 2$?

   (A) -6

   (B) -1

   (C)   1

   (D)   10

   (E)   21

$$PQ = QR \text{ and } \angle PQR = 30°$$

20. What is the measure of ∠QPR?

(A) 30°

(B) 60°

(C) 75°

(D) 120°

(E) 150°

Use the following figure to answer questions 21 through 23.

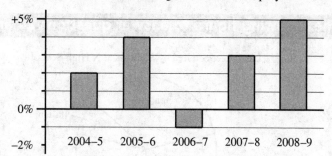

Year-on-Year Change in Profits at Company X

21. What was the overall percentage change in profits at company X from 2007 to 2009?

(A) 2%

(B) 3.15%

(C) 8%

(D) 8.15%

(E) 15%

22. If company X made a profit of $25 million in 2005, what was its profit in 2006?

  (A) $25.04 million

  (B) $25.4 million

  (C) $26 million

  (D) $26.25 million

  (E) $29 million

For this question, indicate all of the answer choices that apply.

23. Which of the following statements are true?

  [A] Company X's change in profits from 2005 to 2007 was exactly the same as from 2007 to 2008.

  [B] If company X made $10 million in profit in 2004, then it lost money from 2006 to 2007.

  [C] If company X made a $15 million profit in 2006, then it made more than $14 million in 2005.

Use the following figure to answer questions 24 and 25.

Languages Studied by Students at X High School

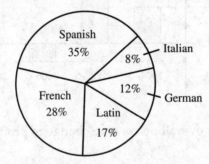

For this question, write your answer in the box.

24. Suppose there are 1,400 students studying foreign languages at X High School and no student studies more than one language. How many study French?

25. What is the angle of the sector representing the students who study Spanish?

   (A) 35°

   (B) 100.8°

   (C) 120°

   (D) 126°

   (E) 135°

STOP.   This is the end of Section 5. Use any remaining time to check your work.

SECTION 6
Quantitative Reasoning
Time: 40 minutes
25 questions

Each of questions 1 through 9 consists of two quantities, Quantity A and Quantity B. You are to compare the two quantities. You may use additional information centered above the two quantities if additional information is given. Choose

(A) if Quantity A is greater;

(B) if Quantity B is greater;

(C) if the two quantities are equal;

(D) if the relationship cannot be determined from the information given.

Quantity A	Quantity B	
1. 30 cents per ounce	5 dollars per pound	(A) (B) (C) (D)

Quantity A	Quantity B	
2. $\dfrac{1}{\sqrt{6}}$	$\dfrac{\sqrt{2}}{2\sqrt{3}}$	(A) (B) (C) (D)

$P(x)$ = the number of distinct prime factors of x

Quantity A	Quantity B	
3. $P(350)$	$P(120)$	(A) (B) (C) (D)

$$x^2 - 3x - 4 = 0 \text{ and } x > 0$$

Quantity A	Quantity B	
4. $3x$	10	Ⓐ Ⓑ Ⓒ Ⓓ

Quantity A	Quantity B	
5. $\sqrt[3]{5^7}$	$\left(\sqrt[3]{5}\right)^7$	Ⓐ Ⓑ Ⓒ Ⓓ

$$2x + 4 > 10$$

Quantity A	Quantity B	
6. $3x + 1$	10	Ⓐ Ⓑ Ⓒ Ⓓ

Quantity A	Quantity B	
7. x	$36°$	Ⓐ Ⓑ Ⓒ Ⓓ

Quantity A	Quantity B	
8. the area of a triangle with height $\frac{2}{3}$ and base $\frac{3}{4}$	the area of a square with side $\frac{1}{2}$	Ⓐ Ⓑ Ⓒ Ⓓ

Data set = {5, 2, 3, 2, 4, 2}

Quantity A	Quantity B	

9.   the mean of the data set   the mode of the data set

Questions 10 through 25 have different formats. Select a single answer choice unless the directions say otherwise. For numeric-entry questions, follow these instructions:

- Enter your answer in the box or boxes provided.
- Your answer may be an integer, a decimal, a fraction, or a negative number.
- If the answer is a fraction, you will be given two boxes: an upper one for the numerator and a lower one for the denominator.
- Equivalent forms of the correct answer, such as 1.6 and 1.60, are all correct. You do not need to reduce fractions to lowest terms.

10.   Which of the following is closest to $\sqrt[3]{60}$?

   (A)   2

   (B)   4

   (C)   8

   (D)   10

   (E)   20

For questions 11 and 12, indicate all of the answer choices that apply.

---

11.   Which of the following points are on the straight line through (1, 4) and (3, −2)?

   [A]   (2, 1)

   [B]   (0, 5)

   [C]   (4, −5)

   [D]   (−1, 8)

   [E]   (5, 5)

12. Which of the following are rational numbers?

A	-3
B	$\frac{4}{3}$
C	0
D	$\sqrt{12}$
E	$\sqrt{16}$
F	π

For this question, write your answer in the box.

13. What is the least common multiple of 21 and 35?

14. If the radius of a circle is increased by 40%, how much will the area increase?

   (A) 16%

   (B) 20%

   (C) 40%

   (D) 80%

   (E) 96%

15. In college basketball, a player awarded a "one-and-one" gets to shoot one free throw and, if successful, shoot a second one. Each successful free throw is worth one point. Suppose a player succeeds at free throws 80% of the time. On average, how many points should this player expect to score for each one-and-one?

   (A) 1

   (B) 1.16

   (C) 1.28

   (D) 1.44

   (E) 1.6

16. When a store processes a credit-card payment, they are charged a fee of 25 cents plus 2.6% of the total. If a store processes 4,000 credit card payments for a total of $150,000, how much will they be charged in fees?

    (A) $4,900

    (B) $7,650

    (C) $13,900

    (D) $40,000

    (E) $103,900

For this question, indicate all of the answer choices that apply.

17. Select all the values of x which make the following true: $2x^4 = 7x^3 + 4x^2$.

    A 0

    B $-\dfrac{1}{2}$

    C -1

    D 2

    E 4

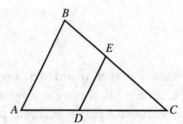

18. Suppose D is the midpoint of $\overline{AC}$ and E is the midpoint of $\overline{BC}$. If triangle DEC has an area of 8 square inches, what is the area of triangle ABC?

    (A) 12

    (B) 16

    (C) 24

    (D) 32

    (E) 64

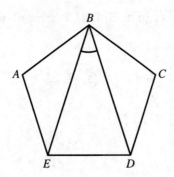

19. If *ABCDE* is a regular pentagon, what is the measure of ∠*EBD*?

   (A) 30°

   (B) 36°

   (C) 45°

   (D) 72°

   (E) 108°

20. Prizes will be randomly awarded to three different people in a room of 50 people. If you are one of these people, what is the probability that you will win one of the prizes?

   (A) 2%

   (B) 3%

   (C) 4%

   (D) 5%

   (E) 6%

For this question, write your answer in the box.

21. Two bids have come in for a printing job. The first will charge a fee of $50 and then $1.50 per copy. The second charges a fee of $30 and then $1.75 per copy. How many copies would be needed for these two bids to cost the same amount?

22. How many diagonals can be drawn on a regular pentagon?

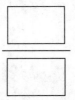

   (A) 5

   (B) 6

   (C) 7

   (D) 8

   (E) 9

For the following question, write your answer in the boxes.

23. If two cards are drawn randomly out of a standard deck of 52 playing cards, what is the probability that both are aces? Write your answer as a fraction.

$$\boxed{} \over \boxed{}$$

Use the following figure to answer questions 24 and 25.

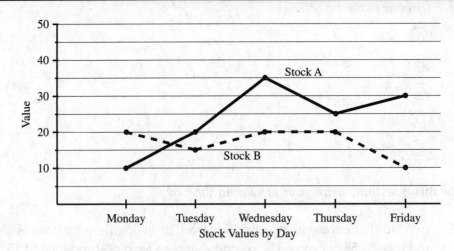

24. On which day was the difference between the values of stock A and stock B greatest?

   (A) Monday

   (B) Tuesday

   (C) Wednesday

   (D) Thursday

   (E) Friday

25. Over which time period did the value of stock A experience the biggest percentage change?

    (A) Monday to Tuesday

    (B) Tuesday to Wednesday

    (C) Wednesday to Thursday

    (D) Thursday to Friday

    (E) More than one of the above

STOP. **This is the end of Section 6. Use any remaining time to check your work.**

GRE Practice Test 6: Answers and Explanations

Analytical Writing: Scoring and Sample Responses

Analyze an Issue: Scoring

Score	Focus	Organization	Conventions
0	Does not address the prompt. Off topic.	Incomprehensible. May merely copy the prompt without development.	Illegible. Nonverbal. Serious errors make the paper unreadable. May be in a foreign language.
1	Mostly irrelevant to the prompt.	Little or no development of ideas. No evidence of analysis or organization.	Pervasive errors in grammar, mechanics, and spelling.
2	Unclear connection to the prompt.	Unfocused and disorganized.	Frequent errors in sentence structure, mechanics, and spelling.
3	Limited connection to the prompt.	Rough organization with weak examples or reasons.	Occasional major errors and frequent minor errors in conventions of written English.
4	Competent connection to the prompt.	Relevant examples or reasons develop a logical position.	Occasional minor errors in conventions of written English.
5	Clear, focused connection to the prompt.	Thoughtful, appropriate examples or reasons develop a consistent, coherent position. Connectors are ably used to mark transitions.	Very few errors. Sentence structure is varied and vocabulary is advanced.
6	Insightful, clever connection to the prompt.	Compelling, convincing examples or reasons develop a consistent, coherent position. The argument flows effortlessly and persuasively.	Very few errors. Sentence structure is varied and vocabulary is precise, well chosen, and effective.

Analyze an Issue:
Sample Response with a Score of 6

In this essay, the writer embraces the postulate presented, using examples to expand upon it. While acknowledging a possible counterargument, the writer bases a strong support for the quotation on personal experience. There are no significant errors in grammar or mechanics.

I came to college, as many of us do, with the mistaken assumption that I would leave in four years "well rounded," a once-empty vessel now filled to the brim with knowledge. After four years, to my chagrin I find that, like the speaker of these words, my formal education has done little but make me aware of my ignorance.

My chagrin derives from my assumption that it would be otherwise. In fact, I now believe that this is the essential role of formal education—to let us know all there is to know that is just out of our reach, around the corner, in the future. It's that understanding that changed me over four years from a scribbling note taker and semiplagiarist to a questioning, critical, eager, lifelong learner.

The quotation may seem too cynical to some. After all, haven't I learned things in my four years? Isn't formal education more valuable for what it imparts rather than for what it reveals? Yes and no. I have learned countless facts, read countless fine works of literature, and taken part in countless fascinating experiments. Yet for every fact, I realized how much more there was to know. For every great book, I recognized how many more there were yet to read. For every experiment that solved a problem, I was left with uncertainty about another problem that was raised by that experiment. It may sound frustrating, but for me, it was both enlightening and electrifying. I took to the academic life like a duck to water, anticipating always another corner to turn, another philosophy to embrace, another question to ask.

A good education, I believe, leaves us with more questions than answers. "The relentless revelation of one's own ignorance" is not a negative; it's an opportunity. If that were not so, if education were finite, what would we graduates have to look forward to?

Analyze an Argument: Scoring

Score	Focus	Organization	Conventions
0	Does not address the prompt. Off topic.	Incomprehensible. May merely copy the prompt without development.	Illegible. Nonverbal. Serious errors make the paper unreadable. May be in a foreign language.
1	Little or no analysis of the argument. May indicate misunderstanding of the prompt.	Little or no development of ideas. No evidence of analysis or organization.	Pervasive errors in grammar, mechanics, and spelling.
2	Little analysis; may instead present opinions and unrelated thoughts.	Disorganized and illogical.	Frequent errors in sentence structure, mechanics, and spelling.
3	Some analysis of the prompt, but some major flaws may be omitted.	Rough organization with irrelevant support or unclear transitions.	Occasional major errors and frequent minor errors in conventions of written English.
4	Important flaws in the argument are touched upon.	Ideas are sound but may not flow logically or clearly.	Occasional minor errors in conventions of written English.
5	Perceptive analysis of the major flaws in the argument.	Logical examples and support develop a consistent, coherent critique. Connectors are ably used to mark transitions.	Very few errors. Sentence structure is varied and vocabulary is advanced.
6	Insightful, clever analysis of the argument's flaws and fallacies.	Compelling, convincing examples and support develop a consistent, coherent critique. The analysis flows effortlessly and persuasively.	Very few errors. Sentence structure is varied and vocabulary is precise, well chosen, and effective.

Analyze an Argument:
Sample Response with a Score of 6

This essay is clear and compelling. The writer points out the county board's faulty reasoning and the pitfalls of such reasoning, ending with a strong admonishment. The argument contains no errors in English usage or mechanics.

Caught between the county administrator's call for a 1 percent reduction in wages and the union's call for a 4 percent increase, the county board compromised on 2.5 percent increase, halfway between the two, as well as a slight take-back by the county in health costs. Although the county board was well meaning, a compromise like this is no compromise at all. It is only reasonable if the answers to the questions "Is the money there?" and "Are the county administrator's numbers fake?" are both "Yes."

The union's position was unreasonable from the start. It is not reasonable to expect what you have received in past years if the money is no longer there. Nevertheless, the union probably started at that place in order to open negotiations.

Unfortunately, the county board fell into a classic middle-ground fallacy, assuming that the middle ground between the two extremes must be the correct place to be. This would only work if the county administrator called for a reduction knowing that it would never fly, and hoping that some middle ground would be reached. There is no evidence that this is the case. The county board, and the union, would have to assume that the county administrator's numbers, as suggested, were the numbers required to avoid layoffs. The county administrator called for the reduction because of the existing budget deficit. Any amount tacked on above that reduced level would, presumably, necessitate layoffs.

By compromising on a 2.5 percent increase, the county board ensured a need for sanitation-worker layoffs. By agreeing as well to a take-back in health costs, the board ensured an even greater impact on their budget in years to come. Since they do represent the county taxpayers, they would have done better to work a bit longer to negotiate a figure closer to that of the county administrator's.

We are used to assuming that the point precisely between A and B is the best compromise between A and B. Children negotiate that way all the time, splitting the difference to avoid hard feelings. Our representatives are not children, and we should require more from them than a simple acceptance of a middle-ground solution.

GRE Practice Test 6: Answer Key

Section 3. Verbal Reasoning

1. **A, D**
2. **B, F**
3. **D, F**
4. **B, C**
5. **A, C**
6. **A**
7. **B, C**
8. **E**
9. **B**
10. **B, E**
11. **C, E**
12. **B**
13. **C**
14. **B, C**
15. **A**

16. His patrons sent him to the University of Padua when he was only 12 years old, and he graduated with a degree in law, although he was far more interested in medicine.
17. **B**
18. **B, F**
19. **C, D, H**
20. **C, F, G**
21. **E**
22. **A, C**
23. **A, B**
24. **E**
25. The dampness implied by the names is simply an illusion; basalt reflects less light than the surrounding rock, making these regions appear shiny and deep.

Section 4. Verbal Reasoning

1. **B, C**
2. **E**
3. His second work of fiction after *Five Weeks in a Balloon*, the manuscript was deemed too pessimistic and dark by his editor, and Verne never revised it, forging ahead instead with such blockbusters as *A Journey to the Center of the Earth* and *Twenty Thousand Leagues Under the Sea*.
4. **B**
5. **E**
6. **A**
7. **C, E**
8. **C, E**
9. **C**
10. **D**
11. **C**
12. **A**
13. Yet in its day, the Boys Choir of Harlem was a marvel of precision and vocal superiority, and its boys traveled the world.
14. **C, E, I**
15. **C, D**
16. **B**
17. **C**
18. **E**
19. **C**
20. **D**
21. **C, F**
22. **A, E**
23. **D, F**
24. **B, F**
25. **D, E**

Section 5. Quantitative Reasoning

1. **C**
2. **A**
3. **B**
4. **B**
5. **B**
6. **A**
7. **B**
8. **B**
9. **B**
10. **A, C, D**
11. **D**
12. **B**
13. **B**
14. **12.5**
15. **A, B**
16. **8,640**
17. **B**
18. **C**
19. **A**
20. **C**
21. **D**
22. **C**
23. **C**
24. **392**
25. **D**

Section 6. Quantitative Reasoning

1. **B**
2. **C**
3. **C**
4. **A**
5. **C**
6. **A**
7. **B**
8. **C**
9. **A**
10. **B**
11. **A, C**
12. **A, B, C, E**
13. **105**

14. **E**
15. **D**
16. **A**
17. **A, B, E**
18. **D**
19. **B**
20. **E**
21. **80**
22. **A**
23. $\dfrac{1}{221}$, or any fraction that reduces to this.
24. **E**
25. **A**

GRE Practice Test 6: Answer Explanations

Section 3. Verbal Reasoning

1. **A, D.** If they were blissful, they were not surprised (choice F) or suspicious (choice C). The two synonyms are *ignorant* (choice A) and *unconscious* (choice D).

2. **B, F.** The mushrooms are not just sought (choice A); they are valued (choice B) or prized (choice F).

3. **D, F.** Look for the words that create similar sentences. A municipal building (choice D) is much the same as a public building (choice F).

4. **B, C.** Again, more than two choices fit the context, but only choices B and C are synonyms.

5. **A, C.** Choose only those statements that are supported by the text. That leaves out choice B, which is never hinted at anywhere in the passage.

6. **A.** The author does not suggest that gasoline is energy efficient (choice F) but rather that ethanol is not, because its production uses lots of gasoline. The best answer is choice A.

7. **B, C.** Both choices B and C are supported by information in the passage. While whistles have been replaced by air horns, whistle posts have not, making choice A incorrect.

8. **E.** First find the main idea. The passage as a whole deals with adaptations that allow water beetles to live in water. Choices A, B, C, and D support this main idea, but choice E does not.

9. **B.** Look back at the sentence about scuba divers. The author is giving you a comparison that helps you better imagine how the water beetle carries air. The best answer is choice B.

10. **B, E.** Once you have one of the blanks filled, the other choice should be obvious here.

11. **C, E.** The citizens are phlegmatic, or indifferent (choice C) rather than superficial (choice A) or biting (choice B). When few people vote, each vote has great ramifications, or consequences (choice E).

12. **B.** As described, the interns serve as menial drudges, or factotums (choice B), not as private soldiers (choice A), equal associates (choice C), officials (choice D), or city dwellers (choice E).

13. **C.** If Maui is the second largest of several islands, it exceeds (choice A) or surpasses (choice B) several others, but it trails (choice C) only one.

14. **B, C.** The author never says anything that would hint at choice A. However, choice B is supported by the first sentence of the passage, and choice C is supported by the last.

15. **A.** The parenthetical element referred to here is the opinion that Casanova was not a good gambler. The author does not go so far as to suggest Casanova would have made a better doctor (choice D), but it's clear that Casanova was not good at making money for himself, so choice A is correct.

16. **His patrons sent him to the University of Padua when he was only 12 years old, and he graduated with a degree in law, although he was far more interested in medicine.** His matriculation at such a young age indicates that he was unusually precocious.

17. **B.** Try filling in the blank without looking at the choices. Then find the choice that is synonymous with your own guess.

18. **B, F.** Read the whole sentence and think about its meaning. Because the Adirondacks resemble (choice F) the Laurentians geologically, geographers may be wrong to regard them (choice B) as part of the Appalachians.

19. **C, D, H.** This is an example of a text completion that may be solved by reading aloud. Reading aloud will prove to you that neither *alluded to* (choice A) nor *talked about* (choice B) fits syntactically, and the other correct answers should fall into place.

20. **C, F, G.** The Prairie School is a style of architecture (choice C), and its horizontal lines call to mind, or evoke (choice F), the horizon rather than reveal it (choice E). A style can have a premise (choice G) more easily than it can have a belief (choice I), and its mood, or tenor (choice H), would not be what is described here.

21. **E.** The purpose of the passage is alluded to in the first sentence—it is a description or explanation of a particular literary form.

22. **A, C.** Choice A is supported by this sentence: "People like polycarbonates for their lightweight clarity and their toughness under fire." Choice C is supported by this sentence: "This chemical, once studied as a potential estrogen replacement, is believed to inhibit the endocrine system and to be especially harmful to young children." Choice B, on the other hand, is belied by this sentence: "Until recently, when a few manufacturers changed their processing, all polycarbonates were found to leach a chemical called bisphenol A (BPA)."

23. **A, B.** Riccioli did not rename objects on the map (choice C); he named them, believing incorrectly that they were liquid (choice B) and thus giving them names better suited to bodies of water (choice A).

24. **E.** The final sentence states: "The dampness implied by the names is simply an illusion; basalt reflects less light than the surrounding rock, making these regions appear dark and deep." The implication is that the mistake was understandable.

25. **The dampness implied by the names is simply an illusion; basalt reflects less light than the surrounding rock, making these regions appear dark and deep.** This sentence explains the error by giving a reason for it.

Section 4. Verbal Reasoning

1. **B, C.** Choice A is attributed in the passage to "most of Verne's science fiction," so it is not specific to *Paris in the Twentieth Century*. The passage does state that, "unlike many of Verne's more mature works, it lacks strong characterization and plot development," making choice B correct. Verne's later works are termed "blockbusters," making choice C correct as well.

2. **E.** The original Luddite, a man named Ned Ludd, was supposed to have destroyed the machinery of his employer. A Luddite is someone who rejects technological change.

3. **His second work of fiction after *Five Weeks in a Balloon*, the manuscript was deemed too pessimistic and dark by his editor, and Verne never revised it, forging ahead instead with such blockbusters as *A Journey to the Center of the Earth* and *Twenty Thousand Leagues Under the Sea*.** In other words, the novel was "lost" because his editor rejected it and Verne set it aside.

4. **B.** The answer is clear from this section of the passage: "The loss of patents he faced if conversion took place would mean a devastating financial blow."

5. **E.** Work backward to fill in the blank. The number of species is limited in very deep waters; therefore, undersea life decreases with increasing depth, and the answer is choice E.

6. **A.** The answer is defined by the phrase that follows: "Each pair of parents stays together for years."

7. **C, E.** *Terminated* (choice A) is not as precise as *resulted* (choice C), which connotes cause and effect. The city was destroyed (choice E); people may be deprived (choice D) or defamed (choice F), but a city cannot.

8. **C, E.** Choose the most logical answers, which often are the simplest. The crust is composed (choice C) of silicates, which contain (choice E) silicon and oxygen.

9. **C.** The newspaper had modest goals (choice A), but they are not presented as a reason for its success. Instead of reaching thousands of readers (choice B), it had a small readership, but those readers were important (choice C).

10. **D.** *La Solidaridad* was published in Spain, not the Philippines (choice A), and Rizal worked in Europe, not in the Philippines (choice C). There is no support for choice B, and the revolution (choice E) came late in the decade. The best inference is choice D.

11. **C.** Choices A, B, and D would not foment revolution among Filipinos, but descriptions of abuses (choice C) might.

12. **A.** Paragraph one introduces the Propaganda Movement, and paragraphs two and three present two examples, one an organization and newspaper, and the other a key leader of the movement.

13. **Yet in its day, the Boys Choir of Harlem was a marvel of precision and vocal superiority, and its boys traveled the world.** This is the only sentence in the passage that presents the author's opinion about the original choir.

14. **C, E, I.** You cannot complete the first blank correctly without reading the entire passage. By reading sentence two, you can see that the roots of air plants are not for moving nutrients. That allows you to choose *rather than* (choice C) instead of *as well as* (choice B). The other two blanks should be fairly easy to fill in after that.

15. **C, D.** If it is "a worldwide and fairly open phenomenon," it is prevalent (choice C). Counterfeit goods are copied, or reproduced (choice D).

16. **B.** Lists of hot spots as described here might be called *inventories* (choice B).

17. **C.** The clue here is "it seems to have been around for all time." That would not describe something radical (choice A) or fresh (choice B), but it could describe something primitive (choice C).

18. **E.** Although *exceptional* may have several of the meanings listed, the best shade of meaning for the context is *extraordinary* (choice E).

19. **C.** Like his son, Hiram I was a Hawaiian missionary. Choices A and D are true of Hiram II; choice B is true of Hiram III. Working backward, you can infer that choice E is more likely true of Hiram II or Hiram III than of Hiram I, who was, in fact, born in 1789.

20. **D.** A final sentence would be more likely to summarize what came before, as choice D does, than to add extraneous or out-of-sequence facts, as the other choices do.

21. **C, F.** When several choices fit the context, look for the synonyms. Only *satisfactory* (choice C) and *acceptable* (choice F) create sentences that share the same meaning.

22. **A, E.** Again, several choices might possibly make sense, but only two are synonyms.

23. **D, F.** The gospel was assumed to have been written by St. Matthew; in other words, it was attributed (choice D) or credited (choice F) to him.

24. **B, F.** Normal retail centers are failing, but e-tailers are doing the opposite—they are multiplying. Both *burgeon* and *proliferate* describe this action.

25. **D, E.** What might cause men to duel? An insult. The words *aspersion* and *defamation* name the kind of slanderous slur that might lead men to fight.

Section 5. Quantitative Reasoning

1. **C.** At $20 per hour, 40 hours per week, for 50 weeks per year, the total yearly income will be $20 \times 40 \times 50 = \$40,000$.

2. **A.** Quantity A simplifies to $\dfrac{\frac{2}{3}+5}{1-\frac{1}{6}} = \dfrac{\frac{2}{3}+\frac{15}{3}}{\frac{6}{6}-\frac{1}{6}} = \dfrac{\frac{17}{3}}{\frac{5}{6}} = \dfrac{17}{3} \times \dfrac{6}{5} = \dfrac{34}{5} = 6.8$. Quantity B simplifies to $\dfrac{8+\frac{1}{4}}{\frac{3}{4}+1} = \dfrac{\frac{32}{4}+\frac{1}{4}}{\frac{3}{4}+\frac{4}{4}} = \dfrac{\frac{33}{4}}{\frac{7}{4}} = \dfrac{33}{4} \times \dfrac{4}{7} = \dfrac{33}{7} \approx 4.71$.

3. **B.** If you add $2y$ to both sides of the inequality, you get $4x + 2y < 3$. Dividing this by 2, you get $2x + y < \dfrac{3}{2}$. Because $\dfrac{3}{2} < 2$, Quantity B is greater.

4. **B.** If you simplify Quantity A, you get $(2x + 1)(2x - 1) - (x^2 + 1) = 4x^2 - 1 - x^2 - 1 = 3x^2 - 2$, which is 2 less than Quantity B.

5. **B.** Because x, $2y$, and $2z - 1$ are consecutive, you know that $2z - 1 > 2y$. Dividing both sides by 2 obtains $z - \dfrac{1}{2} > y$, thus z is greater than y.

6. **A.** The number of ways to choose 2 of 14 girls is $\dfrac{14 \times 13}{2 \times 1} = 91$. The number of ways to choose 3 of 8 boys is $\dfrac{8 \times 7 \times 6}{3 \times 2 \times 1} = 56$.

7. **B.** A circle with diameter 10 has a radius of 5 and an area of $\pi \times 5^2 = 25\pi$, thus two of them have area 50π. A circle with diameter 16 has a radius of 8 and an area of $\pi \times 8^2 = 64\pi$.

8. **B.** Because $PQ = QR$, the triangle PQR is isosceles, so $\angle QRS = \angle QPS$. Since $\angle QSR$ is exterior to the triangle PQS, it has the measure of $\angle QPS + \angle PQS$. It follows that the measure of $\angle QSR$ is greater than that of $\angle QPS$, which equals $\angle QRS$.

9. **B.** The least common multiple of 10 and 12 is 60, so you add: $\dfrac{3}{10} + \dfrac{7}{12} = \dfrac{3 \times 6}{10 \times 6} + \dfrac{7 \times 5}{12 \times 5} = \dfrac{18}{60} + \dfrac{35}{60} = \dfrac{53}{60}$. Similarly, $\dfrac{11}{6} - \dfrac{4}{5} = \dfrac{11 \times 5}{6 \times 5} - \dfrac{4 \times 6}{5 \times 6} = \dfrac{55}{30} - \dfrac{24}{30} = \dfrac{31}{30}$. Because Quantity A is less than 1 and Quantity B is greater than 1, Quantity B is larger.

10. **A, C, D.** These three answer choices simplify to $0.3 \times 200 = 60$, $1.2 \times 80 = 96$, and $0.6 \times 150 = 90$. The other choices are 20% less than 150, which is $0.8 \times 150 = 120$, and 320% of 40, which is $3.2 \times 40 = 128$.

11. **D.** Each set of parentheses contains a -98, -97, and -96. These all cancel out when the two sets of numbers are subtracted; thus the expression simplifies to $(99 - 95) - (100 - 99) = 4 - 1 = 3$.

12. **B.** There are approximately $0.018 \times 23{,}280 \approx 419$ tickets worth $1 and approximately $0.0002 \times 23{,}280 \approx 5$ tickets worth $2. The sum value is thus approximately $419 + \$10 = \$429$, which is closer to $425 than any of the other choices.

13. **B.** Because the mean age of the 14 students is 25, the sum of all their ages is $14 \times 25 = 350$. Because the mean age of the 22 students is 19, the sum of all their ages is $22 \times 19 = 418$. Thus the sum of all the ages of the $14 + 22 = 36$ students is $350 + 418 = 768$, for an overall mean of $768 \div 36 = 21.\overline{3}$.

14. **12.5.** The triangles PQS and PRT are similar because they share $\angle TPR$ and each have a right angle. Because they are similar, the ratios of their heights to their bases are equal: $\dfrac{RT}{PR} = \dfrac{QS}{PQ}$, thus $\dfrac{RT}{15} = \dfrac{5}{6}$. By multiplying both sides of the equation by 15, you get $RT = \dfrac{15 \times 5}{6} = \dfrac{5 \times 5}{2} = 12.5$.

15. **A, B.** Because $n = 6 \times 15$, its prime factorization is $2 \times 3 \times 3 \times 5$, so its only prime factors are 2, 3, and 5.

16. **$8,640.** If the first printing was for B books at C cost (total: BC), then the second printing was for $3B$ books at $0.8C$ (total: $2.4BC$). Together, these total $3.4BC = 12,240$, or $BC = \dfrac{12,240}{3.4} = 3,600$. The second printing thus was $2.4 \times 3,600 = 8,640$.

17. **B.** By the Pythagorean theorem, you calculate $(PR)^2 = 5^2 + 5^2 = 50$, thus $PR = \sqrt{50} = 5\sqrt{2}$. The perimeter is thus $5 + 5 + 5\sqrt{2} = 10 + 5\sqrt{2}$.

18. **C.** When the fraction is factored, the result is $\dfrac{36^x}{3^{11}} = \dfrac{(2^2 3^2)^x}{3^{11}} = \dfrac{2^{2x} 3^{2x}}{3^{11}}$. If this is to be an integer, it must be true that $2x \geq 11$. Thus $x > 5.5$. The smallest integer value of x is thus 6.

19. **A.** Because $x \lozenge y = y^2 - 2x$, it follows that $5 \lozenge 2 = 2^2 - 2(5) = 4 - 10 = -6$.

20. **C.** Because triangle PQR is isosceles, if the measure of $\angle QPR = x$, then the measure of $\angle QRP = x$ also. The sum of all the angles of the triangle is thus $2x + 30° = 180°$, thus $x = 75°$.

21. **D.** From 2007 to 2008, the profits increased by 3%; from 2008 to 2009, the profits increased by 5%. If the profit in 2007 was 100, then in 2008 it was 103 and in 2009 it was $103 \times 1.05 = 108.15$. This is equivalent to an overall increase of 8.15%.

22. **C.** The profits increased by 4% from 2005 to 2006, thus went from $25 million to $25 \times 1.04 = \$26$ million.

23. **C.** The change in profit from 2007 to 2008 was 3%. The change in profit from 2005 to 2006 was 4% and from 2006 to 2007 was −1%. To calculate the overall change, multiply: $1.04 \times 0.99 = 1.0296$. This is slightly less than a 3% increase, thus choice A is false.

   If the company made $10 million in 2004, then it made $10 \times 1.02 = \$10.2$ million in 2005, $10.2 \times 1.04 = \$10.608$ million in 2006, and $10.608 \times 0.99 \approx \$10.5$ million in 2007. With profits consistently over $10 million, company X definitely did not lose money from 2006 to 2007. Thus choice B is false.

If the company made \$15 million in 2006, then in 2005 it made $\dfrac{15}{1.04} \approx \$14.42$ million. Thus choice C is true.

24. **392.** If there are 1,400 students studying foreign languages and 28% study French, a total of $0.28 \times 1{,}400 = 392$ study French.

25. **D.** There are 360° in a full circle, thus a sector that spans 35% of a circle will have a measure of $0.35 \times 360° = 126°$.

Section 6. Quantitative Reasoning

1. **B.** Quantity A, 30 cents per ounce, is equivalent to $30 \times 16 = 480$ cents per pound, which is less than Quantity B.

2. **C.** If you rationalize denominators, Quantity A becomes $\dfrac{1}{\sqrt{6}} \times \dfrac{\sqrt{6}}{\sqrt{6}} = \dfrac{\sqrt{6}}{6}$ and Quantity B becomes $\dfrac{\sqrt{2}}{2\sqrt{3}} \times \dfrac{\sqrt{3}}{\sqrt{3}} = \dfrac{\sqrt{6}}{6}$.

3. **C.** When you factorize, you get $350 = 35 \times 10 = 5 \times 7 \times 2 \times 5$ and $120 = 4 \times 30 = 2 \times 2 \times 3 \times 2 \times 5$. Each of these has three distinct prime factors.

4. **A.** The equation $x^2 - 3x - 4 = 0$ factors into $(x - 4)(x + 1) = 0$, so $x = 4$ or $x = -1$. Because $x > 0$, you conclude that $x = 4$ and thus Quantity A, $3x = 12$, is larger than Quantity B.

5. **C.** If everything is converted into exponents, Quantity A becomes $\sqrt[3]{5^7} = (5^7)^{\frac{1}{3}} = 5^{\frac{7}{3}}$, which is the same as Quantity B, $(\sqrt[3]{5})^7 = (5^{\frac{1}{3}})^7 = 5^{\frac{7}{3}}$.

6. **A.** If you divide both sides by 2, the inequality $2x + 4 > 10$ becomes $x + 2 > 5$, thus $x > 3$ and $3x > 9$, so $3x + 1 > 10$.

7. **B.** The triangle angle adjacent to the one marked 36° measures $180° - 36° = 144°$. The three angles of the triangle must add up to 180°, so x and the leftmost angle must together add up to $180° - 144° = 36°$. Because the leftmost angle cannot be zero, the angle x (Quantity A) must be smaller than 36°, Quantity B.

8. **C.** Quantity A is $\dfrac{1}{2} \times \dfrac{2}{3} \times \dfrac{3}{4} = \dfrac{1}{4}$; Quantity B is $\left(\dfrac{1}{2}\right)^2 = \dfrac{1}{4}$ as well.

9. **A.** The mode of the data set is the most commonly occurring piece of data: 2. The mean is $\dfrac{5 + 2 + 3 + 2 + 4 + 2}{6} = \dfrac{18}{6} = 3$. Thus Quantity A is larger than Quantity B.

10. **B.** The perfect cubes near 60 are $3^3 = 27$ and $4^3 = 64$. Because 60 is closest to 64, you know that $\sqrt[3]{60}$ is closest to $\sqrt[3]{64} = 4$.

11. **A, C.** The slope of the line through (1, 4) and (3, −2) is $m = \dfrac{-2 - 4}{3 - 1} = \dfrac{-6}{2} = -3$. The equation of the line with slope −3 through the point (1, 4) is $y - 4 = -3(x - 1)$, which simplifies to $y = -3x + 7$. If $x = 2$ then $y = -3(2) + 7 = 1$, so (2, 1) is on the line. If $x = 0$ then $y = 7$, so (0, 5) is not on the line. If $x = 4$, then $y = -5$, so (4, −5) is on the line. If $x = -1$, then $y = 10$, so (−1, 8) is not on the line. If $x = 5$, then $y = -8$, so (5, 5) is not on the line.

12. **A, B, C, E.** A rational number is one that can be written as a fraction of integers. The fraction $\dfrac{4}{3}$ is already written in this format. Similarly, $-3 = \dfrac{-3}{1}$, $0 = \dfrac{0}{1}$, and $\sqrt{16} = 4 = \dfrac{4}{1}$. The numbers $\sqrt{12}$ and π are irrational and cannot be represented in this fashion.

13. **105.** When factored into prime numbers, $21 = 3 \times 7$ and $35 = 5 \times 7$. The smallest number which contains both 3×7 and 5×7 is $3 \times 5 \times 7 = 105$. This is the least common multiple of 21 and 35.

14. **E.** A circle with radius r has area πr^2. If the radius increases 40% from r to $1.4r$, the area will increase to $\pi(1.4r)^2 = \pi(1.4r)(1.4r) = 1.96\pi r^2$, an increase of 96%.

15. **D.** The player might earn one point by making the first shot (80% chance) and failing the second (20% chance). The likelihood of this is $0.8 \times 0.2 = 0.16$. The player might also earn two points by making both shots, with a likelihood of $0.8 \times 0.8 = 0.64$. The average expected number of points per one-and-one awarded is thus $0.16 \times 1 + 0.64 \times 2 = 1.44$.

16. **A.** Each of the 4,000 credit-card payments will incur a 25-cent charge, for a total of $4000 \times \$0.25 = \$1,000$ in fees. On top of this, the store will be charged 2.6% of the total of \$150,000, thus $0.026 \times \$150,000 = \$3,900$. The total amount in fees will thus be $\$1,000 + \$3,900 = \$4,900$.

17. **A, B, E.** To factor $2x^4 = 7x^3 + 4x^2$, you move everything to one side of the equation—$2x^4 - 7x^3 - 4x^2 = 0$—then factor out an x^2 to get $x^2(2x^2 - 7x - 4) = 0$, and then factor the quadratic to obtain $x^2(2x + 1)(x - 4) = 0$. From this, you see that $x^2 = 0$ (thus $x = 0$), or else $2x + 1 = 0$ (thus $x = -\dfrac{1}{2}$), or else $x - 4 = 0$ (thus $x = 4$).

18. **D.** $AC = 2DC$ and $BC = 2EC$. Because these are corresponding sides of the triangles ABC and DEC, which share the angle C, this means that the triangles are similar. Furthermore, all of the linear measurements of triangle ABC are exactly double the linear measurements of triangle DEC. This means that if the base and height of triangle DEC are b and h respectively, then the base and height of triangle ABC are $2b$ and $2h$. The area of triangle DEC is $\frac{1}{2}bh = 8$, so the area of triangle ABC is $\frac{1}{2}(2b)(2h) = 4\left(\frac{1}{2}bh\right) = 4 \times 8 = 32$.

19. **B.** The angles of a regular n-sided polygon are $\dfrac{(n-2)180°}{n}$, so each angle of regular pentagon $ABCDE$ measures $\dfrac{(5-2)180°}{5} = 108°$. Triangle ABE is isosceles, so $\angle ABE$ and $\angle AEB$ both measure x. The angles of triangle ABE add up to $180°$, so $x + x + 108° = 180°$, thus $\angle ABE = x = 36°$. Because triangle BCD is congruent to triangle BAE (by side-angle-side), this means that $\angle CBD$ also measures $36°$. If the measure of $\angle EBD = y$, then you know that $\angle ABC$ is formed by $\angle ABE$, $\angle EBD$, and $\angle CBD$, thus $36° + y + 36° = 108°$. You solve to see that $\angle EBD$ measures $y = 36°$.

20. **E.** One way to solve a problem like this is to compute the probability that you do not win a prize. The likelihood that the first prize goes to one of the other 49 people in the room is $\dfrac{49}{50}$. After that person has gotten a prize (and is no longer eligible for another), you will not get the second prize if it is awarded to any of the 48 other people left in contention, with a likelihood of $\dfrac{48}{49}$. Similarly, the likelihood that you would then not win the third prize is $\dfrac{47}{48}$. The likelihood that you do not win anything is thus $\dfrac{49}{50} \times \dfrac{48}{49} \times \dfrac{47}{48} = \dfrac{47}{50} = 0.94$. With a 94% chance of winning nothing, you thus have a 6% chance of winning a prize.

21. **80.** We solve the equation $50 + 1.5x = 30 + 1.75x$, which simplifies to $20 = 0.25x$. Thus $x = 20/0.25 = 80$.

22. **A.** One way to solve this problem would be to draw a pentagon and count the five different diagonals. Another way is to calculate the number of ways two of the five vertices can be chosen: $\dfrac{5 \times 4}{2 \times 1} = 10$. Of these 10 lines, five of them will be the edges of the pentagon. Thus there are five diagonals which can be drawn on a pentagon.

23. $\dfrac{1}{221}$. There are four aces in a standard deck of 52 cards, so the probability of randomly drawing out an ace is $\dfrac{4}{52} = \dfrac{1}{13}$. If that is done successfully, there will be 51 cards left, three of which will be aces. The probability that a second ace is drawn out will thus be $\dfrac{3}{51} = \dfrac{1}{17}$. The probability of randomly drawing out two aces is thus $\dfrac{1}{13} \times \dfrac{1}{17} = \dfrac{1}{221}$. Any fraction that reduces to this is also correct.

24. **E.** The days when the points representing the values of stocks A and B seem furthest apart are Wednesday and Friday. On Wednesday, stock A was worth 35 and stock B was worth 20, a difference of 15. On Friday, stock A was worth 30 and stock B 10, a difference of 20. Thus, the difference was greatest on Friday.

25. **A.** From Monday to Tuesday, stock A went up 10 points, from a value of 10 to a value of 20. Relative to its initial value of 10, this is an increase of $\dfrac{10}{10} = 1 = 100\%$. From Tuesday to Wednesday, stock A went up 15 points from 20 to 35, an increase of $\dfrac{15}{20} = 75\%$. From Wednesday to Thursday, the stock went down 10 points from a base of 35, a change of $\dfrac{-10}{35} \approx -29\%$. From Thursday to Friday, the stock went up 5 points from 25, a change of $\dfrac{5}{25} = 20\%$. Thus, the percentage change from Monday to Tuesday was greater than over all the other time periods.

GRE Practice Test 7

SECTION 1
Analytical Writing

ANALYZE AN ISSUE

30 Minutes

You will have 30 minutes to organize your thoughts and compose a response that represents your point of view on the topic presented. Do not respond to any topic other than the one given; a response to any other topic will receive a score of 0.

You will be required to discuss your perspective on the issue, using examples and reasons drawn from your own experiences and observations.

Use scratch paper to organize your response before you begin writing. Write your response on the pages provided, or type your response using a word processor with the spell and grammar check functions turned off.

Issue Topic

"Campaigns should cease their reliance on polling; relying religiously on polling to determine the direction of a political campaign has become less and less constructive over time and may in fact be detrimental."

Present your viewpoint on the policy suggested above. Consider the consequences of implementing the policy and explain how those consequences affect your position.

SECTION 2
Analytical Writing

ANALYZE AN ARGUMENT

30 Minutes

You will have 30 minutes to organize your thoughts and compose a response that critiques the given argument. Do not respond to any topic other than the one given; a response to any other topic will receive a score of 0.

You are not being asked to discuss your point of view on the statement. You should identify and analyze the central elements of the argument, the underlying assumptions that are being made, and any supporting information that is given. Your critique can also discuss other information that would strengthen or weaken the argument or make it more logical.

Use scratch paper to organize your response before you begin writing. Write your response on the pages provided, or type your response using a word processor with the spell and grammar check functions turned off.

Argument Topic

The city attorney made this recommendation to the City Council:

"Given recent incidents of unlawful behavior around the city reservoir, and given the obvious potential for injury or even drowning, it is evident that our current laissez-faire attitude is neither prudent nor right. Despite the added cost, I would call for round-the-clock surveillance of the property by law enforcement with the ability to halt illegal behaviors and make arrests if needed."

Critique the reasoning used in the argument presented above. Discuss what questions would have to be answered for you to decide whether the recommendation is reasonable and explain how the answers might assist in evaluating the recommendation.

SECTION 3
Verbal Reasoning
Time: 35 minutes
25 questions

Questions 1 through 3 are based on this passage.

What we think of as modern venture capital arose out of a desire to invest in businesses run by returning military men following World War II. George Doriot, an investment banker brigadier general of French descent, taught courses in industrial
Line management at the Harvard Business School. After the war, he returned to Harvard
(5) and founded the American Research and Development Corporation (ARD), arguably the first venture-capital firm open to ordinary potential investors. By the 1960s, the firm he founded had shares listed on the New York Stock Exchange and had invested successfully in such radical new startups as the first minicomputer firm, Digital Equipment Corporation (DEC).

(10)   Today, the sort of private equity that venture capital represents is a common means of identifying and mentoring new businesses. Investors take on risk in the hopes of achieving high return when the business being supported takes off. With luck, the startup may repay that financing in the form of an initial public offering that sells shares to the public or a merger and acquisition that recoups the
(15) investment. One example that is often used to show Doriot's genius is DEC's initial public offering, where shares of the company in which ARD had invested $70,000 ten years before launched at $355 million.

There had always been some models of investment in new companies, of course—the Rockefellers and other wealthy American and European families
(20) had been doing it for years, adding to their portfolios with new airlines and other innovative startups. With the onset of postwar venture-capital firms, however, the average investor suddenly had the option to take on similar risk with the potential for vast reward.

Consider each of the choices separately and select all that apply.

1. Based on the information given in the passage, which are potential benefits of the kind of investment Doriot launched?

    A   Access to capital markets and acquisition of assets

    B   Fostering of entrepreneurship in new technologies

    C   Potentially prodigious return on investment

Select one answer choice.

2. The mention of the Rockefellers is primarily intended to

　Ⓐ　suggest that only the already-rich invest successfully in high-risk ventures

　Ⓑ　draw a contrast between past investments and modern venture capital

　Ⓒ　reveal the rewards ordinary investors may expect from high-tech investments

　Ⓓ　indicate the vast sums needed for initial investments in private equity firms

　Ⓔ　demonstrate one family's ability to overcome odds using startup investments

3. Underline the sentence that suggests that return on investment in a venture-capital outlay may take a long time to achieve.

Question 4 is based on this passage.

In Mr. Stevens, the pompous, repressed, and self-deluded narrator of *The Remains of the Day*, Ishiguro has created a protagonist whom the reader may pity, deride, and be repelled by, often all on the same page. Stevens is a remarkable creation,
(5)　a butler whose loyalty to his master and his profession has eradicated his ability to make human connections. Although at bottom he recognizes the failings of his Nazi-sympathizing employer, Stevens continues to make excuses for him, with only occasional partings of the clouds of denial in which he dwells. The contortions he goes through to convince himself of the rightness of his life choices are dizzying and make for one of the modern age's profoundest portrayals of a man at odds
(10)　with his times.

Select one answer choice.

4. The author of this passage would probably describe Ishiguro's command of character as

　Ⓐ　avant-garde

　Ⓑ　enigmatic

　Ⓒ　superficial

　Ⓓ　masterful

　Ⓔ　salutary

For questions 5 through 8, complete the text by picking the best entry for each blank from the corresponding column of choices.

5. Onondaga Lake in Syracuse, New York, has historical significance as the site of the founding of the Haudenosaunee (Iroquois) Confederacy and literary _____ as the setting for some of the legends of Hiawatha.

Ⓐ	acumen
Ⓑ	pragmatism
Ⓒ	fortitude
Ⓓ	import
Ⓔ	relativism

6. The small, slender predator known as the long-tailed weasel dwells _____ in open fields and meadows with easy access to water, although it may occasionally choose to live in an area that is partially wooded.

Ⓐ	fortuitously
Ⓑ	primarily
Ⓒ	moderately
Ⓓ	annually
Ⓔ	equally

7. In Blackford County, Indiana, the first town to be (i) _____ was Montpelier, settled by Vermonters and named for that state's capital; it also goes by the (ii) _____ of "Oil City."

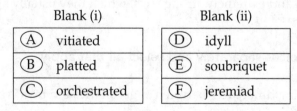

Blank (i)		Blank (ii)	
Ⓐ	vitiated	Ⓓ	idyll
Ⓑ	platted	Ⓔ	soubriquet
Ⓒ	orchestrated	Ⓕ	jeremiad

8. In contrast to a merit system, a political (i) _____ system rewards (ii) _____ with civil service jobs as (iii) _____ for continued support of the party.

Blank (i)	Blank (ii)	Blank (iii)
(A) absolutist	(D) supplicants	(G) forfeiture
(B) demerit	(E) neophytes	(H) recompense
(C) patronage	(F) adherents	(I) compunction

Questions 9 through 12 are based on this passage.

It is not uncommon to mistake an angel shark for a ray; its physiology is such that the comparison is reasonable. Angel sharks are distinctive enough that they are the sole inhabitants of their genus, family, and order.

Line
(5)   The trunk of the angel shark is raylike, with a laterally expanded head and truncated snout. Pectoral and pelvic fins are broad and angular, giving the shark, at least from above, a raylike appearance. Like rays, too, angel sharks lurk along the sand and rocks of the sea floor. They differ from rays in their tubular tails and a lack of venomous spines.

(10)   Angel sharks first appear in the fossil record about 150 million years ago, during the late Jurassic period, and fossils have been located from Europe to Africa to North America. Today there appear to be approximately 20 species left, most vulnerable or endangered, with the subspecies once common in the Atlantic now classified as critically endangered. Because of their tendency as ambush predators to lie along the bottom of the sea floor, from which they snap at passing fish and

(15) crustaceans, angel sharks are easily entangled in trawling nets. Overfishing in their various habitats is the number one challenge for the species. Recent restrictions on net fishing off the coast of California are likely to lead to the recovery of the Pacific angel shark.

    In general, angel sharks pose little danger to humans unless they are cornered.

(20) They do have sharp teeth and extremely strong jaws, which they usually apply to mollusks or bony fish.

Consider each of the choices separately and select all that apply.

9. Which of the following differences between angel sharks and rays is supported by the passage?

    A   Unlike rays, angel sharks are bottom-dwelling predators.

    B   Rays are significantly smaller than the typical angel shark.

    C   Rays produce a toxin in their spines, while angel sharks simply bite.

> For questions 10 through 12, select one answer choice each.

10. In the first sentence of paragraph 3 ("Angel sharks ... North America"), the author implies that

    (A) angel sharks travel regularly from breeding grounds to faraway wintering regions

    (B) at one time in their history, angel sharks lived in both cold and warm waters

    (C) scientists have learned a great deal about the patterns of migration of angel sharks

    (D) angel sharks are not only an ancient animal, but they also had an extensive range

    (E) the appearance and diet of angel sharks have not changed over millions of years

11. From the passage, it can be inferred that classification of angel sharks as endangered is largely due to

    (A) pollution

    (B) climate change

    (C) speciation

    (D) competition

    (E) bycatching

12. Which of the following events would counter the author's argument that Pacific angel sharks are likely to rebound in population?

    (A) Establishment of a protected reef off Santa Barbara

    (B) Continuation of net fishing along the Mexican west coast

    (C) Increased populations of small crustaceans in coastal Pacific waters

    (D) Constraints on the market for shark meat in southeast Asia

    (E) Loosening of restrictions on deep sea rod fishing in California

Question 13 is based on this passage.

The recipient of the first Pulitzer Prize for Criticism, Ada Louise Huxtable was a pioneer, one who, as her longtime employer once wrote about her, "invented a new profession." That profession was that of the architecture critic, and few people were more suited to such an extraordinary career.

Line
(5)   Huxtable was a native Manhattanite, reared on the architecture of that city in the 20s and 30s. She designed stage sets, sold furniture at Bloomingdale's, and married an industrial designer. At the age of 25, she was hired as assistant curator of architecture and design at the Museum of Modern Art, but it was her 1958 article criticizing the way newspapers reported on urban development that
(10) convinced the *Times* to take a chance and hire her to become the first architecture critic in the United States.

Consider each of the choices separately and select all that apply.

13. Which of these facts best supports the suggestion in the passage that Huxtable "invented a new profession"?

A   In 2001, the Columbia School of Journalism listed 37 U.S. newspapers with architecture critics.

B   Art editor and critic Aline Saarinen wrote articles on architecture for the *Times* in the 1940s and early 1950s.

C   *Philadelphia Inquirer* architecture critic Inga Saffron won a Pulitzer Prize in 2014 for her column "Changing Skyline."

For questions 14 through 17, complete the text by picking the best entry for each blank from the corresponding column of choices.

14. Megavitamins are often advertised as offering _____ effects, but medical research suggests that doses in excess of nutritional needs may be toxic or at best quickly excreted.

Ⓐ	equivocal
Ⓑ	salutary
Ⓒ	defamatory
Ⓓ	minuscule
Ⓔ	pernicious

15. A sawtooth eel is fairly uniform in circumference from the head to the base of the tail, where its body begins to _____ gently to a pointed tip.

Ⓐ	waver
Ⓑ	engorge
Ⓒ	recede
Ⓓ	taper
Ⓔ	ascend

16. An underlying weakness in the aorta can lead to the swelling (i) _____ an *aortic aneurism*, which, if left untreated, can rupture and cause a (ii) _____ fatal hemorrhage.

Blank (i)		Blank (ii)	
Ⓐ	before which	Ⓓ	potentially
Ⓑ	known as	Ⓔ	unanimously
Ⓒ	indicated by	Ⓕ	chaotic

17. Whether reflecting upon a (i) _____ hearthside or describing the wings of a small insect, the poet renders the most (ii) _____ aspects of life grand and significant.

Blank (i)		Blank (ii)	
Ⓐ	lambent	Ⓓ	laudatory
Ⓑ	gnarled	Ⓔ	quotidian
Ⓒ	mercurial	Ⓕ	feckless

Questions 18 through 20 are based on this passage.

The toxicity in belladonna derives from agents that inhibit parasympathetic nerve impulses, rendering the human unlucky enough to overdose on any part of the plant unable to regulate a variety of involuntary responses, from perspiration to heart rate.
Line The root is most poisonous, but the berries, flowers, seeds, and leaves are hazardous
(5) as well.

Strangely, belladonna is related to many plants we tolerate quite well, from potatoes to tomatoes to chili peppers. In addition, although it will easily kill pets such as dogs and cats, rabbits seem to eat it with no ill effects whatsoever.

Belladonna's dangers are well documented, yet certain approved medical uses
(10) for the plant's chemicals exist. The atropine in belladonna is used to dilate your eyes at the optometrist, and scopolamine from the plant is occasionally used to treat

irritable bowel syndrome or spastic colon, although pregnant women are warned to avoid it. A variety of homeopathic products also contain belladonna, to the extent that the FDA recently had to order a recall of homeopathic teething products that (15) contained small doses of the toxic substance.

The hallucinations caused by high doses of belladonna lead certain people to try it out as a recreational drug, but reports of belladonna trips online are uniformly terrifying, with people reporting severe dehydration, panic attacks, and complete delirium lasting days.

For questions 18 through 20, select one answer choice each.

---

18. Which of the following best describes the function of paragraph 2 in the passage?

   Ⓐ It rebuts some of the particulars set forth in paragraph 1.

   Ⓑ It provides specifics to support the author's allegation in paragraph 1.

   Ⓒ It qualifies the assertion in paragraph 1 that belladonna is dangerous.

   Ⓓ It connects paragraph 1's introduction to paragraph 3's examples.

   Ⓔ It offers and rejects a counterargument to the ideas set forth in paragraph 1.

19. The author probably mentions homeopathic teething products to

   Ⓐ reassure the reader that homeopathic products are generally safe

   Ⓑ disavow the FDA's intervention in the development of alternative medicines

   Ⓒ signify that belladonna's consumption is widespread and growing

   Ⓓ reveal another potential use for the chemical ingredients of belladonna

   Ⓔ shock the reader regarding the use of a toxin in a product for infants

20. NASA uses scopolamine to combat motion sickness in astronauts. Based solely on the information in this passage, which aspect of the treatment would be most important to regulate?

Ⓐ dosage

Ⓑ delivery method

Ⓒ combination with other drugs

Ⓓ gender of the recipient

Ⓔ natural versus synthetic source

For questions 21 through 25, select two answer choices that (1) complete the sentence in a way that makes sense and (2) produce sentences that are similar in meaning.

---

21. The Los Angeles School District, second-largest in population in the United States, comprises all of the city of Los Angeles and _____ of several adjoining cities.

A institutions

B environs

C management

D portions

E students

F sections

22. Whenever she felt depressed, she found that obtaining a _____ of exercise, even just a walk down the lane, lifted her spirits.

A class

B bit

C trainer

D pleasure

E modicum

F burden

23. The giant crane rose above the cityscape like a _____, swaying slightly as it appeared to ponder its next move.

    [A] malingerer

    [B] behemoth

    [C] leviathan

    [D] contrivance

    [E] babel

    [F] philistine

24. The _____ from the pipe brought with it harmful debris and waste from upstream.

    [A] sputum

    [B] resurgence

    [C] transfiguration

    [D] effluence

    [E] propagation

    [F] emanation

25. The professor's rather _____ prose detracts from our interest in the subject matter.

    [A] pedestrian

    [B] tortuous

    [C] droll

    [D] conciliatory

    [E] prosaic

    [F] effusive

STOP.   This is the end of Section 3. Use any remaining time to check your work.

SECTION 4
Verbal Reasoning
Time: 35 minutes
25 questions

For questions 1 through 4, select two answer choices that (1) complete the sentence in a way that makes sense and (2) produce sentences that are similar in meaning.

1. In an unprecedented act of _____ , the CEO demanded the resignations of his senior staff.

   A gumption

   B irascibility

   C obstinacy

   D truculence

   E consternation

   F epiphany

2. It was _____ indeed that the college had not yet broken ground on the new football stadium when Hurricane Hector rolled in.

   A dubitable

   B providential

   C galvanizing

   D pernicious

   E propitious

   F audacious

3. *Eurycormus* was a bony fish that _____ from the Middle Jurassic epoch until the Late Jurassic epoch, at which point it died out.

[A] amassed

[B] subsisted

[C] procreated

[D] existed

[E] extended

[F] became extinct

4. In badminton, players score points by hitting a shuttlecock with a racquet so that it _____ a net, landing on the opponent's side.

[A] penetrates

[B] bypasses

[C] passes up

[D] passes over

[E] circumvents

[F] clears

Questions 5 and 6 are based on this passage.

Area codes were only added to telephone numbers after World War II. At the time, in order to make a long-distance call, you still needed to dial the operator; that would change slowly over the 1950s and 1960s. As the three-digit area codes were first
Line (5) implemented, codes that covered an entire state had the middle numeral 0, while states that required multiple area codes typically had codes with middle digit 1. Efficiency was key—the biggest cities got the lowest possible number of clicks on a digital phone, with New York City as 212, Los Angeles as 213, and Chicago as 312. If you dialed locally in your city or town, you did not need to use the area code, and the second digit in the seven-digit telephone number you dialed was never 0 or 1,
(10) so operators could easily tell whether a call was long distance or local and treat it accordingly. As demand for telephones increased, the system was unsustainable, and the initial digit 1 was added to calls across area codes, creating an 11-digit phone number.

5. Underline the sentence that suggests that urban population was one motivating factor behind the assignment of area codes.

Select one answer choice.

6. From the information given, it appears likely that area codes

   (A) ranged in the 1960s from 100 to 999

   (B) were originally assigned only to cities

   (C) rapidly eliminated the need for operators

   (D) never began or ended with the numeral 1

   (E) were most efficiently used in city-to-city calls

Question 7 is based on this passage.

The Fluxus artist group of the 1960s and 1970s generated a variety of novel art forms, from computers as a tool for art making to the video art of Nam June Paik. John Cage's vision of art as the interaction between artist and audience influenced the Fluxus group, leading to a variety of effervescent, eclectic performance events in public spaces, as the Fluxus artists never believed that museums or even galleries should be the final arbiter of art. Founder George Maciunas declared Fluxus "anti-art" in its rebellion against and valiant mockery of the elitist, highbrow art of the times.

Line
(5)

Select one answer choice.

7. The author's choice of words indicates an attitude toward Fluxus artists that is

   (A) appreciative

   (B) sardonic

   (C) skeptical

   (D) ironic

   (E) pejorative

Questions 8 and 9 are based on this passage.

The Saffir-Simpson scale classifies hurricanes based solely on wind speed, rating western hemisphere storms from Category 1 (sustained winds of at least 74 mph) to 5 (sustained winds above 156 mph). The structural engineer and meteorologist who developed the scale in the 1970s chose to make the scale simple to comprehend rather than inclusive of all the factors in a hurricane, from rainfall to storm surge. As you might expect of a measurement system devised by a structural engineer, the scale is meant to predict potential property damage, with Category 1 storms expected to snap branches and damage roofs, whereas Category 5 storms destroy framed homes and cause weeks-long power outages.

Line
(5)

Consider each of the choices separately and select all that apply.

8. For which of the following hurricanes would the Saffir-Simpson scale have been least effective in predicting structural damage?

   [A] Hurricane Juan (1985), with wind speeds of 85 mph and up to 17 inches of rain

   [B] Hurricane Isaac (2012), with wind speeds of 80 mph and a surf rise of over 11 feet

   [C] Hurricane Maria (2017), with highest wind speed (1 minute sustained) of 175 mph

Select one answer choice.

9. In the passage, the author is primarily concerned with

   (A) identifying deficiencies of the Saffir-Simpson scale

   (B) defining and explaining the Saffir-Simpson scale

   (C) reviewing the history of the Saffir-Simpson scale

   (D) defending the creators of the Saffir-Simpson scale

   (E) classifying storms according to the Saffir-Simpson scale

---

For questions 10 through 13, complete the text by picking the best entry for each blank from the corresponding column of choices.

---

10. The Akashi Kaikyō Bridge, a span of nearly 4,000 meters, crosses the Akashi Strait, a navigable _____ linking the city of Kobe to Awaji Island.

(A)	basin
(B)	slough
(C)	polder
(D)	narrows
(E)	isthmus

11. The four Strickland sisters—Agnes, Elizabeth, Catharine, and Susanna—were not (i) _____ to resign themselves to the lives of typical eighteenth-century women. Agnes and Elizabeth did historical (ii) _____ and wrote several important biographies, and Catharine and Susanna wrote (iii) _____ about their lives as early settlers in Canada, memoirs that are still read today.

Blank (i)	Blank (ii)	Blank (iii)
(A) able	(D) research	(G) beforehand
(B) content	(E) drama	(H) extensively
(C) supposed	(F) homilies	(I) surreptitiously

12. Although they are (i) _____ the Twin Cities and are often spoken of as a single monolith, Minneapolis and St. Paul have (ii) _____ appearances, populations, and cultural heritages.

Blank (i)	Blank (ii)
(A) dubbed	(D) analogous
(B) considered	(E) noticeable
(C) elected	(F) distinct

13. Animals faced with (i) _____ environmental conditions that provide inadequate energy for growth or (ii) _____ may enter a period of (iii) _____ as an adaptive strategy.

Blank (i)	Blank (ii)	Blank (iii)
(A) corporeal	(D) propagation	(G) senescence
(B) taxing	(E) diminution	(H) prolapse
(C) palpable	(F) aggrandizement	(I) quiescence

Questions 14 through 16 are based on this passage.

Line
(5)

(10)

Hell's Kitchen, once home to poor and working-class Irish Americans and a center of Irish mob activity, now is better known for its prime location next door to the theater district. The crime-ridden, grimy streets of the early and mid-twentieth century gave way in the 1980s to gentrified neighborhoods with any number of reasonably priced restaurants that cater to the hordes of tourists who come to town for Broadway and off-Broadway shows. Arts complexes, including one designed by Frank Gehry, have recently opened there, as have luxury condominiums. Completion of the High Line aerial greenway and the ongoing redevelopment of Hudson Yards have added to Hell's Kitchen's cachet. Indeed, the whole area, once described as "the lowest and filthiest in the city," is now an upscale neighborhood with rents well above average, even for pricey Manhattan. And while many refuse to give up the colorful sobriquet that once described the community, newcomers and some guidebooks now refer to the entire area as "Clinton."

Consider each of the choices separately and select all that apply.

14.   The passage suggests that in the years to come, which of the following will likely happen to Hell's Kitchen?

  [A]   Zoning will keep it from expanding upward and outward.

  [B]   It will continue to draw tourists and affluent inhabitants.

  [C]   Hotels and restaurants will overtake residential areas.

Select one answer choice.

15.   The author probably mentions architect Frank Gehry as a way to

  (A)   illustrate the potential effects of new ideas on old structures

  (B)   show the importance of art as a means of revitalization

  (C)   impress the reader with the prominence of Hell's Kitchen

  (D)   contrast Hell's Kitchen's gritty past with its upscale present

  (E)   reveal the chic new residents of an old Irish neighborhood

16.   Underline the sentence that indicates that some residents are proud of their neighborhood's history.

> For questions 17 through 20, complete the text by picking the best entry for each blank from the corresponding column of choices.

17. Historical _____ is not rare, but perhaps one of the greatest betrayals was that of Julius Caesar by Brutus, the son of Caesar's longtime lover.

(A)	paradox
(B)	synchronicity
(C)	barbarism
(D)	perfidy
(E)	antipathy

18. Anna Anderson's (i) _____ claims to being the long lost daughter of Nicholas II were accepted by some but (ii) _____ by those who had known the royal family; DNA tests after her death confirmed that she had no connection to the Romanovs.

Blank (i)		Blank (ii)	
(A)	spurious	(D)	endorsed
(B)	auspicious	(E)	surmised
(C)	gratuitous	(F)	disparaged

19. A psychoactive drug is one that acts (i) _____ upon the central nervous system, where it (ii) _____ brain function, causing significant changes, for example, in mood or consciousness.

Blank (i)		Blank (ii)	
(A)	moderately	(D)	softens
(B)	primarily	(E)	commences
(C)	uneasily	(F)	alters

20. In the same way that Homer (i) _____ ancient traditions of sung poetry, so did the historian Herodotus use the (ii) _____ of oral storytelling.

Blank (i)		Blank (ii)	
(A)	drew upon	(D)	preferences
(B)	came upon	(E)	conventions
(C)	faced up to	(F)	nuances

Question 21 is based on this passage.

The widening of parameters for the Man Booker Prize for best English-language
fiction led to controversy almost at once, even more when the winners in 2016 and
2017 were U.S. citizens. Prior to 2014, only authors from the Commonwealth, Ireland,

Line   South Africa, and Zimbabwe were eligible.
(5)   This was not the first time the prize was mired in controversy; from the
beginning, its connection to Booker McConnell, Ltd., was seen as problematic.
The firm's dealings in Caribbean rum and sugarcane led one winner to donate his
winnings in protest. In later years, fights between proponents of "readable" versus
"literary" prose have meant that no selection by the committee meets with general

(10)   approval. Nevertheless, the prize is lucrative and ensures substantial profits from
sales, so the Booker marches on.

Select one answer choice.

21.   Based on the information in the passage, it can be inferred that of the following
people, the only one eligible to win the Booker Prize might have been

(A) German Herta Müller for her 1984 stories *Drükender Tango*

(B) New Zealander Keri Hulme for her 1984 novel *The Bone People*

(C) Indian poet Sujata Bhatt for her 1997 collection *Point No Point*

(D) English historian Amanda Vickery for her 1998 work *The Gentleman's Daughter*

(E) American Jennifer Egan for her 2011 novel *A Visit from the Goon Squad*

Question 22 is based on this passage.

A look at the sports programs that have been added and dropped in NCAA colleges
and universities is a simple way to track the popularity of sports through the decades
both with fans and with student athletes. For example, indoor track and field and

Line   lacrosse gained dozens of programs over the past 30 years, but wrestling and water
(5)   polo declined precipitously. In women's sports, soccer grew from 80 programs
in the early 1980s to nearly 1,000 by 2012, while field hockey dropped slightly.
Football grew over that 30-year period, but not nearly as quickly as men's soccer and
basketball did. One wonders whether, despite football fans' wishes, current concerns
over head injuries in football will reverse or stall the trend in that sport's growth and,

(10)   if so, when that change will be noticeable.

Consider each of the choices separately and select all that apply.

22. The author of the passage probably mentions head injuries to

    A   contrast the slow growth of football with the increased popularity of lacrosse

    B   indicate that a sport's popularity need not merely reflect fan appreciation

    C   suggest one potential reason for declining popularity of a sport

Questions 23 through 25 are based on this passage.

Among all bridge designs, one of the loveliest must be the Chinese or Japanese moon bridge. These tall, arched bridges, typically constructed of masonry though occasionally of wood, are unusual for their height, which renders the opening to
Line   the water a semicircle rather than simply an arc. When reflected on the surface
(5)   of the water below, a moon bridge opening forms a perfect, moon-shaped circle. Long approach ramps take the horizontal thrust of the dainty arch; arch bridges are notoriously difficult to build and often unstable due to the careful balance needed to bear their structural loads. Because of their tall arches, moon bridges are meant to carry pedestrians only, and they are often used as decorative elements in formal
(10)   gardens. Among the most famous and popular of the remaining functional moon bridges are the Jindai Bridge in Dahu Park, Taipei, and the Jade Belt Bridge over Kunming Lake in Beijing. The latter bridge's arch was specifically designed in the 1750s to allow the emperor's dragon boat to glide smoothly underneath.

Consider each of the choices separately and select all that apply.

23. Based on the information in the passage, one can infer that moon bridges should not carry automobile traffic due to their

    A   steepness

    B   delicacy

    C   materials

Select one answer choice.

24. The author uses the word *functional* in the second-to-last sentence to

    Ⓐ indicate that the two bridges named are still used for pedestrian traffic

    Ⓑ suggest that most moon bridges are decorative rather than practical

    Ⓒ contrast the bridges in Taipei and Beijing with other operational bridges

    Ⓓ remind the reader that moon bridges are not merely beautiful

    Ⓔ demonstrate how well designed these ancient bridges were

25. Underline the sentence that suggests that moon bridges can last a long time despite their tricky architecture.

STOP.   **This is the end of Section 4. Use any remaining time to check your work.**

SECTION 5
Quantitative Reasoning
Time: 40 minutes
25 questions

Each of questions 1 through 9 consists of two quantities, Quantity A and Quantity B. You are to compare the two quantities. You may use additional information centered above the two quantities if additional information is given. Choose

(A) if Quantity A is greater;
(B) if Quantity B is greater;
(C) if the two quantities are equal;
(D) if the relationship cannot be determined from the information given.

Quantity A	Quantity B	
1. The number of prime numbers p with $1 \leq p \leq 10$	The number of prime numbers p with $10 \leq p \leq 20$	(A) (B) (C) (D)

Quantity A	Quantity B	
2. $\sqrt{x^2}$	x	(A) (B) (C) (D)

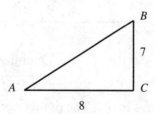

Quantity A	Quantity B	
3. The area of triangle ABC	28	(A) (B) (C) (D)

Quantity A	Quantity B

4. the number of different sequences of 5 letters from an alphabet of 26 letters | the number of different sequences of eight digits   Ⓐ Ⓑ Ⓒ Ⓓ

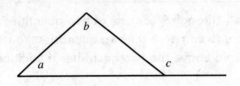

Quantity A	Quantity B

5. $a + b$ c Ⓐ Ⓑ Ⓒ Ⓓ

$$x < 0$$

Quantity A	Quantity B

6. $\dfrac{1}{2^{3x}}$ 4^{-x} Ⓐ Ⓑ Ⓒ Ⓓ

$$0 < x < y < 1$$

Quantity A	Quantity B

7. $\dfrac{x^2}{x+y} - \dfrac{y^2}{x+y}$ $x - y$ Ⓐ Ⓑ Ⓒ Ⓓ

Quantity A	Quantity B

8. The number of ways to choose 8 of 20 people | The number of ways to choose 12 of 20 people   Ⓐ Ⓑ Ⓒ Ⓓ

A random variable X is normally distributed with
a mean of 30 and a standard deviation of 5.

Quantity A	Quantity B

9.   The probability of the   The probability of the   Ⓐ Ⓑ Ⓒ Ⓓ
     event that the value   event that the value
     of X is greater than 38   of X is less than 25

Questions 10 through 25 have different formats. Select a single answer choice unless the directions say otherwise. For Numeric Entry questions, follow these instructions:

• Enter your answer in the box or boxes provided.

• Your answer may be an integer, a decimal, a fraction, or a negative number.

• If the answer is a fraction, you will be given two boxes: an upper one for the numerator and a lower one for the denominator.

• Equivalent forms of the correct answer, such as 1.6 and 1.60, are all correct. You do not need to reduce fractions to lowest terms.

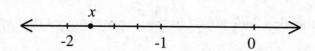

10.   What is the value of x on the number line above?

Ⓐ -2.25

Ⓑ -1.75

Ⓒ -1.25

Ⓓ -2.75

Ⓔ 2.25

11. A rectangular garden measures 10 yards by 36 feet. The gardener would like to cover the whole garden with 3 inches of topsoil. How many cubic yards of topsoil should she order?

Ⓐ   10 yd³

Ⓑ   14 yd³

Ⓒ   30 yd³

Ⓓ   90 yd³

Ⓔ   270 yd³

For this question, indicate all of the answer choices that apply.

12. $|x + 2| = 7$

Which of the following could be the value of x?

[A]   −9

[B]   −5

[C]   3

[D]   5

[E]   7

For this question, indicate all of the answer choices that apply.

13.   Which of the following are in decreasing order?

[A] $0.42, 0.4\overline{2}, 0.\overline{42}$

[B] $\dfrac{3}{7}, 0.\overline{42}, 0.42$

[C] $\dfrac{4}{9}, 0.\overline{42}, 0.4\overline{2}$

[D] $\dfrac{4}{9}, \dfrac{3}{7}, \dfrac{5}{12}$

[E] $\dfrac{5}{12}, 0.4\overline{2}, \dfrac{3}{7}$

14. Let $x_1, x_2, x_3, \ldots$ be an arithmetic sequence. If $x_4 + x_6 + x_{10} + x_{12} = 80$, what is $x_5 + x_{11}$?

    (A) 38

    (B) 40

    (C) 42

    (D) 44

    (E) 46

15. If the two ratios $(x + 1) : (x - 1)$ and 3:2 are proportional, what is the value of x?

    [ ]

16. Suppose that the weights of a certain sort of insect are normally distributed, with a mean of 35 grams and a standard deviation of 10 grams. Approximately what percent of these insects weigh between 25 and 45 grams?

    (A) 29%

    (B) 42%

    (C) 50%

    (D) 68%

    (E) 95%

For this question, write your answer in the boxes.

17. In a sorting process, children are randomly assigned membership to one of four different teams (a 25% probability for each). What is the probability that three friends will all find themselves on the same team? Write your answer in the form of a reduced fraction.

    $\dfrac{[\quad]}{[\quad]}$

18. If we randomly select a nonnegative integer less than 1,000, what is the probability that at least one of its digits is a 5?

　Ⓐ　27%

　Ⓑ　27.1%

　Ⓒ　29%

　Ⓓ　29.7%

　Ⓔ　30%

For this question, indicate all of the answer choices that apply.

19. A scalene triangle $\triangle ABC$ has $AB = 5$ and $AC = 7$. Which of the following could be the perimeter of $\triangle ABC$?

　☐A　15

　☐B　17

　☐C　19

　☐D　21

　☐E　23

　☐F　25

20. In how many different ways can the six members of a wedding party be arranged from left to right if the married couple must stand together?

　Ⓐ　120

　Ⓑ　240

　Ⓒ　360

　Ⓓ　600

　Ⓔ　720

21. What is the mean of all the two-digit positive integers?

　Ⓐ　50

　Ⓑ　54

　Ⓒ　54.5

　Ⓓ　55

　Ⓔ　55.5

For this question, indicate all of the answer choices that apply.

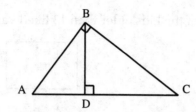

22. Triangle ABC has $\overline{AB} \perp \overline{BC}$. Also, D is the point on side $\overline{AC}$ such that $\overline{BD} \perp \overline{AC}$. Identify all pairs of similar triangles.

    $\boxed{A}$ $\triangle BCA \sim \triangle ADB$

    $\boxed{B}$ $\triangle BCD \sim \triangle ACB$

    $\boxed{C}$ $\triangle BCA \sim \triangle DBA$

    $\boxed{D}$ $\triangle BCD \sim \triangle ABD$

    $\boxed{E}$ $\triangle BCD \sim \triangle ABC$

23. If $\dfrac{1}{x^2 - 1} = \dfrac{1}{x + 1}$, then what are the possible values of x?

    Ⓐ $x = -1$ or $x = 2$

    Ⓑ $x = -1$ or $x = 1$

    Ⓒ $x = 2$

    Ⓓ $x = 2$ or $x = 1$

    Ⓔ $x = -1$

Use the following table to answer questions 24 and 25.

A survey was conducted of 130 children between the ages of 3 and 17 to find out their favorite of three different flavors of ice cream. The results are as follows:

	3–7 years	8–12 years	13–17 years
strawberry	17	10	15
chocolate	23	26	18
vanilla	8	2	11

For this question, write your answer in the box.

24. What percent of the kids older than 13 liked vanilla the best?

25. If one of the kids who liked chocolate best is randomly selected, what is the probability that the child is over 7? Round your answer to the nearest percent.

(A) 27%

(B) 34%

(C) 39%

(D) 66%

(E) 87%

STOP. This is the end of Section 5. Use any remaining time to check your work.

SECTION 6
Quantitative Reasoning
Time: 40 minutes
25 questions

Each of questions 1 through 9 consists of two quantities, Quantity A and Quantity B. You are to compare the two quantities. You may use additional information centered above the two quantities if additional information is given. Choose

Ⓐ if the quantity A is greater;

Ⓑ if the quantity B is greater;

Ⓒ if the two quantities are equal;

Ⓓ if the relationship cannot be determined from the information given.

	Quantity A	Quantity B	
3.	a 20% pay raise followed by a 15% pay cut	a 15% pay cut followed by a 20% pay raise	Ⓐ Ⓑ Ⓒ Ⓓ

$$x > 2$$

	Quantity A	Quantity B	
2.	$3x + 9$	$8x - 5$	Ⓐ Ⓑ Ⓒ Ⓓ

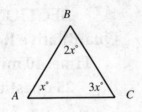

Quantity A	Quantity B	
3. The length AB	Twice the length BC	Ⓐ Ⓑ Ⓒ Ⓓ

$$100^x = 1{,}000^y$$

Quantity A	Quantity B	
4. $2x$	$3y$	Ⓐ Ⓑ Ⓒ Ⓓ

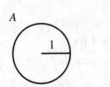

Quantity A	Quantity B	
5. Area of circle A	Area of sector B	Ⓐ Ⓑ Ⓒ Ⓓ

---

p is the probability that event E will happen, and s is the probability that event F will happen. Events E and F are both possible and are mutually exclusive.

Quantity A	Quantity B	
6. p	p^2	Ⓐ Ⓑ Ⓒ Ⓓ

Quantity A   Quantity B

7. Mean of all   Median of all   Ⓐ Ⓑ Ⓒ Ⓓ
    divisors of 20   divisors of 20

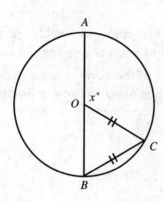

O is the center of circle ABC, and $\overline{BC} \cong \overline{OC}$.

Quantity A   Quantity B

8. $x°$ 130°   Ⓐ Ⓑ Ⓒ Ⓓ

$$a\sqrt{b} = 5$$

Quantity A   Quantity B

9. ab $\dfrac{25}{a}$ Ⓐ Ⓑ Ⓒ Ⓓ

Questions 10 through 25 have different formats. Select a single answer choice unless the directions say otherwise. For Numeric Entry questions, follow these instructions:

- Enter your answer in the box or boxes provided.
- Your answer may be an integer, a decimal, a fraction, or a negative number.
- If the answer is a fraction, you will be given two boxes: an upper one for the numerator and a lower one for the denominator.
- Equivalent forms of the correct answer, such as 1.6 and 1.60, are all correct. You do not need to reduce fractions to lowest terms.

10. $9 - 2 \times 3^2 + 5 =$

    (A) −32

    (B) −22

    (C) −14

    (D) −4

    (E) 2

11. If gasoline costs $2.79 per gallon, then approximately how much will it cost to drive 100 miles in a truck that gets 18 miles per gallon?

    (A) $15

    (B) $20

    (C) $25

    (D) $30

    (E) $35

For this question, write your answer in the box.

12. What is the area of a rectangle with a diagonal of 29 and a perimeter of 82?

13. Let $a * b = a^2 + b^2$. If $a = 2$, for which one of the following values of b will $a * b$ have the least value?

    (A) −5

    (B) −4

    (C) −2

    (D) 1

    (E) 8

For this question, indicate all of the answer choices that apply.

14. $3:2x = x:6$; which of the following could be x?

    [A] −3

    [B] −2

    [C] 1

    [D] 2

    [E] 3

15. In how many different ways can three days of the week be chosen?

    (A) 7

    (B) 14

    (C) 21

    (D) 28

    (E) 35

For this question, indicate all of the answer choices that apply.

16. Points P, Q, and R all lie on a circle. If the coordinates of P are $(-2, 1)$ and the coordinates of Q are $(4, 4)$, what could be the coordinates of R?

    [A] $(0, 2)$

    [B] $(1, 1)$

    [C] $(2, 3)$

    [D] $(2, 4)$

    [E] $(-1, -1)$

17. Suppose that we have enough gasoline to run 8 identical engines for 36 straight hours. If we turn off 3 of these engines, how long can we run the remaining engines using our supply of gasoline?

  (A) 22.5 hours

  (B) 57.6 hours

  (C) 64.3 hours

  (D) 76 hours

  (E) 96 hours

For this question, indicate all of the answer choices that apply.

18. If $0 < |x| < 1 < y$, which of the following inequalities must be true?

  A $\quad x^2 < x$

  B $\quad \dfrac{1}{y} < \dfrac{1}{x^2}$

  C $\quad x + y > 1$

  D $\quad \sqrt{\dfrac{x^2}{y}} > 0$

  E $\quad x^2 y < y^2$

19. Let N be the largest prime factor of $30! - 29!$. Which of the following is N?

  (A) 17

  (B) 19

  (C) 23

  (D) 27

  (E) 29

For this question, write your answer in the box.

20. The three angles of a triangle are distinct integers. The largest angle is 30° more than the smallest angle. What is the smallest possible measurement (in degrees) of the angle that is neither smallest nor largest?

21. A stock went up 5% on Monday, up 8% on Tuesday, down 4% on Wednesday, up 3% on Thursday, and down 10% on Friday. What was the overall change for the whole week, rounded to the nearest percent?

    (A) down 1%

    (B) no change

    (C) up 1%

    (D) up 2%

    (E) up 3%

For this question, write your answer in the boxes.

22. Two socks are randomly taken out of a drawer of 16 socks. If four socks are white and the rest are black, what is the probability that both socks are the same color? Represent your answer as a reduced fraction.

$$\frac{\boxed{}}{\boxed{}}$$

Questions 23 through 25 are based on the following figure.

Number of Airline Flights Taken by the Students of Ms. X's 3rd Grade Class

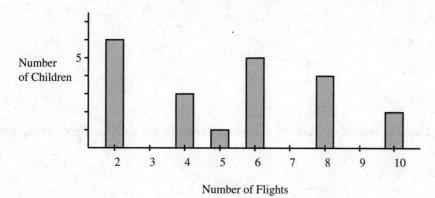

23. What is the mean number of flights taken by the students of Ms. X's third grade class, rounded to the nearest tenth?

(A) 3.2

(B) 4.5

(C) 4.8

(D) 5.1

(E) 5.3

24. What is the median number of flights taken by the students of Ms. X's third grade class?

(A) 4

(B) 4.5

(C) 5

(D) 5.5

(E) 6

25. What is the mode of the number of flights taken by the children of Ms. X's third grade class?

(A) 2

(B) 4

(C) 6

(D) 8

(E) 10

STOP. This is the end of Section 6. Use any remaining time to check your work.

GRE Practice Test 7: Answers and Explanations

Analytical Writing: Scoring and Sample Responses

Analyze an Issue: Scoring

Score	Focus	Organization	Conventions
0	Does not address the prompt. Off topic.	Incomprehensible. May merely copy the prompt without development.	Illegible. Nonverbal. Serious errors make the paper unreadable. May be in a foreign language.
1	Mostly irrelevant to the prompt.	Little or no development of ideas. No evidence of analysis or organization.	Pervasive errors in grammar, mechanics, and spelling.
2	Unclear connection to the prompt.	Unfocused and disorganized.	Frequent errors in sentence structure, mechanics, and spelling.
3	Limited connection to the prompt.	Rough organization with weak examples or reasons.	Occasional major errors and frequent minor errors in conventions of written English.
4	Competent connection to the prompt.	Relevant examples or reasons develop a logical position.	Occasional minor errors in conventions of written English.
5	Clear, focused connection to the prompt.	Thoughtful, appropriate examples or reasons develop a consistent, coherent position. Connectors are ably used to mark transitions.	Very few errors. Sentence structure is varied, and vocabulary is advanced.
6	Insightful, clever connection to the prompt.	Compelling, convincing examples or reasons develop a consistent, coherent position. The argument flows effortlessly and persuasively.	Very few errors. Sentence structure is varied, and vocabulary is precise, well chosen, and effective.

Analyze an Issue:
Sample Response with a Score of 6

In this essay, the writer accepts the position given and provides reasons to support it, while acknowledging a possible counterargument. There are no significant errors in grammar or mechanics.

For years, campaigns relied on polling to determine not only their likelihood of success but also the people's acceptance or distaste for the issues raised by the candidate. In a presidential election year, it was once very common to receive dozens of phone calls from pollsters trying to track the preferences of the citizenry.

Over time, however, it has become clear that polling is not always the predictor one would hope. Results of recent elections both in our state and nationally have belied the late polling by campaigns, and the effect has been damaging both to polling outfits and to the electoral process as a whole.

There are a number of reasons that polls may be skewed or inadequate. A primary reason nowadays is that most polling is done by phone, and many people who used to be subject to polling are now "off the grid" by virtue of having given up their landlines in favor of cell phones. Although polling companies rely on matching phone numbers to addresses, such matching is no longer as easy to do as it once was. In the old days, an area code of 617 referred to a particular part of Massachusetts. Now someone can buy a phone and keep the same number whether he moves to Pittsburgh or San Diego.

So the reliability of polling lessens as people become harder to track, and calling a 617 phone number no longer means what it used to mean. The people with landlines are older, and polling companies start getting skewed results.

If polling cannot be trusted, citizens' belief in the value of polling companies decreases. If media continue to publicize skewed or inaccurate polling results, and those data change voters' minds or even keep them from the polls (in cases where people assume wrongly that a race is won when it is not), the danger is to our democracy.

Many will say that without polling, campaigns are flying blind, and certainly polling may be useful on a small scale, as in a local race where numbers are good or where canvassers are used to go door-to-door to survey trends and conduct direct interviews. For larger races, until we develop new methods by which we can reliably poll sizeable demographics that cross lines involving age, party preference, geography, and so on, we should not continue to rely on polls to do anything more than show a tiny picture of a tiny group's opinions.

Analyze an Argument: Scoring

Score	Focus	Organization	Conventions
0	Does not address the prompt. Off topic.	Incomprehensible. May merely copy the prompt without development.	Illegible. Nonverbal. Serious errors make the paper unreadable. May be in a foreign language.
1	Little or no analysis of the argument. May indicate misunderstanding of the prompt.	Little or no development of ideas. No evidence of analysis or organization.	Pervasive errors in grammar, mechanics, and spelling.
2	Little analysis; may instead present opinions and unrelated thoughts.	Disorganized and illogical.	Frequent errors in sentence structure, mechanics, and spelling.
3	Some analysis of the prompt, but some major flaws may be omitted.	Rough organization with irrelevant support or unclear transitions.	Occasional major errors and frequent minor errors in conventions of written English.
4	Important flaws in the argument are touched upon.	Ideas are sound but may not flow logically or clearly.	Occasional minor errors in conventions of written English.
5	Perceptive analysis of the major flaws in the argument.	Logical examples and support develop a consistent, coherent critique. Connectors are ably used to mark transitions.	Very few errors. Sentence structure is varied, and vocabulary is advanced.
6	Insightful, clever analysis of the argument's flaws and fallacies.	Compelling, convincing examples and support develop a consistent, coherent critique. The analysis flows effortlessly and persuasively.	Very few errors. Sentence structure is varied, and vocabulary is precise, well chosen, and effective.

Analyze an Argument:
Sample Response with a Score of 6

This essay is well organized and to the point. The writer identifies holes in the recommendation and calls for further investigation. There are no real errors in English usage or mechanics.

Before determining whether to accept the city attorney's recommendation of round-the-clock police protection of the reservoir, councilmembers should ask questions regarding unlawful incidents, potential for injury, and cost. The attorney's recommendation is clear but vague. Answers on the following topics would assist the council.

"Unlawful incidents" could refer to a variety of crimes, from Type A misdemeanors on up. If the attorney is concerned about nude sunbathing or occasional drug use, for example, that might not warrant the expense of a police presence. If there have been other, more egregious crimes—for example, assaults or ongoing drug sales—the council might be more inclined to call for law enforcement interference.

The attorney mentions a "potential for injury or even drowning" without giving specifics about actual incidents. Have there been injuries; for example, has someone broken bones while diving from the cliffs surrounding the reservoir? Have there been drownings? The council should call for accident reports going back several years in order to assess this part of the recommendations.

Finally, it is fine to suggest that the recommendation is warranted "despite the added cost," but without knowing what that cost will be, the council cannot and should not act. Presumably a single officer on site would not be enough in the case of a fight or a serious injury; officers might need to be deployed in pairs. For a round-the-clock presence, that might mean three shifts of two officers. Would this require new hires, or could officers be moved from other venues?

The recommendation, while on its face reasonable, is too vague to be accepted without further discussion and exploration. With solid answers about crime, danger, and cost, councilmembers should easily be prepared to vote yes or no.

GRE Practice Test 7: Answer Key

Section 3. Verbal Reasoning

1. **B, C**
2. **B**
3. One example that is often used to show Doriot's genius is DEC's initial public offering, where shares of the company in which ARD had invested $70,000 ten years before launched at $355 million.
4. **D**
5. **D**
6. **B**
7. **B, E**
8. **C, F, H**
9. **C**
10. **D**
11. **D**
12. **B**
13. **A, C**
14. **B**
15. **D**
16. **B, D**
17. **A, E**
18. **C**
19. **E**
20. **A**
21. **D, F**
22. **B, E**
23. **B, C**
24. **D, F**
25. **A, E**

Section 4. Verbal Reasoning

1. **B, D**
2. **B, E**
3. **B, D**
4. **D, F**
5. Efficiency was key—the biggest cities got the lowest possible number of clicks on a digital phone, with New York City as 212, Los Angeles as 213, and Chicago as 312.
6. **D**
7. **A**
8. **A, B**
9. **B**
10. **D**
11. **B, D, H**
12. **A, F**
13. **B, D, I**
14. **B**
15. **D**
16. And while many refuse to give up the colorful sobriquet that once described the community, newcomers and some guidebooks now refer to the entire area as "Clinton."

17. D

18. A, F

19. B, F

20. A, E

21. B

22. B, C

23. A, B

24. A

25. The latter bridge's arch was specifically designed in the 1750s to allow the emperor's dragon boat to glide smoothly underneath.

Section 5. Quantitative Reasoning

1. C

2. D

3. D

4. B

5. C

6. A

7. C

8. C

9. B

10. B

11. A

12. A, D

13. B, C, D

14. B

15. **5**

16. D

17. $\dfrac{1}{16}$

18. B

19. A, D, E

20. B

21. C

22. B, C, D

23. C

24. **25%**

25. D

Section 6. Quantitative Reasoning

1. C

2. D

3. C

4. C

5. C

6. A

7. A

8. B

9. C

10. D

11. A

12. **420**

13. D

14. A, E

15. E

16. B, D, E

17. B

18. B, D, E

19. E

20. **52**

21. C

22. $\dfrac{3}{5}$

23. E

24. E

25. A

GRE Practice Test 7: Answer Explanations

Section 3. Verbal Reasoning

1. **B, C.** The first two sentences of paragraph 2 explain the value of venture-capital investment—mentoring new businesses and achieving high return. The results found in choice A are not mentioned.

2. **B.** The Rockefellers appear in paragraph 3 as an example of old means of investment as contrasted with the new investors in venture capital, who do not require the huge initial means that the Rockefellers had.

3. **One example that is often used to show Doriot's genius is DEC's initial public offering, where shares of the company in which ARD had invested $70,000 ten years before launched at $355 million.** The initial investment took 10 years to show this substantial return.

4. **D.** To answer this question, you need only understand the tone of the passage—the author's attitude toward the subject. Lines such as "Stevens is a remarkable creation" and "one of the modern age's profoundest portrayals" indicate that the author finds Ishiguro's command of character masterful.

5. **D.** The best choice is parallel to "historical significance"; *literary import* (choice D) works best.

6. **B.** Choices A, C, and D lack clear meaning, and choice E would make sense only if fields and meadows were two different places, which they are not.

7. **B, E.** Read the sentence and imagine words that would make sense in context. Then eliminate choices that certainly do not. The word *platted* means "mapped," and the word *soubriquet* means "nickname." None of the other choices fit.

8. **C, F, H.** Again, think about the sentence as a whole, and eliminate choices that do not fit the context. The sentence defines political patronage as a system that rewards adherents, or supporters, with jobs as recompense, or payment.

9. **C.** According to the passage, "They differ from rays in their tubular tails and a lack of venomous spines." They "lurk along the sand and rocks of the sea floor" like rays, making choice A incorrect, and there is no support for choice B.

10. **D.** The sentence does not indicate migration patterns (choices A and C), nor does it mention appearance or diet (choice E). It is not possible to infer choice B from the information given; parts of Europe, Africa, and North America have similar water temperatures and may have done so in the Jurassic period. Only choice D is entirely based on the first sentence of paragraph 3.

11. **D.** Even if you have never heard the word *bycatching*, which means "catching unintentionally while fishing for another species," you should be able to eliminate the other four choices, which find no support in the passage.

12. **B.** The passage states that "Recent restrictions on net fishing off the coast of California are likely to lead to the recovery of the Pacific angel shark." However, if net fishing continues unabated further south in Mexico, there is no clear path to recovery for the shark. A protected reef (choice A), increased populations of food (choice C), and constraints on the market (choice C) all would support rather than counter the author's argument. Choice E would likely have no effect on the population at all.

13. **A, C.** Support would come from indications that the new profession of architecture critic survived after Huxtable started at the *Times*. Choices A and C both support that by giving examples of architecture criticism from after the publication of Huxtable's 1958 article. Choice B mentions an architecture writer from before Huxtable's launch at the *Times*.

14. **B.** *Salutary* means "beneficial." The other choices mean "ambiguous," "insulting," "tiny," and "wicked."

15. **D.** The eel's body remains the same shape but then does something to end in a pointed tip. If it receded (choice C), that would indicate a fading away. It more likely tapers (choice D), which means "comes to a point."

16. **B, D.** The swelling is not indicated by an aneurism (choice C); it is actually called that (choice B). Given the choices for the second blank, only *potentially* (choice D) makes sense.

17. **A, E.** A hearthside is more likely to be lambent, or glowing, than it is to be gnarled (twisted) or mercurial (changeable). The poet renders these quotidian, or ordinary, aspects of life grand and significant.

18. **C.** Paragraph 2 deals first with the fact that belladonna is related to nontoxic plants and that certain animals are immune to belladonna's effects. This does not rebut, or disprove, the particulars in paragraph 1 (choice A), but it does qualify them.

19. **E.** Having set forth the dangers of belladonna, the author provides the shocking information that it is still available in certain homeopathic products, including those for children. The fact that the product has been recalled makes choices A and B incorrect.

20. **A.** The bad effects of overdose are mentioned in paragraphs 1 and 4. There is no support for the other choices.

21. **D, F.** *Environs* (choice B) or even *students* (choice E) might make sense in context, but only *portions* (choice D) and *sections* (choice F) are synonyms.

22. **B, E.** It should be fairly easy to discern that *bit* (choice B) and *modicum* (choice E) are the only synonyms, and the words that make the most sense.

23. **B, C.** A behemoth or leviathan is a huge monster.

24. **D, F.** *Effluence* and *emanation* both refer to a kind of discharge or outflow.

25. **A, E.** Prose that is pedestrian or prosaic is dull and uninspired.

Section 4. Verbal Reasoning

1. **B, D.** Truculence (choice D) is more than simple obstinance (choice C); it involves real anger and meanness, as does irascibility (choice B).

2. **B, E.** Several choices are possible in context, but only choices B and E, meaning "lucky," are synonyms.

3. **B, D.** If you were to fill in the blank without looking at the choices, you might say "lived." Choices B and D are both synonyms for *lived*.

4. **D, F.** Think about badminton. The shuttlecock goes over the net; it does not go through it (choice A) or around it (choices B and E). The best choices are the ones that mean "goes over."

5. **Efficiency was key—the biggest cities got the lowest possible number of clicks on a digital phone, with New York City as 212, Los Angeles as 213, and Chicago as 312.** Numbers were assigned based on population, so large cities were assigned the numerals 1 through 3 for ease of dialing.

6. **D.** You can infer this from the fact that even in the largest cities, where the phone companies wanted the most efficient numbers, the first and third digits were either 2 or 3. There is no support in the passage for the other choices.

7. **A.** To answer this question, think about the author's tone toward her subjects. Adjectives such as *novel*, *effervescent*, and *eclectic* have positive connotations, suggesting an appreciation of the Fluxus group.

8. **A, B.** The Saffir-Simpson scale classifies hurricanes only based on wind speed, so it would be easily able to predict massive damage in Maria (choice C). For the Category 1 hurricanes with substantial potential water damage, the scale would be less effective.

9. **B.** The passage mainly defines and explains the scale; although it points to a potential deficiency in sentence 2 (choice A), that is not its primary concern.

10. **D.** A strait and a narrows are both narrow channels. A basin (choice A) is more like a harbor, a slough (choice B) is a marshy area, and an isthmus (choice E) is a spit of land (and therefore would not be "navigable").

11. **B, D, H.** The sisters probably were supposed to resign themselves to gender roles (choice C), but they chose not to do so (choice B). You would say that they "did" research (choice D), not that they "did" drama (choice E) or homilies (choice F). If they wrote secretly, or surreptitiously (choice I), their work would not be widely read.

12. **A, F.** The cities are nicknamed, or dubbed, the Twin Cities (choice A). The word "although" indicates a contrast, so you can assume that even though they are called twins, they are quite different, as choice F implies.

13. **B, D, I.** Again, make sure that you understand the entire sentence before looking at the choices. Think about the words you might insert to make the sentence logical. Here the environmental conditions are taxing (choice B), or difficult. That prevents growth or propagation (choice D), or reproduction, and leads to a period of quiescence (choice I), or dormancy. *Senescence* (choice G) means "old age," and *prolapse* (choice H) means "collapse of an organ."

14. **B.** Choice A may be true, but there is no support for it in the passage, which only speaks of the neighborhood's development. Similarly, choice C may be true, but the passage refers to growth in condominiums and pricey apartments, so there is no support for the notion that such housing will be overtaken anytime soon. Choice B is the only response with adequate support in the passage.

15. **D.** The mention of a famous architect is not used to impress the reader (choice C) but rather to show how the area has changed and is changing, making choice D the best response.

16. **And while many refuse to give up the colorful sobriquet that once described the community, newcomers and some guidebooks now refer to the entire area as "Clinton."** Some residents of Hell's Kitchen want to cling to the old name, showing that they take pride in the gritty history of the area.

17. **D.** The sentence is about betrayal, so *perfidy,* meaning "disloyalty," is the best choice.

18. **A, F.** Read the whole sentence before choosing. Anderson's claims were disparaged (choice F), or ridiculed, because they were spurious (choice A), or bogus.

19. **B, F.** If the drug causes "significant changes," it does not act moderately (choice A). It acts mostly, or primarily (choice B), on the central nervous system, causing changes or alterations (choice F) in brain function.

20. **A, E.** "In the same way" implies a parallel. Homer used the ancient traditions of poetry; Herodotus used the ancient traditions of storytelling. The choices that best fit the meaning here are *drew upon* (choice A) and *conventions* (choice E).

21. **B.** According to the passage, the prize only goes to English-language fiction from authors in the Commonwealth, Ireland, South Africa, Zimbabwe, and since 2014, the United States. A German author writing in German (choice A) would not be eligible. A poet or historian (choices C and D) would not be eligible. An American work from 2011 (choice E) would not be eligible. As a resident of the Commonwealth and a novelist, Keri Hulme (choice B) was eligible and in fact won for *The Bone People.*

22. **B, C.** Head injuries, the author suggests, may start to limit football's appeal in college, making choice C reasonable. This may take place despite the fans' wishes, meaning that choice B is also possible. Head injuries are not used to contrast one sport with another (choice A).

23. **A, B.** There is no indication that masonry and wood are too feeble to carry automobiles (choice C), but the tall arches lead to steepness (choice A), and the careful balance of the "dainty arch" leads to instability (choice B).

24. **A.** The bridges are still functional in that they are still in use.

25. **The latter bridge's arch was specifically designed in the 1750s to allow the emperor's dragon boat to glide smoothly underneath.** Although it is over 250 years old, the bridge is still used.

Section 5. Quantitative Reasoning

1. **C.** The set of prime numbers $1 \leq p \leq 10$ is $\{2, 3, 5, 7\}$. (Note: 1 is not prime!) The set of prime numbers $10 \leq p \leq 20$ is $\{11, 13, 17, 19\}$.

2. **D.** If x is any positive number, for example $x = 5$, then $\sqrt{5^2} = \sqrt{25} = 5$, making both quantities equal. If x is a negative number, for example $x = -5$, then $\sqrt{(-5)^2} = \sqrt{25} = 5$, which is larger than $x = -5$. In general, $\sqrt{x^2}$ is the absolute value of x; thus there is no way to tell whether the two quantities are equal or not.

3. **D.** If angle C really is right, as it appears in the figure, then the area of the triangle is $\frac{1}{2}(7)(8) = 28$. However, the angle is not marked right, and all figures are not necessarily to scale, so C might be a bit less than $90°$, in which case the area would be less than 28.

4. **B.** For quantity A, there are 26 choices of letter for each of the 5 spaces in the sequence, for a total of $26 \times 26 \times 26 \times 26 \times 26 = 11,881,376$ possibilities. For quantity B, there are 10 choices of digit for each of the 8 spaces, for a total of $10^8 = 100$ million possibilities.

5. **C.** The measure of the unmarked angle adjacent to c is either $180° - c$ (two angles making a straight line) or else $180° - a - b$ (the third angle of a triangle). Because these are the same angle, we conclude that $-c = -a - b$; thus $c = a + b$.

6. **A.** We can rewrite $\frac{1}{2^{3x}} = \frac{1}{\left(2^3\right)^x} = \frac{1}{8^x} = 8^{-x}$. Because $x < 0$, the shared exponent

   of $-x$ is positive. Thus 8^{-x} will be larger than 4^{-x} because its base is larger and the positive exponent is the same.

7. **C.** We can combine the two fractions into $\frac{x^2 - y^2}{x + y}$ and then factor the numerator into $\frac{(x + y)(x - y)}{x + y}$ and reduce (because $x + y \neq 0$ given $0 < x < y$) to $x - y$.

8. **C.** One solution is to compute $\binom{20}{12} = \frac{20!}{12!(20 - 12)!}$ and $\binom{20}{8} = \frac{20!}{8!(20 - 8)!}$

   and then see if they are equal. Another approach is to recognize that the act of picking 8 from 20 is equivalent to selecting 12 to *not* be picked; thus, their numbers must be the same.

9. **B.** The normal distribution is symmetric around the mean of 30, tapering off to either side. Because 38 is further from 30 than 25, the probability that X is greater than 38 will be less than the probability that X is less than 25.

10.   **B.** The number x is clearly between -2 and -1, which rules out choices A, D, and E. Because x is closer to -2 than to -1, the only reasonable choice is B.

11.   **A.** Because 10 yards $= 30$ feet and 3 inches $= 0.25$ feet, the amount of topsoil needed, in cubic feet, is $30 \times 36 \times 0.25 = 270$ ft^3. Each cubic yard measures 3 ft $\times$ 3ft $\times$ 3 ft $= 27$ ft^3, so she will need 10 yd^3.

12.   **A, D.** The absolute value either leaves a positive number unchanged or else makes a negative number positive by multiplying it by -1. Thus the equation $|x + 2| = 7$ is equivalent to either $x + 2 = 7$ or else $x + 2 = -7$, which solve to $x = 5$ and $x = -9$, respectively.

13.   **B, C, D.** If we write out each of the terms, we get $0.4\overline{2} = 0.42222\ldots$, $0.\overline{42} = 0.424242\ldots$, $\frac{3}{7} = 0.42857\ldots$, $\frac{4}{9} = 0.444444\ldots$, and $\frac{5}{12} = 0.416666\ldots$. Put in *decreasing* order, these are $\frac{4}{9}, \frac{3}{7}, 0.\overline{42}, 0.4\overline{2}, 0.42$, and $\frac{5}{12}$. Choices B, C, and D preserve this order, but choices A and E do not.

14.   **B.** In an arithmetic sequence, each term is some constant c greater than the last, so any three consecutive terms will be $a - c$, a, and $a + c$ for some values a and c. The sum of the first and last is $a - c + a + c = 2a$, twice the value in the middle. This means that the sum $x_4 + x_6$ is twice the value of x_5 and $x_{10} + x_{12} = 2x_{11}$. Thus the value of $x_5 + x_{11}$ is half of $x_4 + x_6 + x_{10} + x_{12}$, thus 40.

15.   **5.** We write the ratios as fractions and set them equal: $\frac{x+1}{x-1} = \frac{3}{2}$. By cross-multiplying, we get $2x + 2 = 3x - 3$ or $x = 5$.

16.   **D.** According to the empirical rule, approximately 68% of a normally distributed population will be within the standard deviation of the mean. In this case, the weights that are within 10 grams of 35 grams are all of those from 25 up to 45.

17. $\frac{1}{16}$. The first child can go to any of the four teams. The probability that the second child will go to the same team is $\frac{1}{4}$, as is the probability with the third child. The probability that both join the first friend is thus $\frac{1}{4} \times \frac{1}{4} = \frac{1}{16}$.

18.   **B.** There are 100 numbers of the form 5XY (where X and Y are any digits): 10 options for X and 10 for Y multiplied. Similarly, there are 100 each of the form X5Y and XY5. This is not quite 300, though, because the numbers of the form 55X, 5X5, and X55 (30 in all) have been counted twice. If we subtract $300 - 30 = 270$, we have counted 555 three times and subtracted it three times as well. Adding it back in, we get 271 different numbers, for a probability of $\frac{271}{1000} = 27.1\%$.

19. **A, D, E.** If we subtract $5 + 7 = 12$ from each possible perimeter, we get $3, 5, 7, 9,$ $11,$ and 13 for the third side of the triangle. In choices B and C, this would make the triangle isosceles and not scalene. In choice F, the third side 13 is larger than the other two together, which is impossible.

20. **B.** If we view the married couple as a single unit, we are basically arranging five units (the couple and the four others) freely in any of $5! = 5 \times 4 \times 3 \times 2 = 120$ ways. For each of these, we have two ways to arrange the couple from left to right. Thus there are $120 \times 2 = 240$ options.

21. **C.** The sum of all the numbers from 1 to n is $\dfrac{n(n+1)}{2}$. This means that the sum of all the numbers from 1 to 99 is $\dfrac{99(100)}{2} = 4{,}950$, and the sum of all the numbers from 1 to 9 is $\dfrac{9(10)}{2} = 45$. Thus the sum of all the two-digit positive numbers is $4{,}950 - 45 = 4{,}905$. There are 90 two-digit positive numbers from 10 to 99, and thus their mean is $4{,}905 \div 90 = 54.5$.

22. **B, C, D.** For some number of degrees x, $\angle ABD = x$ and $\angle CBD = 90° - x$ because these two angles together form a right angle. It follows that $\angle BAD = 90° - x$ and $\angle BCD = x$. To see if two triangles are similar, we take care that the letters for the right angles correspond (as fails in choices A and E) as well as the letters for the angle of measure x: $\angle BCA = \angle BCD \cong \angle ABD$. This happens in the remaining cases: B, C, and D.

23. **C.** If we try to replace each x with -1 or 1, then one of the fractions will involve division by zero, which is not possible. Thus, the only working value is $x = 2$ because $\dfrac{1}{2^2 - 1} = \dfrac{1}{3} = \dfrac{1}{2 + 1}$.

24. **25%.** There were $15 + 18 + 11 = 44$ kids over the age of 13 who were surveyed, and 11 of them liked vanilla the best. As a percent, this is $\dfrac{11}{44} = 25\%$.

25. **D.** There were $23 + 26 + 18 = 67$ children who liked chocolate the best. Of these, $26 + 18 = 44$ were over 7 years old. Thus the answer is $\dfrac{44}{67} \approx 66\%$.

Section 6. Quantitative Reasoning

1. **C.** To increase by 20%, we multiply by 1.2. To decrease by 15%, we multiply by 0.85. The end result will be $(1.2)(0.85) = 1.02$, a 2% increase, no matter which is done first: $(0.85)(1.2) = 1.02$.

2. **D.** If you add 5 and subtract $3x$ from both quantities, then A becomes 14 and B becomes $5x$. If you then divide both by 5, A becomes 2.8 and B becomes x. You know that $x > 2$ but not whether it is greater than 2.8. There is no way of telling which quantity is larger.

3. **C.** Solving $x + 2x + 3x = 180°$ results in $x = 30°$; thus, this is a 30-60-90 right triangle. Just as an equilateral triangle can be split in half to produce this triangle, the shortest side BC is exactly half the length of the longest AB, the hypotenuse.

4. **C.** If we write 100 and 1,000 as powers of 10, then $(10^2)^x = (10^3)^y$, so $10^{2x} = 10^{3y}$. Thus $2x = 3y$.

5. **C.** The area of a circle with radius 1 is $\pi(1)^2 = \pi$. The sector is a quarter of a circle with radius 2; thus its area is $\frac{1}{4}\pi(2)^2 = \pi$ as well.

6. **A.** Because events E and F are both possible, $p > 0$ and $s > 0$. Because E and F are mutually exclusive, $p < 1 - s < 1$. Because $0 < p < 1$, we know that $p^2 < p$.

7. **A.** The set of divisors of 20 is $\{1, 2, 4, 5, 10, 20\}$, so the median is $\frac{4+5}{2} = 4.5$ and the mean is $\frac{1+2+4+5+10+20}{6} = \frac{42}{6} = 7$. Thus, the mean is larger than the median.

8. **B.** Segment $\overline{OC}$ is the radius of the circle, as is $\overline{OB}$, so triangle OBC is equilateral. This means that angle COB measures 60°, so $x = 180° - 60° = 120°$.

9. **C.** Squaring both sides of the equation produces $a^2b = 25$. Divide both sides of this by a, and we get $ab = \frac{25}{a}$.

10. **D.** By the order of operations, you must first square the 3 to get $9 - 2 \times 9 + 5$; then multiply to get $9 - 18 + 5$. Addition and subtraction are then done left-to-right, so we first subtract to get $-9 + 5$, and then we add to get -4.

11. **A.** The three numbers in this problem, written as fractions with units, are $\frac{\$2.79}{\text{gal}}$, 100 miles, and $\frac{18\,\text{mi}}{\text{gal}}$. If you multiply the first two with the reciprocal of the third, all of the units except for the dollars will cancel: $\frac{\$2.79}{\text{gal}} \times \frac{100\,\text{mi}}{1} \times \frac{\text{gal}}{18\,\text{mi}} = \frac{\$2.79 \times 100}{18} = \$15.5$. This is closest to \$15.

12. **420.** If the perimeter is 82, then the sum of two adjacent sides must be 41. If one side is x, the other must be $41 - x$. The diagonal of 29 forms a right triangle, so we can use the Pythagorean theorem: $x^2 + (41 - x)^2 = 29^2$. This multiplies out to $x^2 + 41^2 - 82x + x^2 - 29^2 = 0$, or $2x^2 - 82x + 840 = 0$. If we divide everything by 2, we get $x^2 - 41x + 420 = 0$, which can be solved either by factoring into $(x - 20)(x - 21) = 0$ or using the quadratic formula to get $x = 20$ and 21. These are the two sides of the rectangle, so the area is $20 \times 21 = 420$.

13. **D.** The expression $2 \ast b = 2^2 + b^2$ will have the least value when b^2 has the least value. Of all the listed values, the one with the smallest square is 1.

14. **A, E.** When the ratios are written as fractions, the result is $\dfrac{3}{2x} = \dfrac{x}{6}$. When this is cross-multiplied, the result is $18 = 2x^2$, which simplifies to $x^2 = 9$. There are thus two solutions: $x = 3$ and $x = -3$.

15. **E.** The number of ways to choose three of seven days is $\dfrac{7!}{3!(7 - 3)!} = \dfrac{7 \times 6 \times 5 \times 4 \times 3 \times 2 \times 1}{3 \times 2 \times 1 \times 4 \times 3 \times 2 \times 1} = \dfrac{7 \times 6 \times 5}{3 \times 2 \times 1} = 7 \times 5 = 35$.

16. **B, D, E.** Any three different points lie on a circle if they are not in a straight line. The slope from $(-2, 1)$ to $(4, 4)$ is $\dfrac{4 - 1}{4 - (-2)} = \dfrac{3}{6} = \dfrac{1}{2}$, so the equation of the line between them is $y - 4 = \dfrac{1}{2}(x - 4)$ or simply $2y - 8 = x - 4$ or $2y - x = 4$. We plug each candidate point in to see which are collinear: $2(2) - 0 = 4$, $2(1) - 1 = 1$, $2(3) - 2 = 4$, $2(4) - 2 = 6$, and $2(-1) - (-1) = -1$. The points R we want are those that *do not* come out to 4 and thus are not collinear with P and Q.

17. **B.** If 8 engines last 36 hours, then 1 engine will last $36 \times 8 = 288$ hours, and 5 engines will last $\dfrac{288}{5} = 57.6$ hours.

18. **B, D, E.** Because $0 < |x| < 1$, we know that $0 < x^2 < |x| < 1 < y$. We get the same equation by cross-multiplying choice B and by dividing both sides of choice E by y, so those work. Choice D is true because every square root is nonnegative (and both x and y are different from zero). Because x might be negative, we could have something like $x = -0.5$ and $y = 1.1$ so that $x^2 = 0.25$ is not less than -0.5 and $x + y = 0.6$, eliminating the remaining two choices.

19. **E.** We know that $30! = 30(29)(28)\ldots(3)(2)(1)$ and $29!$ is the same, but without the first term; thus we can factor out a $29!$ to get $30! - 29! = 29!(30 - 1) = 29!(29)$. This is a product of 30 terms, the largest of which is the prime number 29.

20. **52.** We can write the three angles in increasing order as $x < y < x + 30°$. As they comprise a triangle, $x + y + x + 30° = 180°$; thus $2x + y = 150$. If we add $2x$ to both sides of the inequality $x < y$, we get $3x < 2x + y = 150°$; thus $x < 50°$. To minimize the measure y of the middle angle, we need x to be as big as possible. As all angles are integers, $x = 49$, so $y = 150 - 2(49) = 52$.

21. **C.** The overall change is $(1.05)(1.08)(0.96)(1.03)(0.9) \approx 1.00917$. Rounded to the nearest percent, this is an increase of 1%.

22. $\frac{3}{5}$. We compute the probability that both socks are white and both socks are black separately. The probability of drawing a white sock randomly is $\frac{4}{16} = \frac{1}{4}$, after which the probability of drawing another white sock is $\frac{3}{15} = \frac{1}{5}$ (three of the 15 remaining socks are white). Together this likelihood is $\frac{1}{4} \times \frac{1}{5} = \frac{1}{20}$. The probability for the first black sock is $\frac{12}{16} = \frac{3}{4}$ and the second is $\frac{11}{15}$, so the odds of two black socks is $\frac{3}{4} \times \frac{11}{15} = \frac{11}{20}$. Together, the probability of one or the other is $\frac{1}{20} + \frac{11}{20} = \frac{12}{20} = \frac{3}{5}$.

23. **E.** The total number of students in the class can be calculated by adding up the heights of all the bars: $6 + 3 + 1 + 5 + 4 + 2 = 21$. Each bar represents a number of flights equal to the product of the number of flights times the number of students. Thus the total number of flights is $2 \times 6 + 4 \times 3 + 5 \times 1 + 6 \times 5 + 8 \times 4 + 10 \times 2 = 111$. The mean is found by dividing $111 \div 21$, which is approximately 5.3.

24. **E.** There are 21 students in the class, so the median (middle) student will be the eleventh, when their numbers of flights are put in order. The first bar on the chart represents 6 students, the next represents 3 students, and the next represents 1 student, for a total of 10. The eleventh student is thus one of the ones who took six flights.

25. **A.** The mode is the most common number that appears. In this case, more students had taken two flights than had taken any other single number of flights.

GRE Practice Test 8

SECTION 1

Analytical Writing

ANALYZE AN ISSUE

30 Minutes

You will have 30 minutes to organize your thoughts and compose a response that represents your point of view on the topic presented. Do not respond to any topic other than the one given; a response to any other topic will receive a score of 0.

You will be required to discuss your perspective on the issue, using examples and reasons drawn from your own experiences and observations.

Use scratch paper to organize your response before you begin writing. Write your response on the pages provided, or type your response using a word processor with the spell and grammar check functions turned off.

Issue Topic

Claim: "Live theater will remain a relevant art form even in our age of individualized, digital entertainment."

Reason: "Nothing can take the place of the audience-actor interaction that takes place in a staged performance."

Present your viewpoint on the claim and reason shown above. Explain the extent to which you agree and disagree both with the claim and with the reason on which the claim is based.

SECTION 2

Analytical Writing

ANALYZE AN ARGUMENT

30 Minutes

You will have 30 minutes to organize your thoughts and compose a response that critiques the given argument. Do not respond to any topic other than the one given; a response to any other topic will receive a score of 0.

You are not being asked to discuss your point of view on the statement. You should identify and analyze the central elements of the argument, the underlying assumptions that are being made, and any supporting information that is given. Your critique can also discuss other information that would strengthen or weaken the argument or make it more logical.

Use scratch paper to organize your response before you begin writing. Write your response on the pages provided, or type your response using a word processor with the spell and grammar check functions turned off.

Argument Topic

Certain pines have always relied on wildfires to spread their seeds. The common Canadian jack pine, for example, has resilient, resin-filled cones that remain dormant until intense heat melts the resin, allowing the seeds to pop out of the opened cone. For that reason, one expects to see jack pine as pioneer trees in the wake of certain wildfires. Students exploring the forest floor in Washington State after a recent rash of forest fires found no evidence of jack pine seedlings and speculated that the fires burned so hot and for so long that they eradicated the seed that burst forth from the cones.

Read the proposed explanation above and suggest one or more alternatives that could instead account for the facts in this argument.

SECTION 3
Verbal Reasoning
Time: 35 minutes
25 questions

For questions 1 through 4, select two answer choices that (1) complete the sentence in a way that makes sense and (2) produce sentences that are similar in meaning.

1. Beat Generation works by Ginsberg and Burroughs led to obscenity trials, which led in turn to the _____ of rules governing what could be published in the United States.

   A   tightening

   B   application

   C   perpetuation

   D   liberalization

   E   instigation

   F   relaxation

2. Unbelievably, the number of orchid species is nearly four times the number of mammal species, with _____ new orchid species added each year.

   A   scores of

   B   assorted

   C   atypical

   D   recurrent

   E   numerous

   F   multihued

3. Not only do the swarms of mosquitoes _____ tourists along the coast, but they also carry with them the possibility of Zika infection.

- [A] blight
- [B] dragoon
- [C] beleaguer
- [D] obviate
- [E] lambaste
- [F] harry

4. Try to avoid _____ in your writing; a more original style will appeal to your readers and ensure them that you do not take them for granted.

- [A] platitudes
- [B] polemics
- [C] plaudits
- [D] salaciousness
- [E] banalities
- [F] stridency

Questions 5 and 6 are based on this passage.

The cultural ancestry of Russia, Ukraine, and Belarus derives from the ancient federation of tribes known as Kievan Rus'. Its origin is a matter of debate, but many historians trace the foundation to the Viking ruler Oleg around 882, when he and his
Line armies took over Slavic villages Smolensk and Kiev. Oleg expanded his kingdom by
(5)   uniting Slavic and Finnish tribes. Other historians mark the founding of the Rurik dynasty as the beginning of Kievan Rus'. Scandinavian prince Rurik and his brothers joined forces to rule over Finnish and Slavic tribes in 862, but within three centuries, the federation had separated into principalities, with each principality ruled by one part of the Rurik clan. While even the origin of the word *Rus'* remains mired
(10) in controversy, it is certainly true that most of the region adhered to Scandinavian traditions for its first century of existence but seemed thoroughly Slavic by the time of ruler Vladimir, who also brought Orthodox Christianity to the region in 988.

Consider each of the choices separately and select all that apply.

5. According to the author, historians seem to differ over which aspects of Kievan Rus'?

   A   The year of its inception

   B   Its Scandinavian origin

   C   The source of its name

Select one answer choice.

6. The most likely reason for the change described in the final sentence is

   Ⓐ   a Viking exodus

   Ⓑ   Christian missionaries

   Ⓒ   war with Constantinople

   Ⓓ   cross-cultural breeding

   Ⓔ   Finnish national pride

Question 7 is based on this passage.

Like stem cells, progenitor cells are marked by their tendency to differentiate into a specific cell type. Unlike stem cells, progenitor cells cannot divide and reproduce indefinitely, and they are limited in the types of cells they may become. Some are
Line   referred to as "committed" progenitor cells; for example, committed progenitor cells
(5)   in the liver will only differentiate into hepatic or bile duct cells. In nature, progenitor cells lie dormant until tissue injury or cell attrition requires their evolution into replacement cells. In medicine, scientists see progenitor cells as potentially useful in rebuilding heart valves or blood vessels and other regenerative tasks.

Consider each of the choices separately and select all that apply.

7. Based on the information in the passage, which of the following might be a potential use for progenitor cells in eye disease?

   A   Replacing dying retinal cells in macular degeneration

   B   Opening blocked drainage canals for glaucoma patients

   C   Restoring a damaged lens after cataract surgery

Questions 8 and 9 are based on this passage.

Unable to produce his own heirs, Cardinal Mazarin, Chief Minister of France during Louis XIV's early reign, surrounded himself at court with the seven daughters of his two sisters. He invited them and their mothers to join him in the hopes of adding to
Line the fractious court some confidants whom he could trust. The young girls, known as
(5) the Mazarinettes, became the talk of Paris due to their unusual Italian features—they were satirized in racist pamphlets for their dark complexions and brazen behavior. At the time, French women of a certain class prided themselves in their pallor, using toxic lead makeup to ensure a delicate white skin that contrasted with that of working-class women.

(10) The cardinal meant to marry each girl off well, thus increasing his family's wealth and guaranteeing his own legacy throughout Europe. The girls were taken in by the queen mother and treated as royal princesses, which ensured their acceptance by the wealthy older men who hovered around the court of the Sun King. Louis himself was attracted to one of the nieces, Marie Mancini, but the queen mother drew
(15) the line there, and Mazarin saw her married off to an Italian prince. Four of the girls became duchesses, two became princesses, and one became a countess, with each marriage expanding the cardinal's influence as he intended.

For questions 8 and 9, select one answer choice each.

---

8. The passage indicates that upper-class French women of the time altered their appearances to

   (A) give themselves a veneer of respectability

   (B) project an air of vulnerability and dreaminess

   (C) contrast with the many foreigners who infiltrated France

   (D) attract courtiers with their conspicuous radiance

   (E) distinguish themselves from women who might toil in the sun

9. The author mentions each of these reasons for Cardinal Mazarin's invitation to his nieces EXCEPT his desire to

   (A) enjoy close alliances in court

   (B) impress European heads of state

   (C) extend his power base

   (D) increase the family treasure

   (E) achieve a lasting legacy

> For questions 10 through 13, complete the text by picking the best entry for each blank from the corresponding column of choices.

10. The other European nations loudly _____ the "hard Brexit" defectors, but nothing they had to say could counteract the June 2016 referendum.

Ⓐ	deprecated
Ⓑ	equivocated
Ⓒ	dissociated
Ⓓ	exculpated
Ⓔ	ballyhooed

11. An ethnographic study of a society may involve any manner of direct, firsthand data collection, including observations, _____, or questionnaires.

Ⓐ	readings
Ⓑ	mapmaking
Ⓒ	interviews
Ⓓ	adaptations
Ⓔ	rituals

12. The Volstead Act, (i) _____ the National Prohibition Act, was actually vetoed by President Wilson, but Congress (ii) _____ his veto the very same day.

Blank (i)		Blank (ii)	
Ⓐ	better known as	Ⓓ	nominated
Ⓑ	keeping in mind	Ⓔ	overrode
Ⓒ	allowing for	Ⓕ	supported

13. The genius of *People* magazine may be its ability to take the (i) _____ details of celebrities' lives and somehow to render them (ii) _____ compared to our own.

Blank (i)		Blank (ii)	
Ⓐ	recreant	Ⓓ	alluring
Ⓑ	quotidian	Ⓔ	incongruous
Ⓒ	debonair	Ⓕ	egregious

Questions 14 through 16 are based on this passage.

"Muck onion" is hardly a pleasant name, but the onions being grown in the muck soil of central New York have become a key agricultural product. Cornell University ranks onions one of the most important vegetable crops in the state, with over 12,000 acres dedicated to their growth.

Line

(5)   The muck that allows the onions to thrive is deep, black soil that is loaded with nutrients—a natural compost that contains up to 80 percent organic matter. The soil holds water readily and maintains heat, making the growing season shorter than for crops in other regions. The source of the muck dates back to the same ancient glaciers that formed the lakes in this region; as the lakes receded, they left behind low-lying

(10)   bogs filled with decayed plant matter. In the early twentieth century, immigrant farmers drained the bogs, leaving behind the rich, black soil. Unfortunately, muck is a finite resource; there is less of it every year, and the tilling and draining of fields speed its disappearance.

Consider each of the choices separately and select all that apply.

14. The passage suggests that growing muck onion long-term would, over time, have which of the following consequences?

   A   The need for farmers to truck in muck from other regions and states

   B   A reduction in the flavor and size of onions grown in central New York

   C   An end to the naturally rich soil in which muck onions currently grow

Select one answer choice.

15. It can be inferred that the author mentions "natural compost" (line 6) primarily to

   Ⓐ contrast the natural muck with store-bought loam

   Ⓑ suggest that all onions grown in this soil are organic

   Ⓒ argue against current uses of synthetic fertilizers

   Ⓓ emphasize the fertile qualities of central New York muck

   Ⓔ classify muck as one means of revitalizing unhealthy soil

16. Underline the sentence that explains why onions grow faster in muck than in other soils.

> For questions 17 through 20, complete the text by picking the best entry for each blank from the corresponding column of choices.

17. Traditionally, windmills were used to grind grain, but their alternative use as water pumps was _____ to the success of ranches and farms on the plains of North America.

Ⓐ	marginal
Ⓑ	perilous
Ⓒ	unrelated
Ⓓ	inimical
Ⓔ	critical

18. Although Felix Mendelssohn was recognized in his youth as a musical (i) _____, his parents were at first (ii) _____ to let him pursue a musical career.

Blank (i)		Blank (ii)	
Ⓐ	prodigy	Ⓓ	reluctant
Ⓑ	vocation	Ⓔ	provoked
Ⓒ	disciple	Ⓕ	expected

19. The ongoing (i) _____ of the coal industry, followed by bankruptcy filings by many large mines and energy companies, have led to (ii) _____ among generations of workers who once clung determinedly to the middle class.

Blank (i)		Blank (ii)	
Ⓐ	emoluments	Ⓓ	privation
Ⓑ	imprecations	Ⓔ	fealty
Ⓒ	vicissitudes	Ⓕ	equanimity

20. The recipe requires the cook to let berries (i) _____ in a sugar-and-brandy solution overnight. The berries are especially (ii) _____ served with a vanilla cream, and the sour berries keep the sweetness from being overly (iii) _____.

Blank (i)		Blank (ii)		Blank (iii)	
Ⓐ	evanesce	Ⓓ	ambrosial	Ⓖ	tangible
Ⓑ	macerate	Ⓔ	fulsome	Ⓗ	feculent
Ⓒ	blanch	Ⓕ	concordant	Ⓘ	cloying

Question 21 is based on this passage.

James Simpson was clearly a brainy fellow; he became a surgeon just out of his teens, was named president of the Royal Medical Society of Edinburgh in 1835 at age 24, and was a full professor by age 28. His specialty was obstetrics, and although he was
Line renowned as a kind and careful doctor and surgeon, he was evidently a scientist at
(5) heart. He worked to improve his field, advocating for monitoring of fetal heart rates and introducing such advances as forceps, acupressure, and anesthesia. Finding ether less than ideal, he turned with his assistants to a new vapor, chloroform, using it to reduce labor pains and introducing it to the medical world as a useful alternative. Queen Victoria chose chloroform during the birth of her eighth child, and
(10) although Simpson was not the queen's physician, his reputation was made.

Select one answer choice.

21. Why does the author say that Simpson was "a scientist at heart"?

Ⓐ He was not satisfied with life as an Edinburgh surgeon.

Ⓑ He was unusually innovative and experimental.

Ⓒ His laboratory work surpassed his surgical work.

Ⓓ He had a passion for investigatory medicine.

Ⓔ He envied the more cerebral work of his lab assistants.

Question 22 is based on this passage.

One might expect that all large mammals on Earth have already been identified and classified, but in fact, a new species of orangutan was just named in 2017. An expedition reported sighting a group of orangutans in an isolated area on Sumatra
Line back in 1997, but the assumption was that these were Sumatran orangutans (*Pongo*
(5) *abelii*) that had simply migrated from the few orangutan habitats on the island. Not until an injured ape was found in the high elevations of Sumatra did scientists manage to analyze the creature and determine that this ape had features distinct from those of the critically endangered Sumatran orangutan. In some respects, it more closely matched the equally endangered Bornean orangutan (*Pongo pygmaeus*)
(10) from 900 miles across the sea, but it was different enough from both that it was given a new name and counted as its own species, *Pongo tapanuliensis*, recently referred to by *National Geographic* as "the rarest great ape on Earth."

Consider each of the choices separately and select all that apply.

22. Which theories, if verified, might explain the fact that *Pongo tapanuliensis* resembles *Pongo pygmaeus* somewhat more than it resembles *Pongo abelii*?

    [A] *Pongo abelii* on Sumatra lived together prior to a drastic event that divided them.

    [B] The three species comprise discrete evolutionary lineages from a long-ago ancestor.

    [C] Changes in sea levels during the Ice Age allowed for movement among landmasses.

Questions 23 through 25 are based on this passage.

The theremin is an electronic instrument that makes music without being touched by the player. The original versions consisted of an oscillator with two metal rod antennas, one of which controlled amplitude and the other of which controlled
Line pitch. By fluttering and waving their fingers, hands, and arms, theremin players
(5) are able to create haunting, eerie sounds reminiscent of a stringed instrument. The effect is magical—the players look as though they are dancing, and the sound comes not from fingers on a keyboard or bows on strings but from movements through the air. To make music rather than noise, theremin players must rely on their ears more than other musicians do; there are no frets or keys to give clues
(10) about correct tone.

Early theremins were produced by RCA in the 1930s and were popular as a curiosity for some time. Robert Moog parlayed his boyhood interest in building theremins into the development of the Moog synthesizer, which radically altered electronic music.

Consider each of the choices separately and select all that apply.

23. Based on the information in the passage, early theremins were most likely

    [A] monophonic

    [B] digital

    [C] acoustic

Select one answer choice.

24. Based on the description in the passage, an early theremin most closely resembled a

    (A) violin

    (B) computer

    (C) radio receiver

    (D) alarm clock

    (E) pipe organ

25. Underline the sentence that suggests the difficulty of playing the theremin.

STOP. **This is the end of Section 3. Use any remaining time to check your work.**

SECTION 4
Verbal Reasoning
Time: 35 minutes
25 questions

Questions 1 through 3 are based on this passage.

"Remember, remember, the Fifth of November" goes one nursery rhyme popular in England since the seventeenth century. The event to be remembered is the Gunpowder Plot, a dastardly but daring 1605 attempt to blow up Parliament and assassinate the entire House of Lords and the king. Military expert Guy Fawkes was put in charge of the explosives, and the conspirators got as far as planting 36 barrels of gunpowder in a cellar under the building.

Line
(5)

The plot was foiled when someone sent an anonymous letter to a Catholic member of the House of Lords warning him to stay home. Most of the plotters—disgruntled Catholics enraged by the failure of the king to end religious persecution—were chased and killed in a shootout, but Fawkes was arrested and leapt from the gallows to his death rather than be hanged. The 36 barrels were never ignited, anti-Catholic fervor spread, and England became even more resolutely Protestant.

(10)

Consider each of the choices separately and select all that apply.

1. The author hints that the Gunpowder Plot failed due to

    A   dissension among the leadership of the conspiracy

    B   failure of the gunpowder to ignite when lit

    C   one plotter's desire to save the life of a Catholic

Select one answer choice.

2. Based on information from the passage, what is the likeliest outcome of the plot had it succeeded?

    Ⓐ   A military takeover led by Guy Fawkes

    Ⓑ   Inclusion of Catholics in the House of Lords

    Ⓒ   The installation of a new, Catholic king from Europe

    Ⓓ   Backlash against Catholics and a religious civil war

    Ⓔ   The replacement of the House of Lords by the House of Commons

3. Underline the sentence that suggests the author's opinion of the Gunpowder Plot.

Question 4 is based on this passage.

Water is a fact of life in the Netherlands; the country is surrounded, most of it lies below sea level, and its soaked landmass is slowly sinking. Because of this, the little European nation has become something of the world's expert in protection
Line from the seawater inundation that accompanies climate change. Rather than build
(5) higher and higher sea walls to hold back the water, the Dutch are working with the water as they have for centuries, using canals and reinventing plazas as retention ponds, widening rivers and channels to reduce flooding. Small changes such as removal of concrete to allow for rain to be absorbed by the earth and shoring up the famous dikes help to give water a place to go that does not harm people's homes
(10) and livelihoods. There are even experiments involving floating houseboats that are reminiscent of post-apocalyptic scenes from *Waterworld*.

Select one answer choice.

4. Based on the information given in the passage, which of these statements about Dutch plans for climate change is accurate?

   Ⓐ They feel protected from storm surge and are focusing on increased precipitation.

   Ⓑ They expect continued sea level rise and are working to divert and absorb water.

   Ⓒ They believe that continuing to build along the shoreline should be discouraged.

   Ⓓ They anticipate more danger from superstorms than from sea level rise.

   Ⓔ They have done what they can in the interior and are now shoring up harbors.

   > For questions 5 through 8, complete the text by picking the best entry
   > for each blank from the corresponding column of choices.

5. At the _____ of King Salman, women in Saudi Arabia received the right to drive automobiles in the fall of 2017.

Ⓐ	keystone
Ⓑ	latitude
Ⓒ	behest
Ⓓ	prerogative
Ⓔ	disavowal

6. In the world of finance, deviations from the average stock price are expected to _____ to the mean over a given period of time.

Ⓐ	transpose
Ⓑ	renege
Ⓒ	contravene
Ⓓ	revert
Ⓔ	ratiocinate

7. The Appalachian Trail is (i) _____ by a loose collection of citizen groups, environmental organizations, individual (ii) _____, and government agencies.

Blank (i)		Blank (ii)	
Ⓐ	housed	Ⓓ	summits
Ⓑ	maintained	Ⓔ	collectives
Ⓒ	hiked	Ⓕ	volunteers

8. Although the Faeroe Islands are largely (i) _____, the Kingdom of Denmark still (ii) _____ their military defense and legal affairs.

Blank (i)		Blank (ii)	
Ⓐ	uninhabited	Ⓓ	disallows
Ⓑ	progressive	Ⓔ	oversees
Ⓒ	autonomous	Ⓕ	disputes

Questions 9 through 12 are based on this passage.

The publishing house known as Ticknor and Fields began in the Old Corner Bookstore in Boston, Massachusetts. Its literary talents included Horatio Alger, Ralph Waldo Emerson, Henry Wadsworth Longfellow, Harriet Beecher Stowe, Mark
Line Twain, Henry David Thoreau, Nathaniel Hawthorne, and John Greenleaf Whittier—a
(5) venerable collection of American greats. Thanks to William Davis Ticknor's business acumen and James Thomas Fields's ability to recognize genius, the imprint became the most important American publisher of the nineteenth century.

In addition to publishing books in English, the firm purchased and published two significant literary and cultural magazines, the *Atlantic Monthly* and the *North*
(10) *American Review*. Those magazines often debuted key works of both new and familiar American authors. The influence, then, of Ticknor and Fields on the reading public in the mid-1800s cannot be overstated.

(15) The publishing house survived the death of Ticknor and the retirement of Fields. It went on to be the major publisher of works by Sara Orne Jewett, Bret Hart, and William Dean Howells before merging with Hurd & Houghton in 1878. Now known as Houghton Mifflin Harcourt, the company retains its headquarters in Boston but has branches all over the world.

Consider each of the choices separately and select all that apply.

9. The passage primarily demonstrates the influence of Ticknor and Fields by

   [A] describing its inception

   [B] listing its key authors

   [C] aggrandizing its founders

For questions 10 through 12, select one answer choice each.

---

10. With which of the following statements would the author of the passage probably agree?

    (A) Ticknor and Fields owed its success to its compensation of authors.

    (B) Ticknor and Fields was a rare amalgam of high and low art.

    (C) Ticknor and Fields suffered a decline in importance in the late 1800s.

    (D) Ticknor and Fields was wise not to depart from English-language texts.

    (E) Ticknor and Fields holds a significant place in American cultural history.

11. Which is the best summary of the passage as a whole?

    (A) A businessman and a literary sage joined forces in 1800s Boston to become the publisher of new and exciting American works.

    (B) Not only did Ticknor and Fields publish Hawthorne in the early 1800s and Jewett in the late 1800s, but it also continues its success today.

    (C) Boston publisher Ticknor and Fields grew to be a preeminent arbiter of literary culture in 1800s America and continues today under a different name.

    (D) Without the combined expertise of William Ticknor and his partner James Fields, American publishing might have lagged behind British publishing.

    (E) Important American writers such as Hawthorne and Twain found a helpful, supportive haven under the auspices of Ticknor and Fields.

12. In paragraph 3 of the passage, the first sentence introduces the topic, and the other sentences provide

    (A) examples in support

    (B) examples in refutation

    (C) reasons for an opinion

    (D) causes and effects

    (E) comparisons and contrasts

Question 13 is based on this passage.

Parametric modeling builds a model from known parameters regarding a particular population. Unlike with nonparametric modeling, this type of algorithm is fairly inflexible; it can work well if all assumptions about the data are correct but may prove to be far off the mark if any of the assumptions is wrong. This conundrum is easy to see if you picture a linear regression. Imagine dependent variable y, representing people's heights, and $x1$ and $x2$, representing their ages and IQs. You may plot points for a few subjects and then draw a line to represent the function, but since the underlying relationship is specious, the resulting model will be dubious as well.

Line

(5)

13. Underline the sentence that names one form of parametric modeling.

For questions 14 through 17, complete the text by picking the best entry for each blank from the corresponding column of choices.

---

14. Topanga Canyon, with its (i) _____, desert roads ascending into the Santa Monica Mountains, has been an artists' (ii) _____ for decades. Today, a mix of musicians, filmmakers, painters, and potters live and work along the (iii) _____, which provide stunning views as well as separating canyon dwellers from the city below.

Blank (i)	Blank (ii)	Blank (iii)
(A) tortuous	(D) oeuvre	(G) jetties
(B) verdant	(E) hiatus	(H) parapets
(C) transitory	(F) enclave	(I) coulees

15. Shin guards are protective gear worn in a (i) _____ of sports, from ice hockey to rugby, to protect against (ii) _____ leg injuries.

Blank (i)	Blank (ii)
Ⓐ variety	Ⓓ significant
Ⓑ phenomenon	Ⓔ frivolous
Ⓒ training	Ⓕ indefinite

16. The Joint Chiefs of Staff were not officially assembled until after World War II, but they _____ from an earlier attempt by Theodore Roosevelt to create a board that would work and plan jointly across the armed forces.

Ⓐ	counteracted
Ⓑ	increased
Ⓒ	altered
Ⓓ	evolved
Ⓔ	accrued

17. Labrador retrievers make particularly good service dogs because they are not only _____ but also quite clever.

Ⓐ	astute
Ⓑ	tenable
Ⓒ	corpulent
Ⓓ	tractable
Ⓔ	senescent

Questions 18 through 20 are based on this passage.

In his essay "On Denoting," logician and philosopher Bertrand Russell distinguishes between quantifying phrases such as "some man" or "every man" and descriptive phrases such as "that man in the gray suit." Within those phrases, a phrase may
Line   denote a specific object, as in "the junior senator from Massachusetts"; it may
(5)   denote an object that does not exist, as in "the young king of Massachusetts"; or it may denote an ambiguity, as in "a man," which does not name a specific man or a group of men but instead refers to an ambiguous, unnamed man. Russell goes on to characterize those sentences containing a denoting phrase that refers to a nonexistent object as false; a sentence such as "The young king of Massachusetts played poker
(10)   with the junior senator" would be false in Russell's analysis because no such

person exists to play poker or socialize with the junior senator. In "On Referring," philosopher P. F. Strawson shoots down this argument, declaring that such a statement is neither true nor false, right nor wrong, and that Russell has confused meaning with referring. According to Strawson, people, not expressions, provide
(15) meaning.

> **For questions 18 through 20, select one answer choice each.**

18. Based on information in the passage, which of these sentences would Russell automatically view as false?

    (A)   The governor of Alabama has served more than one term.

    (B)   A dentist in Alabama charges less than a dentist in Illinois.

    (C)   The Alabama legislature is composed of a House and a Senate.

    (D)   Birmingham, Alabama, was named in honor of Birmingham, England.

    (E)   The first American pope was born in Birmingham in 1955.

19. Based on information in the passage, which of these would be an ambiguous phrase?

    (A)   The car on the right

    (B)   That green car

    (C)   All cars

    (D)   Some cars

    (E)   Those noisy cars

20. Which of the following best describes the function of the final sentence of the passage?

    (A)   It presents a conclusion drawn from the examples in the other sentences.

    (B)   It puts forward a thesis that contradicts the main thesis in the passage.

    (C)   It offers the author's opinion about Russell's linguistic analysis.

    (D)   It connects the rest of the passage to information that will follow.

    (E)   It reaffirms the topic that the other sentences in the passage support.

For questions 21 through 25, select two answer choices that (1) complete the sentence in a way that makes sense and (2) produce sentences that are similar in meaning.

21. Neighborhoods with a _____ of grocery stores, and especially of fresh produce, are termed "food deserts" by the USDA.

    A   schism

    B   bastion

    C   paucity

    D   scintilla

    E   plenitude

    F   dearth

22. Those who lost their shirts in the sudden deflation of the dot-com bubble were understandably _____ about reinvesting in tech stocks.

    A   chary

    B   circumspect

    C   euphoric

    D   obdurate

    E   stoic

    F   querulous

23. Thoreau posited that being _____ was required of anyone who hoped to achieve true liberty.

    A   cursory

    B   sanguine

    C   venal

    D   sapient

    E   recalcitrant

    F   contumacious

24. The composer of our national anthem was just an amateur poet; his real _____ was the law.

    A fortune

    B pastime

    C vocation

    D fascination

    E profession

    F authorization

25. Harare, the largest and most important city in Zimbabwe, is also one of the continent's most modern, with its _____ industries, transportation, and communications.

    A advanced

    B productive

    C impressive

    D spotless

    E abundant

    F sophisticated

STOP.   This is the end of Section 4. Use any remaining time to check your work.

SECTION 5
Quantitative Reasoning
Time: 40 minutes
25 questions

Each of questions 1 through 9 consists of two quantities, Quantity A and Quantity B. You are to compare the two quantities. You may use additional information centered above the two quantities if additional information is given. Choose

(A) if the quantity in Column A is greater;

(B) if the quantity in Column B is greater;

(C) if the two quantities are equal;

(D) if the relationship cannot be determined from the information given.

	Quantity A	Quantity B	
1.	$9^{1.5}$	18	(A) (B) (C) (D)

$$x^2 > x$$

	Quantity A	Quantity B	
2.	x	1	(A) (B) (C) (D)

	Quantity A	Quantity B	
3.	Probability of rolling a sum of 5 with two 6-sided dice	Probability of dropping three coins and having all land "heads"	(A) (B) (C) (D)

A random variable X is normally distributed.

	Quantity A	Quantity B	
4.	Mode of X	Median of X	Ⓐ Ⓑ Ⓒ Ⓓ

The real number A is such that line $5y + Ax = 2$ is perpendicular to line l.

	Quantity A	Quantity B	
5.	Slope of line l	$5A^{-1}$	Ⓐ Ⓑ Ⓒ Ⓓ

	Quantity A	Quantity B	
6.	$2^{21} \times 5^{15}$	10^{17}	Ⓐ Ⓑ Ⓒ Ⓓ

In parallelogram $\square ABCD$, E is a point of side $\overline{CD}$.

	Quantity A	Quantity B	
7.	Area of $\triangle ABC$	Area of $\triangle ABE$	Ⓐ Ⓑ Ⓒ Ⓓ

$$\frac{x+1}{x-1} = x$$

	Quantity A	Quantity B	
8.	$|x-1|$	$\sqrt{2}$	Ⓐ Ⓑ Ⓒ Ⓓ

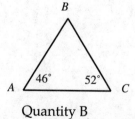

	Quantity A	Quantity B	
9.	Length AC	Mean of lengths AB and BC	Ⓐ Ⓑ Ⓒ Ⓓ

Questions 10 through 25 have different formats. Select a single answer choice unless the directions say otherwise. For Numeric Entry questions, follow these instructions:

- Enter your answer in the box or boxes provided.
- Your answer may be an integer, a decimal, a fraction, or a negative number.
- If the answer is a fraction, you will be given two boxes: an upper one for the numerator and a lower one for the denominator.
- Equivalent forms of the correct answer, such as 1.6 and 1.60, are all correct. You do not need to reduce fractions to lowest terms.

10. How many times larger is 1.4 million than 20,000?

(A) 7

(B) 28

(C) 70

(D) 280

(E) 700

11. How many different primes are in the factorization of $2^{\left(3^4\right)}$?

(A) 1

(B) 2

(C) 3

(D) 4

(E) 12

12. How many diagonals can be drawn from one vertex of a regular octagon?

(A) 4

(B) 5

(C) 6

(D) 7

(E) 8

For this question, write your answer in the box.

13. The area of a circle (in square inches) is 6 times the circumference (in inches). How many feet is the diameter of the circle?

14. What percent of a 1-meter square lies within 4 centimeters of the perimeter (outer edge)? Round your answer to the nearest percent.

  (A) 4%

  (B) 8%

  (C) 11%

  (D) 15%

  (E) 16%

For this question, indicate all of the answer choices that apply.

15. If $N > 2$ is a positive integer, which of the following could NOT be prime?

  A $3N$

  B $4N + 6$

  C $N^2 - 1$

  D $N^2 + 1$

  E $N + 1$

16. Cylinder A has 3 times the height and 5 times the diameter of cylinder B. How many times larger is the volume of cylinder A than the volume of cylinder B?

  (A) 8

  (B) 15

  (C) 45

  (D) 75

  (E) 225

For this question, indicate all of the answer choices that apply.

$$2x^2 + 5x - 3 = 0$$

17. Check all the possible values of x.

    [A] -3

    [B] $\dfrac{1}{2}$

    [C] $\dfrac{3}{2}$

    [D] 2

    [E] 3

18. A hospital has two backup generators. The first is maintained every 75 days. The second is maintained every 81 days. How often are both maintained on the same day? Round your answer to the nearest tenth of a year.

    (A) 0.4 year

    (B) 1.1 years

    (C) 3.5 years

    (D) 5.5 years

    (E) 16.6 years

19. In how many ways can the letters of the word *APOLLO* be rearranged?

    (A) 90

    (B) 180

    (C) 360

    (D) 540

    (E) 720

For this question, indicate all of the answer choices that apply.

20. Triangle *PQR* is isosceles and angle *PQR* measures 50°. Which of the following could be the measure of angle *PRQ*?

    A   60°

    B   65°

    C   80°

    D   100°

    E   130°

21. Suppose that the 25 numbers in data set *S* have mean 7 and standard deviation 3. If each of the numbers in *S* is multiplied by 4 to form a new data set *T*, what is the standard deviation of *T*?

    Ⓐ 3

    Ⓑ $3\sqrt{2}$

    Ⓒ 6

    Ⓓ 9

    Ⓔ 12

Use the following table to answer questions 22 through 25.

Annual Rate of Return

	2006	2007	2008	2009	2010
S&P	+16%	+5%	−37%	+26%	+15%
Dow Jones	+16%	+6%	−34%	+19%	+11%
Nasdaq	+10%	+10%	−41%	+44%	+17%
Hang Seng	+34%	+39%	−48%	+52%	+5%
Shanghai	+130%	+97%	−65%	+80%	−14%

For Question 23 and 24, write your answer in the box.

22. What single percent increase would be required to offset the loss to the Dow Jones in 2008? Write your answer as a percent rounded to the nearest whole number.

    [   ] %

23. What was the overall rate of change in the Nasdaq from 2008 to 2010 inclusive?

    Ⓐ −0.6%

    Ⓑ +20%

    Ⓒ +44%

    Ⓓ −3%

    Ⓔ +1.3%

24. If $20,000 were invested in the S&P at the start of 2006, how much would it be worth at the end of 2008? Round your answer to the nearest dollar.

25. Which of the above stock indices had the largest variance in rates of return for the years listed in the chart?

    Ⓐ S&P

    Ⓑ Dow Jones

    Ⓒ Nasdaq

    Ⓓ Hang Seng

    Ⓔ Shanghai

STOP. This is the end of Section 5. Use any remaining time to check your work.

SECTION 6
Quantitative Reasoning
Time: 40 minutes
25 questions

Each of questions 1 through 9 consists of two quantities, Quantity A and Quantity B. You are to compare the two quantities. You may use additional information centered above the two quantities if additional information is given. Choose

- (A) if Quantity A is greater;
- (B) if Quantity B is greater;
- (C) if the two quantities are equal;
- (D) if the relationship cannot be determined from the information given.

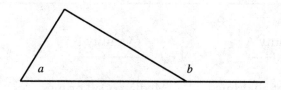

Quantity A	Quantity B	
1. a	b	(A) (B) (C) (D)

$$A^2 > B^2 \quad \text{and} \quad B > 0$$

Quantity A	Quantity B	
2. A	B	(A) (B) (C) (D)

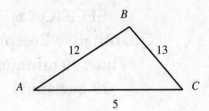

Quantity A	Quantity B	
3. Area of triangle *ABC*	50	Ⓐ Ⓑ Ⓒ Ⓓ

Quantity A	Quantity B	
4. 4π meters	1,250 centimeters	Ⓐ Ⓑ Ⓒ Ⓓ

Quantity A	Quantity B	
5. Mean of all primes less than 20	Median of all primes less than 20	Ⓐ Ⓑ Ⓒ Ⓓ

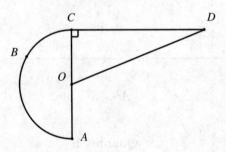

Point *O* is the center of semicircle *ABC* and $\overline{OC} \perp \overline{CD}$. The length of $\overline{CD}$ is the same as the arclength of $\overset{\frown}{ABC}$.

Quantity A	Quantity B	
6. Area of semicircle *ABC*	Area of triangle *COD*	Ⓐ Ⓑ Ⓒ Ⓓ

The random variable X is normally distributed
with mean 180 and standard deviation 20.

Quantity A	Quantity B	
7. Probability of the event that the value of X is less than 160	$\dfrac{1}{10}$	 Ⓐ Ⓑ Ⓒ Ⓓ

Quantity A	Quantity B	
8. $4^{-\frac{1}{2}}$	0.5	Ⓐ Ⓑ Ⓒ Ⓓ

$$2 < x < 3$$

Quantity A	Quantity B	
9. $\dfrac{x+7}{x+1}$	$\dfrac{x+3}{x-1}$	Ⓐ Ⓑ Ⓒ Ⓓ

> **Questions 10 through 25 have different formats. Select a single answer choice unless the directions say otherwise. For Numeric Entry questions, follow these instructions:**
>
> • **Enter your answer in the box or boxes provided.**
>
> • **Your answer may be an integer, a decimal, a fraction, or a negative number.**
>
> • **If the answer is a fraction, you will be given two boxes: an upper one for the numerator and a lower one for the denominator.**
>
> • **Equivalent forms of the correct answer, such as 1.6 and 1.60, are all correct. You do not need to reduce fractions to lowest terms.**

10. What is the last digit of 3^{108}?

    Ⓐ 1

    Ⓑ 3

    Ⓒ 6

    Ⓓ 7

    Ⓔ 9

For this question, write your answer in the box.

11. A stock portfolio that was originally worth $15,000 has increased in value by $10,000. By what percentage of the original value has the portfolio increased? Give your answer rounded to the nearest whole percent.

 %

12. For which of the following values of x does $\dfrac{x+5}{x-2}$ have the greatest value?

(A) 0

(B) 1

(C) 3

(D) 4

(E) 5

For this question, indicate all of the answer choices that apply.

13. If $-\dfrac{N}{7}$ is a positive integer, which of the following MUST be true?

[A] N is even.

[B] N is odd.

[C] N is positive.

[D] N is negative.

[E] N is not prime.

14. The x-intercept of a straight line is twice that of the y-intercept. Which of the following could be the slope of the line?

(A) -2

(B) $-\dfrac{1}{2}$

(C) 0

(D) $\dfrac{1}{2}$

(E) 2

15. A fund loses 30% of its value one year and then increases in value by 10% each subsequent year. How many years of these 10% increases will it take to overcome the initial loss (have the overall growth, including the initial loss, be positive)?

   (A) 1 year

   (B) 2 years

   (C) 3 years

   (D) 4 years

   (E) 5 years

For this question, write your answer in the box.

16. What is the twentieth term of this arithmetic sequence?

$$5, 9, 13, \ldots$$

17. Three liters of a 2% salt solution are mixed with two liters of a 5% salt solution. What is the percentage of salt in the resulting solution?

   (A) 2.8%

   (B) 3.2%

   (C) 3.5%

   (D) 3.8%

   (E) 7%

18. How many different six-digit numbers are there?

   (A) 99,999

   (B) 900,000

   (C) 999,999

   (D) 1,000,000

   (E) 1,000,001

For this question, indicate all of the answer choices that apply.

19. Suppose that a number N is divisible by 3. If the third digit is replaced by the letter A, we get 8,2A3,711. Which of the following could be the value of the digit replaced by the A?

    [A] 1

    [B] 2

    [C] 3

    [D] 4

    [E] 5

20. It is 2:50 p.m., and Amy is driving at 50 mph. At this rate, she will reach her destination at 5:26 p.m. of the same day. If she instead drives at 65 mph, when will she reach her destination?

    (A) 4:45 p.m.

    (B) 4:50 p.m.

    (C) 4:56 p.m.

    (D) 5:06 p.m.

    (E) 5:11 p.m.

21. A motorboat always travels at 12 mph. A river flows downstream at a steady 3 mph. The motorboat travels downstream to a location and then returns immediately. If the full round trip took 1 hour, how far was the location from the starting point? Give your answer in feet.

    (A) 29,500 ft

    (B) 29,700 ft

    (C) 30,100 ft

    (D) 30,300 ft

    (E) 30,500 ft

Use the following table to answer questions 22 through 25.

	Sun	Mercury	Earth	Mars	Jupiter
Diameter (10³ km)	1,391	5	13	7	143
Distance to sun (10⁶ km)	0	58	150	228	779
Density (kg/m³)	1,410	5,427	5,514	3,933	1,326

22. In a scale model of the solar system, the Earth is represented by a marble with a diameter of 1 inch. What is the diameter of the sphere representing the sun?

    (A) 3 feet, 4 inches

    (B) 5 feet, 7 inches

    (C) 8 feet, 11 inches

    (D) 24 feet, 2 inches

    (E) 115 feet, 11 inches

23. In the same scale model, where the Earth has a 1-inch diameter, how far away from the sun is the model of Mars? Round your answer to the nearest foot.

    (A) 228 feet

    (B) 975 feet

    (C) 1462 feet

    (D) 2,964 feet

    (E) 17,538 feet

24. What is the mass of the Earth? Give your answer in kilograms, rounded to two significant digits.

    (A) 6.3×10^{12} kg

    (B) 6.3×10^{15} kg

    (C) 6.3×10^{18} kg

    (D) 6.3×10^{21} kg

    (E) 6.3×10^{24} kg

25. How much more dense is Mars than the sun?

   (A) 179% more

   (B) 204% more

   (C) 279% more

   (D) 291% more

   (E) 391% more

STOP. This is the end of Section 6. Use any remaining time to check your work.

GRE PRACTICE TEST 8
Answers and Explanations

Analytical Writing: Scoring and Sample Responses

Analyze an Issue: Scoring

Score	Focus	Organization	Conventions
0	Does not address the prompt. Off topic.	Incomprehensible. May merely copy the prompt without development.	Illegible. Nonverbal. Serious errors make the paper unreadable. May be in a foreign language.
1	Mostly irrelevant to the prompt.	Little or no development of ideas. No evidence of analysis or organization.	Pervasive errors in grammar, mechanics, and spelling.
2	Unclear connection to the prompt.	Unfocused and disorganized.	Frequent errors in sentence structure, mechanics, and spelling.
3	Limited connection to the prompt.	Rough organization with weak examples or reasons.	Occasional major errors and frequent minor errors in conventions of written English.
4	Competent connection to the prompt.	Relevant examples or reasons develop a logical position.	Occasional minor errors in conventions of written English.
5	Clear, focused connection to the prompt.	Thoughtful, appropriate examples or reasons develop a consistent, coherent position. Connectors are ably used to mark transitions.	Very few errors. Sentence structure is varied, and vocabulary is advanced.
6	Insightful, clever connection to the prompt.	Compelling, convincing examples or reasons develop a consistent, coherent position. The argument flows effortlessly and persuasively.	Very few errors. Sentence structure is varied, and vocabulary is precise, well chosen, and effective.

Analyze an Issue:
Sample Response with a Score of 6

In this essay, the writer decides to disagree with the claim and the reason presented. The essay is clear and well argued, whether you believe in its premise or not. There are no significant errors in grammar or mechanics.

Given the question whether live theater continues to be a relevant art form in our age of individualized, digital entertainment, I must come down on the negative side, especially when the reason given has to do with the importance of audience-actor interaction. My reasons for this have something to do with the fascinating technology I recently witnessed at HyperCon in Dallas.

At the convention, I was given a headset that allowed me to participate in an event taking place miles away, in Austin. Audience engagement software enabled me not only to see what was happening but also to react to it in real time. The event was live, but I was not there. Nevertheless, I had the sort of audience-speaker interaction I would have had by being in the very same room.

Another demonstration showed me how virtual reality could transport me to La Scala for live opera. An immersive project allowed groups in the same room to have the same experiences without wearing headsets at all.

My friends and I can already use apps to watch movies together without being in the same room or even in the same state. It is not much of a stretch to imagine watching theater performances, whether live or taped, in a similar way.

So if we consider viewing live theater as remaining relevant because of its social advantages, I would say that the benefits of sitting elbow to elbow in overpriced, dusty seats are not clear to me—not when I can have social interaction with art from the comfort of my home. The three-dimensional aspects of staged performances are now easily replicated digitally, as are the audiovisual sensations, down to the coughing of (fake) audience members.

I recognize that this may not be a popular opinion; many people get a particular enjoyment out of shelling out a lot of money, dressing up, and traveling to a theater. However, I would posit that the advantages of digital and virtual technology will be that the enjoyment of *Death of a Salesman* will no longer be limited to wealthy city dwellers and tourists but instead will be available to anyone with access to the technology needed. This universal availability more than compensates for any diminution of traditional audience-actor interaction.

Analyze an Argument: Scoring

Score	Focus	Organization	Conventions
0	Does not address the prompt. Off topic. May fail to choose between the two prompts.	Incomprehensible. May merely copy the prompt without development.	Illegible. Nonverbal. Serious errors make the paper unreadable. May be in a foreign language.
1	Little or no analysis of the argument. May indicate misunderstanding of the prompt.	Little or no development of ideas. No evidence of analysis or organization.	Pervasive errors in grammar, mechanics, and spelling.
2	Little analysis; may instead present opinions and unrelated thoughts.	Disorganized and illogical.	Frequent errors in sentence structure, mechanics, and spelling.
3	Some analysis of the prompt, but some major flaws may be omitted.	Rough organization with irrelevant support or unclear transitions.	Occasional major errors and frequent minor errors in conventions of written English.
4	Important flaws in the argument are touched upon.	Ideas are sound but may not flow logically or clearly.	Occasional minor errors in conventions of written English.
5	Perceptive analysis of the major flaws in the argument.	Logical examples and support develop a consistent, coherent critique. Connectors are ably used to mark transitions.	Very few errors. Sentence structure is varied, and vocabulary is advanced.
6	Insightful, clever analysis of the argument's flaws and fallacies.	Compelling, convincing examples and support develop a consistent, coherent critique. The analysis flows effortlessly and persuasively.	Very few errors. Sentence structure is varied, and vocabulary is precise, well chosen, and effective.

Analyze an Argument:
Sample Response with a Score of 6

*This essay is clear and logical. The writer points out the potential flaws in the students'
analysis and counters with two possible alternatives to their explanation. The argument
contains no errors in English usage or mechanics.*

The students' speculation that a lack of jack pine seedlings
arose due to prolonged heat from forest fires is interesting,
but it is certainly not the only possible explanation. Without
further proof that extreme heat or extreme duration of fire
could kill jack pine seeds, I would want to consider simpler
explanations for the lack of such seedlings in the Washington
forests.

The range of the jack pine is never described, but the fact
that it is referred to as "Canadian" could imply a range that
begins to the north of the fires in Washington State. If that
were the case, then jack pines may never have existed in the
forests students were exploring, and the failure of seedlings
to thrive would be simply explained by the fact that they were
never there to begin with.

No indication is given of the length of time between the
fires and the students' visit to the forests, nor is there
any indication of the length of time it might take a jack
pine seedling to sprout once the forest floor cools. It is
certainly possible that the students arrived in the forest too
early to view optimum seedling growth.

Before jumping to conclusions about the effect of prolonged
heat on jack pine sprouts or seedlings, it would be useful to
know whether jack pines are an expected pioneer in Washington
State forests. It would also be helpful to know the typical
timeframe between a forest fire and the sprouting of pioneer
species.

GRE Practice Test 8: Answer Key

Section 3. Verbal Reasoning

1. D, F
2. A, E
3. C, F
4. A, E
5. A, C
6. D
7. A, C
8. E
9. B
10. A
11. C
12. A, E
13. B, D
14. C
15. D
16. The soil holds water readily and maintains heat, making the growing season shorter than for crops in other regions.
17. E
18. A, D
19. C, D
20. B, D, I
21. B
22. B, C
23. A
24. C
25. To make music rather than noise, theremin players must rely on their ears more than other musicians do; there are no frets or keys to give clues about correct tone.

Section 4. Verbal Reasoning

1. C
2. D
3. The event to be remembered is the Gunpowder Plot, a dastardly but daring 1605 attempt to blow up Parliament and assassinate the entire House of Lords and the king.
4. B
5. C
6. D
7. B, F
8. C, E
9. B
10. E
11. C
12. A
13. This conundrum is easy to see if you picture a linear regression.
14. A, F, I
15. A, D
16. D
17. D

18. E
19. D
20. B
21. C, F

22. A, B
23. E, F
24. C, E
25. A, F

Section 5. Quantitative Reasoning

1. A
2. D
3. B
4. C
5. C
6. B
7. C
8. C
9. A
10. C
11. A
12. B
13. 2 feet

14. D
15. A, B, C
16. D
17. A, B
18. D
19. B
20. B, C
21. C
22. 52
23. A
24. $15,347
25. E

Section 6. Quantitative Reasoning

1. B
2. D
3. B
4. A
5. A
6. C
7. A
8. C
9. B
10. A
11. 67%
12. C
13. D, E

14. B
15. D
16. 81
17. B
18. B
19. B, E
20. B
21. B
22. C
23. C
24. E
25. A

GRE Practice Test 8: Answer Explanations

Section 3. Verbal Reasoning

1. **D, F.** Several of the choices make sense in context, but only *liberalization* (choice D) and *relaxation* (choice F) lead to sentences that mean the same thing.

2. **A, E.** Again, when in doubt, look for the synonyms. Both choices A and E mean "many."

3. **C, F.** The mosquitoes pester the tourists; choices C and F are the only synonyms in the set.

4. **A, E.** Platitudes (choice A) and banalities (choice E) are trite, dull words that should be avoided in writing. Some of the other choices should also be avoided, but no two of them are synonyms.

5. **A, C.** Although many historians trace the foundation to 882, not all do, meaning that they differ on its inception (choice A). According to the passage, "even the origin of the word" is mired in controversy, making choice C also correct. Since the region "adhered to Scandinavian traditions," the Scandinavian connection (choice B) does not seem to be in doubt.

6. **D.** The answer is not directly given; the question asks for your best guess as to why the region turned from Scandinavian to Slavic. Of the choices given, the likeliest is choice D; if Vikings took over Slavic villages, they might impose their culture for a while, but eventually interbreeding would result in a reversion to the original culture of the region.

7. **A, C.** Progenitor cells perform regenerative tasks, so either choice A or choice C might be a possible job for such cells.

8. **E.** The women "of a certain class" used lead makeup to create white skin that "contrasted with that of working-class women." Choices A, B, C, and D may well be true, but they are not directly supported by information in the passage.

9. **B.** The cardinal invited his family "in the hopes of adding ... some confidants" (choice A). By marrying them off, he hoped to increase "his family's wealth" (choice D), guarantee "his own legacy" (choice E), and expand "the cardinal's influence" (choice C). Only choice B is never mentioned.

10. **A.** What did the other nations do? They denounced (choice A) the defectors. They did not hesitate (choice B), disconnect (choice C), excuse (choice D), or praise (choice E) them.

11. **C.** The clue is "direct, firsthand data collection." This would not include readings (choice A), mapmaking (choice B), or adaptations (choice D). Rituals (choice E) would be observed; they would not be the form of collecting data. Interviews (choice C) are a form of direct, firsthand data collection.

12. **A, E.** The word "but" sets up a contrast—the bill was vetoed, but that veto was overridden (choice E).

13. **B, D.** The magazine takes ordinary daily details (choice B) and makes them seem fascinating (choice D).

14. **C.** The passage points out that "muck is a finite resource," so excess farming will eventually lead to its disappearance (choice C). There is no indication that muck exists in other regions besides the lake region (choice A), and the passage does not suggest any changes in the qualities of onions over time (choice B).

15. **D.** Go back and reread the line to see the author's intent. She is explaining the fertile qualities of the muck. None of the other choices is supported by the context.

16. **The soil holds water readily and maintains heat, making the growing season shorter than for crops in other regions.** In other words, the onions grow fast thanks to the soil's heat and water retention.

17. **E.** The use of windmills as pumps was important, or critical (choice E), to the success of Western farms.

18. **A, D.** Mendelssohn was a musical wonder, or prodigy (choice A), but his parents weren't sure they wanted that career for him; they were reluctant (choice D).

19. **C, D.** In other words, the ongoing changes in the coal industry have led to hardship for workers.

20. **B, D, I.** The berries do not vanish (choice A) or lighten (choice C); they steep (choice B). They are not excessive (choice E) or consistent (choice F); they are delicious and fragrant (choice D). Their sweetness is kept from being overly sugary (choice I), not overly touchable (choice C) or dirty (choice D).

21. **B.** The author contrasts Simpson's doctoring with his interest in working to improve the field through experiment. His experimentation was not exactly "investigatory medicine" (choice D), and there is no suggestion that he disliked being a surgeon (choice A) or was bad at it (choice C).

22. **B, C.** The new species resembles one on Borneo rather than one on its own island of Sumatra. This might be due to a common ancestor and different evolutionary paths (choice B) or because at one time orangutans could move freely between islands (choice C). If the new species were divided from Sumatran orangutans by a drastic event (choice A), it would not explain their similarity to Bornean orangutans.

23. **A.** Early theremins were still electrified, not acoustic (choice C). They were electronic but not computerized (choice B). Because they had only two antennas, one for pitch, they were surely monophonic, producing a single melodic line (choice A).

24. **C.** The description is of an object without strings but with two antennas and an oscillator.

25. **To make music rather than noise, theremin players must rely on their ears more than other musicians do; there are no frets or keys to give clues about correct tone.** The movements involved may not be difficult, but getting a pure sound on pitch clearly is.

Section 4. Verbal Reasoning

1. **C.** There is no support for choice A or B, but the anonymous letter to a Catholic mentioned in paragraph 2 supports choice C.

2. **D.** Guy Fawkes was not a leader (choice A), and there already was at least one Catholic in the House of Lords (choice B). No support exists for choices C and E. However, the backlash that took place when the plot was revealed is enough to suggest that choice D might have been the outcome had it succeeded.

3. **The event to be remembered is the Gunpowder Plot, a dastardly but daring 1605 attempt to blow up Parliament and assassinate the entire House of Lords and the king.** In the author's opinion, the plot was both dastardly and daring.

4. **B.** The passage suggests that the Dutch are clear about their situation but are working with the water rather than avoiding it or blocking it. Most of the examples given involve diversion or absorption of excess water. Some of this has to do with rainfall (choice A), but seawater inundation is also still a problem. There is no support in the passage for choices C, D, and E.

5. **C.** Women can drive due to the behest, or directive, of King Salman.

6. **D.** Even if you are not familiar with the term "revert to the mean," you should be able to eliminate choices that mean "reorder" (choice A), "break a promise" (choice B), "disobey" (choice C), and "form judgments" (choice E).

7. **B, F.** Once again, it helps to read the whole sentence before choosing words to complete it. An agency cannot hike a trail (choice C), and collectives (choice E) cannot be individual. Choices B and F complete the sentence in a logical way.

8. **C, E.** "Although" indicates a contrast. Denmark still has charge of (choice E) the Faeroe Islands' defense and legal affairs, even though they are pretty much self-governing (choice C).

9. **B.** The passage does describe the publishing house's inception (choice A), but that does not really demonstrate the influence of the publisher. It does not aggrandize, or overstate the importance of, the founders (choice C), but it does list key authors who wrote both for the founders and after their departures, making choice B the best answer.

10. **E.** To answer a question of this sort, think about the author's attitude toward the subject as well as the key details included in the passage. There is no discussion of compensation (choice A), and the author does not suggest that Ticknor and Fields sponsored any low art (choice B). Rather than suffering a decline, the publisher kept going through the late 1800s (choice C), and although the author might possibly agree with choice D, there is nothing in the passage to support that. Choice E has a great deal of support, from the use of descriptive words such as *venerable*, *important*, *significant*, *key*, and *major* to the statement that the influence of the publisher "cannot be overstated."

11. **C.** A good summary contains key details without extending beyond the material in the passage. Only choice C is both broad enough and specific enough to fulfill that role. Choice A covers only the early years, choices B and E are too specific, and choice D makes a leap beyond what is stated.

12. **A.** Return to the paragraph to check. The first sentence states that the publishing company survived. The other sentences give specifics supporting that statement.

13. **This conundrum is easy to see if you picture a linear regression.** A linear regression is presented as one form of parametric modeling.

14. **A, F, I.** The desert roads are tortuous, or winding (choice A). The artists live in an enclave, or community (choice F). They work along the coulees, or ravines (choice I).

15. **A, D.** Choices A and D are the only ones that complete the sentence in a logical way.

16. **D.** Think about the meaning of the sentence as a whole: Theodore Roosevelt tried to create a board that worked jointly across the armed forces, and the Joint Chiefs of Staff developed, or evolved (choice D), from that plan.

17. **D.** The correct answer should not mean the same thing as clever, making choice A incorrect. You would not want a fat (choice C) or old (choice E) service dog; you would want one that is trainable (choice D).

18. **E.** Any of the sentences might be proved either true or false, but only choice E is automatically false in Russell's view because it denotes a nonexistent object, an American pope.

19. **D.** "All cars" (choice C) is not ambiguous because it includes the entire set of cars, making it specific. Most of the other choices denote a particular set of cars, but "some cars" is ambiguous.

20. **B.** The final sentence gives Strawson's opinion in refutation to Russell's ideas.

21. **C, F.** Both *paucity* and *dearth* mean "lack."

22. **A, B.** If you lose at a gamble, you are likely to be cautious and on guard the next time. Both *chary* and *circumspect* describe this kind of guarded attitude.

23. **E, F.** Although several of the choices might make sense in context, the synonyms are *recalcitrant* (choice E) and *contumacious* (choice F), meaning "disobedient" or "noncompliant."

24. **C, E.** On the one hand, he was an amateur poet; on the other hand, he was a professional lawyer—his vocation (choice C) or profession (choice E) was the law.

25. **A, F.** The words "most modern" are a clue to the answer: Harare has advanced (choice A) or sophisticated (choice F) industries, transportation, and communications.

Section 5. Quantitative Reasoning

1. **A.** Quantity A is $9^{1.5} = 9^1 \times 9^{\frac{1}{2}} = 9 \times \sqrt{9} = 9 \times 3 = 27$.

2. **D.** The equation $x^2 > x$ is true if $x > 1$ or if x is a negative number.

3. **B.** There are 6 different ways that the first die can land and 6 ways the second can land, for a total of $6 \times 6 = 36$ different outcomes. Of these, 4 results in a sum of 5; the first die can be a 1, 2, 3, or 4, and the second die must make the sum 5. Thus the probability of rolling a sum of 5 is $\dfrac{4}{36} = \dfrac{1}{9}$. The probability that a coin lands "heads" is $\dfrac{1}{2}$, so the probability that three coins all land "heads" is $\dfrac{1}{2} \times \dfrac{1}{2} \times \dfrac{1}{2} = \dfrac{1}{8}$. Because $\dfrac{1}{8} > \dfrac{1}{9}$, quantity B is larger than quantity A.

4. **C.** In a normal distribution, the mean, median, and mode all equal the same center value.

5. **C.** We solve $5y + Ax = 2$ for $y = -\dfrac{A}{5}x + \dfrac{2}{5}$, so the slope of this line is $-\dfrac{A}{5}$.

    The slope of perpendicular line l will be the negative reciprocal: $\dfrac{5}{A} = 5A^{-1}$.

6. **B.** Rewrite $2^{21} \cdot 5^{15} = 2^{6}\left(2^{15} \cdot 5^{15}\right) = 2^{6} \cdot 10^{15}$. Because $2^{6} = 64 < 100$, this means that $2^{6} \cdot 10^{15} < 100 \cdot 10^{15} = 10^{17}$.

7. **C.** The two triangles have the same base $\overline{AB}$. Their heights are the same as the height of the parallelogram, the vertical distance between the line segments $\overline{AB}$ and $\overline{CD}$ (which contains E). With the same base and the same height, these two triangles have the same area.

8. **C.** We cross-multiply $\dfrac{x+1}{x-1} = x$ to get $x + 1 = x^2 - x$, which simplifies to $x^2 - 2x - 1 = 0$. Using the quadratic formula $x = \dfrac{-(-2) \pm \sqrt{(-2)^2 - 4(1)(-1)}}{2(1)} = \dfrac{2 \pm \sqrt{8}}{2}$. Since $\sqrt{8} = 2\sqrt{2}$, this reduces to $x = 1 \pm \sqrt{2}$. Thus $|x - 1| = \left|\left(1 \pm \sqrt{2}\right) - 1\right| = |\pm\sqrt{2}| = \sqrt{2}$.

9. **A.** The angle opposite side $\overline{AC}$ measures $180° - 46° - 52° = 82°$. Because this is the biggest angle of the three, the opposite side $\overline{AC}$ is thus the largest of the triangle. When the two smaller sides are averaged, their mean will also be less than AC.

10. **C.** Just divide $1{,}400{,}000 \div 20{,}000 = 70$.

11. **A.** This number is 2^{81}, whose prime factorization has only one prime, the number 2.

12. **B.** From one vertex of an octagon, there are seven other vertices to which a line could be drawn. Two of these lines will trace edges. The remaining five lines will all be diagonals of the octagon.

13. **2 feet.** If the radius of the circle is R, the area is πR^2, and the circumference is $2\pi R$. We are given $\pi R^2 = 6(2\pi R)$. If we divide both sides by πR, we get $R = 12$ inches. Thus the diameter is 2 feet.

14. **D.** If we draw lines parallel to each edge and 4 centimeters away, the resulting smaller square in the center will consist of all points greater than 4 cm from the border. Its dimensions are 92 cm $\times$ 92 cm; thus $(0.92 \text{ m})^2 = 0.8464 \text{ m}^2$. Thus the rest of the square is $1 - 0.8464 = 0.1536 \approx 15\%$.

15. **A, B, C.** We can factor the first three possibilities: $3 \times N$, $2(2N + 3)$, and $(N + 1)(N - 1)$, so they couldn't possibly be prime. The last two could; for example, if $N = 4$, then $4^2 + 1 = 17$ and $4 + 1 = 5$.

16. **D.** If A has height h and diameter $2r$, it has volume $\pi r^2 h$. Cylinder B will have height $3h$ and diameter $5(2r) = 10r$; thus its radius is $5r$. The volume of B is thus $\pi(5r)^2(3h) = 75\pi r^2 h$, which is 75 times as great as the volume of A.

17. **A, B.** The equation $2x^2 + 5x - 3 = 0$ factors into $(2x - 1)(x + 3) = 0$; thus $2x - 1 = 0$ or $x + 3 = 0$. The first simplifies to $x = \dfrac{1}{2}$; the other to $x = -3$.

18. **D.** We are looking for the least common multiple of $75 = 3 \times 5^2$ and $81 = 3^4$, which clearly must have two 5s and four 3s in its prime factorization: $3^4 \times 5^2 = 81 \times 25 = 2{,}025$ days. The answer is $\dfrac{2{,}025}{365} \approx 5.5$ years.

19. **B.** There are $6! = 6 \times 5 \times 4 \times 3 \times 2 \times 1 = 720$ ways in which the letters can be arranged. However, because there are two O's in the word, switching their order does not make a different arrangement, so we must divide by 2 to avoid double counting. Similarly, the two L's also lead to double counting. Thus the answer is $\dfrac{720}{2 \times 2} = 180$.

20. **B, C.** An isosceles triangle will have two angles of the same measure. If these each measure 50°, then the third angle is $180° - 2 \times 50° = 80°$. If the two equal angles measure $x \neq 50°$, then $2x + 50° = 180°$, so $x = 65°$.

21. **C.** If S is $x_1, x_2, \ldots, x_{25}$, then $\dfrac{x_1 + x_2 + \cdots + x_{25}}{25} = 7$ is the mean, and T is

$4x_1, 4x_2, \ldots, 4x_{25}$ with mean $\dfrac{4x_1 + 4x_2 + \cdots + 4x_{25}}{25} = 4\left(\dfrac{x_1 + x_2 + \cdots + x_{25}}{25}\right) = 28$.

The standard deviation of T is $\sqrt{\dfrac{(4x_1 - 28) + (4x_2 - 28) + \cdots + (4x_{25} - 28)}{25}}$

$= \sqrt{4\left[\dfrac{(x_1 - 7) + (x_2 - 7) + \cdots + (x_{25} - 7)}{25}\right]}$, which is $\sqrt{4} = 2$ times the standard

deviation of S. Thus the standard deviation of T is 6.

22. **52.** In 2008, the Dow Jones dropped 34%, taking it from 100% of its value to 66%. To regain these 34 percentage points, the Dow Jones would have to grow the relative amount $\dfrac{34}{66} \approx 51.51\%$, which rounds to 52%.

23. **A.** The overall change was $(1 - 0.41)(1 + 0.44)(1 + 0.17) = 0.994032$, a loss of approximately 0.6%.

24. **$15,347.** We compute $20{,}000(1.16)(1.05)(1 - 0.37) = \$15{,}346.80$ and then round to get this answer.

25. **E.** Even without computing the variance, we can see that the Shanghai index experienced the highest rates of growth and the biggest drops and thus must have the largest variance.

Section 6. Quantitative Reasoning

1. **B.** The measure of angle b is the sum of both a and the top angle of the triangle, the one not adjacent to b. Assuming that all three angles of the triangle have a positive measure, this means that b is larger than a.

2. **D.** We might have $A = 10$ and $B = 1$, but we might also have $A = -10$ and $B = 1$.

3. **B.** This is a right triangle because its sides satisfy the Pythagorean theorem: $5^2 + 12^2 = 25 + 144 = 169 = 13^2$. The two smaller sides are the legs, so the area of the triangle is $\dfrac{1}{2}(5)(12) = 30$.

4. **A.** Because $\pi \approx 3.14$ and a meter is 100 cm, 4π m $\approx 4(3.14)(100 \text{ cm}) = 1{,}256$ cm.

5. **A.** The set of all primes less than 20 is 2, 3, 5, 7, 11, 13, 17, and 19. The median

   is the average of the two in the middle: $\dfrac{7+11}{2} = 9$, while the mean is

   $\dfrac{2+3+5+7+11+13+17+19}{8} = \dfrac{77}{8}$, which is more than 9.

6. **C.** If we label $OC = r$, the radius of the circle, then the area of semicircle

   ABC is $\dfrac{1}{2}\pi r^2$. We are told the base CD is half the circle's circumference,

   $CD = \dfrac{1}{2}(2\pi r) = \pi r$, so the area of triangle COD is $\dfrac{1}{2}bh = \dfrac{1}{2}(\pi r)(r) = \dfrac{1}{2}\pi r^2$ as

   well.

7. **A.** Using the quick 68-95-99.7 empirical rule, we know that roughly 68% of X is
   180 ± 20 and that the remaining 32% is evenly distributed between above 200
   and below 160. Thus, the amount below 160 is 16%, which is bigger than $\dfrac{1}{10}$.

8. **C.** The negative exponent puts the 4 in the denominator, and the exponent of ½

   takes the square root: $4^{-\frac{1}{2}} = \dfrac{1}{4^{\frac{1}{2}}} = \dfrac{1}{\sqrt{4}} = \dfrac{1}{2}$. As a decimal: 0.5.

9. **B.** Quantity A is the quotient of a number between 9 and 10 divided by a

   number between 3 and 4, so it could be anywhere between $\dfrac{9}{3} = 3$ and $\dfrac{10}{4} = 2.5$.

   Quantity B is the quotient of a number between 5 and 6 divided by a number

   between 1 and 2, so it could be anywhere between $\dfrac{5}{1} = 5$ and $\dfrac{6}{2} = 3$. In any case,
   Quantity B is larger.

10. **A.** The best way to approach this problem is to look for a pattern in the first few
    powers of 3. The first several powers of 3 are $3^1 = 3$, $3^2 = 9$, $3^3 = 27$, $3^4 = 81$, and
    $3^5 = 243$. The next power 3^6 will end in a 9 (the result of multiplying the last 3
    by 3). The next power will end in a 7, resulting from the multiplication of the
    last 9 and the 3. The pattern of the last digits is thus 3, 9, 7, 1, 3, 9, 7, 1, and so
    on, repeating every four powers. The power of 108 is a multiple of 4, and thus
    3^{108} will end in 1, just as with every fourth power of 3 (3^4, 3^8, etc.).

11. **67%.** The percent increase is $\dfrac{10,000}{15,000} = \dfrac{2}{3} = 0.66\overline{6} \approx 0.67 = 67\%$.

12. **C.** When $x = 0$, the fraction is $-\dfrac{5}{2}$. When $x = 1$, the fraction is -6. When $x = 3$,

    the fraction is 8. When $x = 4$, the fraction is $\dfrac{9}{2} = 4.5$. When $x = 5$, the fraction is
    $\dfrac{10}{3} \approx 3.33$.

13. **D, E.** Because $-\dfrac{N}{7}$ is positive, we know that N must be negative, choice D. Because all prime numbers are positive, choice E is correct. The fact that N is divisible by 7 requires neither an even ($N = -21$) nor an odd ($N = -28$) number.

14. **B.** If the y-intercept is 5, then the x-intercept is 10. The slope through these two points, (0, 5) and (10, 0), is $\dfrac{0-5}{10-0} = -\dfrac{1}{2}$.

15. **D.** We need to find the whole number n for which $(0.7)(1.1)^n$ is greater than 1. With a calculator, we see that $0.7(1.1) = 0.77$, $0.7(1.1)^2 = 0.847$, $0.7(1.1)^3 = 0.9317$, and $0.7(1.1)^4 = 1.02487$. Thus, after 4 years of the 10% growth, the overall change will be an increase over the initial value by 2.487%.

16. **81.** An arithmetic sequence adds a constant k each time, so $9 = 5 + k$ and $13 = 9 + k$; thus $k = 4$. The twentieth term involves adding 4 *nineteen* times and thus, will be $5 + 19(4) = 81$.

17. **B.** The three liters weigh 3,000 grams, of which $0.02(3,000) = 60$ grams are salt. The two liters weigh 2,000 grams, of which $0.05(2,000) = 100$ grams are salt. Mixed together, we have 160 grams of salt in 5,000 grams of mixture and thus a $\dfrac{160}{5,000} = 0.032 = 3.2\%$ salt solution.

18. **B.** There are 9 options for the first digit because it cannot begin with a zero. Each of the remaining 5 digits can have any of the 10 different digits. We multiply all these options together to get the answer: $9 \times 10^5 = 900,000$.

19. **B, E.** If we add the digits of a number that is divisible by 3, we will always get a number that is also divisible by 3. Thus $8 + 2 + A + 3 + 7 + 1 + 1 = 22 + A$ must be a multiple of 3. This happens with $A = 2$ and $A = 5$.

20. **B.** From 2:50 to 5:26 is 2 hours and 36 minutes, which is $2\dfrac{36}{60} = 2.6$ hours. At 50 mph, this means that Amy is $50 \times 2.6 = 130$ miles from her destination. At 65 mph, this will take exactly 2 hours, so she will arrive at 4:50 p.m.

21. **B.** The boat travels at $12 + 3 = 15$ mph downstream and $12 - 3 = 9$ mph upstream. If the distance is D, then the full duration of the trip will be $\dfrac{D}{15} + \dfrac{D}{9} = \dfrac{24D}{15 \times 9} = \dfrac{8D}{45}$. We set $\dfrac{8D}{45} = 1$ and get $D = \dfrac{45}{8}$ miles $= \left(\dfrac{45}{8}\right)5,280 = 29,700$ feet.

22. **C.** The ratio of the Sun's diameter to that of the Earth is $\dfrac{1,391}{13} = 107$. Thus, the scale model of the sun will be 107 inches in diameter, which is 8 feet and 11 inches.

23. **C.** Because the diameter of the Earth is 13×10^3 km, represented by 1 inch, the distance 228×10^6 km to Mars will be represented by $\left(228 \times 10^6 \text{ km}\right)\left(\dfrac{1 \text{ in}}{13 \times 10^3 \text{ km}}\right) = \dfrac{228}{13} \times 10^3$ in. In feet, $\dfrac{228}{13 \times 12} \times 10^3 \approx 1{,}462$.

24. **E.** The mass (kg) of the Earth is the density (kg/m^3) times the volume (m^3). The volume of a sphere with radius r is $\dfrac{4}{3}\pi r^3$, so with $r = \dfrac{1}{2}D = \left(\dfrac{1}{2}\right)13 \times 10^3 \approx 6{,}500 \text{ km} = 6.5 \times 10^6 \text{ m}$, the Earth's volume is $\dfrac{4}{3}\pi\left(6.5 \times 10^6\right)^3 \approx \left(\dfrac{4}{3}\right)\pi\left(6.5\right)^3 \times 10^{18} \approx 1{,}150 \times 10^{18} \text{ m}^3$. Thus, its mass is $(1.15 \times 10^{21} \text{ m}^3)(5{,}514 \text{ kg/m}^3) \approx 6{,}341 \times 10^{21} \approx 6.3 \times 10^{24}$.

25. **A.** Mars is $3{,}933 - 1{,}410 = 2{,}523 \text{ km/m}^3$ more dense than the Sun. Relative to the density of the sun, this increase is $\dfrac{2{,}523}{1{,}410} \approx 1.789 \approx 179\%$ more.